ANNUAL EDITIONS

Personal Growth and Behavior

Twenty-Third Edition

Dover Memorial Library
Gardner-Webb University
P.O. Box 836
Boiling Springs, N.C. 28017

EDITOR

Karen G. Duffy

SUNY at Geneseo (Emerita)

Karen G. Duffy holds a doctorate in psychology from Michigan State University, and she is an emerita Distinguished Service Professor of State University of New York at Geneseo. Dr. Duffy continues to work on her books and research, and she is also involved in several community service projects both in the United States and Russia.

McGraw-Hill/Dushkin

530 Old Whitfield Street, Guilford, Connecticut 06437

Visit us on the Internet
http://www.dushkin.com

Credits

1. **Becoming a Person: Foundations**
   Unit photo—© 2003 by PhotoDisc, Inc.
2. **Determinants of Behavior: Motivation, Environment, and Physiology**
   Unit photo—WHO photo.
3. **Problems Influencing Personal Growth**
   Unit photo—Courtesy of McGraw-Hill/Dushkin.
4. **Relating to Others**
   Unit photo—Courtesy of McGraw-Hill/Dushkin.
5. **Dynamics of Personal Adjustment: The Individual and Society**
   Unit photo—© 2003 by Cleo Freelance Photography.
6. **Enhancing Human Adjustment: Learning to Cope Effectively**
   Unit photo—© 2003 by Cleo Freelance Photography.

BF
698
.A1
P47
2003-04

Copyright

Cataloging in Publication Data
Main entry under title: Annual Editions: Personal Growth and Behavior. 2003/2004.
1. Personal Growth and Behavior—Periodicals. I. Duffy, Karen G., *comp.* II. Title: Personal Growth and Behavior.
ISBN 0–07–254834–7   658'.05   ISSN 0732–0779

© 2003 by McGraw-Hill/Dushkin, Guilford, CT 06437, A Division of The McGraw-Hill Companies.

Copyright law prohibits the reproduction, storage, or transmission in any form by any means of any portion of this publication without the express written permission of McGraw-Hill/Dushkin, and of the copyright holder (if different) of the part of the publication to be reproduced. The Guidelines for Classroom Copying endorsed by Congress explicitly state that unauthorized copying may not be used to create, to replace, or to substitute for anthologies, compilations, or collective works.

Annual Editions® is a Registered Trademark of McGraw-Hill/Dushkin, A Division of The McGraw-Hill Companies.

Twenty-third Edition

Cover image © 2003 PhotoDisc, Inc.
Printed in the United States of America   1234567890BAHBAH543   Printed on Recycled Paper

Editors/Advisory Board

Members of the Advisory Board are instrumental in the final selection of articles for each edition of ANNUAL EDITIONS. Their review of articles for content, level, currentness, and appropriateness provides critical direction to the editor and staff. We think that you will find their careful consideration well reflected in this volume.

EDITOR

Karen G. Duffy
SUNY at Geneseo (Emerita)

ADVISORY BOARD

Sonia L. Blackman
California State Polytechnic University

Linda Corrente
Community College of Rhode Island

Robert DaPrato
Solano Community College

Mark J. Friedman
Montclair State University

Roger Gaddis
Gardner-Webb University

Richard A. Kolotkin
Minnesota State University, Moorhead

Angela J.C. LaSala
Community College of Southern Nevada

David M. Malone
Duke University

Karla K. Miley
Black Hawk College

Terry F. Pettijohn
Ohio State University

Victor L. Ryan
University of Colorado, Boulder

Pamela E. Stewart
Northern Virginia Community College

Robert S. Tomlinson
University of Wisconsin, Eau Claire

Charmaine Wesley-Hartman
Modesto Junior College

Lois J. Willoughby
Miami Dade Community College - Kendall

Staff

EDITORIAL STAFF

Ian A. Nielsen, Publisher
Roberta Monaco, Senior Developmental Editor
Dorothy Fink, Associate Developmental Editor
Iain Martin, Associate Developmental Editor
Addie Raucci, Senior Administrative Editor
Robin Zarnetske, Permissions Editor
Marie Lazauskas, Permissions Assistant
Diane Barker, Proofreader
Lisa Holmes-Doebrick, Senior Program Coordinator

TECHNOLOGY STAFF

Richard Tietjen, Senior Publishing Technologist
Jonathan Stowe, Executive Director of eContent
Marcuss Oslander, Sponsoring Editor of eContent
Christopher Santos, Senior eContent Developer
Janice Ward, Software Support Analyst
Angela Mule, eContent Developer
Michael McConnell, eContent Developer
Ciro Parente, Editorial Assistant
Joe Offredi, Technology Developmental Editor

PRODUCTION STAFF

Brenda S. Filley, Director of Production
Charles Vitelli, Designer
Mike Campell, Production Coordinator
Laura Levine, Graphics
Tom Goddard, Graphics
Eldis Lima, Graphics
Nancy Norton, Graphics
Juliana Arbo, Typesetting Supervisor
Karen Roberts, Typesetter
Jocelyn Proto, Typesetter
Cynthia Powers, Typesetter
Cathy Kuziel, Typesetter
Larry Killian, Copier Coordinator

To the Reader

In publishing ANNUAL EDITIONS we recognize the enormous role played by the magazines, newspapers, and journals of the public press in providing current, first-rate educational information in a broad spectrum of interest areas. Many of these articles are appropriate for students, researchers, and professionals seeking accurate, current material to help bridge the gap between principles and theories and the real world. These articles, however, become more useful for study when those of lasting value are carefully collected, organized, indexed, and reproduced in a low-cost format, which provides easy and permanent access when the material is needed. That is the role played by ANNUAL EDITIONS.

Have you ever watched children on a playground? Some children are reticent; watching the other children play, they sit demurely on the sidelines and shun becoming involved in the fun. Some children readily and happily interact with their playmates. They take turns, share their toys, and follow the rules of the playground. Other children are bullies who brazenly taunt the playing children and aggressively take others' possessions. What makes each child so different? Do these childhood behaviors forecast adult behaviors? Can children's (or adults') behaviors, especially antisocial ones, be changed?

These questions are not new. Lay persons and social scientists alike have always been curious about human nature. The answers to our questions, though, are incomplete, because attempts to address these issues are relatively new or just developing. Psychology, the science that can and should answer questions about individual differences, is the primary focus of this book, and has existed for well over 100 years. That may seem old to you, but psychology is young when other disciplines are considered. Mathematics, medicine, and philosophy are thousands of years old.

By means of psychology and related sciences, this anthology will help you explore the issues of individual differences and their origins, methods of coping, personality change, and other matters of human adjustment. The purpose of this anthology is to compile the newest, most complete and readable articles that examine individual behavior and adjustment as well as the dynamics of personal growth and interpersonal relationships. The readings in this book offer interesting insights into both the everyday and scientific worlds, a blend welcomed by most of today's specialists in human adjustment. The anthology is revised each year to reflect both traditional viewpoints and emerging perspectives about people's behavior. Thanks to the editorial board's valuable advice, the present edition has been completely revised and includes a large number of new articles representing the latest thinking in the field.

Annual Editions: Personal Growth and Behavior 03/ 04 comprises six units, each of which serves a distinct purpose. The first unit is concerned with theories and philosophies related to self-identity. For example, one theory, humanism, hypothesizes that self-concept and self-esteem—our feelings about who and how worthy we are—represent the most valuable components of personality.

This unit includes articles that supplement the theoretical articles by providing applications of, or alternate perspectives on, popular theories about personal growth and human adjustment. These include all of the classic and major theories of personality: humanistic, psychoanalytic, behavioral, and trait theories.

The second unit provides information on how and why a person develops in a particular way—in other words, what factors determine or direct individual growth: biology, heredity, experience, or some combination. The third unit pertains to problems commonly encountered in the different stages of development: infancy, childhood, adolescence, middle age, and adulthood.

The fourth and fifth units are similar in that they address social problems of adjustment—problems that occur in interpersonal relationships and issues that are endemic to society or culture. Unit 4 concerns interpersonal topics such as friendship and shyness, while unit 5 discusses broader societal issues such as racism, evolving gender roles, and changing work habits. The final unit focuses on adjustment or how most people cope with problems of daily existence or various mental disorders.

Annual Editions: Personal Growth and Behavior 03/ 04 will challenge you and interest you on a variety of topics. It will provide you with many answers, but it will also stimulate many questions. Perhaps it will inspire you to continue your study of the burgeoning field of psychology, which is responsible for exploring personal growth and behavior. As has been true in the past, your feedback on this edition would be valuable for future revisions. Please take a moment to fill out and return the postage-paid article rating form on the last page. Thank you.

Karen Groves Duffy

Karen G. Duffy
Editor

Contents

UNIT 1
Becoming a Person: Foundations

Five unit selections discuss the psychosocial development of an individual's personality. Attention is given to values, emotions, lifestyles, and self-concept.

The concepts in bold italics are developed in the article. For further expansion, please refer to the Topic Guide and the Index.

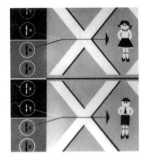

UNIT 2
Determinants of Behavior: Motivation, Environment, and Physiology

Eight articles in this section examine the effects of culture, genes, and emotions on an individual's behavior.

The concepts in bold italics are developed in the article. For further expansion, please refer to the Topic Guide and the Index.

UNIT 3
Problems Influencing Personal Growth

This unit's ten articles consider aging, development, self-image, and social interaction, and their influences on personal growth.

The concepts in bold italics are developed in the article. For further expansion, please refer to the Topic Guide and the Index.

UNIT 4
Relating to Others

Ten unit articles examine some of the dynamics involved in relating to others. Topics discussed include friendship, love, the importance of family ties, and self-esteem.

The concepts in bold italics are developed in the article. For further expansion, please refer to the Topic Guide and the Index.

UNIT 5
Dynamics of Personal Adjustment: The Individual and Society

Eight selections discuss some of the problems experienced by individuals as they attempt to adjust to society.

The concepts in bold italics are developed in the article. For further expansion, please refer to the Topic Guide and the Index.

UNIT 6
Enhancing Human Adjustment: Learning to Cope Effectively

Six selections examine some of the ways an individual learns to cope successfully within today's society. Topics discussed include therapy, depression, and interpersonal relations.

The concepts in bold italics are developed in the article. For further expansion, please refer to the Topic Guide and the Index.

Topic Guide

This topic guide suggests how the selections in this book relate to the subjects covered in your course. You may want to use the topics listed on these pages to search the Web more easily.

On the following pages a number of Web sites have been gathered specifically for this book. They are arranged to reflect the units of this *Annual Edition.* You can link to these sites by going to the DUSHKIN ONLINE support site at *http://www.dushkin.com/online/.*

ALL THE ARTICLES THAT RELATE TO EACH TOPIC ARE LISTED BELOW THE BOLD-FACED TERM.

World Wide Web Sites

The following World Wide Web sites have been carefully researched and selected to support the articles found in this reader. The easiest way to access these selected sites is to go to our DUSHKIN ONLINE support site at *http://www.dushkin.com/online/*.

AE: Personal Growth and Behavior 03/04

The following sites were available at the time of publication. Visit our Web site—we update DUSHKIN ONLINE regularly to reflect any changes.

General Sources

National Institute of Child Health and Human Development (NICHD)
http://www.nichd.nih.gov

The NICHD conducts and supports research on the reproductive, neurobiologic, developmental, and behavioral processes that determine and maintain the health of children and adults.

Psychnet
http://www.apa.org/psychnet/

Get information on psychology from this Web site through the site map or by using the search engine. Access *APA Monitor,* the American Psychological Association newspaper; APA Books on a wide range of topics; PsychINFO, an electronic database of abstracts on over 1,350 scholarly journals; and HelpCenter for information on dealing with modern life problems.

UNIT 1: Becoming a Person: Foundations

Abraham A. Brill Library
http://plaza.interport.net/nypsan/service.html

The Abraham A. Brill Library, perhaps the largest psychoanalytic library in the world, contains data on over 40,000 books, periodicals, and reprints in psychoanalysis and related fields. Its holdings span the literature of psychoanalysis from its beginning to the present day.

JungWeb
http://www.cgjungboston.com/

Dedicated to the work of Carl Jung, this site is a comprehensive resource for Jungian psychology. Links to Jungian psychology, reference materials, graduate programs, dreams, multilingual sites, and related Jungian themes are available.

Sigmund Freud and the Freud Archives
http://plaza.interport.net/nypsan/freudarc.html

Internet resources related to Sigmund Freud can be accessed through this site. A collection of libraries, museums, and biographical materials, as well as the Brill Library archives, can be found here.

UNIT 2: Determinants of Behavior: Motivation, Environment, and Physiology

American Psychological Society (APS)
http://www.psychologicalscience.org

APS membership includes a diverse group of the world's foremost scientists and academics working to expand basic and applied psychological science knowledge. Links to teaching, research, and graduate studies resources are available.

Federation of Behavioral, Psychological, and Cognitive Science
http://www.thefederationonline.org/welcome.html

At this site you can hotlink to the National Institutes of Health's medical database, government links to public information on mental health, a social psychology network, and the Project on the Decade of the Brain.

Max Planck Institute for Psychological Research
http://www.mpipf-muenchen.mpg.de/BCD/bcd_e.htm

Several behavioral and cognitive development research projects are available on this site.

The Opportunity of Adolescence
http://www.winternet.com/~webpage/adolescencepaper.html

This paper calls adolescence the turning point, after which the future is redirected and confirmed, and goes on to discuss the opportunities and problems of this period to the individual and society, using quotations from Erik Erikson, Jean Piaget, and others.

Psychology Research on the Net
http://psych.hanover.edu/APS/exponnet.html

Psychologically related experiments on the Internet can be found at this site. Biological psychology/neuropsychology, clinical psychology, cognition, developmental psychology, emotions, general issues, health psychology, personality, sensation/perception, and social psychology are addressed.

Serendip
http://serendip.brynmawr.edu/serendip/

Organized into five subject areas (brain and behavior, complex systems, genes and behavior, science and culture, and science education), Serendip contains interactive exhibits, articles, links to other resources, and a forum area for comments and discussion.

UNIT 3: Problems Influencing Personal Growth

Adolescence: Changes and Continuity
http://www.personal.psu.edu/faculty/n/x/nxd10/adolesce.htm

This site offers a discussion of puberty, sexuality, biological changes, cross-cultural differences, and nutrition for adolescents, including obesity and its effects on adolescent development.

Ask NOAH About: Mental Health
http://www.noah-health.org/english/illness/mentalhealth/mental.html

This enormous resource contains information about child and adolescent family problems, mental conditions and disorders, suicide prevention, and much more.

Facts for Families
http://www.aacap.org/info_families/index.htm

The American Academy of Child and Adolescent Psychiatry provides concise, up-to-date information on issues that affect teenagers and their families. Fifty-six fact sheets include many teenager's issues.

www.dushkin.com/online/

Mental Health Infosource: Disorders
http://www.mhsource.com/disorders/

This no-nonsense page lists hotlinks to psychological disorders pages, including anxiety, panic, phobic disorders, schizophrenia, and violent/self-destructive behaviors.

Mental Health Risk Factors for Adolescents
http://education.indiana.edu/cas/adol/mental.html

This collection of Web resources is useful for parents, educators, researchers, health practitioners, and teens. It covers a great deal, including abuse, conduct disorders, and stress.

Suicide Awareness: Voices of Education
http://www.save.org

This is the most popular suicide site on the Internet. It is very thorough, with information on dealing with suicide (both before and after), along with material from the organization's many education sessions.

UNIT 4: Relating to Others

CYFERNET-Youth Development
http://www.cyfernet.mes.umn.edu/youthdev.html

An excellent source of many articles on youth development, this site includes a statement on the concept of normal adolescence and impediments to healthy development.

Hypermedia, Literature, and Cognitive Dissonance
http://www.engr.ncsu.edu/TDE_Workshop/1997/abstracts/gingher.html

This article, subtitled *The Heuristic Challenges of Connectivity*, discusses EQ (emotional intelligence) in adults and offers an interactive study, the Metatale Paradigm, that is linked to story sources. Click on *http://www.uncg.edu/~rsginghe/metatext.htm* for access.

Emotional Intelligence Discovery
http://www.cwrl.utexas.edu/~bump/Hu305/3/3/3/

This site has been set up by students to talk about and expand on Daniel Goleman's book, *Emotional Intelligence*. There are links to many other EI sites.

The Personality Project
http://www.personality-project.org/personality.html

The Personality Project of William Revelle, director of the Graduate Program in Personality at Northwestern University, is meant to guide those interested in personality theory and research to the current personality research literature.

UNIT 5: Dynamics of Personal Adjustment: The Individual and Society

AFF Cult Group Information
http://www.csj.org/index.html

Information about cults, cult groups, and psychological manipulation is available at this page sponsored by the secular, not-for-profit, tax-exempt research center and educational organization, American Family Foundation.

Explanations of Criminal Behavior
http://www.uaa.alaska.edu/just/just110/crime2.html

An excellent outline of the causes of crime, including major theories, which was prepared by Darryl Wood at the University of Alaska, Anchorage, can be found at this site.

National Clearinghouse for Alcohol and Drug Information
http://www.health.org

This is an excellent general site for information on drug and alcohol facts that might relate to adolescence and the issues of peer pressure and youth culture. Resources, referrals, research

and statistics, databases, and related Internet links are among the options available at this site.

Schools Health Education Unit (SHEU)
http://www.sheu.org.uk/sheu.htm

SHEU is a research unit that offers survey, research, and evaluation services on health and social development for young people.

UNIT 6: Enhancing Human Adjustment: Learning to Cope Effectively

John Suler's Teaching Clinical Psychology Site
http://www.rider.edu/users/suler/tcp.html

This page contains Internet resources for clinical and abnormal psychology, behavioral medicine, and mental health.

Health Information Resources
http://www.health.gov/nhic/Pubs/tollfree.htm

Here is a long list of toll-free numbers that provide health-related information. None offer diagnosis and treatment, but some do offer recorded information; others provide personalized counseling, referrals, and/or written materials.

Knowledge Exchange Network (KEN)
http://www.mentalhealth.org

The CMHS National Mental Health Services Exchange Network (KEN) provides information about mental health via toll-free telephone services, an electronic bulletin board, and publications. It is a one-stop source for information and resources on prevention, treatment, and rehabilitation services for mental illness, with many links to related sources.

Mental Health Net
http://www.mentalhealth.net

This comprehensive guide to mental health online features more than 6,300 individual resources. It covers information on mental disorders, professional resources in psychology, psychiatry, and social work, journals, and self-help magazines.

Mind Tools
http://www.mindtools.com/

Useful information on stress management can be found at this Web site.

NetPsychology
http://netpsych.com/index.htm

This site explores the uses of the Internet to deliver mental health services. This is a basic cybertherapy resource site.

We highly recommend that you review our Web site for expanded information and our other product lines. We are continually updating and adding links to our Web site in order to offer you the most usable and useful information that will support and expand the value of your Annual Editions. You can reach us at: *http://www.dushkin.com/annualeditions/*.

UNIT 1

Becoming a Person: Foundations

Unit Selections

1. **The Benefits of Positive Psychology**, Michael Craig Miller
2. **The Trouble With Self-Esteem**, Lauren Slater
3. **Repression Tries for Experimental Comeback**, Bruce Bower
4. **Why Our Kids Are Out of Control**, Jacob Azerrad with Paul Chance
5. **In Search of a Leader**, Linda S. Demorest and Deona Grady

Key Points to Consider

- Is it possible to trace the history of psychological thought? Why or why not? Where do you think psychological and psychiatric thinking will head in the future? Will events at any given point in world history influence the theories of psychologists and psychiatrists? Explain.

- Is self-concept the most important human construct? Do you think that the development of self is driven by biology? Why or why not? What else do you think prompts the development of self-concept? How do you think evaluations from others affect our self-concept, especially self-esteem? What are the consequences of low self-esteem? What are the consequences of over-inflated self-esteem. Explain what a person with too low or too high esteem could do to alter his or her perception of self-worth.

- Do you believe in the unconscious and repression? Why or why not? If yes, can you provide examples from your own life of their influence? What other concepts are important to Sigmund Freud's conceptualization of humans? Define and give examples of each. What contributions, if any, has Freud made to our understanding of human nature?

- What is behaviorism? To what general principles do behavioral theorists subscribe? Should we utilize punishment to alter or manage children's behaviors? Why or why not? Which is most preferred—reinforcement or punishment? Why? What do parents do that perpetuates children's misconduct? What should parents do differently?

- What is a personality trait? Do you think personality traits remain stable over a lifetime? Explain. Do traits remain stable across situations; that is, are they carried from church to school, for example? What traits do you possess? Would your friends agree with you? What traits do leaders possess? Do any of your traits overlap with those of leaders? Describe what you think are important leadership traits not included in the article on leaders.

- Which theory of human personality (humanistic, behavioral, psychoanalytic, or trait) do you think is best and why? How do these theories differ from one another; for example, how does each deal with the "nature" (goodness or badness) of humans? What part of our life experience is most important according to each theory?

 **Links: www.dushkin.com/online/**
These sites are annotated in the World Wide Web pages.

Abraham A. Brill Library
  http://plaza.interport.net/nypsan/service.html
JungWeb
  http://www.cgjungboston.com/
Sigmund Freud and the Freud Archives
  http://plaza.interport.net/nypsan/freudarc.html

A baby sits in front of a mirror and looks at himself. A chimpanzee sorts through photographs while its trainer carefully watches its reactions. A college student answers a survey about how she feels about herself. What does each of these events share with the others? All are examples of techniques used to investigate self-concept.

That baby in front of the mirror has a red dot on his nose. Researchers watch to see if the baby reaches for the dot in the mirror or touches his own nose. Recognizing the fact that the image he sees in the mirror is his own, the baby touches his real nose, not the nose in the mirror. Scientists thus claim that the baby has some conceptualization of himself.

The chimpanzee has been trained to sort photographs into two piles—human pictures or animal pictures. If the chimp has been raised with humans, the researcher wants to know into which pile (animal or human) the chimp will place its own picture. Is the chimp's concept of itself animal or human? Or does the chimp have no concept of self at all?

The college student taking the self-survey answers questions about her self image, whether she thinks she is fun to be with, whether she spends large amounts of time in fantasy, and what her feelings are about her personality and intelligence.

These research projects are designed to investigate how self-concept develops and, in turn, guides our behaviors and thoughts. Most psychologists believe that people develop a personal identity or a sense of self, which is a sense of who we are, our likes and dislikes, our characteristic feelings and thoughts, and an understanding of why we behave as we do. Self-concept is our knowledge of our gender, race, and age, as well as our sense of self-worth and more. Strong positive or negative feelings are usually attached to this identity. Psychologists are studying how and when this sense of self develops. Most psychologists do not believe that infants are born with a sense of self but rather that children slowly develop self-concept as a consequence of their experiences.

This unit delineates some of the popular viewpoints regarding how sense of self, personality, and behavior develop and how, or whether, they guide behavior. This knowledge of how self develops provides an important foundation for the rest of the units in this book. This unit explores major theories or forces in psychology: self or humanistic, behavioral, psychoanalytic, and trait theories. The last article is included because it references an important element that many of these theories ignore—culture.

The first article reviews the interesting and circuitous history of theories in the area of personal growth and development. In "The Benefits of Positive Psychology," the recent evolution of psychology from focusing on human foibles and problems to an emphasis on the more positive aspects of human existence is discussed. The human quality of optimism is given a central role in this article. You will find "positive psychology" reminiscent of humanistic psychology.

The next series of articles introduces to the reader some of the various theories about human nature. In the first article, the reader is provided with a critique of the concept of self-esteem. As noted earlier, some theorists, namely the humanists, believe that self-concept is the crux or glue of personality. Self-esteem is a related concept and refers to our perceived self-worth. In

"The Trouble With Self-Esteem," high and low self-esteem are analyzed. While psychologists have long thought that low esteem was problematic—perhaps leading to suicide—scientists are now discovering that individuals with inflated self-esteem also host their own set of difficulties.

The next article in this unit relates to a different theory, the psychoanalytic theory of Sigmund Freud. Psychoanalysis, a theory as well as a form of therapy, proposes that individuals possess a dark, lurking unconscious that often motivates negative behaviors such as guilt and defensiveness. This notion is quite a contrast to the more positive thinking of the humanists. This article reviews an important construct in this theory—repression. Contemporary psychologists, using sophisticated research techniques, are attempting to establish that repression indeed occurs.

The next article pertains to a third theory—behaviorism. Behaviorism expunges thought, emotion, and abstract concepts such as self from psychological philosophy. In "Why Our Kids Are Out of Control," the author discusses how, by means of rewards, parents often perpetuate a child's misbehavior.

The next essay in this unit offers a contrasting viewpoint on human nature, known as the trait or dispositional approach. Trait theories in general hold that personality is composed of various traits that perhaps may be bound together by self-concept. This theory claims that most personality traits remain constant over time, a view that is in sharp contrast to other theories—humanistic theories that propose continued growth, the psychoanalytic stage theory of Freud, and the behavior change model of learning theories and behaviorism. While most trait theorists often propose that we are all individually different, the penultimate article in this unit, "In Search of a Leader," reveals which traits leaders share in common.

The Benefits of Positive Psychology

It may seem like a strange time to write about optimism. After the disaster of last September, we considered delaying this article. But perhaps a historical moment of pessimism and fear is also a suitable moment to consider the benefits of positive psychology.

This subject has evolved from a kind of secular evangelism—the famous "power of positive thinking"—into a formal discipline and intellectual movement. One of the movement's leaders and spokesmen, Martin E.P. Seligman, has described its aims most clearly. Researchers in positive psychology seek a detailed understanding of positive human experience at both individual and social levels. They are interested in individual attributes like the ability to engage in satisfying and joyful activities, maintain an optimistic outlook, and live in accord with positive values. They are also concerned about the qualities that make for good citizenship, which Seligman describes as "responsibility, nurturance, altruism, civility, moderation, tolerance, and work ethic." After the September terror attack, journalists described such qualities emerging in our society, at least in the short run.

Optimism does not suffice in a crisis, especially if it is defined as the inclination to put the most favorable construction upon things or anticipate the best possible outcome. That might imply blindness to painful realities—hardly a useful attitude. Seligman's list shows that positive psychology involves more than optimism. It requires an ability to grapple with real problems.

Realism can strike either a negative or positive note. Aldous Huxley, the British novelist and essayist, wrote, "Cynical realism—it's the intelligent man's best excuse for doing nothing in an intolerable situation." The French author and filmmaker Jean Cocteau, put a different spin on the subject: "True realism consists in revealing the surprising things which habit keeps covered and prevents us from seeing."

Given these conflicting sentiments, it's reasonable to ask when realism is advantageous and when it is not. On the most basic evolutionary level, success must depend in large part on a realistic appraisal of risks. Some experimental psychologists have noted the paradox that depressed and even pessimistic people are more realistic than average (see "Depressive Realism: Sadder but Wiser?" Harvard Mental Health Letter, Vol. 11, No. 10, April 1995). Does this mean there is some advantage to being depressed? Perhaps temporarily, in some circum-

stances, but not if the depression continues and causes persistent passivity and helplessness. Fortunately, whether or not depression promotes realism, there is no evidence that the converse is true; we cannot say that realism causes depression or pessimism. This should be reassuring at a time when the reality of the world's dangers is so clear.

Researchers have recently been studying the impact of optimism on health and well-being. Some of their work demonstrates what seems intuitively obvious—people with a positive outlook tend to have better morale and a greater adaptive capacity. Because they are more resilient in the face of stress, adversity, or loss, they actually suffer less even in the worst circumstances. They respond to challenges more flexibly and creatively. They are likely to be ready for trouble when it comes, and they have learned how to confront and overcome rather than avoid it. Their outlook allows them to work through difficulties effectively rather than impulsively. They succeed because they persevere. Their personal relationships are satisfying, and they are confident of receiving help from friends, family members, co-workers, and the community when they need it.

Although it's slightly less obvious, a positive disposition also seems to be good for physical health. In several studies, optimists have been found to live longer, while pessimists suffer what some researchers call "excess mortality," not a good thing by anyone's standard. The evidence suggests that avoiding pessimism is more important than boosting optimism. Pessimistic, anxious, and depressed people are more likely to develop high blood pressure. Their immune systems are not as effective, and they recover from surgery more slowly and less completely. For example, a study of 650 patients in the Veterans Administration system found that a positive attitude was correlated with vitality, freedom from pain, and a feeling of being healthier in general. In a study of 300 heart patients, researchers found that optimists were less likely than pessimists to need rehospitalization after coronary bypass surgery.

Further evidence comes from a long-term study of 800 men and women who had answered a well-known psychological questionnaire, the Minnesota Multiphasic Personality Inventory (MMPI), in the 1960s. Investigators used the MMPI results along with the concept of "explanatory style," derived from Seligman's work, to sort out pessimists and optimists. The subjects with a pessimistic explanatory style were those with a tendency to anticipate catastrophe and blame themselves when things went wrong. Thirty years on, their physical health was worse than average, their death rate was higher than average, and they made more use of both medical and mental health services.

The authors suggest that pessimists may have been taking an unproductive approach to medical care—perhaps doing a poor job of seeking or using their doctors' advice. Or the disadvantage may have been biological; for example, their immune systems may have been weaker. Another study found that people with a pessimistic explanatory style did have lower concentrations of immunoglobulin A (IgA), one of the chemicals that is vital for an effective immune response.

But unrealistic optimism may also be a danger to health. In a recent Australian study, investigators asked 164 women about their attitudes toward breast cancer screening and 200 men about prostate cancer screening. The majority of both men and women thought they were less likely than average to develop one of these illnesses—although, of course, only half of them could be right. Such attitudes may cause people to neglect necessary cancer screening. The results of a study conducted in Hong Kong bear out this conclusion—high optimism scores were correlated with less concern about taking action to prevent illness.

Turn the question around. Are people who engage in risky behavior overoptimistic? Do they underestimate the likelihood of a bad outcome? Apparently they don't. In a study of 74 college students, the ones who took more risks did not judge the probability of trouble to be lower. They had just decided that certain risks were worth taking.

This evidence is not conclusive, partly because many different human factors must be considered, but it is worth noting. The correlation between a positive attitude and good physical health seems to be real. There's also good reason to believe the connection is causal—constructive, realistically optimistic attitudes toward life's painful events are physically as well as emotionally healthful—although it's not yet clear exactly how the relationship works out in psychological and biological terms.

These data offer further encouragement to the study of positive psychology. A resurgence of positive human values in America may have been one byproduct of the tragic events of September 2001, but we can hope to arrive at the same place by other, happier routes. We have ample reason to be interested in all potential ways of promoting resilience, the ability to stay engaged in satisfying pursuits, and a sensible balance of optimism and realism.

—Michael Craig Miller, M.D.

For Further Reading

Achat, H., Kawachi, I. Spiro, A. 3rd, DeMolles, D.A., and Sparrow, D. "Optimism and Depression as Predictors of Physical and Mental Health Functioning: The Normative Aging Study," Annals of Behavioral Medicine (2000):Vol. 22, pp.127–30.

Clarke, V.A., Lovegrove, H., Williams, A. and Machpherson, M. "Unrealistic Optimism and the Health Belief Model," Journal of Behavioral Medicine (2000): Vol. 23, pp. 367–76.

Maruta, T., Colligan, R.C., Malinchoc, M. and Offord, K.P. "Optimists vs. Pessimists: Survival Rate Among Medical Patients Over a 30-Year Period," Mayo Clinic Proceedings (2000): Vol. 75, pp.140–3.

Raikkonen, K., Matthews, K.A., Flory, J.D., Owens, J.F., and Gump, B.B. "Effects Of Optimism, Pessimism, and Trait Anxiety on Ambulatory Blood Pressure and Mood During Everyday Life," Journal of Personality and Social Psychology (1999): Vol. 76, pp. 104–13.

Seligman, M.E.P. "Positive Psychology, Positive Prevention, and Positive Therapy," Handbook of Positive Psychology. Oxford University Press (in press).

From *The Harvard Mental Health Letter,* January 2002. © 2002 by President and Fellows of Harvard College. Reprinted by permission.

The Trouble With Self-Esteem

Maybe thinking highly of yourself is the real problem.

By Lauren Slater

Take this test:
1. On the whole I am satisfied with myself.
2. At times I think that I am no good at all.
3. I feel that I have a number of good qualities.
4. I am able to do things as well as most other people.
5. I feel I do not have much to be proud of.
6. I certainly feel useless at times.
7. I feel that I am a person of worth, at least the equal of others.
8. I wish I could have more respect for myself.
9. All in all, I am inclined to feel that I am a failure.
10. I take a positive attitude toward myself.

Devised by the sociologist Morris Rosenberg, this questionnaire is one of the most widely used self-esteem assessment scales in the United States. If your answers demonstrate solid self-regard, the wisdom of the social sciences predicts that you are well adjusted, clean and sober, basically lucid, without criminal record and with some kind of college cum laude under your high-end belt. If your answers, on the other hand, reveal some inner shame, then it is obvious: you were, or are, a teenage mother; you are prone to social deviance; and if you don't drink, it is because the illicit drugs are bountiful and robust.

It has not been much disputed, until recently, that high self-esteem—defined quite simply as liking yourself a lot, holding a positive opinion of your actions and capacities—is essential to well-being and that its opposite is responsible for crime and substance abuse and prostitution and murder and rape and even terrorism. Thousands of papers in psychiatric and social-science literature suggest this, papers with names like "Characteristics of Abusive Parents: A Look At Self-Esteem" and "Low Adolescent Self-Esteem Leads to Multiple Interpersonal Problems." In 1990, David Long published "The Anatomy of Terrorism," in which he found that hijackers and suicide bombers suffer from feelings of worthlessness and that their violent, fluorescent acts are desperate attempts to bring some inner flair to a flat mindscape.

This all makes so much sense that we have not thought to question it. The less confidence you have, the worse you do; the more confidence you have, the better you do; and so the luminous loop goes round. Based on our beliefs, we have created self-esteem programs in schools in which the main objective is, as Jennifer Coon-Wallman, a psychotherapist based in Boston, says, "to dole out huge heapings of praise, regardless of actual accomplishment." We have a National Association for Self-Esteem with about a thousand members, and in 1986, the State Legislature of California founded the "California Task Force to Promote Self-Esteem and Personal and Social Responsibility." It was galvanized by Assemblyman John Vasconcellos, who fervently believed that by raising his citizens' self-concepts, he could divert drug abuse and all sorts of other social ills.

It didn't work.

In fact, crime rates and substance abuse rates are formidable, right along with our self-assessment scores on paper-and-pencil tests. (Whether these tests are valid and reliable indicators of self-esteem is a subject worthy of inquiry itself, but in the parlance of social-science writing, it goes "beyond the scope of this paper.") In part, the discrepancy between high self-esteem scores and poor social skills and academic acumen led researchers like Nicholas Emler of the London School of Economics and Roy Baumeister of Case Western Reserve University to consider the unexpected notion that self-esteem is overrated and to suggest that it may even be a culprit, not a cure.

"There is absolutely no evidence that low self-esteem is particularly harmful," Emler says. "It's not at all a cause of poor academic performance; people with low self-esteem seem to do just as well in life as people with high self-esteem. In fact, they may do better, because they often try harder." Baumeister takes Emler's findings a bit further, claiming not only that low self-esteem is in most cases a socially benign if not beneficent condition but also that its opposite, high self-regard, can maim and even kill. Baumeister conducted a study that found that some people with favorable views of themselves were more likely to administer loud blasts of ear-piercing noise to a subject than those more tepid, timid folks who held back the horn. An earlier experiment found that men with high self-esteem were more willing to put down victims to whom they had administered electric shocks than were their low-level counterparts.

Last year alone there were three withering studies of self-esteem released in the United States, all of which had the same central message: people with high self-esteem pose a greater threat to those around them than people with low self-esteem and feeling bad about yourself is not the cause of our country's biggest, most expensive social problems. The research is original and compelling and lays the groundwork for a new, important kind of narrative about what makes life worth living—if we choose to listen, which might be hard. One of this country's most central tenets, after all, is the pursuit of happiness, which has been strangely joined to the pursuit of self-worth. Shifting a paradigm is never easy. More than 2,000 books offering the attainment of self-esteem have been published; educational programs in schools designed to cultivate self-esteem continue to proliferate, as do rehabilitation programs for substance abusers that focus on cognitive realignment with self-affirming statements like, "Today I will accept myself for who I am, not who I wish I were." I have seen therapists tell their sociopathic patients to say "I adore myself" every day or to post reminder notes on their kitchen cabinets and above their toilet-paper dispensers, self-affirmations set side by side with waste.

W ILL WE GIVE these challenges to our notions about self-esteem their due or will the research go the way of the waste? "Research like that is seriously flawed," says Stephen Keane, a therapist who practices in Newburyport, Mass. "First, it's defining self-esteem according to very conventional and problematic masculine ideas. Second, it's clear to me that many violent men, in particular, have this inner shame; they find out early in life they're not going to measure up, and they compensate for it with fists. We need, as men, to get to the place where we can really honor and expand our natural human grace."

Keane's comment is rooted in a history that goes back hundreds of years, and it is this history that in part prevents us from really tussling with the insights of scientists like Baumeister and Emler. We have long held in this country the Byronic belief that human nature is essentially good or graceful, that behind the sheath of skin is a little globe of glow to be harnessed for creative uses. Benjamin Franklin, we believe, got that glow, as did Joseph Pulitzer and scads of other, lesser, folks who eagerly caught on to what was called, in the 19th century, "mind cure."

Mind cure augurs New Age healing, so that when we lift and look at the roots, New Age is not new at all. In the 19th century, people fervently believed that you were what you thought. Sound familiar? Post it above your toilet paper. You are what you think. What you think. What you think. In the 1920's, a French psychologist, Émile Coué, became all the rage in this country; he proposed the technique of autosuggestion and before long had many citizens repeating, "Day by day in every way I am getting better and better."

But as John Hewitt says in his book criticizing self-esteem, it was maybe Ralph Waldo Emerson more than anyone else who gave the modern self-esteem movement its most eloquent words and suasive philosophy. Emerson died more than a century ago, but you can visit his house in Concord, Mass., and see his bedroom slippers cordoned off behind plush velvet ropes

and his eyeglasses, surprisingly frail, the frames of thin gold, the ovals of shine, perched on a beautiful desk. It was in this house that Emerson wrote his famous transcendentalist essays like "On Self-Reliance," which posits that the individual has something fresh and authentic within and that it is up to him to discover it and nurture it apart from the corrupting pressures of social influence. Emerson never mentions "self-esteem" in his essay, but his every word echoes with the self-esteem movement of today, with its romantic, sometimes silly and clearly humane belief that we are special, from head to toe.

Self-esteem, as a construct, as a quasi religion, is woven into a tradition that both defines and confines us as Americans. If we were to deconstruct self-esteem, to question its value, we would be, in a sense, questioning who we are, nationally and individually. We would be threatening our self-esteem. This is probably why we cannot really assimilate research like Baumeister's or Emler's; it goes too close to the bone and then threatens to break it. Imagine if you heard your child's teacher say, "Don't think so much of yourself." Imagine your spouse saying to you, "You know, you're really not so good at what you do." We have developed a discourse of affirmation, and to deviate from that would be to enter another arena, linguistically and grammatically, so that what came out of our mouths would be impolite at best, unintelligible at worst.

Why have we so conflated the two quite separate notions—a) self and b) worth?

IS THERE A WAY to talk about the self without measuring its worth? Why, as a culture, have we so conflated the two quite separate notions—a) self and b) worth? This may have as much to do with our entrepreneurial history as Americans, in which everything exists to be improved, as it does, again, with the power of language to shape beliefs. How would we story the self if not triumphantly, redemptively, enhanced from the inside out? A quick glance at amazon.com titles containing the word "self" shows that a hefty percentage also have -improvement or -enhancement tucked into them, oftentimes with numbers—something like 101 ways to improve your self-esteem or 503 ways to better your outlook in 60 days or 604 ways to overcome negative self-talk. You could say that these titles are a product of a culture, or you could say that these titles and the contents they sheathe shape the culture. It is the old argument: do we make language or does language make us? In the case of self-esteem, it is probably something in between, a synergistic loop-the-loop.

On the subject of language, one could, of course, fault Baumeister and Emler for using "self-esteem" far too unidimensionally, so that it blurs and blends with simple smugness. Baumeister, in an attempt at nuance, has tried to shade the issue by referring to two previously defined types: high *unstable* self-esteem and high *well-grounded* self-esteem. As a psychologist, I remember once treating a murderer, who said, "The problem with me, Lauren, is that I'm the biggest piece of [expletive] the world revolves around." He would have scored high on a self-esteem inventory, but does he really "feel good" about himself?

And if he doesn't really feel good about himself, then does it not follow that his hidden low, not his high, self-esteem leads to violence? And yet as Baumeister points out, research has shown that people with overt low self-esteem aren't violent, so why would low self-esteem cause violence only when it is hidden? If you follow his train of thinking, you could come up with the sort of silly conclusion that covert low self-esteem causes aggression, but overt low self-esteem does not, which means concealment, not cockiness, is the real culprit. That makes little sense.

"The fact is," Emler says, "we've put antisocial men through every self-esteem test we have, and there's *no* evidence for the old psychodynamic concept that they secretly feel bad about themselves. These men are racist or violent because they don't feel bad *enough* about themselves." Baumeister and his colleagues write: "People who believe themselves to be among the top 10 percent on any dimension may be insulted and threatened whenever anyone asserts that they are in the 80th or 50th or 25th percentile. In contrast, someone with lower self-esteem who regards himself or herself as being merely in the top 60 percent would only be threatened by the feedback that puts him or her at the 25th percentile.… In short, the more favorable one's view of oneself, the greater the range of external feedback that will be perceived as unacceptably low."

Perhaps, as these researchers are saying, pride really is dangerous, and too few of us know how to be humble. But that is most likely not the entire reason why we are ignoring flares that say, "Look, sometimes self-esteem can be bad for your health." There are, as always, market forces, and they are formidable. The psychotherapy industry, for instance, would take a huge hit were self-esteem to be re-examined. After all, psychology and psychiatry are predicated upon the notion of the self, and its enhancement is the primary purpose of treatment. I am by no means saying mental health professionals have any conscious desire to perpetuate a perhaps simplistic view of self-esteem, but they are, we are (for I am one of them, I confess), the "cultural retailers" of the self-esteem concept, and were the concept to falter, so would our pocketbooks.

Really, who would come to treatment to be taken down a notch? How would we get our clients to pay to be, if not insulted, at least uncomfortably challenged? There is a profound tension here between psychotherapy as a business that needs to retain its customers and psychotherapy as a practice that has the health of its patients at heart. Mental health is not necessarily a comfortable thing. Because we want to protect our patients and our pocketbooks, we don't always say this. The drug companies that underwrite us never say this. Pills take you up or level you out, but I have yet to see an advertisement for a drug of deflation.

If you look at psychotherapy in other cultures, you get a glimpse into the obsessions of our own. You also see what a marketing fiasco we would have on our hands were we to dial down our self-esteem beliefs. In Japan, there is a popular form of psychotherapy that does not focus on the self and its worth. This psychotherapeutic treatment, called Morita, holds as its central premise that neurotic suffering comes, quite literally, from extreme self-awareness. "The most miserable people I know have been self-focused," says David Reynolds, a Morita practitioner in Oregon. Reynolds writes, "Cure is not defined by the alleviation of discomfort or the attainment of some ideal state (which is impossible) but by taking constructive action in one's life which helps one to live a full and meaningful existence and not be ruled by one's emotional state."

Morita therapy, which emphasizes action over reflection, might have some trouble catching on here, especially in the middle-class West, where folks would be hard pressed to garden away the 50-minute hour. That's what Morita patients do; they plant petunias and practice patience as they wait for them to bloom.

Like any belief system, Morita has its limitations. To detach from feelings carries with it the risk of detaching from their significant signals, which carry important information about how to act: reach out, recoil. But the current research on self-esteem does suggest that we might benefit, if not fiscally then at least spiritually, from a few petunias on the Blue Cross bill. And the fact that we continue, in the vernacular, to use the word "shrink" to refer to treatment means that perhaps unconsciously we know we sometimes need to be taken down a peg.

Down to… what? Maybe self-control should replace self-esteem as a primary peg to reach for. I don't mean to sound Puritanical, but there is something to be said for discipline, which comes from the word "disciple," which actually means to comprehend. Ultimately, self-control need not be seen as a constriction; restored to its original meaning, it might be experienced as the kind of practiced prowess an athlete or an artist demonstrates, muscles not tamed but trained, so that the leaps are powerful, the spine supple and the energy harnessed and shaped.

There are therapy programs that teach something like self-control, but predictably they are not great moneymakers and they certainly do not attract the bulk of therapy consumers, the upper middle class. One such program, called Emerge, is run by a psychologist named David Adams in a low-budget building in Cambridge, Mass. Emerge's clients are mostly abusive men, 75 percent of them mandated by the courts. "I once did an intake on a batterer who had been in psychotherapy for three years, and his violence wasn't getting any better," Adams told me. "I said to him, 'Why do you think you hit your wife?' He said to me, 'My therapist told me it's because I don't feel good about myself inside.'" Adams sighs, then laughs. "We believe it has *nothing* to do with how good a man feels about himself. At Emerge, we teach men to evaluate their behaviors honestly and to interact with others using empathy and respect." In order to accomplish these goals, men write their entire abuse histories on 12-by-12 sheets of paper, hang the papers on the wall and read them. "Some of the histories are so long, they go all around the room," Adams says. "But it's a powerful exercise. It gets a guy to really concretely *see*." Other exercises involve having the men act out the abuse with the counselor as the victim. Unlike traditional "suburban" therapies, Emerge is under no pressure to keep its customers; the courts do that for them. In return, they are free to pursue a path that has to do with "balanced confrontation," at the heart of which is critical reappraisal and self—no, not esteem—responsibility.

While Emerge is for a specific subgroup of people, it might provide us with a model for how to reconfigure treatment—and maybe even life—if we do decide the self is not about how good it feels but how well it does, in work and love. Work and love. That's a phrase fashioned by Freud himself, who once said the successful individual is one who has achieved meaningful work and meaningful love. Note how separate this sentence is from the notion of self. We blame Freud for a lot of things, but we can't blame that cigar-smoking Victorian for this particular cultural obsession. It was Freud, after all, who said that the job of psychotherapy was to turn neurotic suffering into ordinary suffering. Freud never claimed we should be happy, and he never claimed confidence was the key to a life well lived.

I remember the shock I had when I finally read this old analyst in his native tongue. English translations of Freud make him sound maniacal, if not egomaniacal, with his bloated words like id, ego and superego. But in the original German, id means under-I, ego translates into I and superego is not super-duper but, quite simply, over-I. Freud was staking a claim for a part of

the mind that watches the mind, that takes the global view in an effort at honesty. Over-I. I can see. And in the seeing, assess, edit, praise and prune. This is self-appraisal, which precedes self-control, for we must first know both where we flail and stumble, and where we are truly strong, before we can make disciplined alterations. Self-appraisal. It has a certain sort of rhythm to it, does it not? Self-appraisal may be what Baumeister and Emler are actually advocating. If our lives are stories in the making, then we must be able to edit as well as advertise the text. Self-appraisal. If we say self-appraisal again and again, 101 times, 503 times, 612 times, maybe we can create it. And learn its complex arts.

Lauren Slater is a psychologist. Her memoir, "Love Works Like This," will be published by Random House in May.

From *The New York Times Magazine,* February 3, 2002. © 2002 by The New York Times Company. Reprinted by permission.

Repression tries for experimental comeback

Sigmund Freud and his theoretical heirs have held that people are capable of pushing unwanted memories into a kind of unconscious cold-storage, where they're gone but not forgotten. Many memory researchers view this mental process, called repression, as a fanciful idea lacking empirical support.

In the March 15 NATURE, researchers describe an everyday form of induced forgetting that may provide a scientific footing for Freudian repression.

When people consistently try to forget a memory in the face of reminders, they often succeed rather well at it, say psychologists Michael C. Anderson and Collin Green of the University of Oregon in Eugene. Successful forgetting increases with practice at avoiding a memory, Anderson and Green say.

"Everyday mechanisms of memory inhibition provide a viable model of repression," Anderson says. His view counters that of some clinicians, who hold that repression exists but only as a special process for dealing with traumas.

Anderson's work was inspired by the finding that kids who have been sexually abused by a trusted caregiver forget that experience far more often than do kids abused by a stranger. Children can willingly use indirect reminders, such as the abuser's presence, as cues to avoid thinking about the actual abuse, according to Anderson.

He and Green had 32 college students learn arbitrary word pairs, such as "ordeal-roach." Volunteers then saw a series of single words from those pairs. Words were shown once, eight times, 16 times, or not at all. On each presentation, participants saw a signal to either remember and say aloud the associated word or to avoid thinking about it.

On an ensuing memory test, students recalled nearly all of the words that they had tried to remember. Volunteers recalled progressively fewer other words, the more chances they had to try to forget them. On average, they recalled about 80 percent of words they tried to forget.

Similar findings emerged when participants saw new words and cues intended to jog their memories, such as "insect-r__" to spur recall of "roach." Again, memory suffered for words that students had tried to forget. These findings indicate that volunteers forgot specific words deliberately blocked, not word pairs.

Comparable memory losses emerged for students told that trying to forget a word would make them think about it more. For instance, people told not to think about, say, a white bear, can't think of anything but that white bear.

In Anderson's studies, however, volunteers used cues such as "ordeal" to anticipate and fend off unwanted memories. The white bear never showed its face.

The new data suggest that brain networks that restrain communication "could give rise to the type of repression proposed by Freud to underlie neuroses," says Martin A. Conway of the University of Bristol in England.

Elizabeth F. Loftus of the University of Washington in Seattle notes that memory was still pretty good for those who tried to forget words. She doesn't regard the study as evidence of repression.

Anderson's findings are "broadly consistent" with Freudian repression, remarks Daniel L. Schacter of Harvard University. Still, he cautions, it's too early to conclude that willful forgetting applies to emotionally sensitive experience.

—*B. Bower*

From *Science News*, March 17, 2001, p. 164. © 2001 by the Science Service, 1719 N Street, N.W., Washington, D.C. 20036; www.sciserv.org. Reprinted by permission of Bruce Bower.

Why
Our Kids Are
Out of Control

Whiny, arrogant, rude, violent. America's children are showing their bad side. Child psychologist Jacob Azerrad, Ph.D., and Paul Chance, Ph.D., show us what we can do to save our children.

By Jacob Azerrad, Ph.D., with Paul Chance, Ph.D.

MICHAEL IS OUT OF CONTROL. HE HAS SEVERAL TEMPER TAN-trums a day, throws food during meals, deliberately breaks toys and household items, hits and bites his younger brother and sister and refuses to comply with reasonable requests. Asked to put away his toys or go to bed, the 5-year-old replies, "No. And you can't make me." He is, in truth, a very unpleasant child. He is also very unhappy: No one can behave as he does and feel good about himself or be pleased with life.

We seem to be in the midst of an epidemic of Michaels. I have been a child psychologist for 35 years, and each year I see parents dealing with more and more severe problems. Their children are not just ill-mannered, they are whiny, selfish, arrogant, rude, defiant and violent. Most of them are also miserable, as are their parents.

Such disgraceful behavior in young children predicts serious problems later in life. As adolescents they are more likely to drop out of school, use drugs, engage in de-linquency and be clinically depressed. And when I read newspaper articles about road rage, commuter rage and office rage it seems to me that many out-of-control chil-dren are growing up to be out-of-control adults.

Why are there so many out-of-control children today? Many explanations have been proposed: high-sugar di-ets, environmental toxins, allergies, television, psychiat-ric disorders. In considering these theories, it is useful to note that the rise in outrageous child behavior is largely an American phenomenon. Psychologist Tiffany Field, Ph.D., of the University of Miami School of Medicine, found that in France, for example, 3-year-olds behave ad-mirably in restaurants. They sit quietly and talk and eat their meals like "little adults." They do not argue or throw food or refuse to eat as many American children do.

In a separate study, Field noted another major differ-ence in the behavior of French and American preschool-ers: On playgrounds, French youngsters were aggressive toward their playmates only 1 percent of the time; Amer-ican preschoolers, by contrast, were aggressive 29 percent of the time. It is probably not a coincidence that France has the lowest murder rate in the industrialized world, and the United States has the highest.

Can such dramatic differences in behavior between ad-vanced, industrialized nations be accounted for by differ-ences in diet, toxins, allergies, television or psychiatric disorders? It seems extremely unlikely, and I have found no scientific evidence to support these theories. I suggest that the fundamental reason behind so many more Amer-ican children running amuck is child-rearing practices.

Let me explain: Studies have consistently shown that the problem behavior of children is typically the result of misplaced adult attention. In a study done many years ago, psychologist Betty Hart, Ph.D., and her colleagues at the University of Washington, studied the effects of atten-tion on Bill, a 4-year-old "crybaby" enrolled in a morning preschool. Each morning Bill had between five and 10 crying spells: He cried when he fell, bumped his head or if another child took away a toy. Each time Bill cried a teacher went to him to offer comfort. Hart and her col-leagues reasoned that this adult attention, though in-tended to reassure and comfort Bill, might actually be the reason for all his crying.

To test their hypothesis, the researchers asked the teachers to try a new strategy. Now when Bill cried, the teachers glanced at him to be sure he was not injured but did not go to him, speak to him or look at him. If he hap-pened to cry when a teacher was nearby, she turned her

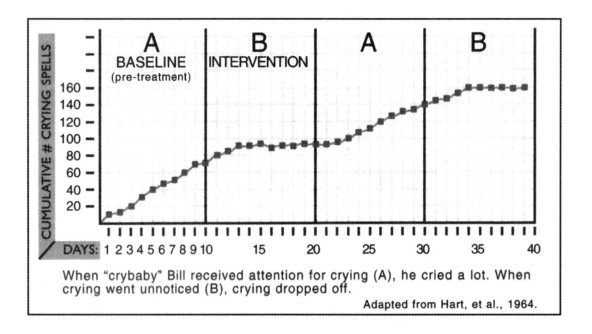

When "crybaby" Bill received attention for crying (A), he cried a lot. When crying went unnoticed (B), crying dropped off.

Adapted from Hart, et al., 1964.

back or walked away. Teachers paid special attention to Bill only when he suffered a mishap without crying. If he fell, for example, and went about his business without a whimper, a teacher would go to him and compliment him on his grown-up behavior. The result of this new approach: In five days the frequency of Bill's crying spells fell from an average of about seven per morning to almost zero.

"IT MAY SEEM ODD THAT REPRIMANDS, THREATS AND CRITICISM CAN REWARD BAD BEHAVIOR, BUT SUCH IS THE POWER OF ADULT ATTENTION."

To be certain that Bill's change in behavior was because of the new strategy, Hart and colleagues asked the teachers to once again pay attention to Bill when he cried. Bill returned to crying several times a day. When the teachers again ignored the crying and attended to Bill only when he acted maturely, the crying spells dropped sharply (see figure). Hart and her coworkers repeated this experiment with another "crybaby," Alan, and got nearly identical results. Similarly, researchers have shown that the disruptive behavior of school children is often a result of adult attention. In studies of elementary school classrooms, for example, researchers found some students repeatedly left their seats without good reason. Typically the teacher interrupted the lesson to reprimand them. But these efforts often increased the frequency of wandering.

When the teacher ignored children who wandered and paid attention to those who worked hard, the frequency of the problem behavior usually fell sharply. It may seem odd that reprimands, threats and criticism can actually reward bad behavior, but such is the tremendous power of adult attention. When children can get attention by behaving well, they do.

Unfortunately, many adults are far more likely to attend to annoying behavior than they are to desirable behavior. Glenn Latham, Ed.D., a family and educational consultant, has found that adults typically ignore 90 percent or more of the good things children do. Instead, they pay attention to children when they behave badly.

I believe that Americans attend more to bad behavior than to good behavior because they have come under the spell of self-described child-rearing authorities. These kiddie gurus—who include pediatrician Benjamin Spock, M.D., child psychiatrists T. Barry Brazelton, M.D., and Stanley Turecki, M.D., and child psychologist Ross W. Greene, Ph.D., among others—repeatedly urge parents to give special attention to children when they behave badly. Consider the following example.

In *Dr. Spock's Baby and Child Care* (Pocket Books, 1998), a book that has sold 40 million copies, Dr. Spock recommends this approach in dealing with aggressive behavior:

"If your child is hurting another or looks as if he were planning murder, pull him away in a matter-of-fact manner and get him interested in something else."

Given what research shows about the effects of adult attention, getting a child "interested in something else" whenever he is aggressive is a sure formula for producing a highly aggressive child.

If a child gets angry and throws or smashes things, Dr. Brazelton suggests the following:

TIME OUT THE RIGHT WAY

Most of the annoying things children do can be dealt with very effectively by ignoring them and attending to children when they behave more maturely. However, when the behavior is particularly immature or poses a risk of injury to the child or others, it may be necessary to turn to punishment. In these instances, Time Out usually does the trick.

Time Out is probably the most widely researched technique for dealing with unwanted behavior in young children. Unfortunately, it is often used incorrectly. It is therefore worth noting that Time Out means removing the child from all rewarding activities for a short period. The common practice of sending a child to his room, where he can play computer games, watch TV or talk with friends on the telephone, is not Time Out, nor is sitting on the couch with the child and discussing the merits of his behavior. Time Out means exposing the child to a very boring, unrewarding environment. For the sake of illustraiton, let's assume that your child has bitten someone. Here is a simple, highly effective way of discouraging this behavior:

1. Say to her: "We do not bite." Say nothing more than this—give no further description of the behavior, no explanation of what you are doing. Say nothing except, "We do not bite."

2. Take her by the hand and seat her in a small chair facing a blank wall. Stand close enough so that if she attempts to leave the chair you can immediately return her to it.

3. Keep her in the chair for three minutes. (Do not tell her how long she will be in the chair. Say nothing.) If she screams, kicks the wall, asks questions or says she has to go to the bathroom, ignore her. It is absolutely essential that you say nothing.

4. At the end of the three minutes, keep her in the chair until she has been quiet and well-behaved for five more seconds. When she does so, tell her she has been good and may now leave the chair. Never let her leave until she has been well-behaved for at least a few seconds.

5. Following Time Out, say nothing about it. Do not discuss the punished behavior or the fairness of the punishment. Say nothing except, "We do not bite."

Once the child realizes that you mean business, that she cannot manipulate you into providing attention for bad behavior, Time Out will proceed more smoothly and quickly and there will be far fewer times when you need to use it.

"Sit down with her in your lap until she's available to you. Then, discuss why you think she needed to do it, why she can't do it and how badly you know she feels for this kind of destructive, out-of-control behavior."

If your child has a particularly intense tantrum, Dr. Turecki gives this advice:

"With these tantrums you should be physically present with your child, with your arms around him if he'll permit it or just be there with him as a comforting physical presence in the room. Be calm and say reassuring things: 'I know you're upset, but it will be okay.'"

If the child has a tantrum that is not so intense, Turecki recommends being "menacing and firm." In other words, having a mild tantrum doesn't pay off, but having a severe tantrum does. I can scarcely imagine a more effective way of teaching a child to have severe tantrums.

Many of the most popular child-rearing books are full of such nonsense. They repeatedly urge parents to hold, soothe, comfort and talk to a child who bites, hits, screams, throws or breaks things, ignores or refuses parental requests or otherwise behaves in obnoxious, infantile ways. Common sense and a truckload of research argue solidly against this practice. Yet these experts seem to be unaware of the well-established fact that children do what gets noticed, that adult attention usually makes behavior more likely to occur, not less.

Nevertheless, thousands of parents follow the bad advice of these and like-minded child-rearing gurus every day. And the more faithfully they follow the advice, the worse their children become. Some of these parents eventually find their way to my office, desperate for help. I advise them to redirect their attention from infantile behavior to grown-up behavior. They are often amazed by the change in their children.

"IT IS A SAD REALITY THAT MANY (PERHAPS MOST) FORMS OF CHILD PSYCHOTHERAPY ARE A CONSUMER RIP-OFF."

—R. CHRISTOPHER BARDEN, PH.D., J.D., PRESIDENT, NATIONAL ASSOCIATION FOR CONSUMER PROTECTION IN MENTAL HEALTH PRACTICES

Take Dennis, for example. Ten-year-old Dennis was a "born liar," according to his mother, who added, "he wouldn't tell the truth if his life depended on it." Dennis had several siblings, but he was the only chronic liar. Why Dennis? With several children in the family, there was a good deal of competition for adult attention. Dennis wanted more than his share, and he got it by lying: His mother spent a lot of time with him trying to separate fact from fiction and trying to understand why he lied. Mom didn't realize it, but all this attention just encouraged dishonesty.

The solution was to give Dennis attention when it was clear he was telling the truth and to ignore him when he might be lying. When Mom knew that Dennis had given her the right amount of change after a purchase, or when a discrete call to his teacher proved that he really had been kept after school, he got time with Mom and approval for telling the truth. Instead of "tell a lie, get attention," the rule became, "tell the truth, get attention." When the rule changed, so did Dennis.

Five-year-old Debbie offered a different sort of challenge, but the solution was essentially the same. She woke up every night screaming because of nightmares about "the big germ" and "the terrible lion." Every night her parents rushed to her side to comfort her and assure her there were no big germs or terrible lions in the house. During the day, Debbie talked about her nightmares with anyone who would listen. Her mother encouraged this behavior because she thought it would be therapeutic for Debbie to get her fears "out in the open." In fact, all this attention to her fears made them worse, not better. From Debbie's standpoint, the lesson was: "If Mom and Dad are so interested in what I say about the big germ and the terrible lion, these monsters must really exist."

The solution to Debbie's problem was to pay less attention to talk about nightmares and more attention to grown-up behavior. When Mom and Dad started saying things like, "I appreciated it when you helped me set the table today" and "I heard you taking the phone message from Mrs. Smith. You were very grown up," they provided Debbie with better ways of getting attention than screaming in the night and complaining about monsters.

"THESE KIDDIE GURUS URGE PARENTS TO GIVE SPECIAL ATTENTION TO CHILDREN WHEN THEY BEHAVE BADLY."

Even Michael, the screaming, out-of-control boy who made life miserable for himself and everyone near him, soon became a happy, self-disciplined child. He was more challenging than most children, but once again the most important step to turning him around was giving him the attention he wanted when he gave his parents the behavior they wanted.

It sounds easier than it is. Parents who have fallen into the habit of offering attention for disagreeable behavior often have a hard time shifting their focus to agreeable behavior. Over the years I have devised a simple procedure to help parents do this. I call it the Nurture Response:

1. Be on the alert for behavior that indicates growing maturity: Taking disappointment calmly, performing spontaneous acts of kindness and demonstrating an interest in learning. When you see this kind of grown-up behavior, make a mental note of it. Perhaps Margaret, who usually responds to disappointments with a tantrum, is unperturbed when told her favorite breakfast cereal is unavailable. Maybe Sam, who is typically selfish with his belongings, shares his toys with the neighbor's child.

SEVEN TO 25 PERCENT OF PRESCHOOLERS MEET THE CRITERION FOR ODD— OPPOSITIONAL-DEFIANT DISORDER.

2. Some time later (anywhere from five minutes to five hours after the event), remind the child of the behavior you observed. You might say, "Do you remember when Harry's bike fell over and he couldn't straighten it because it was too heavy for him? You went over and helped him. Do you remember doing that?"

3. When you're sure the child remembers the event in question, praise her for it. You might say, "It was very good of you to help Harry with his bike. I'm proud of you." Often the highest praise you can offer children is to tell them they acted like an adult. You might say, "I know you were disappointed that you couldn't go to the mall, but you were very grown up about it. I was impressed."

Don't mix the praise with criticism. Don't say, for example, "I was proud of the way you helped Harry; you're usually so mean to him," or even, "I'm glad you were finally nice to Harry."

"THE FUNDAMENTAL REASON BEHIND SO MANY MORE AMERICAN CHILDREN RUNNING AMUCK IS CHILD-REARING PRACTICES."

4. Immediately after praising the child, spend some time with him in an activity he enjoys. Do this in a spontaneous way, without suggesting that it is payment for the grown-up behavior. You might play a favorite game, go for a walk, or read a story. Remember that nothing is more important to a child than the undivided attention of a parent, so give the child your full attention for these few minutes.

The nurture response is not a panacea, of course. Some dangerous or extremely annoying forms of behavior, such as knocking other children down or having screaming tantrums, may require additional measures, including punishment. But it is amazing how much can be accomplished by simply ignoring the behavior you don't want and noticing the behavior you do want.

For decades many child-rearing icons have urged parents to pay special attention to troublesome behavior, to offer sympathy, understanding and reassurance when children behave in outrageous ways. This view so pervades our society that scarcely anyone questions it. Both common sense and scientific evidence tell us, however, that this approach is bound to backfire, and it does.

Parents should think of themselves as gardeners. A good gardener encourages desirable plants and discourages undesirable ones. In the same way, a good parent encourages desirable acts and discourages undesirable ones.

Do you want your children to be well-behaved and happy? Then ignore experts who tell you to shower attention on children when they are badly behaved and miserable. Remember that gardeners must nurture the flowers, not the weeds.

Jacob Azerrad, Ph.D., has been a child psychologist for 35 years.

Paul Chance, Ph.D., is the book review editor of Psychology Today.

Reprinted with permission from *Psychology Today*, September/October 2001, pp. 42-48. © 2001 by (Sussex Publishers, Inc.).

In search of a leader

Abstract
Leadership ability is demonstrated through a variety of personality traits and abilities, including applied intelligence, charisma, effective communication and motivational skills, persistence, ethical standards of conduct, and a positive mental attitude.

Linda S. Demorest and Deona Grady

During the course of your career you may be called upon to hire a manager for your organization, or you may be asked to act in a leadership capacity. Whether you are seeking a leader or seeking to become a leader, you must first have an understanding of the skills necessary to the person in whom authority resides.

Leadership ability is demonstrated through a variety of personality traits and abilities. They include: applied intelligence, charisma, effective communication and motivational skills, persistence, ethical standards of conduct, and a positive mental attitude. Although the traits can be examined individually, successful leaders consistently exhibit all of these characteristics.

Applied Intelligence and Education

Intelligence is the ability to acquire knowledge. It also enables a person to be capable of original thought, imagination and innovation. Applied intelligence is a combination of academic learning and life experiences, with what is often referred to as common sense. Lifelong learning, through formal educational institutions and professional seminars is crucial to subject knowledge and critical thinking skills. Sociologists refer to our society as a "credential society." Employers often use diplomas and degrees to determine who is eligible for a job. A college degree is one significant way for a leader to establish credibility.

The ability to brainstorm and have new ideas is a strong leadership quality. Nobel Prize winning chemist Linus Pauling said, "The best way to get a good idea is to get lots of ideas." By successfully applying the best of your ideas, you can stay ahead of competition.

A good leader also recognizes when she has made mistakes and will learn from them. By examining a mistake from a lab experiment, Alexander Fleming discovered penicillin. He changed the course of medical history, and won the Nobel Prize in Medicine.

Charisma

The definition of charisma according to Webster's dictionary is "a special quality conferring to extraordinary powers of leadership and the ability to inspire veneration: a personal magnetism that enables an individual to attract or influence people." When seeking a quality leader, I strongly suggest you take Webster's definition to heart. People follow people they like. A person may have brilliant ideas, but if he cannot inspire others to follow he is likely to be worthless to your organization. If his people skills are weak, it could prove to be a grave detriment, costing the organization valuable employees who may choose to leave rather then tolerate working under the leadership of someone they dislike.

Effective Communication Skills

Richard Weaver, a central figure in the development of established persuasive techniques said, "Language is sermonic and we are all preachers in public and private capacities." In order to motivate others to think, feel and act in accordance with organizational goals, a leader must show effective communication skills. The ability to listen and truly hear what others are saying is as important as a full vocabulary and the verbal skills necessary to articulate thought. Speaking ability can be an innate talent or one developed through education and practice. A leader should excel in several communication forums:

- interpersonal communication in both formal interactions (demonstrated by the interview) and informal conversations

- public communication that may include business presentations, staff meetings, and representation of the organization within the community

- intercultural communication, a skill that has become mandatory as businesses expand to serve the needs of our global society

Having a sense of humor that people can identify with also is a valuable communication tool for a leader.

Motivational and Management Skills

There is a psychology to knowing how to motivate different individuals. The carrot on the stick may work for a while, but many people are motivated by more than chasing after a financial goal. John Kilcullen, founder and chief executive officer of IDG books (books "for Dummies") said, "My job as the leader is to make sure that the team has the tools and is nurtured so they can realize the company's vision." Michael Dell of Dell Computers uses a similar leadership style, abandoning the traditional vertical structure of corporations. He encourages employees to ask questions, and he deals directly with people responsible for problems instead of handling the situation through middle management. This hands-on approach is also acted out when Dell attends brown bag lunch sessions with his employees, monitors customer-service phone calls, and anonymously logs into chat rooms where users write about Dell and its competitors (talk about a fly on the wall!). Your corporate culture will determine the management style most valued by your organization, but a leader in any capacity must understand the importance of motivational skills and share the "core values" held in high regard by the organization she represents.

Persistence and Commitment

A leader must be persistent, focused and committed to goals. Writer Theodore Geisel, known throughout the world as Dr. Seuss, tried unsuccessfully for years to get his first book published. Editors believed his books lacked moral lessons. Educators thought the words he used were nonsensical and silly, and would confuse children just learning to read. Dr. Seuss did not change his style, and his first book was published only after a chance meeting with an old college buddy who worked in publishing. He became a best selling author of children's books, selling more than 200 million copies worldwide.

He also was very hard working, another criterion for leadership. Theodore Geisel, whom his biographer calls "the original workaholic" began his workday at around 10 a.m. and often worked past mid-night. He would take breaks to draw or read to keep his creative juices flowing, but he kept working on the project until finishing it.

The story of Gertrude Elion exemplifies another leader who was persistent, focused and committed to goals. She graduated from college with honors in chemistry in 1937, but could not find a job because employers felt a woman chemist would be "a distraction in the lab." She worked without compensation in a research lab until 1944, when she was offered a position as lab assistant at Burroughs Wellcome. Gertrude Elion worked at Burroughs Wellcome for 54 years. She discovered numerous drugs to treat serious illnesses, including a drug to fight transplant rejection. She was one of three co-recipients of the Nobel Prize in medicine in 1988.

You may not be able to find another Gertrude Elion for your organization, but look for several of the fundamental qualities of a good leader. Look for someone who is passionate about his or her work, someone who shows a history of overcoming obstacles and who believes in his or her ability to achieve goals.

Ethical Standards

It should go without saying that leaders must be honest and willing to adhere to personal and professional ethics. A leader in any capacity will make decisions and lead people to act. These actions will have consequences. It is imperative that the people you choose to lead have a clear understanding of the rules, of ethics that govern your industry and personal ethics that will set an example to other employees and garner respect from everyone that he or she comes into contact with. Thomas Paine, political philosopher said, "Character is much easier kept than recovered." It's an age-old dilemma. Many people seem to think

it is acceptable to get ahead by using whatever means necessary, without regard to ethical considerations. Do not allow a person with this mentality to lead your organization.

An error in judgment in regard to the ethics of your chosen leader has the potential to devastate your organization through the loss of respect from employees, competitors and clients, and this will translate into lost revenue that may never be recouped.

Positive Mental Attitude

Henry Ford said, "Whether you think you can or you think you can't, you are usually right." Self-image affects all aspects of whatever we do. It's like an aura of positive energy, or a stinky cloud of negative, self-defeating static. Your leader's attitude will affect all those under his or her leadership. It is imperative that you bring a positive attitude into your organization through positive leadership. Look for signs of a positive attitude in the candidate's posture, ability to make eye contact, speech and general presentation.

A charismatic leader with strong communication skills, but lacking education and or ethics may be initially effective but ultimately destructive. I encourage you take seriously your commitment to recognize leadership ability in others and within yourself. For better or worse, the person empowered to lead wields a mighty sword that can carry an organization to victory or leave it permanently severed.

Linda has been a member of ABWA since 1997 and is president of the Chintimini Chapter located in Corvallis, Ore. For two years, she has been writing professionally while returning to college to complete undergraduate requirements in preparation for law school. Prior to returning to school, she was an account executive. Deona lives in Belton, Mo., and is currently a stay-at-home mom. Prior to the birth of her three children she held a career in management.

From *Women in Business,* March/April 2002, pp. 11, 25. © 2002 by Women in Business.

UNIT 2

Determinants of Behavior: Motivation, Environment, and Physiology

Unit Selections

Key Points to Consider

- What evidence do we have that biology is not the only influence on our psychological being? How much of a role do you think the environment plays compared to biology? Explain.

- Based on your experience observing children, which would you say most contributes to personal growth: physiological or environmental factors? Defend your choice.

- What is schizophrenia? What are some of its symptoms? How can two brothers both have the disorder, yet the causes for each brother's psychosis differ? How common do you think it is to see mental disorder throughout a family tree? Is a familial disorder learned or inherited?

 **Links: www.dushkin.com/online/**
These sites are annotated in the World Wide Web pages.

American Psychological Society (APS)
   http://www.psychologicalscience.org
Federation of Behavioral, Psychological, and Cognitive Science
   http://www.thefederationonline.org/welcome.html
Max Planck Institute for Psychological Research
   http://www.mpipf-muenchen.mpg.de/BCD/bcd_e.htm
The Opportunity of Adolescence
   http://www.winternet.com/~webpage/adolescencepaper.html
Psychology Research on the Net
   http://psych.hanover.edu/APS/exponnet.html
Serendip
   http://serendip.brynmawr.edu/serendip/

On the front page of every newspaper, in practically every newscast, and on many magazine covers the problems of substance abuse in America haunt us. Innocent children are killed when caught in the crossfire of the guns of drug lords or even of their own classmates. Prostitutes selling their bodies for drug money spread the deadly AIDS virus. The white-collar middle manager loses his job because he embezzled company money to support his cocaine habit.

Why do people turn to drugs? Why doesn't the publicity about the ruination of human lives diminish the drug problem? Why can some people consume two cocktails and stop, while others feel helpless against the inebriating seduction of alcohol? Why do some people crave heroin as their drug of choice, while others choose cigarettes or caffeine?

The causes of individual behavior such as drug and alcohol abuse are the focus of this section. If physiology—either biochemistry, the nervous system, or genes—is the determinant of our behavior, then solutions to such puzzles as alcoholism lie in the field of psychobiology, the study of behavior in relation to biological processes, and in human medicine. However, if experience as a function of our environment and learning creates personality and coping ability and thus causes subsequent behavior, normal or not, then researchers must take a different tack and explore features of the environment responsible for certain behaviors. A third explanation is that the ability to adjust to change is produced by some complex interaction or interplay between experience and biology. If this interaction accounts for individual differences in personality and ability to cope, scientists then have a very complicated task ahead of them.

Conducting research designed to unravel the determinants of behavior is difficult. Scientists must call upon their best design skills to develop studies that will yield useful and replicable findings. A researcher hoping to examine the role of experience in personal growth and behavior needs to be able to isolate one or two stimuli or environmental features that seem to control a particular behavior. Imagine trying to delimit the complexity of the world sufficiently so that only one or two events stand out as the cause of an individual's alcoholism. Likewise, researchers interested in psychobiology also need refined, technical knowledge. Suppose a scientist hopes to show that a particular form of mental illness is inherited. She cannot merely examine family genetic histories, because family members can also learn maladaptive behaviors from one another. The researcher's ingenuity will be challenged; she must use intricate techniques such as comparing children to their adoptive parents as well as to their biological parents. Volunteer subjects may be difficult to find, and, even then, the data may be hard to interpret.

The first two articles in this unit offer general information on the interaction of nature and nurture. The first article, by Paul Ehrlich, explores the joint contributions of nature and nurture.

The article discusses the contributions of genes as well as the relative influence of the environment or culture. The author clearly and succinctly provides a general overview of the nature/nurture controversy.

A companion article discusses schizophrenia as an exemplar of the nature/nurture issue. From where does schizophrenia originate? An interesting case history of two brothers with schizophrenia examines how each brother developed the disorder. The complex unraveling of the nature and nurture of each brother's case is fascinating, because each brother's disorder seems to derive from different causes.

We next examine the role of nature, in particular of genetics in determining our behaviors. The first article, on personality genes, assesses how DNA exerts an influence on our developing personalities, one particular aspect of human nature. The article concludes with the understanding that genes do exert significant influence.

A companion article, "Where We Come From," points out that an individual's ancestral roots can often be traced through DNA. Another companion article, "The Secrets of Autism," discusses how such a disorder is usually tied to the action of multiple genes. The article is also interesting because it divulges information about this baffling and intriguing childhood disorder—autism—and provides some case studies as well.

The nervous system is also an important component of the biological determinants of our personal tendencies and behaviors. Three articles provide information about the brain, which is the focal point of the nervous system. In the first article, "Altered States of Consciousness," author Susan Greenfield asserts that the brain is very complex and that each part of the brain plays a different role in our thought processes. She deduces that understanding the brain and building computational models of the brain will be very difficult.

The influence of the brain on the expression of specific aspects of the human psyche is discussed in the next two articles. In the first, Ruth Palombo Weiss explores brain-based learning. Scientific information about the functioning of the brain now allows trainers and teachers to tailor their methods toward higher quality learning experiences for students and learners.

We next turn our attention away from psychobiology to human motivation—an entirely different determinant of human behavior and growth. Motivation, in general, guides and directs our behaviors. In "Resolved: No More Dumb Resolutions," Jennifer Huget discusses why people often set goals but don't achieve them. She offers very practical advice about how to set goals and unflinchingly attain them.

In summary, this unit covers factors that determine our behavior and thoughts, in other words, factors that are moderated by experience, genes, the nervous system, biochemistry, motives, or some combination of these.

The Tangled Skeins of Nature and Nurture in Human Evolution

By Paul R. Ehrlich

WHEN we think about our behavior as individuals, "Why?" is a question almost always on the tips of our tongues. Sometimes that question is about perceived similarities: why is almost everyone religious; why do we all seem to crave love; why do most of us like to eat meat? But our differences often seem equally or more fascinating: why did Sally get married although her sister Sue did not, why did they win and we lose, why is their nation poor and ours rich? What were the fates of our childhood friends? What kinds of careers did they have; did they marry; how many children did they have? Our everyday lives are filled with why's about differences and similarities in behavior, often unspoken, but always there. Why did one of my closest colleagues drink himself to death, whereas I, who love wine much more than he did, am managing to keep my liver in pretty good shape? Why, of two very bright applicants admitted to our department at Stanford University for graduate work, does one turn out pedestrian science and another have a spectacular career doing innovative research? Why are our natures often so different, and why are they so frequently the same?

The background needed to begin to answer all these *whys* lies within the domain of human biological and cultural evolution, in the gradual alterations in genetic and cultural information possessed by humanity. It's easy to think that evolution is just a process that sometime in the distant past produced the physical characteristics of our species but is now pretty much a matter of purely academic, and local school board, interest. Yet evolution is a powerful, ongoing force that not only has shaped the attributes and behaviors shared by all human beings but also has given every single individual a different nature.

A study of evolution does much more than show how we are connected to our roots or explain why people rule Earth—it explains why it would be wise to limit our intake of beef Wellington, stop judging people by their skin color, concern ourselves about global warming, and reconsider giving our children antibiotics at the first sign of a sore throat. Evolution also provides a framework for answering some of the most interesting questions about ourselves and our behavior.

When someone mentions evolution and behavior in the same breath, most people think immediately of the power of genes, parts of spiral-shaped molecules of a chemical called DNA. Small wonder, considering the marvelous advances in molecular genetics in recent decades. New subdisciplines such as evolutionary medicine and evolutionary psychology have arisen as scientists have come to recognize the importance of evolution in explaining contemporary human beings, the network of life that supports us, and our possible fates. And the mass media have been loaded with stories about real or imagined links between every conceivable sort of behavior and our genes.

Biological evolution—evolution that causes changes in our genetic endowment—has unquestionably helped shape human natures, including human behaviors, in many ways. But numerous commentators expect our genetic endowment to accomplish feats of which it is incapable. People don't have enough genes to program all the behaviors some evolutionary psychologists, for example, believe that genes control. Human beings have something on the order of 100,000 genes, and human brains have more than one *trillion* nerve cells, with about 100–1,000 trillion connections (synapses) between them. That's at least one *billion* synapses per gene, even if each and every gene did nothing but control the production of synapses (and it doesn't). Given that ratio, it would be quite a trick for genes typically to control more than the most general aspects of human behavior. Statements such as "Understanding the genetic roots of personality will help you 'find yourself' and relate better to others" are, at today's level of knowledge, frankly nonsensical.

The notion that we are slaves to our genes is often combined with reliance on the idea that all problems can be solved by dissecting them into ever smaller components—the sort of reductionist approach that has been successful in much of science but is sometimes totally unscientific. It's like the idea that knowing the color of every microscopic dot that makes up a picture of your mother can explain why you love her. Scientific problems have to be approached at the appropriate level of organization if there is to be a hope of solving them.

There are important "coevolutionary" interactions between culture and genetics. For example, our farming practices change our physical environment in ways that alter the evolution of our blood cells.

That combination of assumptions—that genes are destiny at a micro level and that reductionism leads to full understanding—is now yielding distorted views of human behavior. People think that coded into our DNA are "instructions" that control the details of individual and group behavior: that genetics dominates, heredity makes us what we are, and what we are is changeable only over many generations as the genetic endowment of human populations evolves. Such assertions presume, as I've just suggested, that evolution has produced a level

of genetic control of human behavior that is against virtually all available evidence. For instance, ground squirrels have evolved a form of "altruistic" behavior—they often give an alarm call to warn a relative of approaching danger. Evidence does indicate that this behavior is rooted in their genes; indeed, it probably evolved because relatives have more identical genes than do unrelated individuals. But some would trace the "altruistic" behavior of a business executive sending a check to an agency helping famine victims in Africa, or of a devout German Lutheran aiding Jews during the Holocaust, to a genetic tendency as well. In this view, we act either to help relatives or in the expectation of reciprocity—in either case promoting the replication of "our" genes. But experimental evidence indicates that not all human altruistic behavior is self-seeking—that human beings, unlike squirrels, are not hereditarily programmed only to be selfish.

ANOTHER FALSE ASSUMPTION of hereditary programming lies behind the belief that evolution has resulted in human groups of different quality. Many people still claim (or secretly believe), for example, that blacks are less intelligent than whites and women less "logical" than men, even though those claims are groundless. Belief in genetic determinism has even led some observers to suggest a return to the bad old days of eugenics, of manipulating evolution to produce ostensibly more skilled people. Advocating programs for the biological "improvement of humanity"—which in the past has meant encouraging the breeding of supposedly naturally superior individuals—takes us back at least to the days of Plato, more than two millennia ago, and it involves a grasp of genetics little more sophisticated than his.

Uniquely in our species, changes in culture have been fully as important in producing our natures as have changes in the hereditary information passed on by our ancestors. Culture is the nongenetic information (socially transmitted behaviors, beliefs, institutions, arts, and so on) shared and exchanged among us. Indeed, our evolution since the invention of agriculture, about 10,000 years ago, has been overwhelmingly cultural because, as we shall see, cultural evolution can be much more rapid than genetic evolution. There is an unhappy predilection, especially in the United States, not only to overrate the effect of genetic evolution on our current behavior but also to underrate that of cultural evolution. The power of culture to shape human activities can be seen immediately in the diversity of languages around the world. Although, clearly, the ability to speak languages is a result of a great deal of genetic evolution, the specific languages we speak are just as clearly products of cultural evolution. Furthermore, genetic evolution and cultural evolution are not independent. There are important "coevolutionary" interactions between them. To take just one example, our farming practices (an aspect of our culture) change our physical environment in ways that alter the evolution of our blood cells.

Not only is the evolution of our collective nongenetic information critical to creating our natures, but also the rate of that evolution varies greatly among different aspects of human cul-

ture. That, in turn, has profound consequences for our behavior and our environments. A major contemporary human
problem, for instance, is that the rate of cultural evolution in
science and technology has been extraordinarily high in contrast with the snail's pace of change in the social attitudes and
political institutions that might channel the uses of technology
in more beneficial directions. No one knows exactly what
sorts of societal effort might be required to substantially re-
dress that imbalance in evolutionary rates, but it is clear to me
that such an effort, if successful, could greatly brighten the
human prospect.

Science has already given us pretty good clues about the reasons for the evolution of some aspects of our natures; many
other aspects remain mysterious despite a small army of very
bright people seeking reasons. Still others (such as why I ordered duck in the restaurant last night rather than lamb) may remain unanswerable—for human beings have a form of free will.
But even to *think* reasonably about our natures and our prospects, some background in basic evolutionary theory is essential. If Grace is smarter than Pedro because of her genes, why
did evolution provide her with "better" genes? If Pedro is actually smarter than Grace but has been incorrectly evaluated by an
intelligence test designed for people of another culture, how did
those cultural differences evolve? If I was able to choose the
duck for dinner because I have free will, what exactly does that
mean? How did I and other human beings evolve that capacity
to make choices without being complete captives of our histories? Could I have exercised my free will to eat a cockroach
curry had we been in a restaurant that served it (as some in
Southeast Asia do)? Almost certainly not—the very idea nause-
ates me, probably because of an interaction between biological
and cultural evolution.

Trying to separate nature and nurture
is like trying to separate the
contributions of length and width to
the area of a rectangle, which at first
seems easy. When you think about it,
though, it proves impossible.

Every attribute of *every* organism is, of course, the product
of an interaction between its genetic code and its environment. Yes, the number of heads an individual human being
possesses is specified in the genes and is the same in a vast
diversity of environments. And the language or languages a
child speaks (but not her capacity to acquire language) is determined by her environment. But without the appropriate internal environment in the mother's body for fetal
development, there would be no head (or infant) at all; and
without genetically programmed physical structures in the
larynx and in the developing brain, there would be no ca-

pacity to acquire and speak language. Beyond enabling us to
make such statements in certain cases, however, the relative
contributions of heredity and environment to various human
attributes are difficult to specify. They clearly vary from attribute to attribute. So although it is informative to state that
human nature is the product of genes interacting with environments (both internal and external), we usually can say
little with precision about the processes that lead to interesting behaviors in adult human beings. We can't partition
the responsibility for aggression, altruism, or charisma between DNA and upbringing. In many such cases, trying to separate the contributions of nature and nurture to an attribute is
rather like trying to separate the contributions of length and
width to the area of a rectangle, which at first glance also
seems easy. When you think about it carefully, though, it
proves impossible.

Diverse notions of inherited superiority or inferiority and of
characteristic innate group behaviors have long pervaded
human societies: beliefs about the divine right of kings; "natural" attributes that made some people good material for
slaves or slave masters; innate superiority of light-skinned
people over dark-skinned people; genetic tendencies of Jews
to be moneylenders, of Christians to be sexually inhibited, and
of Asians to be more hardworking than Hispanics; and so on.
Consider the following quote from a recent book titled *Living
With Our Genes*, which indicates the tone even among many
scientists: "The emerging science of molecular biology has
made startling discoveries that show beyond a doubt that
genes are the single most important factor that distinguishes
one person from another. We come in large part ready-made
from the factory. We accept that we *look* like our parents and
other blood relatives; we have a harder time with the idea we
act like them."

In fact, the failure of many people to recognize the fundamental error in such statements (and those in other articles and
books based on genetic determinism, such as Richard J. Herrn-
stein and Charles Murray's famous *The Bell Curve*) is itself an
environmental phenomenon—a product of the cultural milieu in
which many of us have grown up. Genes do not shout commands to us about our behavior. At the very most, they whisper
suggestions, and the nature of those whispers is shaped by our
internal environments (those within and between our cells)
during early development and later, and usually also by the external environments in which we mature and find ourselves as
adults.

How do scientists know that we are not simply genetically
programmed automata? First, biological evolution has produced what is arguably the most astonishingly adaptable device
that has ever existed—the human nervous system. It's a system
that can use one organ, the brain, to plan a marriage or a murder,
command muscles to control the flight of a thrown rock or a
space shuttle, detect the difference between a 1945 Mouton and
a 1961 Latour, learn Swahili or Spanish, and interpret a pattern
of colored light on a flat television screen as a three-dimen-
sional world containing real people. It tries to do whatever task
the environment seems to demand, and it usually succeeds—
and because many of those demands are novel, there is no way

that the brain could be preprogrammed to deal with them, even if there were genes enough to do the programming. It would be incomprehensible for evolution to program such a system with a vast number of inherited rules that would reduce its flexibility, constraining it so that it could not deal with novel environments. It would seem equally inexplicable if evolution made some subgroups of humanity less able than others to react appropriately to changing circumstances. Men and people with white skin have just as much need of being smart and flexible as do women and people with brown skin, and there is every reason to believe that evolution has made white-skinned males fully as capable as brown-skinned women.

A SECOND TYPE OF EVIDENCE that we're not controlled by innate programs is that normal infants taken from one society and reared in another inevitably acquire the behaviors (including language) and competences of the society in which they are reared. If different behaviors in different societies were largely genetically programmed, that could not happen. That culture dominates in creating intergroup differences is also indicated by the distribution of genetic differences among human beings. The vast majority (an estimated 85 percent) is not between "races" or ethnic groups but *between individuals within groups*. Human natures, again, are products of similar (but not identical) inherited endowments interacting with different physical and cultural environments.

Thus, the genetic "make-brain" program that interacts with the internal and external environments of a developing person doesn't produce a brain that can call forth only one type of, say, mating behavior—it produces a brain that can engage in any of a bewildering variety of behaviors, depending on circumstances. We see the same principle elsewhere in our development; for instance, human legs are not genetically programmed to move only at a certain speed. The inherited "make-legs" program normally produces legs that, fortunately, can operate at a wide range of speeds, depending on circumstances. Variation among individuals in the genes they received from their parents produces some differences in that range (in any normal terrestrial environment, I never could have been a four-minute miler—on the moon, maybe). Environmental variation produces some differences, too (walking a lot every day and years of acclimatization enable me to climb relatively high mountains that are beyond the range of some younger people who are less acclimatized). But no amount of training will permit any human being to leap tall buildings in a single bound, or even in two.

Similarly, inherited differences among individuals can influence the range of mental abilities we possess. Struggle as I might, my math skills will never approach those of many professional mathematicians, and I suspect that part of my incapacity can be traced to my genes. But environmental variation can shape those abilities as well. I'm also lousy at learning languages (that may be related to my math incompetence). Yet when I found myself in a professional environment in which it

would have been helpful to converse in Spanish, persistent study allowed me to speak and comprehend a fair amount of the language. But there are no genetic instructions or environmental circumstances that will allow the development of a human brain that can do a million mathematical calculations in a second. That is a talent reserved for computers, which were, of course, designed by human minds.

Are there any behavioral instructions we can be sure are engraved in human DNA? If there are, at least one should be the urge to have as many children as possible. We should have a powerful hereditary tendency to maximize our genetic contributions to future generations, for that's the tendency that makes evolution work. Yet almost no human beings strictly obey this genetic "imperative"; environmental factors, especially cultural factors, have largely overridden it. Most people choose to make smaller genetic contributions to the future—that is, have fewer children—than they could, thus figuratively thwarting the supposed maximum reproduction "ambitions" of their genes.

If genes run us as machines for reproducing themselves, how come they let us practice contraception? We are the only animals that deliberately and with planning enjoy sex while avoiding reproduction. We can and do "outwit" our genes—which are, of course, witless. In this respect, our hereditary endowment made a big mistake by "choosing" to encourage human reproduction not through a desire for lots of children but through a desire for lots of sexual pleasure.

There are environments (sociocultural environments in this case) in which near-maximal human reproduction has apparently occurred. For example, the Hutterites, members of a Mennonite sect living on the plains of western North America, are famous for their high rate of population growth. Around 1950, Hutterite women over the age of 45 had borne an average of 10 children, and Hutterite population growth rates exceeded 4 percent per year. Interestingly, however, when social conditions changed, the growth rate dropped from an estimated 4.12 percent per year to 2.91 percent. Cultural evolution won out against those selfish little genes.

Against this background of how human beings can overwhelm genetic evolution with cultural evolution, it becomes evident that great care must be taken in extrapolating the behavior of other animals to that of human beings. One cannot assume, for example, that because marauding chimpanzees of one group sometimes kill members of another group, selection has programmed warfare into the genes of human beings (or, for that matter, of chimps). And although both chimp and human genetic endowments clearly can interact with certain environments to produce individuals capable of mayhem, they just as clearly can interact with other environments to produce individuals who are not aggressive. Observing the behavior of nonhuman mammals—their mating habits, modes of communication, intergroup conflicts, and so on—can reveal patterns we display in common with them, but those patterns certainly will not tell us which complex behaviors are "programmed" inalterably into our genes. Genetic instructions are of great importance to our natures, but they are not destiny.

THERE are obviously limits to how much the environment ordinarily can affect individual characteristics. No known environment, for example, could have allowed me to mature with normal color vision: like about 8 percent of males, I'm colorblind—the result of a gene inherited from my mother. But the influence on many human attributes of even small environmental differences should not be underestimated. Consider the classic story of the "Siamese twins" Chang and Eng. Born in Siam (now Thailand) on May 11, 1811, these identical twins were joined at the base of their chests by an arm-like tube that in adulthood was five or six inches long and about eight inches in circumference. They eventually ended up in the United States, became prosperous as sideshow attractions, and married sisters. Chang and Eng farmed for a time, owned slaves before the Civil War, and produced both many children and vast speculation about the circumstances of their copulations. They were examined many times by surgeons who, working before the age of X-rays, concluded that it would be dangerous to try to separate them.

From our perspective, the most interesting thing about the twins is their different natures. Chang was slightly shorter than Eng, but he dominated his brother and was quick-tempered. Eng, in contrast, was agreeable and usually submissive. Although the two were very similar in many respects, in childhood their differences once flared into a fistfight, and as adults on one occasion they disagreed enough politically to vote for opposing candidates. More seriously, Chang drank to excess and Eng did not. Partly as a result of Chang's drinking, they developed considerable ill will that made it difficult for them to live together—they were constantly quarreling. In old age, Chang became hard of hearing in both ears, but Eng became deaf only in the ear closer to Chang. In the summer of 1870, Chang suffered a stroke, which left Eng unaffected directly but bound him physically to an invalid. On January 17, 1874, Chang died in the night. When Eng discovered his twin's death, he (although perfectly healthy) became terrified, lapsed into a stupor, and died two hours later, before a scheduled surgical attempt was to have been made to separate the two. An autopsy showed that the surgeons had been correct—the twins probably would not have survived an attempt to separate them.

Chang and Eng demonstrated conclusively that genetic identity does not necessarily produce identical natures, even when combined with substantially identical environments—in this case only inches apart, with no sign that their mother or others treated them differently as they grew up. Quite subtle environmental differences, perhaps initiated by different positions in the womb, can sometimes produce substantially different behavioral outcomes in twins. In this case, in which the dominant feature of each twin's environment clearly was the other twin, the slightest original difference could have led to an escalating reinforcement of differences.

The nature-nurture dichotomy, which has dominated discussions of behavior for decades, is largely a false one—all characteristics of all organisms are truly a result of the simultaneous influences of both. Genes do not dictate destiny in most cases (exceptions include those serious genetic defects that at present cannot be remedied), but they often define a range of possibilities in a given environment. The genetic endowment of a chimpanzee, even if raised as the child of a Harvard professor, would prevent it from learning to discuss philosophy or solve differential equations. Similarly, environments define a range of developmental possibilities for a given set of genes. There is no genetic endowment that a child could get from Mom and Pop that would permit the youngster to grow into an Einstein (or a Mozart or a García Marquez—or even a Hitler) as a member of an isolated rain-forest tribe without a written language.

Attempts to dichotomize nature and nurture almost always end in failure. Although I've written about how the expression of genes depends on the environment in which the genes are expressed, another way of looking at the development of a person's nature would have been to examine the contributions of three factors: genes, environment, *and* gene-environment interactions. It is very difficult to tease out these contributions, however. Even under experimental conditions, where it is possible to say something mathematically about the comparative contributions of heredity and environment, it can't be done completely because there is an "interaction term." That term cannot be decomposed into nature or nurture because the effect of each depends on the contribution of the other.

To construct an artificial example, suppose there were a gene combination that controlled the level of a hormone that tended to make boys aggressive. Further, suppose that watching television also tended to make boys aggressive. Changing an individual's complement of genes so that the hormone level was doubled and also doubling the television-watching time might, then, quadruple some measure of aggressiveness. Or, instead, the two factors might interact synergistically and cause the aggression level to increase fivefold (perhaps television is an especially potent factor when the viewer has a high hormone level). Or the interaction might go the other way—television time might increase aggression only in those with a relatively low hormone level, and doubling both the hormone level and the television time might result in only a doubling of aggression. Or perhaps changing the average *content* of television programming might actually reduce the level of aggressiveness so that even with hormone level and television time doubled, aggressiveness would decline. Finally, suppose that, in addition, these relationships depended in part on whether or not a boy had attentive and loving parents who provided alternative interpretations of what was seen on television. In such situations, there is no way to make a precise statement about the contributions of "the environment" (television, in this case) to aggressiveness. This example reflects the complexity of relationships that has been demonstrated in detailed studies of the ways in which hormones such as testosterone interact with environmental factors to produce aggressive behavior.

The best one can ordinarily do in measuring what genes contribute to attributes (such as aggressiveness, height, or I.Q. test score) is calculate a statistical measure known as heritability. That statistic tells how much, on average, offspring resemble their parents in a particular attribute *in a particular set of environments*. Heritability, however, is a measure that is difficult to make and difficult to interpret. That is especially true in determining heritability of human traits, where it would be unethical or impossible to create the conditions required to estimate it, such as random mating within a population.

Despite these difficulties, geneticists are gradually sorting out some of the ways genes and environments can interact in experimental environments and how different parts of the hereditary endowment interact in making their contribution to the development of the individual. One of the key things they are learning is that it is often very difficult for genetic evolution to change just one characteristic. That's worth thinking about the next time someone tells you that human beings have been programmed by natural selection to be violent, greedy, altruistic, or promiscuous, to prefer certain facial features, or to show male (or white) dominance. At best, such programming is difficult; often it is impossible.

TODAY'S DEBATES about human nature—about such things as the origins of ethics; the meanings of consciousness, self, and reality; whether we're driven by emotion or reason; the relationship between thought and language; whether men are naturally aggressive and women peaceful; and the role of sex in society—trace far back in Western thought. They have engaged thinkers from the pre-Socratic philosophers, Plato, and Aristotle to René Descartes, John Locke, Georg Wilhelm Friedrich Hegel, Charles Sanders Peirce, and Ludwig Wittgenstein, just to mention a tiny handful of those in the Western tradition alone.

What exactly *is* this human nature we hear so much about? The prevailing notion is that it is a single, fixed, inherited attribute—a common property of all members of our species. That notion is implicit in the universal use of the term in singular form. And I think that singular usage leads us astray. To give a rough analogy, *human nature* is to *human natures* as *canyon is to canyons*. We would never discuss the "characteristics of canyon." Although all canyons share certain attributes, we always use the plural form of the word when talking about them in general. That's because even though all canyons have more characteristics in common with one another than any canyon has with a painting or a snowflake, we automatically recognize the vast diversity subsumed within the category *canyons*. As with *canyon*, at times there is reason to speak of human nature in the singular, as I sometimes do when referring to what we all share—for example, the ability to communicate in language, the possession of a rich culture, and the capacity to develop complex ethical systems. After all, there are at least *near*-universal aspects of our natures and our genomes (genetic endowments), and the variation within them is small in relation to the differences between, say, human and chimpanzee natures or human and chimpanzee genomes.

I argue, contrary to the prevailing notion, that human nature is not the same from society to society or from individual to individual, nor is it a permanent attribute of *Homo sapiens*. Human natures are the behaviors, beliefs, and attitudes of *Homo sapiens* and the changing physical structures that govern, support, and participate in our unique mental functioning. There are many such natures, a diversity generated especially by the overwhelming power of cultural evolution—the super-rapid kind of evolution in which our species excels. The human nature of a Chinese man living in Beijing is somewhat different from the human nature of a Parisian woman; the nature of a great musician is not identical with that of a fine soccer player; the nature of an inner-city gang member is different from the nature of a child being raised in an affluent suburb; the nature of someone who habitually votes Republican is different from that of her identical twin who is a Democrat; and my human nature, despite many shared features, is different from yours.

The differences among individuals and groups of human beings are, as already noted, of a magnitude that dwarf the differences within any other nondomesticated animal species. Using the plural, *human natures*, puts a needed emphasis on that critical diversity, which, after all, is very often what we want to understand. We want to know why two genetically identical individuals would have different political views; why Jeff is so loud and Barbara is so quiet; why people in the same society have different sexual habits and different ethical standards; why some past civilizations flourished for many centuries and others perished; why Germany was a combatant in two horrendous 20th-century wars and Switzerland was not; why Julia is concerned about global warming and Juliette doesn't know what it is. There is no single human nature, any more than there is a single human genome, although there are features common to all human natures and all human genomes.

But if we are trying to understand anything about human society, past or present, or about individual actions, we must go to a finer level of analysis and consider human nature*s* as actually formed in the world. It is intellectually lazy and incorrect to "explain" the relatively poor school performance of blacks in the United States, or the persistence of warfare, or marital discord, by claiming that nonwhites are "naturally" inferior, that all people are "naturally" aggressive, or that men are "naturally" promiscuous. Intellectual performance, aggression, and promiscuity, aside from being difficult to define and measure, all vary from individual to individual and often from culture to culture. Ignoring that variance simply hides the causative factors—cultural, genetic, or both—that we would like to understand.

Permanence is often viewed as human nature's key feature; after all, remember, "you can't change human nature." But, of course, we *can*—and we do, all the time. The natures of Americans today are very different from their natures in 1940. Indeed, today's human natures everywhere are diverse products of change, of long genetic and, especially, cultural evolutionary processes. A million years ago, as paleoanthropologists, archaeologists, and other scientists have shown, human nature was a radically different, and presumably much more uniform, attribute. People then had less nimble brains, they didn't have a language with fully developed syntax, they had not developed formal strata in societies, and they hadn't yet learned to attach worked stones to wooden shafts to make hammers and arrows.

Human natures a million years in the future will also be unimaginably different from human natures today. The processes that changed those early people into modern human beings will continue as long as there are people. Indeed, with the rate of cultural evolution showing seemingly continuous acceleration, it would be amazing if the broadly shared aspects of human natures were not quite different even a million *hours* (about a hundred years) in the future. For example, think of how Internet commerce has changed in the past million or so minutes (roughly two years).

As evolving mental-physical packages, human natures have brought not only planetary dominance to our species but also great triumphs in areas such as art, music, literature, philosophy, science, and technology. Unhappily, though, those same packages—human behavioral patterns and their physical foundations—are also the source of our most serious current problems. War, genocide, commerce in drugs, racial and religious prejudice, extreme economic inequality, and destruction of society's life-support systems are all products of today's human natures, too. As Pogo so accurately said, "We have met the enemy, and they is us." But nowhere is it written that those problems have to be products of tomorrow's human natures. It is theoretically possible to make peace with ourselves and with our environment, overcome racial and religious prejudice, reduce large-scale cruelty, and increase economic equality. What's needed is a widespread understanding of the evolutionary processes that have produced our natures, open discourse on what is desirable about them, and conscious collective efforts to steer the cultural evolution of the more troublesome features of our natures in ways almost everyone would find desirable. A utopian notion? Maybe. But considering progress that already has been made in areas such as democratic governance and individual freedom, race relations, religious tolerance, women's and gay rights, and avoidance of global conflict, it's worth a try.

Paul R. Ehrlich is a professor of population studies and of biological sciences at Stanford University. This essay is adapted from his Human Natures: Genes, Cultures, and the Human Prospect, *published by Island Press in August 2000.*

From *The Chronicle of Higher Education,* September 22, 2000, pp. B7-B11. © 2000 by The Chronicle of Higher Education. Reprinted with permission of the author. This article may not be posted, published, or distributed without permission from *The Chronicle.*

Nature vs. Nurture:
Two Brothers With Schizophrenia

Norman L. Keltner; Christopher A. James; Rani J. Darling; Lisa S. Findley; Kelli Oliver

One of the great debates in 20th century psychiatry centered on etiology: Is upbringing (nurturing) or biology (nature) at the root of mental illness? In the late 19th century, Kraepelinian thinking, which postulated an organic causation, dominated psychiatric thought. As the new century dawned, however, this view quickly gave way to what Cohn (1974) called the Freudian revolution. By the time of Freud's death in 1939, psychoanalytic thought was well on its way to achieving all its goals. It was the application of these principles during World War II that firmly entrenched psychoanalysis, and by extension psychodynamic assumptions, into the heart and soul of our culture. "From the end of World War II until the mid-1970s, a broadly conceived psychosocial model, informed by psychoanalytic and sociological thinking, was the organizing model of American psychiatry" (Wilson, 1993, p. 400).

While the nurture advocates held sway for most of the century, clearly as the millennium closed the proponents of a biological view had won the day. These biologically oriented theorists, in contrast to their more dynamically inclined colleagues, dominated influential academic positions, controlled research direction and subsequent funding, and offered the public some reprieve from the family-blaming psychodynamic models.

The quintessential point in this circling back to a Kraepelinian-like viewpoint was the development of the third edition of the *Diagnostic and Statistical Manual (DSM-III)* (American Psychiatric Association [APA], 1980). Strauss, Yager, and Strauss (1984), summarizing psychiatrists' opinions, stated it was the most important psychiatric publication to appear during the 1970s. Wilson (1993) suggests this document led to the 're-medicalization" of psychiatry: "The history of the development of *DSM-III* is a story about the changing power base, as well as the changing knowledge base, within American psychiatry" (p. 408). With this background in mind, the authors present an interesting case review of two brothers with schizophrenia. Rea-

soning suggests a nature perspective (i.e., genetic causation), and that may well be the most fruitful model to embrace. Yet after working with these individuals, we are attracted to a more holistic framework that accounts for the significance of heredity-environment interactions. Andreasen (1999) likens this approach to the model used to understand cancer: "schizophrenia probably occurs as a consequence of multiple 'hits' which include some combination of inherited genetic factors and external, nongenetic factors that affect the regulation and expression of genes governing brain function or that injure the brain directly" (p. 645).

Schizophrenia

Schizophrenia is one of the most common causes of psychosis, affecting about 1% of the adult population (Regier et al., 1993). It is a biological brain disorder typically emerging in late adolescence or early adulthood, is exacerbated by stress, and responds to dopamine receptor antagonists (Weinberger, 1987). It is a thought disorder; symptoms include hallucinations, delusions, withdrawal, poor rapport, and difficulties in communication (APA, 1994; Keltner, Folks, Palmer, & Powers, 1998). It affects men and women almost equally, but men have an earlier age of onset by approximately 4 to 6 years. Though schizophrenia most likely first occurs early in life, a significant minority of women have a first-time episode perimenopausally; this bimodal expression is thought to be estrogen related. Since schizophrenia is thought to be neurodevelopmental rather than neurodegenerative (there is no evidence of gliosis as found in degenerative disorders), influences that disrupt brain development at critical times have been postulated to cause downstream effects, many of which are not evident for years.

These effects include subtle cerebral abnormalities (e.g., enlarged lateral ventricles; enlarged third ventricle; reductions in cortical gray matter in frontal, thalamic, limbic, and hippo-

Table 1. Genetic Risk for Schizophrenia

Familial Relationship	Risk Schizophrenia
* Identical twin affected	50%
* Fraternal twin affected	15%
* Sibling affected	10%
* One parent affected	15%
* Both parents affected	35%
* Second-degree relative affected	2%–3%
* No affected relative	1%
* General population	1%

Source: Roberts, Leigh, & Weinberger (1993)

campal structures); disrupted neural circuitry (e.g., dopaminergic afferents to the dorsolateral prefrontal cortex); and altered neurotransmitter systems. Disruptive influences can be divided into three causative categories: genetic, shared environmental, and individual-specific environmental influences (Kendler, Myers, & Neale, 2000; Tsuang, 2000). When reviewing the cases of the brothers in this article, it will become evident that all three categories are potentially involved.

Genetic Considerations in Schizophrenia

Individuals with schizophrenia inherit a predisposition to this disorder, hence schizophrenia runs in families (Mortensen et al., 1999; Stall et al., 2000). Cardino and colleagues (1999) estimate 85% of the susceptibility to schizophrenia is genetic. Roberts, Leigh, and Weinberger (1993) outline the genetic risks for relatives of people with schizophrenia (Table 1).

As is clear from Table 1, individuals related to people with schizophrenia have a significantly higher likelihood of developing schizophrenia (2%–50%) than do members of the general population (1%). Twin studies are crucial to our understanding of the impact of heredity. Studies among monozygotic twin groups have repeatedly demonstrated high concordancy rates (50% per Table 1). While compelling indeed, a pure genetic causation would predict even higher concordancy rates among individuals who share the exact same genetic blueprint. The fact that there is not 100% concordancy suggests nongenetic variables influence schizophrenogenesis.

There are multiple nongenetic factors that influence the development of schizophrenia (Andreasen, 1999; McNeil, Cantor-Graae, & Weinberger, 2000; Nicolson et al., 1999; Rapoport, 2000; Sherman, 1999). For example, the following have been implicated in schizophrenia causation: birth during the winter, infection during pregnancy, famine (e.g., the Dutch Hunger Winter, 1944–45), exposure to toxins (e.g., alcohol) prenatally, obstetrical complications, exposure to radiation, and maternal exposure to great stress (e.g., natural disasters).

Of particular interest to this article is the high incidence of schizophrenia among individuals raised in homes in which one or both parents suffered from schizophrenia. This high incidence (15%–35%) may be partially accounted for by poor parenting (Rosen, 1978). In other words, in a home with (a) disabled parent(s), childrearing may be so inadequate that what might appear to be a clear-cut biological process is hopelessly confounded by nurturing issues. As will become evident, these brothers were raised by disabled parents.

Case Reviews

The following case reviews are presented because they are compelling, filled with pathos, and instructive. The destructive forces of poor parenting and mistreatment are the backdrop for boys with apparent genetic predisposition to severe mental illness. Within the context of a disordered biology interacting with a malicious environment, we attempt to reconstruct lives forever assigned to the periphery of "normal" society. We refer to these brothers as Al and Pete.

Al. Many of us think back to our childhood and remember birthday parties, hide and seek, baseball games, etc. Al thinks back to his past and remembers molestation, cruelty, and punishment. Al has been diagnosed with undifferentiated schizophrenia since the age of 20.

Al is the next to youngest of eight children. According to Al, more than half these siblings suffer from major mental illness. Al stated, "My mama had schizophrenia for 10 years, then God saved her." When asked about his relationship with his mother now, Al states she left the rest of the family after "daddy" died. When questioned about his father, Al speaks of how his father used to beat his mother and the children. Al recalls seeing his father beat one brother so severely he thought the boy might die. Al further described a beating he received from his father that left him bleeding. When asked why he thought his father beat him, Al responded, "He got mad a lot. I forgot to get firewood like he asked me to." In discussing his illness, Al was asked to describe when he first started hearing voices. He replied, "When I was little, after those boys did that to me. I was out fixing my bicycle and I heard the devil talk to me over and over." Al reported numerous incidents of abuse during his life. At one point during the interview, Al stated his belief that his schizophrenia was God's punishment for what he had done.

Al's first documented psychiatric episode occurred in the early 1980s when he was in his early 20s. In the psychological evaluation emanating from this experience, the psychiatrist noted the presence of hallucinations and delusions; Al described spaceships, command hallucinations, and stated he had killed Christ. His condition deteriorated further and he was committed to a public hospital. During that hospitalization Al was diagnosed as having undifferentiated schizophrenia.

Today, Al lives in a residential group home and attends day treatment. He continues to manifest both auditory and visual hallucinations. Though prescribed two atypical antipsychotic drugs, symptom control varies from day to day.

Pete. Pete is older than Al and has a diagnosis of chronic undifferentiated schizophrenia. His psychiatric symptoms began after his father died suddenly. It was more than 10 years later before he was given a formal diagnosis. Presumably his family and the community were able to absorb his behaviors during those intervening years. He was self-supporting for a while, working in a country store, before being let go for out-of-control behavior.

Pete has a good memory, yet it is fairly selective in that there are certain life experiences he repeatedly shares with others. Some of the stories could be entirely true but are unverifiable, and one has the sense of delusional or grandiose embellishment. He does not admit to hearing voices but frequently complains of seeing flashing lights of different colors.

Pete had a turbulent childhood as well, but a portion of his childhood was spent in the home of a relative. Though he also experienced his father's wrath, he was spared some of the more difficult years in the household. As noted, Pete's symptoms emerged after the death of his physically and emotionally abusive father. When asked about his childhood, Pete is less apt to remember the negative. He states that his dad "loved me with all his heart." He also remembers his mother as loving him.

Pete did not altogether escape the stranger trauma experienced by his brother. Pete reports being robbed at gunpoint when he was a resident of a psychiatric boarding home. The event, as would be expected, was very traumatic and left an indelible scar.

Pete does not maintain close contact with family members. At one time he tried to maintain contact but circumstances beyond his control led to his curtailing any future, meaningful contact. Pete states that he has "a spiritual mother who speaks to him through his soul."

Today, Pete lives in a residential group home and attends day treatment. The only relative he sees on a regular basis is his brother Al.

Commentary

This brief review of two brothers with schizophrenia provides support for what may be the most compelling model for explaining causative agents of schizophrenia: a multifactorial view (Andreasen, 1999). This model is perhaps best captured by Kendler et al. (2000) and Tsuang (2000) as they divide disruptive influences associated with schizophrenia into genetic,

shared environmental, and individual-specific environmental causes. As evidenced by the histories of the brothers, their mental disabilities may be directly linked to all the aforementioned causative factors.

Although many calamitous situations and crises have been shared by these brothers, both have had life experiences that are psychologically traumatic in their own right. One was a victim of sexual abuse while the other was subject to robbery (i.e., individual-specific issues). Kendler et al. (2000) state that shared environmental factors affect family members "through several mechanisms that cluster in families, including parental monitoring, religious and cultural values, community organizations, and drug availability. Undoubtedly, these areas were absent while shared dysfunctional events occurred with regularity.

The individual stressors compounded by an abusive home life seem to be logical grounds from which to mount the nurture argument. The nature argument, however, is not to be ignored. From reviewing charts and performing interviews, it was revealed that at least one of the parents may have had a history of schizophrenia. A family with this many mentally dysfunctional people is of etiologic significance because epidemiological studies suggest a high concordancy rate when a parent or sibling suffers from schizophrenia. An increase beyond these "normal" morbidity rates could be expected when several members of one family are diagnosed with this condition.

In examining the cohesiveness among the above factors (i.e., genetics, shared and individual-specific environmental factors), one can see that each of these variables could have played an active role in the development of schizophrenia for these men. Using Kendler and associates' (2000) views, we are able to speculate on the synergistic effects with which these variables/ stressors may have converged to predispose these men to this disability. Further, this view provokes these questions:

- If multifactorial causation is indeed the explanation for schizophrenia, could the severity of the brothers' illnesses have been diminished by removing one or more factors?
- Which factor must be removed?
- How many factors must be present before schizophrenia develops?

Each brother has developed differing severities in the pathology of the illness, along with differing symptoms and dates of onset. These variances are reminders of the unfortunate troth that there is much to learn regarding the disease process of schizophrenia and its causes.

Nursing Implications

These two case studies chronicle a modern American tragedy. The tragedy is experienced at both individual and family levels. First, as individuals, these men have suffered directly from their illness and have missed out on life experiences others take for granted (an indirect consequence). Second, this family has never experienced the "normal" family life. One can only imagine the degree of angst and misery generated in a family with this level of dysfunction. In response to such dysfunction (individual and familial) the nurse is called on to bolster strengths and minimize/prevent deterioration.

Nurses can play a pivotal role in applying prevention strategies across a variety of practice settings. Research links poor prenatal care, second-trimester viruses, and other intrauterine insults to the subsequent development of disorders including schizophrenia (Hultman & Ohman, 1998). Advanced practice psychiatric nurses can contribute to this level of prevention by consultation and collaboration with their colleagues in antepartal, obstetric, and pediatric nursing. Education and outreach services to pregnant women would be a primary prevention effort to decrease the prevalence rates of schizophrenia caused by prenatal risk factors.

Also pertinent to primary prevention efforts are the studies that implicate early childhood trauma in the later development of psychiatric illnesses such as depression, posttraumatic stress disorder, and even schizophrenia. This line of research addresses how experiences alter neurocircuitry, thereby increasing vulnerability to neurotransmitter malfunction (Yehuda, 2000). Child abuse detection, reporting, and prevention efforts are another area in which nurses can have a potential impact on the morbidity of schizophrenia.

A final primary prevention strategy that nurses can provide is in management of the schizophrenic patient's stress factors. Evidence to support the effects of stress on schizophrenia has been found in the life experiences of people with the disorder, who have been shown to experience a higher rate of environmental stressors prior to episodes of illness. Schizophrenia patients suffer from disturbances in emotional processing and in their reactions to stressful events (Walker & Diforio, 1997). Peplau (1952) wrote about the psychotherapeutic management of delusions and hallucinations through the use of the interpersonal problem-solving approach and management of anxiety. These techniques are well known and used by psychiatric nurses.

Secondary prevention strategies would address stabilization of illness and minimization of disability. It is speculated that the neuroanatomical abnormalities worsen over time in first-episode patients with schizophrenia, and that earlier, more intense interventions produce better outcomes (Larsen, Johannessen, & Opjordsmoen, 1998; Linszen, Lenior, De Haan, Dingemans, & Gersons, 1998). Nurses can facilitate patient recovery and improve outcomes by intervening in the early phases of illness. Engaging the patient in psychoeducational groups while closely supervising medication adherence and response also has proved effective (Castle, 1997; O'Connor, 1991). Given the high propensity for comorbid substance-abuse problems among patients with schizophrenia (Dixon, 1999; Kessler et al., 1997), education about the effects of substance use on illness course would be an important aspect of the psychoeducational program (Holland, Baguley, & Davies, 1999). Some of the most hopeful news in schizophrenia research is emerging in the field of psychosocial rehabilitation. Nurses are learning to incorporate these principles in working with schizophrenic patients to improve their hope for recovery and successful community living (Farrell & Deeds, 1997; Kirkpatrick et al., 1995).

While one's genetic heritage creates a predisposition toward schizophrenia, other factors such as the home environment, the prenatal environment, dietary factors, and others may determine whether the disease is manifested. The NIMH is providing funding for this area of research. There are a number of indicators that can be detected in children who have been associated with the later development of schizophrenia. Case finding and tracking of high-risk individuals across periods of vulnerability would permit the creation of a database for subsequent prevention strategies and/or research by nurses and other colleagues in mental health.

References

Acocella, J. (2000, May). The empty couch. *The New Yorker*, 8, 112–118.

American Psychiatric Association. (1980). *Diagnostic and statistical manual of mental disorders* (3rd ed.). Washington, DC: Author.

American Psychiatric Association. (1994). *Diagnostic and statistical manual of mental disorders* (4th ed.). Washington, DC: Author.

Andreasen, N.C. (1999). Understanding causes of schizophrenia. *New England Journal of Medicine*, 340, 645–647.

Cardino, A.G., Marshall, E.J., Coid, B., Gottesman, I., Farmer, A., McGuffin, P., Reveley, A., & Murray, R. (1999). Heritability estimates for psychotic disorders. *Archives of General Psychiatry, 56,* 162–168.

Castle, L. (1997). Beyond medication. What else does the patient with schizophrenia need to reintegrate into the community? *Journal of Psychosocial Nursing and Mental Health Services, 35*(9), 18–21.

Cohn, J.H. (1974). The decline of psychoanalysis: The end of an era, or here we go again. *JAMA*, 228, 711–712.

Dixon, L. (1999). Dual diagnosis of substance abuse in schizophrenia: Prevalence and impact on outcomes. *Schizophrenia Research, 35*(Suppl.), 93–100.

Farrell, S.P., & Deeds, E.S. (1997). The clubhouse model as exemplar: Merging psychiatric nursing and psychosocial rehabilitation. *Journal of Psychosocial Nursing and Mental Health Services, 35*(1), 27–34.

Holland, M., Baguley, I., & Davies, T. (1999). Hallucinations and delusions: A dual diagnosis case study. *British Journal of Nursing, 8,* 1095–1102.

Hultman, C.M., & Ohman, A. (1998). Perinatal characteristics and schizophrenia: Electrodermal activity as a mediating link in a vulnerability-stress perspective. *International Journal of Developmental Neuroscience, 16,* 307–316.

Keltner, N.L., Folks, D.G., Palmer, C.A., & Powers, R.E. (1998). *Psychobiological foundations of psychiatric care*. St. Louis: Mosby.

Kendler, K.S., Myers, J.M., & Neale, M.C. (2000). A multidimensional twin study of mental health in women. *American Journal of Psychiatry, 157,* 506–513.

Kessler R.C., Crum, R.M., Warner, L.A., Nelson, C.B., Schulenberg, J., & Anthony, J.C. (1997). Lifetime co-occurrence of DSM-III-R alcohol abuse and dependence with other psychiatric disorders in the National Comorbidity Survey. *Archives of General Psychiatry, 54,* 313–321.

Kirkpatrick, H., Landeen, J., Byrne, C., Woodside, H., Pawlick, J., & Bernardo, A. (1995). Hope and schizophrenia: Clinicians identify hope-instilling strategies. *Journal of Psychosocial Nursing and Mental Health Services, 33*(6), 15–19.

Larsen, T.K., Johannessen, J.O., & Opjordsmoen, S. (1998). First-episode schizophrenia with long duration of untreated psychosis. Pathways to care. *British Journal of Psychiatry, 33*(Suppl. 172), 45–52.

Linszen, D., Lenior, M., De Haan, L., Dingemans, P., & Gersons, B. (1998). Early intervention, untreated psychosis and the course of early schizophrenia. *British Journal of Psychiatry, 33*(Suppl. 172), 84–89.

McNeil, T.F., Cantor-Graae, E., & Weinberger, D.R. (2000). Relationship of obstetric complications and differences in size of brain structures in monozygotic twin pairs discordant for schizophrenia. *American Journal of Psychiatry, 157*, 203–212.

Mortensen, P., Pedersen, C., Westergaard, T., Wohlfahrt, J., Ewald, H., Mors, O., Andersen, P., & Melbye, M. (1999). Effects of family history and place and season of birth on the risk of schizophrenia. *New England Journal of Medicine, 340*, 603–608.

Nicolson, R., Malaspina, D., Giedd, J.N., Hamburger, S., Lenane, M., Bedwell, J., Fernandez, T., Berman, A., Susser, E., & Rapoport, J. (1999). Obstetrical complications and childhood-onset schizophrenia. *American Journal of Psychiatry, 156*, 1650–1652.

O'Connor, F. (1991). Symptom monitoring for relapse prevention in schizophrenia. *Archives of Psychiatric Nursing, 5*, 193–201.

Peplau, H. (1952). Interpersonal relations in nursing. New York: Putnam.

Rapoport, J.L. (2000). The development of neurodevelopmental psychiatry. *American Journal of Psychiatry, 157*, 159–161.

Regier, D.A., Narrow, W.E., Rae, D.S., Manderscheid, R.W., Locke, B., & Goodwin, F. (1993). The de facto US mental and addictive disorders service system: Epidemiologic catchment area prospective 1-year prevalence rates of disorders and services. *Archives of General Psychiatry, 50*, 85–94.

Roberts, G.W., Leigh, P.N., & Weinberger, D.R. (1993). *Neuropsychiatric disorders*. London: Mosby Europe.

Rosen, H. (1978). A guide to clinical psychiatry. Coral Gables, FL: Mnemosyne.

Sherman, C. (1999). Natural catastrophe linked to rise in schizophrenia rate. *Clinical Psychiatry News, 27*(9), 24.

Stall, W.G., Pol, H.E.H., Schnack, H.G., Hoogendoorn, M., Jellema, K., & Kahn, R. (2000). Structural brain abnormalities in patients with schizophrenia and their healthy siblings. *American Journal of Psychiatry, 157*, 416–420.

Strauss, D.G., Yager, J., & Strauss, G.E. (1984). The cutting edge in psychiatry. *American Journal of Psychiatry, 141*, 38–43.

Tsuang, M.T. (2000). Genes, environment, and mental health wellness. *American Journal of Psychiatry, 157*, 489–491.

Walker, E.F., & Diforio, D. (1997). Schizophrenia: A neural diathesis-stress model. *Psychological Review, 104*, 667–685.

Weinberger, D.R. (1987). Implications of normal brain development for the pathogenesis of schizophrenia. *Archives in General Psychiatry, 44*, 660–668.

Wilson, M. (1993). DSM-III and the transformation of American psychiatry: A history. *American Journal of Psychiatry, 150*, 399–410.

Yehuda, R. (2000). Biology of posttraumatic stress disorder. *Journal of Clinical Psychiatry, 61*(Suppl. 7), 14–21.

Norman L. Keltner, EdD, RN, is Professor, University of Alabama School of Nursing, Birmingham, AL. Christopher A. James, MEd, is Coordinator II, Chilton-Shelby Mental Health, Clanton, AL. Rani J. Darling, BSN, RN, is currently attending school in Europe; Lisa S. Findley, BSN, RN, is Staff Nurse, University of Alabama Hospital; and Kelli Oliver, BSN, RN, is Staff Nurse, East Alabama Medical Center, Opelika, AL.

Reprinted from *Perspectives in Psychiatric Care*, July-September 2001, p. 88. © 2001 by NurseCom.

THE PERSONALITY
GENES

Does DNA shape behavior?
A leading researcher's behavior is a case in point

By J. MADELEINE NASH

MOLECULAR BIOLOGIST DEAN Hamer has blue eyes, light brown hair and the goofy sense of humor of a stand-up comic. He smokes cigarettes, spends long hours in a cluttered laboratory at the National Institutes of Health, and in his free time clambers up cliffs and points his skis down steep, avalanche-prone slopes. He also happens to be openly, matter-of-factly gay.

What is it that makes Hamer who he is? What, for that matter, accounts for the quirks and foibles, talents and traits that make up anyone's personality? Hamer is not content merely to ask such questions; he is trying to answer them as well. A pioneer in the field of molecular psychology, Hamer is exploring the role genes play in governing the very core of our individuality. To a remarkable extent, his work on what might be called the gay, thrill-seeking and quit-smoking genes reflects his own genetic predispositions.

That work, which has appeared mostly in scientific journals, has been gathered

into an accessible and quite readable form in Hamer's provocative new book, *Living with Our Genes* (Doubleday; $24.95). "You have about as much choice in some aspects of your personality," Hamer and coauthor Peter Copeland write in the introductory chapter, "as you do in the shape of your nose or the size of your feet."

Until recently, research into behavioral genetics was dominated by psychiatrists and psychologists, who based their most compelling conclusions about the importance of genes on studies of identical twins. For example, psychologist Michael Bailey of Northwestern University famously demonstrated that if one identical twin is gay, there is about a 50% likelihood that the other will be too. Seven years ago, Hamer picked up where the twin studies left off, homing in on specific strips of DNA that appear to influence everything from mood to sexual orientation.

Hamer switched to behavioral genetics from basic research; after receiving his

Ph.D. from Harvard, he spent more then a decade studying the biochemistry of metallothionein, a protein that cells use to metabolize heavy metals like copper and zinc. As he was about to turn 40, however, Hamer suddenly realized he had learned as much about metallothionein as he cared to. "Frankly, I was bored," he remembers, "and ready for something new."

Instrumental in Hamer's decision to switch fields was Charles Darwin's *The Descent of Man, and Selection in Relation to Sex*. "I was fascinated to learn that Darwin seemed so convinced that behavior was partially inherited," he remembers, "even though when he was writing, genes had not been discovered, let alone DNA." Homosexual behavior, in particular, seemed ripe for exploration because few scientists had dared tackle such an emotionally and politically charged subject. "I'm gay," Hamer says with a shrug, "but that was not a major motivation. It was more of a question of intellectual curios-

Nature or Nurture?

Many aspects of personality may have a genetic component—such as sexual orientation, anxiety, a tendency to take chances and ...

IMPULSIVENESS   OPENNESS

ILLUSTRATIONS FOR TIME BY SCOTT MENCHIN

ity—and the fact that no one else was doing this sort of research."

The results of Hamer's first foray into behavioral genetics, published by the journal *Science* in 1993, ignited a furor that has yet to die down. According to Hamer and his colleagues, male homosexuality appeared to be linked to a stretch of DNA at the very tip of the X chromosome, the chromosome men inherit from their mothers. Three years later, in 1996, Hamer and his collaborators at NIH seconded an Israeli group's finding that linked a gene on chromosome 11 to the personality trait psychologists called novelty seeking. That same year Hamer's lab helped pinpoint another gene, this time on chromosome 17, that appears to play a role in regulating anxiety.

Unlike the genes that are responsible for physical traits, Hamer emphasizes, these genes do not cause people to become homosexuals, thrill-seeking rock climbers or anxiety-ridden worrywarts. The biology of personality is much more complicated than that. Rather, what genes appear to do, says Hamer, is subtly bias the psyche so that different individuals react to similar experiences in surprisingly different ways.

Intriguing as these findings are, other experts caution that none has been unequivocally replicated by other research teams. Why? One possibility is that, despite all of Hamer's work, the links between these genes and these particular personality traits do not, in fact, exist. There is, however, another, more tantalizing possibility. Consider the genes that give tomatoes their flavor, suggests Hamer's colleague Dr. Dennis Murphy of the National Institute of Mental Health. Even a simple trait like acidity is controlled not by a single gene but by as many as 30 that operate in concert. In the same way, he speculates, many genes are in-volved in setting up temperamental traits and psychological vulnerabilities; each gene contributes just a little bit to the overall effect.

Hunting down the genes that influence personality remains a dauntingly difficult business. Although DNA is constructed out of a mere four chemicals—adenine, guanine, cytosine, thymine—it can take as many as a million combinations to spell out a single human gene. Most of these genes vary from individual to individual by only one chemical letter in a thousand, and it is precisely these minute differences that Hamer and his colleagues are trying to identify. Of particular interest are variations that may affect the operation of such brain chemicals as dopamine and serotonin, which are well-known modulators of mood. The so-called novelty-seeking gene, for example, is thought to affect how efficiently nerve cells absorb dopamine. The so-called anxiety gene is postulated to affect serotonin's action.

How can this be? After all, as Hamer and Copeland observe in their book, "... genes are not switches that say 'shy' or 'outgoing' or 'happy' or 'sad.' Genes are simply chemicals that direct the combination of more chemicals." What genes do is order up the production of proteins in organs like the kidney, the skin and also the brain. Thus, Hamer speculates, one version of the novelty-seeking gene may make a protein that is less efficient at absorbing dopamine. Since dopamine is the chemical that creates sensations of pleasure in response to intense experiences, people who inherit this gene might seek to stimulate its production by seeking out thrills.

Still, as critics emphasize and Hamer himself acknowledges, genes alone do not control the chemistry of the brain. Ultimately, it is the environment that deter-mines how these genes will express themselves. In another setting, for example, it is easy to imagine that Hamer might have become a high school dropout rather than a scientist. For while he grew up in an affluent household in Montclair, N.J., he was hardly a model child. "Today," he chuckles, "I probably would have been diagnosed with attention-deficit disorder and put on Ritalin." In his senior year in high school, though, Hamer discovered organic chemistry and went from being an unruly adolescent to a first-rate student. What people are born with, Hamer says, are temperamental traits. What they can acquire through experience is the ability to control these traits by exercising that intangible part of personality called character.

Over the coming decade, Hamer predicts, scientists will identify thousands of genes that directly and indirectly influence behavior. A peek inside the locked freezer in the hallway outside his own lab reveals a rapidly expanding stash of plastic tubes that contain DNA samples from more than 1,760 volunteers. Among them: gay men and their heterosexual brothers, a random assortment of novelty seekers and novelty avoiders, shy children and now a growing collection of cigarette smokers.

Indeed, while Hamer has maintained a professional distance from his studies, it is impossible to believe he is not also driven by a desire for self-discovery. Soon, in fact, his lab will publish a paper about a gene that makes it harder or easier for people to stop smoking. Judging by the pack of cigarettes poking out of his shirt pocket, Hamer would seem to have drawn the wrong end of that genetic stick. He has tried to stop smoking and failed, he confesses, dozens of times. "If I quit," he says, "it will be an exercise of character." And not, it goes without saying, of his genes.

From *Time*, April 27, 1998, pp. 60–61. © 1998 by Time Inc. Magazine Company. Reprinted by permission.

Where We Come From

Recent advances in genetics are starting to illuminate the wanderings of early humans

BY NANCY SHUTE

Andy Carvin is a pioneer on the strange frontier of DNA genealogy. The 29-year-old Internet policy analyst had built his family tree back to ancestors in Busk, Ukraine, but that's where the trail went cold. Then he read about research tracing the Y sex chromosome, which is passed intact from father to son, all the way back to the time of Aaron, the single progenitor of the priestly *cohen* caste 3,000 years ago. More than once, his father had told him their family was *cohanim*. "I was really curious," Carvin says, "to see if there was even a small possibility that the oral tradition was true."

On the Internet, Carvin located Family Tree DNA, a small Houston firm created to answer such questions. He mailed in a sample of his DNA, gathered by swabbing the inside of his cheek, and waited. In late October, he got a call from Bennett Greenspan, president of Family Tree DNA. Not only did his Y chromosome have the *cohanim* markers—small genetic variations—but other markers matched with those of another man in the database, making it likely that they share a forefather within the past 250 years.

So, just before Thanksgiving, Carvin set off on a DNA-induced family reunion. He took the train from his home in Washington, D.C., to Philadelphia and met Bill Swersky, a 59-year-old federal official. "We immediately hit it off," says Carvin. "I felt like I was visiting one of my uncles." Over smoked whitefish and bagels, they paged through family photos. Andy's dad looks like Bill's father. Bill's son looks like Andy when he was younger. "He's a hell of a lot better looking than I am," Swersky says of his new relative. "I'm jealous."

It's exceedingly unusual to find such treasure in the genetic attic. Humans are very much alike genetically, with most of the variation within—rather than between—ethnic groups. Carvin and Swersky struck gold because they're part of the small *cohanim* group, which is itself a subset of an insular group, Jews. Finns, Sardinians, and Basques are among other groups with small founding populations that also have highly distinctive genetic pedigrees. By contrast, most people of European origin are so genetically mixed that it's impossible to tell German from Frenchman, Bosnian from Serb.

But the tools of biotechnology have become so powerful that it's now possible to deduce ancient human history from a drop of blood or a few shed skin cells. This molecular view of the past is already being employed to trace the cause of ailments such as cancer and heart disease, as well as aiding individuals like Carvin in tracking their roots. Most significantly for scientists studying past human life and culture, it offers the best insight yet into the abiding mystery of how modern *Homo sapiens* arose out of archaic hominids who first left Africa about 1.7 million years ago."It's a very exciting time," says Colin Renfrew, a professor of archaeology at the University of Cambridge. "In the next 10 years the whole course of early human history is going to become very much clearer."

Indeed, in recent months, two groups of geneticists have published sweeping chronicles of the peopling of Europe, one tracing maternal DNA lineages, the other, paternal. These findings portray the majority of European forebears arriving from the Middle East as hunter-gatherers 25,000 to 40,000 years ago. During the last Ice Age, these first Europeans fled south to Iberia, Ukraine, and the Balkans. As the ice retreated, the Ice Age survivors spread out and flourished.The last major migration from the East 9,000 years ago brought agriculture and domestic animals but did not displace the earlier settlers, as some researchers had thought.

Genetic clock. The European studies are among the first to capitalize on a new ability to compare the migrations of males and females, which don't always follow the same path through history. Over the past 20 years, researchers have been able to track women's wanderings through mitochondria—tiny energy-producing bodies that cluster by the hundreds in human cells. Mitochondria have very odd DNA. They contain genetic material only from the maternal line, unlike the cell nucleus,which is a mix of DNA from both parents. This means that all children, male and female, carry copies of their mother's mitochondrial DNA.

That peculiarity gave geneticists a key tool for learning the movements of ancient populations. That's because as mitochondrial DNA is passed along, tiny, harmless mutations occur. By comparing the mutations among people, it's possible to calculate how closely they're related. And by calculating the mutation rate, researchers can deduce how far back in time different groups split apart. Douglas Wallace, director of the center for molecular medicine at Emory University Medical School, says: "You literally have a genetic clock." Wallace proved that point in 1980, when he was able to differentiate people from Europe, Asia, and Africa by comparing their DNA.

The realization that there is a map and a clock of human history in every cell completely transformed the small, highly technical field of population genetics. Scientists had been searching for human history in the genes at least since World War I, when two Polish immunologists discovered that different armies had very different proportions of various blood types.(Type B blood, for example, is more common in East Asians and Africans than it is in Europeans. Since blood type is hereditary, controlled by a single gene, a blood type can be used as a crude form of genealogy.) Blood types were used to prove that the Romany, or Gypsies, were correct when they claimed they originally came from the Indian subcontinent, not Europe.

But although researchers kept cataloging genetic markers in blood proteins, the number identified was far fewer than the millions of inherited mutations that must exist. "There just weren't enough data to answer the interesting questions," says Kenneth Kidd, a genetics professor at Yale University School of Medicine. Times changed. Since the mid-1980s, technology has unleashed a flood of new data, so much that researchers struggle to keep pace. Restriction enzymes allow scientists to snip DNA into tiny, easy-to-read bits. The 1983 invention of the polymerase chain reaction, or PCR, made it possible to make unlimited copies of a DNA strand in a test tube. PCR made it possible to decode the human genome. And for students of human history, it is opening the window to the past further than anyone imagined.

Enter Eve. In 1987, Allan Wilson, Rebecca Cann, and Mark Stoneking, researchers at the University of California-Berkeley, catapulted mitochondrial DNA into the headlines worldwide when they announced that they had traced it back 200,000 years to the oldest female ancestor of living humans—an African woman quickly dubbed Eve. Eve's debut rocked the archaeological community, which had been arguing for decades over whether modern humans evolved on more than one continent or instead swept out of Africa to replace more archaic hominids around the world. Wilson's group was attacked for sloppy science, and in fact there were problems with the original calculations. But genetic data from dozens of researchers have since almost universally supported the "Out of Africa" theory. "History has made a pretty consistent stamp on populations," says Lynn

Jorde, a geneticist at the University of Utah, who has found African roots in nuclear DNA as well as in mitochondria and the Y. "Looking at more and more of the nuclear DNA is going to clarify the picture."

Questions remain about the nature of the early human diaspora. For instance, lively debate continues over whether Neanderthals and modern humans mated [box, "Ancient History in the DNA"]. And some remain skeptical about the Out of Africa theory itself. This month researchers at Australian National University published the results of mitochondrial DNA testing on a 60,000-year-old skeleton called Lake Mungo 3. The DNA didn't match that of living humans, suggesting that the Mungo lineage evolved in Australia, not Africa. But it could simply mean that the Mungo lineage went extinct, as have many others.

Indeed, there have been many Adams, and many Eves. The genetic record reflects only those whose offspring survived and reproduced. For instance, the earliest forefather identified so far is 20,000 to 30,000 years younger than Eve. "It's rather distressing to find that Eve could not be the wife of Adam," says Luigi Luca Cavalli-Sforza, a professor emeritus at Stanford University and pioneer of population genetics. The bulk of the genetic data suggests that a small population of modern humans, as few as 10,000, left Africa 100,000 or so years ago, wandering into the Middle East and on to Asia and Europe. Their genetic footprints lead all the way to Tierra del Fuego.

Emory's Wallace has spent the past decade tracking mitochondrial markers from Africa to Asia and the Americas—and fueling a robust dispute over just when humans first arrived in the New World. For much of the past 50 years, archaeologists thought that people tramped across the Bering Land Bridge and through a gap in the glaciers about 14,000 years ago. But Wallace thinks there were other migrations, one as early as 30,000 years ago. Archaeological sites in Pennsylvania, Virginia, and Chile support this earlier migration, although the notion remains hotly contested.Wallace's newest and most surprising discovery is a set of genetic markers found only in the Ojibwa and other tribes living near the Great Lakes; the markers are not found in any other native Americans or in Asia. "We just don't know how it got there," Wallace says, "but it's clearly related to the European population." The simple answer would be that the DNA arrived with European colonists, but the strain is different enough from the existing European lineage that it must have left the Old World long before Columbus. The lineage could have passed through Asia and later died out there. But Dennis Stanford, a paleoarchaeologist at the Smithsonian Institution, says this mystery strain, dubbed Haplogroup X, bolsters his theory that a hardy band of Europeans left Iberia and navigated the North Atlantic ice pack 15,000 years ago."During colder time periods the sea ice was as far south as the Bay of Biscay," Stanford says, adding that the ice edge would have been ideal for hunting and fishing, just as it is in the Arctic today.

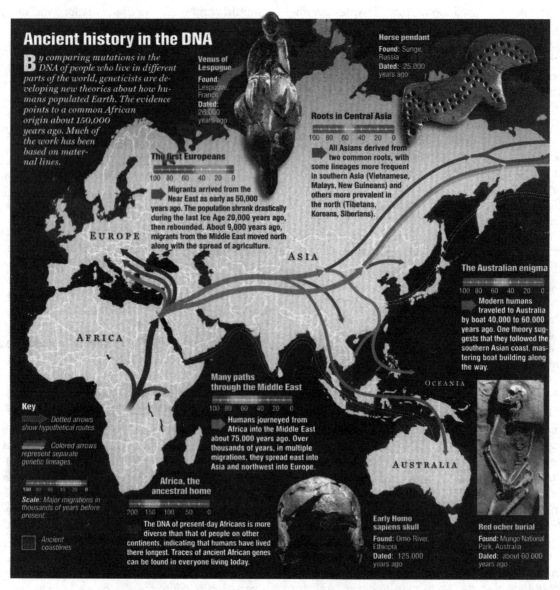

Ancient history in the DNA

By comparing mutations in the DNA of people who live in different parts of the world, geneticists are developing new theories about how humans populated Earth. The evidence points to a common African origin about 150,000 years ago. Much of the work has been based on maternal lines.

Venus of Lespugue
Found: Lespugue, France
Dated: 26,000 years ago

Horse pendant
Found: Sungir, Russia
Dated: 25,000 years ago

Roots in Central Asia
100 80 60 40 20 0
All Asians derived from two common roots, with some lineages more frequent in southern Asia (Vietnamese, Malays, New Guineans) and others more prevalent in the north (Tibetans, Koreans, Siberians).

The first Europeans
100 80 60 40 20 0
Migrants arrived from the Near East as early as 50,000 years ago. The population shrank drastically during the last Ice Age 20,000 years ago, then rebounded. About 9,000 years ago, migrants from the Middle East moved north along with the spread of agriculture.

EUROPE

ASIA

The Australian enigma
100 80 60 40 20 0
Modern humans traveled to Australia by boat 40,000 to 60,000 years ago. One theory suggests that they followed the southern Asian coast, mastering boat building along the way.

AFRICA

OCEANIA

Many paths through the Middle East
100 80 60 40 20 0
Humans journeyed from Africa into the Middle East about 75,000 years ago. Over thousands of years, in multiple migrations, they spread east into Asia and northwest into Europe.

Key
Dotted arrows show hypothetical routes.
Colored arrows represent separate genetic lineages.
100 80 60 40 20 0
Scale: Major migrations in thousands of years before present.
Ancient coastlines

AUSTRALIA

Africa, the ancestral home
200 150 100 50 0
The DNA of present-day Africans is more diverse than that of people on other continents, indicating that humans have lived there longest. Traces of ancient African genes can be found in everyone living today.

Early Homo sapiens skull
Found: Omo River, Ethiopia
Dated: 125,000 years ago

Red ocher burial
Found: Mungo National Park, Australia
Dated: about 60,000 years ago

CLOCKWISE FROM TOP LEFT: SCALA /ART RESOURCE; KENNETH GARRETT—NATIONAL GEOGRAPHIC IMAGE COLLECTION; J.M. MCAVOY—NOTTTOWAY RIVER SURVEY; KENNETH GARRETT—NATIONAL GEOGRAPHIC IMAGE COLLECTION; AUSTRALIAN NATIONAL UNIVERSITY/REUTERS/ARCHIVE; DAVID L. BRILL

While Wallace and others were finding remarkable stories in mitochondrial DNA, scientists seeking similar tales in the Y chromosome were met with silence. It was particularly frustrating because the Y—passed intact from father to son—seemed like an ideal tool for tracking human origins. But unlike mitochondrial DNA, the male chromosome shows little variation, and searching for markers was excruciating work. Michael Hammer, a geneticist at the University of Arizona who first identified key Y markers, started looking for a *cohanim* marker in 1995, after he got a call from Karl Skorecki, an Israeli physician. Skorecki was wondering if the very different looking men he saw reading the Torah in shul could possibly all be sons of Aaron, as the Bible said. Intrigued, Hammer started searching the DNA of Skorecki and other Jewish men who according to oral tradition were *cohanim*, the priest caste. Hammer identified markers that are often shared by men who think they are *cohanim*, including Andy Carvin and Bill Skwersky. By comparing the variations, Hammer determined that the *cohanim* had a common male ancestor 84 to 130 generations ago—which includes the time of the exodus from Egypt and the original *cohen*, Aaron.

Brothers and enemies. Since then, other researchers have used the *cohanim* markers to ascertain that the Lemba, a Bantu-speaking people in Southern Africa who have traditionally claimed Jewish ancestry, do indeed have Semitic roots. And last June, Hammer published results showing that although Palestinian and Jewish men may be political foes, they are also brethren, so closely related as to be genetically indistinguishable.

The Y chromosome is starting to yield other intriguing tales as well. Last November, Peter Underhill, a Stanford

Stone tools
Found: Cactus
Hill, Virginia
Dated: 15,000
to 18,000
years ago

*Land bridge
between
continents*

The X factor
A small group of Indians
near the Great Lakes has
a lineage (haplogroup "X")
unlike those of other American Indians, but related to
a European strain. Some
archaeologists think that
the colonists came from
Iberia about 15,000 years
ago, crossing the North
Atlantic ice pack to Green-
land. Others believe the X
factor is the remnant of a
vanished Asian lineage.

**A bridge to
the New World**

100 80 60 40 20 0

The first inhabitants
of the New World
migrated from central
Siberia 20,000 to 30,000
years ago along the Bering
land bridge. They may have
been joined by a second
migration 15,000 years ago
that skirted the coast. Na-
Dene people, who include
the Athabascans, Apaches,
and Navajos, are genetically distinct from the first
American Indians, and
came from northern Siberia
about 9,000 years ago. Es-
kimos and Aleuts arrived
4,000 to 6,000 years later.

NORTH
AMERICA

For most of the past 65,000
years, sea levels have been
lower than today. During the
last Ice Age 20,000 years
ago, sea levels were about
400 feet lower.

**Along the Andes
to Tierra del Fuego**

100 80 60 40 20 0

The earliest migration swept
from Siberia to Tierra del Fuego, traveling along the Andes.
Another route curved farther east,
to present-day Brazil.

SOUTH
AMERICA

Sources: Douglas Wallace,
Michael Brown, and Marie
Lott, Emory University;
David Anderson, Paula
Dunbar, NOAA; Theodore
Schurr, Southwest Founda-
tion for Biomedical Re-
search; *The Human Career*

**Throwing
stone**
Found: Monte
Verde, Chile
Dated: 14,800
years ago

SOURCES: DOUGLAS WALLACE, MICHAEL BROWN, AND MARIE LOTT, EMORY UNUVERSITY;
DAVID ANDERSON, PAULA DUNBAR, NOAA; THEODORE SCHURR, SOUTHWEST FOUNDATION
FOR BIOMEDICAL RESEARCH; *THE HUMAN CAREER*

University researcher, published a list of 87 new Y markers, which he used to draw a tree that sorts all the world's
men into just 10 branches. Indeed, men's lineages have
much crisper divisions than women's, perhaps because
men move into an area and kill or expel the men already
there. "You get this alpha male effect," Underhill says.

Women, by contrast, move because they've married
into a new family and village. Generation after generation, daughters marry and move out, while sons stay put,
making women's DNA often more well traveled than
men's. People living near Medellín, Colombia, have almost exclusively Native American mitochondrial DNA
and European—specifically, Spanish—Y chromosome
DNA. The story is familiar, and tragic: The Spanish colonists killed or supplanted the native men and married the
native women.

For all its dazzle—or perhaps because of it—molecular
anthropology is not without critics. "The molecular stuff
has been very important," says Milford Wolpoff, an anthropology professor at the University of Michigan and a
leading critic of the Out of Africa theory of human origins. "But in the end it has the same problem fossils
have—the sample size is very small." Earlier this month,
the journal *Science* published a Wolpoff study of early human skulls, which suggests that Africans may have
mixed with earlier hominids rather than supplanting
them. The small number of living humans sampled by geneticists, Wolpoff says, and the effects of natural selection
over the millennia, make it foolhardy to say with assurance that Out of Africa is right. The geneticists, for their
part, readily admit that they need more samples, more
markers, and more precise calculations. But they also say

that even with today's imperfect science, the DNA is right. And in places like India and China, where the fossil record is scanty, the genetic history will be the only history. "Genetics is moving so fast," says Chris Stringer, a paleoanthropologist at the Natural History Museum in London. "It's well ahead of the fossil and historical record."

Gene-based anthropology also struggles with the specter of racism. Australia has banned researchers from publishing work involving Aboriginal DNA, and India bars the export of its citizens' genetic matter. Geneticists are dismayed by these attitudes; if there's one thing the genes show, they say, it is that there is no such thing as race. The external differences that most people would use in defining race—skin color, eye shape, height—are genetically inconsequential, minor variations that evolved in response to the environment, the genetic equivalent of a sunburn. For instance, a change in just one gene accounts for Northern Europeans' fair skin, which may have developed to better absorb sunlight and synthesize vitamin D. "We are all brothers," says Stanford's Underhill, "and we're all different."

Genealogy by the genes

For-profit genetic genealogy services are springing up, but they can answer only limited questions.

• **Family Tree** DNA (713-828-4200, *www.familytreedna.com*) helps connect distantly related "genetic cousins."

• **GeneTree** (888-404-4363, *www.genetree.com*) tests whether families with the same surname are related.

• **Oxford Ancestors** (*www.oxfordancestors.com*) groups people into ancient maternal and paternal lineages.

Custom medicine. The differences may be minor, but they matter a lot to medical researchers. African-Americans are more apt to get sickle-cell anemia; some people with Eastern European roots have a gene that confers resistance to AIDS; women with Scottish ancestry are predisposed to one form of breast cancer. So researchers are using molecular anthropology to seek the origins of disease and then using that knowledge to create customized treatments. They're looking increasingly at nuclear DNA—the DNA of genes and inherited traits—which mingles with every generation. "Go back five generations," says Yale's Kidd. "You have 32 ancestors. At each nuclear locus you may have a gene from a different set of two of those ancestors." Thus nuclear DNA paints a much fuller picture of the past than mitochondrial and Y, which represent only two ancestors in any generation. Kidd is now studying nuclear DNA in 33 populations around the world, seeking a better understanding of schizophrenia, Tourette's syndrome, and alcoholism. Science is far from being able to simply scan the human genome to find the

causes of complex diseases like these. But the day will come, and soon, when it will be possible to pinpoint the genetic roots of disease without the geographic history. "Who cares where patients come from?" asks Aravinda Chakravarti, head of the institute of genetic medicine at Johns Hopkins University. "We'll be looking at what kind of diabetes is there, not whether they came from Timbuktu or Thailand or Towson."

NEANDERTHAL MYSTERY

Did early man mix it up?

Humans have been arguing about Neanderthals ever since an unusual skeleton with a beetled brow was dug up in a quarry by Germany's River Neander in 1856. Were these the bones of ancestors of modern *Homo sapiens*? More recent evidence that humans and Neanderthals both lived in Europe up to 26,000 years ago raised a more startling question: Did Neanderthals and humans have sex?

Since 1997, researchers have managed to extract mitochondrial DNA from three Neanderthal skeletons. The genes appear to have diverged from the modern human lineage about 500,000 years ago, way too early for Stone Age whoopee.

But in 1998, the skeleton of a child with human and Neanderthal features was found in Lagar Velho, Portugal. Washington University anthropologist Erik Trinkaus who is researching the find, says the 24,500-year-old bones are clear evidence of admixture. Both geneticists and archaeologists could be right with any mixed DNA lost by chance over the millennia. "We can't say anything about sexual practices in the Pleistocene." says Svante Pääbo, the geneticist at the Max Planck Institute for Evolutionary Anthropology in Leipzig who analyzed the Neanderthal DNA.

The thought of Neanderthal-human hybrids fascinates more than a few humans. Three years after the Lagar Velho find, Trinkaus still gets E-mails from people writing: "That explains Uncle George." –N.S.

But for some people, knowing where they came from matters a lot. Alice Petrovilli, a 71-year-old Aleut living in Anchorage, says she was eager to participate in a University of Kansas study on Aleut origins, even though other Aleut elders refused. "I think it's important. People always acted like because we were so far away we were a substandard species. It proves we were out here for a long, long time." Her DNA helps establish the Aleuts as people who migrated through Alaska and arrived in the Aleutian Islands 4,000 to 6,000 years ago and are genetically related to the Chukchi of northeast Russia.

Pearl Duncan is also interested in where her genes have been. The 51-year-old Jamaica-born writer had exhaustively researched her family history through genealogical records and traced several nicknames to Ghanaian dialects. But the trail ended there, lost in the Middle Passage when her slave ancestors were brought from Africa to the New World. So she tested her father's Y against DNA she gathered from members of Ghanaian churches in New York, where she lives, and found a match. "I really traced a cultural voice that is missing from the African-American narrative," says Duncan, who is writing a book about her search. She is incorporating her Ghanaian history with that of John Smellie, her Scottish ancestor 12 generations back.

No lifeguards. But geneticists fear that for every Pearl Duncan who boldly dives into the gene pool, at home with her mixed racial history, other more naive searchers may be dismayed at what they find. "Five percent of the people in America are sending Father's Day cards to the wrong guy," says Martin Tracey, a professor of genetics at Florida International University in Miami. What's more, mitochondrial and Y DNA reveal just a tiny slice of family history. Only one out of four great-grandfathers is represented on the Y, for instance, and only one great-grandmother in mitochondrial DNA. Go back just five generations, and only one of 16 forefathers is revealed. Thus someone seeking African roots could have DNA tests come back purely European, even though the person has largely African ancestors. "It's really dangerous to market a single locus as a statement of identity," says Emory's Wallace, who counsels patients with devastating genetic diseases. "I don't want to say to someone, 'I believe you're a Native American, but your mitochondria are European.'"

Indeed, few genetic genealogists will experience the same thrill as Adrian Targett, a schoolteacher in Cheddar, England, who discovered through DNA testing that he's a blood relative of Cheddar Man, a 9,000-year-old skeleton found in a nearby cave. But some people, those who seek answers to very specific questions, say they get their money's worth (box, "Genealogy by the Genes"). Doug Mumma, a 65-year-old retired nuclear physicist in Livermore, Calif., searched out strangers with his surname all over the world and paid $170 per sample to have their Y chromosomes tested. Many turned out to have no genetic link to Mumma, but he did locate several blood relatives in Germany. Mumma says, "To me it's cheap for what I want to do."

From *U.S. News & World Report*, January 29, 2001, pp. 34-41. © 2001 by U.S. News & World Report, L.P. Reprinted by permission.

SCIENCE

THE SECRETS OF AUTISM

THE NUMBER OF CHILDREN DIAGNOSED WITH AUTISM AND ASPERGER'S IN THE U.S. IS EXPLODING. WHY?

By J. MADELEINE NASH

Tommy Barrett is a dreamy-eyed fifth-grader who lives with his parents, twin brothers, two cats and a turtle in San Jose, Calif., the heart of Silicon Valley. He's an honor-roll student who likes math and science and video games. He's also a world-class expert on Animorph and Transformer toys. "They're like cars and trains and animals that transform into robots or humans—I love them!" he shouts exuberantly.

And that is sometimes a problem. For a time, in fact, Tommy's fascination with his toys was so strong that when they weren't around he would pretend to *be* the toys, transforming from a truck into a robot or morphing into a kitten. He would do this in the mall, in the school playground and even in the classroom. His teachers found this repetitive pantomime delightful but disturbing, as did his mother Pam.

Autistic disorders may afflict nearly 300,000 kids in the U.S. alone

By that point, there were other worrisome signs. Pam Barrett recalls that as a 3-year-old, Tommy was a fluent, even voluble talker, yet he could not seem to grasp that conversation had reciprocal rules, and, curiously, he avoided looking into other people's eyes. And although Tommy was obviously smart—he had learned to read by the time he was 4—he was so fidgety and unfocused that he was unable to participate in his kindergarten reading group.

When Tommy turned 8, his parents finally learned what was wrong. Their bright little boy, a psychiatrist informed them, had a mild form of autism known as Asperger syndrome. Despite the fact that children with

Asperger's often respond well to therapy, the Barretts, at that moment, found the news almost unbearable.

That's because just two years earlier Pam and her husband Chris, operations manager of a software-design company, had learned that Tommy's twin brothers Jason and Danny were profoundly autistic. Seemingly normal at birth, the twins learned to say a few words before they spiraled into their secret world, quickly losing the abilities they had just started to gain. Instead of playing with toys, they broke them; instead of speaking, they emitted an eerie, high-pitched keening.

Up to 20 genes may be involved in autism, but they're not the only factors

First Jason and Danny, now Tommy. Pam and Chris started to wonder about their children's possible exposure to toxic substances. They started scanning a lengthening roster of relatives, wondering how long autism had shadowed their family.

The anguish endured by Pam and Chris Barrett is all too familiar to tens of thousands of families across North America and other parts of the world. With a seeming suddenness, cases of autism and closely related disorders like Asperger's are exploding in number, and no one has a good explanation for it. While many experts believe the increase is a by-product of a recent broadening of diagnostic criteria, others are convinced that the surge is at least in part real and thereby cause for grave concern.

In the Barretts' home state of California, for instance, the number of autistic children seeking social services has more than quadrupled in the past 15 years, from fewer than 4,000 in 1987 to nearly 18,000 today. So common are

The Geek Syndrome

At Michelle Winner's social-skills clinic in San Jose, Calif., business is booming. Every week dozens of youngsters with Asperger syndrome file in and out of therapy sessions while their anxious mothers run errands or chat quietly in the waiting room. In one session, a rosy-cheeked 12-year-old struggles to describe the emotional reactions of a cartoon character in a video clip; in another, four little boys (like most forms of autism, Asperger's overwhelmingly affects boys) grapple with the elusive concept of teamwork while playing a game of 20 Questions. Unless prompted to do so, they seldom look at one another, directing their eyes to the wall or ceiling or simply staring off into space.

Yet outside the sessions the same children become chatty and animated, displaying an astonishing grasp of the most arcane subjects. Transformer toys, video games, airplane schedules, star charts, dinosaurs. It sounds charming, and indeed would be, except that their interest is all consuming. After about five minutes, children with Asperger's, a.k.a. the "little professor" or "geek" syndrome, tend to sound like CDs on autoplay. "Did you ask her if she's interested in astrophysics?" a mother gently chides her son, who has launched into an excruciatingly detailed description of what goes on when a star explodes into a supernova.

Although Hans Asperger described the condition in 1944, it wasn't until 1994 that the American Psychiatric Association officially recognized Asperger syndrome as a form of autism with its own diagnostic criteria. It is this recognition, expanding the definition of autism to include everything from the severely retarded to the mildest cases, that is partly responsible for the recent explosion in autism diagnoses.

There are differences between Asperger's and high-functioning autism. Among other things, Asperger's appears to be even more strongly genetic than classic autism, says Dr. Fred Volkmar, a child psychiatrist at Yale. About a third of the fathers or brothers of children with Asperger's show signs of the disorder. There appear to be maternal roots as well. The wife of one Silicon Valley software engineer believes that her Asperger's son represents the fourth generation in just such a lineage.

It was the Silicon Valley connection that led *Wired* magazine to run its geek-syndrome feature last December. The story was basically a bit of armchair theorizing about a social phenomenon known as assortative mating. In university towns and R.-and-D. corridors, it is argued, smart but not particularly well-socialized men today are meeting and marrying women very like themselves, leading to an overload of genes that predispose their children to autism, Asperger's and related disorders.

Is there anything to this idea? Perhaps. There is no question that many successful people—not just scientists and engineers but writers and lawyers as well—possess a suite of traits that seem to be, for lack of a better word, Aspergery. The ability to focus intensely and screen out other distractions, for example, is a geeky trait that can be extremely useful to computer programmers. On the other hand, concentration that is too intense—focusing on cracks in the pavement while a taxi is bearing down on you—is clearly, in Darwinian terms, maladaptive.

But it may be a mistake to dwell exclusively on the genetics of Asperger's; there must be other factors involved. Experts suspect that such variables as prenatal positioning in the womb, trauma experienced at birth or random variation in the process of brain development may also play a role.

Even if you could identify the genes involved in Asperger's, it's not clear what you would do about them. It's not as if they are lethal genetic defects, like the ones that cause Huntington's disease or cystic fibrosis. "Let's say that a decade from now we know all the genes for autism," suggests Bryna Siegel, a psychologist at the University of California, San Francisco. "And let's say your unborn child has four of these genes. We may be able to tell you that 80% of the people with those four genes will be fully autistic but that the other 20% will perform in the gifted mathematical range."

Filtering the geeky genes out of the high-tech breeding grounds like Silicon Valley, in other words, might remove the very DNA that made these places what they are today.

—By J. Madeleine Nash.
With reporting by Amy Bonesteel/Atlanta

cases of Asperger's in Silicon Valley, in fact, that *Wired* magazine coined a cyber-age term for the disorder, referring to its striking combination of intellectual ability and social cluelessness as the "geek syndrome." *Wired* went on to make a provocative if anecdotal case that autism and Asperger's were rising in Silicon Valley at a particularly alarming rate—and asked whether "math-and-tech genes" might be to blame (*see box*).

Yet the rise in autism and Asperger's is hardly confined to high-tech enclaves or to the children of computer programmers and software engineers. It occurs in every job category and socioeconomic class and in every state. "We're getting calls from school systems in rural Georgia," observes Sheila Wagner, director of the Autism Resource Center at Atlanta's Emory University. "People are saying, 'We never had any kids with autism before, and now we have 10! What's going on?'"

It's a good question. Not long ago, autism was assumed to be comparatively rare, affecting as few as 1 in 10,000 people. The latest studies, however, suggest that as many as 1 in 150 kids age 10 and younger may be affected by autism or a related disorder—a total of nearly 300,000 children in the U.S. alone. If you include adults, according to the Autism Society of America, more than a million people in the U.S. suffer from one of the autistic disorders (also known as pervasive developmental disorders or PDDs). The problem is five times as common as Down syndrome and three times as common as juvenile diabetes.

No wonder parents are besieging the offices of psychologists and psychiatrists in their search for remedies. No wonder school systems are adding special aides to help teachers cope. And no wonder public and private research institutions have launched collaborative initiatives aimed at deciphering the complex biology that produces such a dazzling range of disability.

In their urgent quest for answers, parents like the Barretts are provoking what promises to be a scientific revolution. In response to the concerns they are raising, money is finally flowing into autism research, a field that five years ago appeared to be stuck in the stagnant backwaters of neuroscience. Today dozens of scientists are racing to identify the genes linked to autism. Just last month, in a series of articles published by *Molecular Psychiatry*, scientists from the U.S., Britain, Italy and France reported that they are beginning to make significant progress.

Meanwhile, research teams are scrambling to create animal models for autism in the form of mutant mice. They are beginning to examine environmental factors that might contribute to the development of autism and using advanced brain-imaging technology to probe the deep interior of autistic minds. In the process, scientists are gaining rich new insights into this baffling spectrum of disorders and are beginning to float intriguing new hypotheses about why people affected by it develop minds that are strangely different from our own and yet, in some important respects, hauntingly similar.

AUTISM'S GENETIC ROOTS

AUTISM WAS FIRST DESCRIBED IN 1943 BY JOHNS HOPKINS psychiatrist Leo Kanner, and again in 1944 by Austrian pediatrician Hans Asperger. Kanner applied the term to children who were socially withdrawn and preoccupied with routine, who struggled to acquire spoken language

---

GUIDE FOR PARENTS
How do you tell if your child is autistic? And what should you do if he or she is?

WHAT TO LOOK FOR

SIGNS OF AUTISM

(Usually apparent in toddlers; watch for cluster of symptoms)
- No pointing by 1 year
- No babbling by 1 year; no single words by 16 months; no two-word phrases by 24 months
- Any loss of language skills at any time
- No pretend playing
- Little interest in making friends
- Extremely short attention span
- No response when called by name; indifference to others
- Little or no eye contact
- Repetitive body movements, such as hand flapping, rocking
- Intense tantrums
- Fixations on a single object, such as a spinning fan
- Unusually strong resistance to changes in routines
- Oversensitivity to certain sounds, textures or smells

SIGNS OF ASPERGER'S

(Usually diagnosed at 6 or older)
- Difficulty making friends
- Difficulty reading or communicating through nonverbal social cues, such as facial expressions
- No understanding that others may have thoughts or feelings different from his or her own
- Obsessive focus on a narrow interest, such as reciting train schedules
- Awkward motor skills
- Inflexibility about routines, especially when changes occur spontaneously
- Mechanical, almost robotic patterns of speech

(Even "normal" children exhibit some of these behaviors from time to time. The symptoms of autism and Asperger's, by contrast, are persistent and debilitating.)
                                   —*By Amy Lennard Goehner*

---

yet often possessed intellectual gifts that ruled out a diagnosis of mental retardation. Asperger applied the term to children who were socially maladroit, developed bizarre obsessions and yet were highly verbal and seemingly

GUIDE FOR PARENTS *continued*

Snapshots from the Autistic Brain

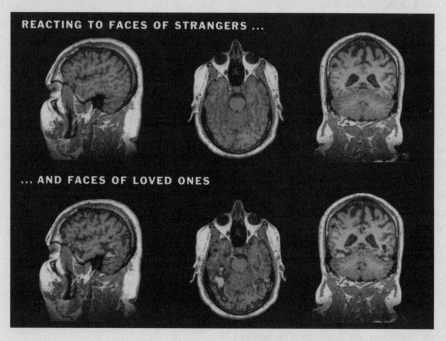

Neuroimaging studies confirm what scientists long suspected: autistic brains don't react to facial cues the way normal brains do. But in one regard the conventional wisdom was wrong. In a breakthrough study, Karen Pierce at the University of California at San Diego has shown that when faces of strangers are replaced by faces of loved ones, the autistic brain lights up like an explosion of Roman candles.

WHERE TO START

GET AN EVALUATION: Take your child to a developmental pediatrician with expertise in autism or Asperger syndrome. The pediatrician will evaluate your child with a team of specialists (speech therapists, occupational therapists, behavior therapists) to determine the areas in which your child needs help.

EARLY INTERVENTION: Every state is mandated to provide a free evaluation and early-intervention services for children. To find out whom to contact in your state, consult the National Information Center for Children and Youth with Disabilities (funded by the Department of Education) at 800-695-0285 or *nichcy.org/index.html*. Ask about support groups in your area.

HOW TO TREAT IT

There is no cure for autism, but there are many treatments that can make a difference:
SPEECH THERAPY: Can help overcome communication and language barriers
OCCUPATIONAL THERAPY: Helps with sensory integration and motor skills
BEHAVIORAL THERAPY: Improves cognitive skills and reduces inappropriate behavior
EDUCATIONAL THERAPY: A highly structured approach works best
MEDICATION: Can reduce some symptoms
SPECIAL DIETS: Eliminating certain food groups, such as dairy, helps some children

HELPFUL WEBSITES
ONLINE ASPERGER SYNDROME INFORMATION AND SUPPORT *www.aspergersyndrome.org*
AUTISM SOCIETY OF AMERICA *autism-society.org*
FAMILIES FOR EARLY AUTISM TREATMENT *www.feat.org*
AUTISM RESOURCES *autism-info.com*
YALE CHILD STUDY CENTER *info.med.yale.edu/chldstdy/autism*

Network: Other parents can be great sources in finding the right treatments.

quite bright. There was a striking tendency, Asperger noted, for the disorder to run in families, sometimes passing directly from father to son. Clues that genes might be central to autism appeared in Kanner's work as well.

VACCINES

Are the Shots Safe?

Ask the parents of autistic children whether they believe childhood vaccines can cause autism, and the answer will probably be yes. They have heard of too many cases of babies who were perfectly normal until they got their measles, mumps and rubella (MMR) shot and then, within weeks—if not days—started throwing tantrums, losing language skills and generally tuning out.

Ask doctors the same question, and they are likely to cite the panel of experts convened by the Institute of Medicine last year. They studied the evidence but found no explanation for how vaccines might possibly cause autism. Included in the review were studies that showed no significant difference in the incidence of autism disorders before and after MMR immunization became routine in 1988 in Britain. "We bent over backward to look for the biological mechanisms that would support a link," says the panel's chairwoman, Dr. Marie McCormick of the Harvard School of Public Health.

But failing to prove that something can happen is not the same as proving it doesn't, and the issue is still a matter of furious debate. The only scientific evidence against childhood vaccines comes from Dr. Andrew Wakefield, formerly at the Royal Free Hospital in London. His theory is that autism stems from a severe immune reaction to something in the vaccine. In February he published a paper showing that immunized children with autism and bowel disorders have higher levels of measles particles in their intestinal tissue than normal children do. The evidence is not entirely persuasive, however; measles particles in the tissues do not necessarily mean that the virus—or the vaccine—causes autism.

What about all the children whose symptoms appeared shortly after their MMR? The association may be purely coincidental. The shots are given at 15 months, which is when behavior and speech patterns in babies usually become sufficiently pronounced for parents to start noticing that something is wrong. Most of the evidence suggests that autism is primarily a genetic disorder. It may be that some symptoms appear immediately after birth but are too subtle to be spotted in the first year or so of life.

To get more definitive answers, the National Institutes of Health and the Centers for Disease control have each launched their own investigations. Karyn Seroussi of Poughkeepsie, N.Y., for one, supports this research. "If it's the shots, I want to know," says Seroussi, an autism advocate and parent of an autistic son. "If it's not, I want to know what the heck it is that's causing autism." On that, both parents and doctors can agree.

—By Alice Park

But then autism research took a badly wrong turn. Asperger's keen insights languished in Europe's postwar turmoil, and Kanner's were overrun by the Freudian juggernaut. Children were not born autistic, experts insisted, but became that way because their parents, especially mothers, were cold and unnurturing.

In 1981, however, British psychiatrist Dr. Lorna Wing published an influential paper that revived interest in Asperger's work. The disorder Asperger identified, Wing observed, appeared in many ways to be a variant of Kanner's autism, so that the commonalities seemed as important as the differences. As a result, researchers now believe that Asperger and Kanner were describing two faces of a highly complicated and variable disorder, one that has its source in the kaleidoscope of traits encoded in the human genome. Researchers also recognize that severe autism is not always accompanied by compensatory intellectual gifts and is, in fact, far likelier to be characterized by heartbreaking deficits and mental retardation.

Perhaps the most provocative finding scientists have made to date is that the components of autism, far more than autism itself, tend to run in families. Thus even though profoundly autistic people rarely have children, researchers often find that a close relative is affected by some aspect of the disorder. A sister may engage in odd repetitive behavior or be excessively shy; a brother may have difficulties with language or be socially inept to a noticeable degree. In similar fashion, if one identical twin has autism, there is a 60% chance that the other will too and a better than 75% chance that the twin without autism will exhibit one or more autistic traits.

How many genes contribute to susceptibility to autism? Present estimates run from as few as three to more than 20. Coming under intensifying scrutiny, as the papers published by *Molecular Psychiatry* indicate, are genes that regulate the action of three powerful neurotransmitters: glutamate, which is intimately involved in learning and memory, and serotonin and gamma-aminobutiric acid (GABA), which have been implicated in obsessive-compulsive behavior, anxiety and depression.

Those genes hardly exhaust the list of possibilities. Among the suspects are virtually all the genes that control brain development and perhaps cholesterol and immune-system function as well. Christopher Stodgell, a developmental toxicologist at New York's University of Rochester, observes that the process that sets up the brain resembles an amazingly intricate musical score, and there are tens of thousands of genes in the orchestra. If these genes do what they're supposed to do, says Stodgell, "then you have a Mozart's *Concerto for Clarinet*. If not, you have cacophony."

A DIFFERENCE OF MIND

AUTISTIC PEOPLE OFTEN SUFFER FROM A BEWILDERING ARRAY of problems—sensory disturbances, food allergies, gas-

FIRST PERSON

My Brother

KARL TARO GREENFELD

My autistic brother Noah and I once played together. He was two, and I was a year older. We wrestled, and I tickled him. He responded in a high-pitched giggle, halfway between a baby's gurgle and a child's laughter. I can't remember ever playing with him again. Noah stayed forever a baby, profoundly retarded, always dependent, never very communicative. And my role changed, much too early, from playmate to steward. There was barely any sibling rivalry. There were no battles to be fought. He would always be the center of attention.

I was treated as a sort of supporting player. Because my father had written a trilogy of books about our family with Noah as the title character (starting with *A Child Called Noah*; 1972), I would often be asked what it was like having an autistic brother. I never figured out how to respond. The answer I always gave—that I had never known any other life or any other brother—seemed cryptic and somehow unsatisfactory.

But that remains the only answer I can give. Noah, who can't speak, dress or go to the bathroom completely unassisted, will always be the center of our family. He never earned that role; his needs dictated it. I wasn't consciously resentful of this as a child. There was no more reason to be angry about this than there was about the rigid laws of basic arithmetic.

I accepted the fact that Noah and his problems could fill a battleship of parental duty and obligation, leaving my mother and father too spent to worry about the more banal problems of their normal son. But at some point in my early teens, in the confusing years of adolescence, I stopped having friends over. Noah's condition dictated what we ate and when we slept and to a great degree how we lived. We never had fancy furniture because he chewed on the couch cushions and spit on the carpets. He would pull apart anything more complicated than a pencil. I was ashamed of our home and family. Already marked as different by virtue of being Asian American in a predominantly white community, I came to see Noah as an additional stigmatizing mark.

My father used to say every family has a skeleton in its closet. Only ours was out in the open. I don't even remember if I talked about Noah in school. My friends knew about him, but after the first few questions, there wasn't much to say. Noah didn't change. Autism is a condition, I knew from close up, for which there are no miraculous cures. So he always stayed Noah. This kid who shared the same black hair and brown eyes as I had but couldn't talk and wanted to be left alone. So what was there to say about Noah? He was my brother who was never going to grow up.

Noah is 35 now and has been living in institutions since he was 18. My parents visit him every weekend at the state-run Fairview Developmental Center in Costa Mesa, Calif. I go whenever I am in town. (Currently I live in Hong Kong.) We bring Noah his favorite foods: sushi, fresh fruit and Japanese crackers and take him for a walk or a ride. Sometimes he lashes out at me. Spitting. Scratching. Pulling hair. but he knows me; I can tell by the wary squint he gives me. We're brothers, after all.

My parents are now in their 70s. My father underwent open-heart surgery a few years ago. Eventually, the responsibility for Noah will fall solely upon me. I imagine I may have to move my own family back to California to visit him every weekend, so that those caring for him will know that despite Noah's temper tantrums and violent outbursts, he is loved; he is a brother and part of a family. He is still the center of my life. My travels, from Los Angeles to New York City to Paris to Tokyo to Hong Kong, will always bring me back to him. I don't know any other life. I have no other brother.

Greenfeld is the editor of TIME ASIA.

trointestinal problems, depression, obsessive compulsiveness, subclinical epilepsy, attention-deficit hyperactivity disorder. But there is, researchers believe, a central defect, and that is the difficulty people across the autistic spectrum have in developing a theory of mind. That's psychologese for the realization, which most children come to by the age of 4, that other people have thoughts, wishes and desires that are not mirror images of their own. As University of Washington child psychologist Andrew Meltzoff sees it, the developmental stage known as the terrible twos occurs because children—normal children, anyway—make the hypothesis that their parents have independent minds and then, like proper scientists, set out to test it.

Children on the autistic spectrum, however, are "mind blind"; they appear to think that what is in their mind is identical to what is in everyone else's mind and that how they feel is how everyone else feels. The notion that other people—parents, playmates, teachers—may take a different view of things, that they may harbor concealed motives or duplicitous thoughts, does not readily occur. "It took the longest time for Tommy to tell a lie," recalls Pam Barrett, and when he finally did, she inwardly cheered.

FIRST PERSON

My Son

AMY LENNARD GOEHNER

I didn't know the world that my friends with normal—or, as we call them, typically developing—kids live in until recently. Two and a half years ago, my husband and I adopted our second child, Joey. And as he has grown to be a toddler, every milestone he has reached has been bittersweet—a celebration but also a painful reminder of all the milestones our 8-year-old son Nate has never reached.

Before Joey could talk, he pointed—as if to say, "Hey, Mom, look at that dog over there"—the way kids do to engage you. I flashed back to the evaluation forms we filled out for Nate when we were taking him to specialists. One question that appeared on every form was "Does your child point?" It's a major developmental step, a gesture that communicates a child's desire to share something outside himself. Nate never pointed.

When Nate was 2 and not talking, we took him to a big New York City hospital to get him evaluated. The neurologist gave us his diagnosis almost apologetically, in a very quiet voice. I remember just two words: "Maybe autistic."

When I stopped crying, I went to my office and called everyone I had ever met who was in any way connected to the world of special-needs kids. We made a lot of mistakes before finding the perfect match for Nate (and us)—a wonderful speech therapist whom we later dubbed our captain. When she met Nate, he was nonverbal and running around her office like a self-propelled buzz saw. She looked at us calmly and said, "Let's get busy. We've got work to do."

We've been working ever since. In addition to continual speech, behavior and occupational therapy, we have dabbled in what one of our doctors called "the flavor of the week"—vitamins and supplements and other "can't miss" cures. We shelled out a small fortune for every must-have tool that Lori, Nate's occupational therapist, mentioned even casually, including weighted vests (to help "ground" Nate) and special CDs (to help desensitize him to loud sounds). "Every time Lori opens her mouth, it costs me a hundred bucks," my husband once said.

Recently I read Joey a picture book that contained illustrations of fruit. Joey pretended to pick the fruit off the page and eat it, offering me a bit. Again I flashed back to those evaluation forms: "Does your child engage in pretend/imaginative play?" Nate's idea of play is to drop sticks and small stones into a drain at the playground. He could do this for hours if we let him. Last week Joey took a long noodle from his bowl of soup, dragged it across the table and said, "Look, it's a train. There's the freight car." Then Nate took a noodle from his soup. He tossed it onto the ceiling.

Yet maybe because I entered motherhood through the special-needs world, I somehow feel more a part of it than I do the "normal" one. The challenges in this world are greater, but the accomplishments—those firsts—are that much sweeter.

The other day I heard Joey singing a song about trains, and I realized that I couldn't remember the first time I heard my second son sing. I just took it for granted. With Nate, I never take anything for granted.

When Nate was 6, I was invited to hear his class put on a concert. I had no idea what to expect, as Nate doesn't sing. What he does do is make loud, repetitive noises, occasionally while rocking back and forth. But I went anyway. And when the music teacher approached Nate and began to sing a song Nate loved to listen to, Nate looked down, stared at his hands and very quietly chimed in, "A ram sam sam, a ram sam, gooly, gooly, gooly… " The other moms rushed to hand me tissues as tears streamed town my face. I was listening to Nate sing. For the first time.

Goehner is head arts reporter at TIME

Meltzoff believes that this lack can be traced to the problem that autistic children have in imitating the adults in their lives. If an adult sits down with a normal 18-month-old and engages in some interesting behavior—pounding a pair of blocks on the floor, perhaps, or making faces—the child usually responds by doing the same. Young children with autism, however, do not, as Meltzoff and his colleague Geraldine Dawson have shown in a series of playroom experiments.

The consequences of this failure can be serious. In the early years of life, imitation is one of a child's most powerful tools for learning. It is through imitation that children learn to mouth their first words and master the rich nonverbal language of body posture and facial expression. In this way, Meltzoff says, children learn that drooping shoulders equal sadness or physical exhaustion and that twinkling eyes mean happiness or perhaps mischievousness.

For autistic people—even high-functioning autistic people—the ability to read the internal state of another person comes only after long struggle, and even then most of them fail to detect the subtle signals that normal individuals unconsciously broadcast. "I had no idea that other

FIRST PERSON

Myself

TEMPLE GRANDIN

I was 2 ½ years old when I began to show symptoms of autism: not talking, repetitious behavior and tantrums. Not being able to communicate in words was a great frustration, so I screamed. Loud, high-pitched noises hurt my ears like a dentist's drill hitting a nerve. I would shut out the hurtful stimuli by rocking or staring at sand dribbling through my fingers.

As a child, I was like an animal with no instincts to guide me. I was always observing, trying to work out the best ways to behave, yet I never fit in. When other students swooned over the Beatles, I called their reaction an ISP—interesting social phenomenon. I wanted to participate but did not know how. I had a few friends who were interested in the same things I was, such as skiing and riding horses. But friendship always revolved around what I did rather than who I was.

Even today personal relationships are something I don't really understand. I still consider sex to be the biggest, most important "sin of the system," to use my old high school term. From reading books and talking to people at conventions, I have learned that autistic people who adapt most successfully in personal relationships either choose celibacy or marry someone with similar disabilities.

Early education and speech therapy pulled me out of the autistic world: Like many autistics, I think in pictures. My artistic abilities became evident when I was in first and second grade, and they were encouraged. I had a good eye for color and painted watercolors of the beach.

But words are like a foreign language to me. I translate them into full-color movies, complete with sound, which run like a videotape in my head. When I was a child, I believed that everybody thought in pictures. Not until I went to college did I realize that some people are completely verbal and think only in words. On one of my earliest jobs I thought the other engineer was stupid because he could not "see" his mistakes on his drawings. Now I understand his problem was a lack of visual thinking and not stupidity.

Autistics have trouble learning things that cannot be thought about in pictures. The easiest words for an autistic child to learn are nouns because they relate directly to pictures. Spatial words such as *over* and *under* had no meaning for me until I had a visual image to fix them in my memory. Even now, when I hear the word under by itself, I automatically picture myself getting under the cafeteria tables at school during an air-raid drill, a common occurrence on the East Coast in the early 1950s.

Teachers who work with autistic children need to understand associative thought patterns. But visual thinking is more than just associations. Concepts can also be formed visually. When I was little, I had to figure out that small dogs were not cats. After looking at both large and small dogs, I realized that they all had the same nose. This was a common visual feature of all the dogs but none of the cats.

I credit my visualization abilities with helping me understand the animals I work with. One of my early livestock design projects was to create a dip-vat and cattle-handling facility for a feed yard in Arizona. A dip vat is a long, narrow, 7-ft.-deep swimming pool through which cattle move in single file. It is filled with pesticide to rid the animals of ticks, lice and other external parasites. In 1978 dip-vat designs were very poor. The animals often panicked because they were forced into the vat down a steep, slick decline. They would refuse to jump into the vat and would sometimes flip over backward and drown.

The first thing I did when I arrived at the feedlot was put myself inside a cow's head and see with its eyes. Because their eyes are on the sides of their head, cattle have wide-angle vision. Those cattle must have felt as if they were being forced to jump down an airplane escape slide into the ocean.

One of the first steps was to convert the ramp from steel to concrete. If I had a calf's body and hooves, I would be very scared to step on a slippery metal ramp. The final design had a concrete ramp at a 25° downward angle. Deep grooves in the concrete provided secure footing. The ramp appeared to enter the water gradually, but in reality it abruptly dropped away below the water's surface. The animals could not see the drop-off because the dip chemicals colored the water. When they stepped out over the water, they quietly fell in because their center of gravity had passed the point of no return.

Owners and managers of feedlots sometimes have a hard time comprehending that if devices such as dip vats and restraint chutes are properly designed, cattle will voluntarily enter them. Because I think in pictures, I assume cattle do too. I can imagine the sensations the animals feel. Today half the cattle in the U.S. are handled in equipment I have designed.

Grandin is an assistant professor of animal sciences at Colorado State University.

people communicated through subtle eye movements," says autistic engineer Temple Grandin, "until I read it in a magazine five years ago" (*see box*).

At the same time, it is incorrect to say autistic people are cold and indifferent to those around them or, as conventional wisdom once had it, lack the high-level trait known as empathy. Last December, when Pam Barrett felt overwhelmed and dissolved into tears, it was Danny, the most deeply autistic of her children, who rushed to her side and rocked her back and forth in his arms.

Another misperception about people with autism, says Karen Pierce, a neuroscientist at the University of California at San Diego, is the notion that they do not register faces of loved ones as special—that, in the words of a prominent brain expert, they view their own mother's face as the equivalent of a paper cup. Quite the contrary, says Pierce, who has results from a neuroimaging study to back up her contention. Moreover, the center of activity in the autistic mind, she reported at a conference held in San Diego last November, turns out to be the fusiform gyrus, an area of the brain that in normal people specializes in the recognition of human faces.

In a neuroimaging study, Pierce observed, the fusiform gyrus in autistic people did not react when they were presented with photographs of strangers, but when photographs of parents were substituted, the area lit up like an explosion of Roman candles. Furthermore, this burst of activity was not confined to the fusiform gyrus but, as in normal subjects, extended into areas of the brain that respond to emotionally loaded events. To Pierce, this suggests that as babies, autistic people are able to form strong emotional attachments, so their social aloofness later on appears to be the consequence of a brain disorganization that worsens as development continues.

In so many ways, study after study has found, autistic people do not parse information as others do. University of Illinois psychologist John Sweeney, for example, has found that activity in the prefrontal and parietal cortex is far below normal in autistic adults asked to perform a simple task involving spatial memory. These areas of the brain, he notes, are essential to planning and problem solving, and among their jobs is keeping a dynamically changing spatial map in a cache of working memory. As Sweeney sees it, the poor performance of his autistic subjects of the task he set for them—keeping tabs on the location of a blinking light—suggests that they may have trouble updating that cache or accessing it in real time.

To Sweeney's collaborator, University of Pittsburgh neurologist Dr. Nancy Minshew, the images Sweeney has produced of autistic minds in action are endlessly evocative. They suggest that essential connections between key areas of the brain either were never made or do not function at an optimal level. "When you look at these images, you can see what's not there," she says, conjuring up an experience eerily akin to looking at side-by-side photographs of Manhattan with and without the Twin Towers.

A MATTER OF MISCONNECTIONS

DOES AUTISM START AS A GLITCH IN ONE AREA OF THE brain—the brainstem, perhaps—and then radiate out to affect others? Or is it a widespread problem that becomes more pronounced as the brain is called upon to set up and utilize increasingly complex circuitry? Either scenario is plausible, and experts disagree as to which is more probable. But one thing is clear: very early on, children with autism have brains that are anatomically different on both microscopic and macroscopic scales.

For example, Dr. Margaret Bauman, a pediatric neurologist at Harvard Medical School, has examined postmortem tissue from the brains of nearly 30 autistic individuals who died between the ages of 5 and 74. Among other things, she has found striking abnormalities in the limbic system, an area that includes the amygdala (the brain's primitive emotional center) and the hippocampus (a seahorse-shaped structure critical to memory). The cells in the limbic system of autistic individuals, Bauman's work shows, are atypically small and tightly packed together, compared with the cells in the limbic system of their normal counterparts. They look unusually immature, comments University of Chicago psychiatrist Dr. Edwin Cook, "as if waiting for a signal to grow up."

An intriguing abnormality has also been found in the cerebellum of both autistic children and adults. An important class of cells known as Purkinje cells (after the Czech physiologist who discovered them) is far smaller in number. And this, believes neuroscientist Eric Courchesne, of the University of California at San Diego, offers a critical clue to what goes so badly awry in autism. The cerebellum, he notes, is one of the brain's busiest computational centers, and the Purkinje cells are critical elements in its data-integration system. Without these cells, the cerebellum is unable to do its job, which is to receive torrents of information about the outside world, compute their meaning and prepare other areas of the brain to respond appropriately.

Several months ago, Courchesne unveiled results from a brain-imaging study that led him to propose a provocative new hypothesis. At birth, he notes, the brain of an autistic child is normal in size. But by the time these children reach 2 to 3 years of age, their brains are much larger than normal. This abnormal growth is not uniformly distributed. Using MRI-imaging technology, Courchesne and his colleagues were able to identify two types of tissue where this mushrooming in size is most pronounced.

These are the neuron-packed gray matter of the cerebral cortex and white matter, which contains the fibrous connections projecting to and from the cerebral cortex and other areas of the brain, including the cerebellum. Perhaps, Courchesne speculates, it is the signal overload caused by this proliferation of connections that injures the Purkinje cells and ultimately kills them. "So now," says Courchesne, "a very interesting question is, What's driv-

46

ing this abnormal brain growth? If we could understand that, then we might be able to slow or stop it."

A proliferation of connections between billions of neurons occurs in all children, of course. A child's brain, unlike a computer, does not come into the world with its circuitry hard-wired. It must set up its circuits in response to a sequence of experiences and then solder them together through repeated neurological activity. So if Courchesne is right, what leads to autism may be an otherwise normal process that switches on too early or too strongly and shuts off too late—and that process would be controlled by genes.

Currently Courchesne and his colleagues are looking very closely at specific genes that might be involved. Of particular interest are the genes encoding four brain-growth regulators that have been found in newborns who go on to develop mental retardation or autism. Among these compounds, as National Institutes of Health researcher Dr. Karin Nelson and her colleagues reported last year, is a potent molecule known as vasoactive intestinal peptide. VIP plays a role not only in brain development but in the immune system and gastrointestinal tract as well, a hint that other disorders that so frequently accompany autism may not be coincidental.

The idea that there might be early biomarkers for autism has intrigued many researchers, and the reason is simple. If one could identify infants at high risk, then it might become possible to monitor the neurological changes that presage the onset of behavioral symptoms, and someday perhaps even intervene in the process. "Right now," notes Michael Merzenich, a neuroscientist at the University of California, San Francisco, "we study autism after the catastrophe occurs, and then we see this bewildering array of things that these kids can't do. What we need to know is how it all happened."

The genes that set the stage for autistic disorders could derail developing brains in a number of ways. They could encode harmful mutations like those responsible for single-gene disorders—cystic fibrosis, for instance, or Huntington's disease. They could equally well be garden-variety variants of normal genes that cause problems only when they combine with certain other genes. Or they could be genes that set up vulnerabilities to any number of stresses encountered by a child.

A popular but still unsubstantiated theory blames autism on the MMR (measles, mumps and rubella) vaccine, which is typically given to children at around 15 months (*see box*). But there are many other conceivable culprits. Researchers at the University of California at Davis have just launched a major epidemiological study that will test the tissues of both autistic and nonautistic children for residues of not only mercury but also PCBs, benzene and other heavy metals. The premise is that some children

may be genetically more susceptible than others to damage by these agents, and so the study will also measure a number of other genetic variables, like how well these children metabolize cholesterol and other lipids.

Drugs taken by some pregnant women are also coming under scrutiny. At the University of Rochester, embryologist Patricia Rodier and her colleagues are exploring how certain teratogens (substances that cause birth defects) could lead to autism. They are focusing on the teratogens' impact on a gene called HOXA1, which is supposed to flick on very briefly in the first trimester of pregnancy and remain silent ever after. Embryonic mice in which the rodent equivalent of this gene has been knocked out go on to develop brainstems that are missing an entire layer of cells.

In the end, it is not merely possible but likely that scientists will discover multiple routes—some rare, some common; some purely genetic, some not—that lead to similar end points. And when they do, new ideas for how to prevent or correct autism may quickly materialize. A decade from now, there will almost certainly be more effective forms of therapeutic intervention, perhaps even antiautism drugs. "Genes," as the University of Chicago's Cook observes, "give you targets, and we're pretty good at designing drugs if we know the targets."

Paradoxically, the very thing that is so terrible about autistic disorders—that they affect the very young—also suggests reason for hope. Since the neural connections of a child's brain are established through experience, well-targeted mental exercises have the potential to make a difference. One of the big unanswered questions, in fact, is why 25% of children with seemingly full-blown autism benefit enormously from intensive speech- and social-skills therapy—and why the other 75% do not. Is it because the brains of the latter are irreversibly damaged, wonders Geraldine Dawson, director of the University of Washington's autism center, or is it because the fundamental problem is not being adequately addressed?

The more scientists ponder such questions, the more it seems they are holding pieces of a puzzle that resemble the interlocking segments of Tommy Barrett's Transformer toys. Put the pieces together one way, and you end up with a normal child. Put them together another way, and you end up with a child with autism. And as one watches Tommy's fingers rhythmically turning a train into a robot, a robot into a train, an unbidden thought occurs. Could it be that some dexterous sleight of hand could coax even profoundly autistic brains back on track? Could it be that some kid who's mesmerized by the process of transformation will mature into a scientist who figures out the trick?

—With reporting by Amy Bonesteel/Atlanta

From *Time*, May 6, 2002, pp. 46-56. © 2002 by Time, Inc. Magazine Company. Reprinted by permission.

Altered States of Consciousness

Susan Greenfield

EVERYONE would claim to be an individual; everyone would claim they were different from everyone else. And yet the macabre idea is that if we all took our brains out, they would look pretty much the same. Just looking at the brain is not very helpful. If you were to look at the heart, you would see it pumping, and if you saw the lungs, they would be inflating like bellows, and that would inspire some idea as to how both function. But if you look at the brain, it does not move. The brain has no intrinsic moving parts, so you cannot actually guess by looking at it how it is working, and, even worse, you certainly cannot tell how one person might be individual from another.

What you can see clearly, if you do look at the brain, are the different bits to it. So you have that cauliflower thing on the back, like a little brain, that is called the cerebellum; you have the stalky part, continuous with the spinal cord, and the "cortex," so named after the Latin for bark because it wraps around the brain like its arboreal namesake around a tree. But what do these structures actually do? That is the first question if we are to understand how brains work or how an individual's brain works: How are the functions that we have, the awesome range of mental activities that we are capable of performing, embedded and related to this structural variation?

One idea is that each brain region has its own function—that the brain is really a set of minibrains. But with this idea we would simply enter an infinite regress that miniaturizes the problem but does not solve it.

Instead, we know that the brain functions like an orchestra, where different instruments each play a different part. Or it is like a stew or some complex food, where each ingredient plays its own part. With the advent of scanning techniques, this holistic organization has become clear. In a test a subject was asked to passively view, listen to, and speak words, or to generate verbs—all fairly subtle. But even a single "function" like language is, in terms of the brain, subtly different. Scans show that the brain divides different aspects of the task according to constellations of different brain regions. But the important take-home message is that there is no single brain area lighting up for language, and there is certainly, no single brain area lighting up even for aspects of language. The regions are working like instruments in an orchestra or like ingredients of some complex dish.

How is this organized? Let us look at how the brain is put together, because there is far more to your brain than mere gross brain regions. We start with consciousness. That is the ultimate and blanket function of the brain. What is consciousness? We will come to that later, because it is a very hard question. It is the first-person world as it seems to you. It is the world that no one can hack into directly. No one knows what you are experiencing or feeling at this moment.

Of course you can have aspects of consciousness that go wrong, dysfunctions such as depression, schizophrenia, or anxiety that would be described as a constellation of different features that would then be described as forms of consciousness. And language, or your memory, or the way you think, or even sometimes your senses, which can become distorted, are indeed functions of the brain. These can be divided even further; for example, vision has 30 different brain regions in the brain. And even within those regions one has so-called parallel processing, where the brain processes vision in parallel, dealing with form, color, and motion simultaneously. We have yet to discover how those different aspects of vision are brought back together again but we know that it is shared around.

We come then to the brain regions themselves that we have looked at. If you were to open up a brain region, you would arrive at large-scale assemblies of brain cells or neurons. These could be broken down further to isolated circuits. And then, beyond the circuits, you could look at one connection between one brain cell and another, across a narrow gap, which is called a synapse. And across the synapse you could start looking at the machinery that enables one brain cell to communicate with another. And then, finally—and only finally—do you come to the subject of much biomedical science, which is causing such delirium at the moment, and that is the gene. The genes will express a protein that is part of the biochemical machinery for working across the synapse.

So the brain is organized in a nested hierarchy. It is not just a brain region functioning as some final unit; you can break it down further and further and further. Let us look at how far you can break it down and try to discover where the secret of your individuality might lie, because it does not lie at the level of the gross brain regions. Instead, let us look at the networks of neurons that make up a brain region. You have 100 billion neurons, as many trees as there are in the Amazon rain forest. But even more awesome than that are the connections between your brain cells.

You have up to 100,000 connections onto any one brain cell. If you were to count them at one a second in the outer layer of the brain, in the cortex alone, it would take 32 million years to accomplish the task. If you wanted to work out the permutations and combinations, it would exceed the particles in the universe.

Why are they so important? Let us go back again to see where they fit in. I will remind you they are midway between the genes and the gross brain regions. The number of genes you have is about 10^5. Even if one makes the assumption—which is completely wrong—that every single gene in your body was accounting for a brain connection, you can see that you have about 10^{15} brain connections, so you would be out by 10^{10}. You just do not have enough genes to determine your brain connectivity. People who hope one day to manipulate their genes so that they are good at housekeeping or cooking or being witty or not being shy—all these other things that people fondly hope they can start targeting with molecular biology—should bear this number in mind. There is far more to your brain than your genes.

I am not saying that genes are not important and I am not saying that if a gene goes wrong you will not have some kind of terrible malfunction. What I am saying is that there is far more above and beyond the single genes that is really important. And I am talking, of course, about nurture, not just nature, because the most marvelous thing about being born human is that as you grow your brain connections grow with you. So, although you are born with pretty much all the brain cells you will ever have, it is the growth of the connections after birth that accounts for the growth of your brain.

The reason this is so exciting, and the reason I have been emphasizing the connections, is because this means, if the connections are growing as you are growing, then they will mirror what happens to you. This means that even if you are a clone (that is, even if you are an identical twin), you will have a unique configuration of brain cell connections that will trigger your reactions to events and will mirror your experiences such that you will see the whole world in terms of your brain cell connections.

Let us look at some evidence for that. London taxi drivers, as you may know, are masters at remembering. Every working day they must remember how to get from one place to another—and not only the configurations of the streets but also the one-way systems and how best to navigate round the streets of London. In a fascinating study, scientists scanned the brains of London taxi drivers and compared them with scans of other people of a similar age. Surprisingly, they found that the hippocampus was enlarged in taxi drivers compared to people of a similar age. Now, could it be that people with an enlarged hippocampus are disposed to become taxi drivers? No, because it was found that the longer they had been plying their trade the more marked this structural difference was. It was a result of what they were doing—what they were physically doing—that their brains had physically changed.

Your brain will relate to whatever you do. Here is another simple example. Human subjects were asked to practice five-finger piano exercises. The study found that with physical practice of even only five days, an enormous enhancement occurred in areas of the brain relating to the digits—just by engaging in five-finger piano exercises. But more remarkable still is a comparable change in brain territory when people were not practicing the piano but were imagining they were practicing. In real terms you can see that brain territory reflects every mental processes, and it is physically measurable, which is why we now wish to shoot down the myth between mental activity and brain activity, as if airy fairy thoughts were something that floated free, beamed in from Planet Zog or somewhere. Everything that happens to you, everything you are thinking, has a physical basis rooted in your physical brain. What we are realizing now is how exquisitely sensitive the brain is to your experiences and what you do, and therefore how it makes you the individual you are.

Even into old age, one's brain remains continuously "plastic"; that is, it is constantly dynamic, constantly evolving and changing, mirroring whatever happens to you. Sadly, sometimes things can go wrong. For example, dementia (which is a name for confusion and memory loss that characterizes Alzheimer's disease) is not a natural consequence of aging; when it strikes a brain cell in the vulnerable region, the main part of the cell (the cell body) remains, but the branches (dendrites) with which it makes contact with other cells have atrophy. Therefore, as one becomes senile—and I stress this is not going to happen to everyone, it is a particular illness—it is almost like becoming a child again. As the brain connections are dismantled, you retrace back. Where, just as in childhood the world means more and more, so this time the world means less and less. It means less because you cannot see things in terms of other things anymore because the connections are no longer there.

This prompts me to ask the question—which is not a scientific question at all, but is one I think puzzles many people: What is a mind? We are clear what brains are, but why do people now talk about minds as opposed to brains? I myself do not subscribe to the idea that it is some alternative to the biological squalor that scientists work in. I would like to suggest that mind has a very clear physical basis in the brain. We have seen that you are born with almost all your brain cells. The growth of the connections between cells accounts for the growth of the brain after birth. These connections reflect your experience, and in turn they will influence your further perception so that you see the world in terms of what has happened to you. You are born, in the words of the great William James, into a world that is a "booming, buzzing confusion," where you judge the world in terms of how sweet, how fast, how cold, how hot, how loud, how bright. You judge it in terms of its pure sensory qualities. But as you get older, the sweet, the bright, the noisy, the loud, the fast, the cold, the hot acquire labels; they become objects or people or processes or phenomena. They have labels, then they have memories and associations attached to them, and gradually you can no longer deconstruct the world (unless you are some brilliant artist) in terms of colors and noises and abstract shapes; instead, you see it with a meaning, a meaning that is special to you. That is how it continues to occur and, as we have seen, the brain connections remain highly dynamic. I think this is what the mind is: the personalization of the brain.

As you go through life the world acquires a highly personalized significance, built up by "hardwired circuits" in the brain. But although we have this mind rooted in personalized circuits in the brain and we therefore see the world in a certain way, this organization is not always accessed.

Let us consider "blowing the mind." Here people are not using their mind: they are engaged in a mindless pursuit. Sadly, with dementia you are losing your mind on a permanent basis, but, amazingly, some people pay money to lose their minds or "let themselves go." The very word ecstasy means "to stand outside of yourself." I think phrases like "lose your mind," "blow your mind," "out of your mind," "let yourself go" are exactly what we are talking about.

But what about accessing the mind or otherwise? I think this is the real challenge to anyone with aspirations to model the brain on a computer and, indeed, to neuro-science in general. Because what I am talking about is of course "consciousness." Consciousness and the mind are very different things, although of course one will be related to the other. You can lose your mind but still be conscious. Tonight, when you lose your consciousness, I

imagine you are not expecting to lose your mind. So the two concepts are separate and can be differentiated. What I want to turn to now—having looked at how the brain is hardwired and how it is reflecting experience—is the much harder question: Why do we sometimes access those connections but sometimes not? For people at a rave, for example, what is actually changing in the brain? That really is the much harder question.

Some people, like MIT AI expert Marvin Minsky, believe that it is going to be possible to build computers that are conscious. My own view is that at the moment biological brains are not like computers—and I am using the word "computer" to mean in general artificial intelligence and not just the laptop. I am not saying that in the future it is not going to be possible, since that would be an arrogant assertion; you cannot say something is not going to happen. But I cannot see how it is going to happen, especially in light of the way people are dealing with the problem at the moment.

First, the brain is based on chemicals. Chemical transmission is the absolute cornerstone of brain function; it is the most basic principle there is, and yet it is not allowed for in modeling. This is important because it gives a qualitative dimension, because you have many chemical messengers that are not found in computer modeling, and, more important, we have access to manipulating those chemicals with drugs. If you are to start manipulating at this level, which is a basic level, imagine how you would be manipulating the mind quite dramatically, and hence perhaps even consciousness, by doing that. Every psychoactive drug works on the principle of modifying chemical transmission in the brain in different ways to different extents. We thus have chemically based events in the brain and we know that if you take a drug like morphine, it will give you a dreamlike euphoria; it is manipulating your emotions. We know it works at the chemical level, and therefore emotions must be chemically based, which is something as yet not modeled in computers. As Stuart Sutherland, the psychologist, once said, he would believe a computer was conscious when it ran off with his wife. It is not good enough to have learning and memory machines. We already have that— a Cray Computer makes a very good learning and memory machine—but it is not conscious. Are we not missing the point here that it is not all about learning a memory and building up the mind? That it is about something that you had before you have a mind even— when you are a one-day-old baby—and that is an emotion?

The final important point about biological brains and computers is the issue of responses. I am sure you may be familiar with the so-called Turing test devised by the great computer pioneer Alan Turing. He said a computer would be conscious if it satisfied the following test: if a person given impartial access to a computer or a person and allowed to ask any question he or she liked could not tell from the answers whether it was a computer or a person, then the computer would have succeeded in being conscious. At the moment there are modified versions of the Turing test because the test is still too hard for a computer to do, but the modified versions make it easy by having limited subject matter to ask the computer. But even then there is no computer yet that has passed the Turing test (although, rather amusingly, there is a human being who has failed it). My own worry is that you do not even have to point to the Turing test because responses are not key. Therefore, you can be conscious without making responses, and, indeed, as we know from speak-your-weight machines, responses can occur without consciousness. The fact that you have a computer that does things is not a testament to the fact that there is a consciousness inside the computer. Instead, we have this wonderful personal world that only you can experience firsthand.

What unique property is in the brain that generates consciousness? It is not the hardwired connections; it is not our learning ability. It might have something to do with chemicals; my own contention is that it has a lot to do with feelings—but then, of course, feelings and consciousness are very similar, if not often synonymous.

So what is the basis for that? Why is it unique to the brain and why is it not possible in machines? We have seen that there is no such thing as a center for this or a center for that, and certainly, therefore, there is no such thing as a center for consciousness. We have seen already that autonomous brains within brains make no sense. Now I can show you, scientifically, additional evidence against this idea. If you look at brain imaging again and give subjects anesthesia, thus removing their consciousness, you can see that no single area of the brain shuts down. There is no one brain area that has just stopped. There is no center for consciousness.

If there is no center for consciousness, where is it? Let me compound this by introducing another concept. Is a dog conscious? If so, what is the difference between dogs and us? And how does that give us a clue as to what is special about the brain for generating consciousness?

More controversially, let us extend the riddle to that of the fetus. It is still a commonly held belief that the fetus is not conscious. But if it is not conscious, when does it become conscious? When does a baby become conscious? At the time of birth? Fine, but when is a baby born? Some babies are born prematurely, and they are conscious. You would not for two months just ignore the baby in the incubator in the hospital and say, "Ah, 40 weeks are up, it is going to be conscious today. Now we can go and visit." That would not be likely. Even less likely would you do it after the birth and say, "Ah, a few weeks have gone now, it is coming up to six months from birth, it might be conscious." It does not make sense.

Or is it the manner of birth, squeezing down the birth canal? That is tough on babies born by Caesarean section, if this is the case, because they will never be conscious. Clearly the manner and the timing of birth, because it is

so variable, cannot determine, cannot be the trigger, for consciousness. To my mind, it is a much more logical deduction that the fetus must be conscious.

But, for our purposes, we say, "OK, so this is a bit like the problem with cats and dogs or, indeed, rats or other animals: How is it different from consciousness?" When would the fetus become conscious? What would it be conscious of? I think the big problem here, and one that stops us from developing the idea, is that we normally think of consciousness as all or none. I myself defined it as "the thing you are going to lose tonight." But what if I was wrong? What if instead of consciousness being all or none, on or off, what if consciousness grew as brains grew? What if, therefore, it gradually developed? And so a fetus was conscious, but not as conscious as a child, and a baby was conscious but not as conscious as an adult, and a cat was conscious but not as conscious as a primate, and a monkey was conscious but not as conscious as a human.

If consciousness grows as brains grow, two interesting issues are raised. One is that you as an adult human being are more conscious at some times than at other times. If you think about it, we talk about raising our consciousness or deepening our consciousness—it does not matter which way you go, you can go up or down—consciousness is something that is variable. If that is the case, science finally has purchase on the problem, because, instead of looking for some magic brain region or some magic gene or some magic chemical, we can look for something that varies in degree, something we can measure. We can look for something conceivably that ebbs and flows within your brain, something that changes in size within your brain. Now, what could that be?

Let us look at the properties of consciousness. We have seen there is no special brain region; consciousness is spatially multiple, many brain regions must be contributing to it, but you have only one consciousness at any time. I would like to think that you see only one thing at one time. Although it is a complex pattern, you will see it as a pattern. Think of those famous vases and profiles, where either you see the profiles or you see the vase; which is true? Both are valid, but looking at it one way negates for that moment looking at it the other. You have only one at a time. I have just suggested to you that it is continuously variable.

Finally, we are always conscious of something. When we become very sophisticated, of course, we have an inner hope, fear, dream, thought, or fantasy: you can close your eyes and have consciousness triggered internally. But in the simplest form we have momentary states triggered by the changing input from the sensory world.

Let me suggest a metaphor to capture how these properties might be accommodated in the brain. Imagine a stone falling in a puddle. The stone is fixed; if the "stone" in the brain is a hub of brain circuits, then it could be, if you like, hardwired. You can see where this is leading. It could be a fixed thing, but, when a stone is thrown, it generates, just for a moment, ripples that are highly transient, that are vastly bigger in their extent than the size of the stone itself; and those ripples can vary enormously according to the size of the stone, the height from which it is thrown, the force with which it is thrown, and the degree of competition from other stones coming in. All these factors will determine the extent of the ripples. What I am suggesting is that in the brain you do have the equivalent of stones: hardwired little circuits, as we have seen, riddling your adult brain, which are sometimes accessed, sometimes not. The equivalent of throwing the stone would be, for example, me seeing my husband. That would then go through certain parts of my brain and start activating the circuitry that is related to my husband. Still, I would not be conscious of him. What would happen then? How could we now get ripples occurring in the brain? Amazingly enough, you have something very special in your brain: you have chemical fountains, not just circuits, and these chemical fountains actually emanate from those primitive parts of your brain and access the cortex and other areas. These are the chemicals that are targeted, for example, by Ecstasy or by Prozac, and these are the chemicals that vary during sleep-wakefulness and during high arousal, and these chemicals fulfill a very special function: they put brain cells on red alert.

Imagine I see my husband. That is the equivalent of throwing the stone. It activates the hub of hardwired circuitry, established over long experience of married life. If that is coincidental with a group of brain cells being sprayed upon by a fountain of chemicals related to arousal, then that would predispose those adjacent cells to be corralled just for that moment, and just for that moment this very active hub will activate a much larger group of cells, and that larger group of cells will determine the extent of my consciousness at that particular moment. That is the model.

How do we know the brain works like that? How do we know that you can get ripples in the brain. I was very fortunate to visit Israel and meet Arnivam Grinvald, who works at the Weizmann Institute. He showed me experiments—not on humans because it is invasive—but using optical dyes that register the voltage of brain cells. Arnivam showed that even to a flash of light there is indeed the neuron equivalent of ripples. These ripples (in this particular experiment to a simple flash of light) are extending over 10 million neurons, and they are extending very quickly, in less than a quarter of a second, or about 230 milliseconds. So this means that in your brain you can have tens, even hundreds of millions of brain cells corralled into transient working assembly in less than a quarter of a second and then it is all gone again, just like a ripple. That, in my view, is the best place to look if we are trying to find out about consciousness.

As a kind of interim thought on the physical basis of consciousness, I would like to suggest that there is no magic ingredient. The critical factor is not qualitative but quantitative: the larger the assembly of brain cells, the greater the depth of your consciousness.

Let us play around with that idea. What would happen if you had an abnormally small assembly of brain cells? Let us just think about what kind of consciousness you might have, because the advantage of this model is that there are different reasons for which you could have an abnormally small assembly of brain cells. For example, if the connectivity was modest, or if the epicenter was weak or only weakly activated (as a tiny pebble laid very gently on the surface of the water), or if the fountains of chemicals malfunctioned, or, indeed, if there was competition from new, rapidly forming assemblies—all these factors could give you different types of consciousness. Modest connectivity occurs in childhood, as we have seen. What do we know about children? Very young children are living in the moment. They are not doing vast learning and memory tasks, the world does not "mean" much to them; they judge the world literally at face value, on how fast and cold and sweet and so on. They have a literally sensational time. They are judging the world not in terms of associations but on the impact of their senses at that very moment. Let's look at an example of when the center is weakly activated. A particular example is one that we are most likely to experience tonight, and that is a dream. A dream could be a small assembly because in your sleeping state your senses are not working heavily, so they are therefore not able to recruit a very large assembly and you are thus dependent on the small spontaneous activity of brain cells. That is why in dreaming the world seems to be highly emotional, not very logical; you have ruptures in your logic like with schizophrenic states.

We know also that children have a much greater predisposition to dreaming than people who are older. It seems that these different states all have one element in common. They are caused for different reasons, but dreaming, along with fast-paced sports and childhood, are all characterized by living in the moment, by having a strong emphasis on the senses, and by not putting a great premium on anything you have learned or remembered; that is, not using your mind. The mind is not accessed in any of these states.

Let me summarize: childhood, dreaming, schizophrenia, fast-paced sports, and, dare I say it, raves are all examples of where the mind is not being accessed. It is not being accessed for different reasons: lack of connectivity (childhood), lack of strong sensory stimulation (dreams), an imbalance with those fountains of chemicals (schizophrenia), or a degree of competition from other stimulations (fast-paced sports and also raves, where, for good measure, people are flooding their brains with a drug that deliberately confuses those fountaining chemicals).

This brings us to pleasure—indeed, it brings us to the opposite of that—to what would occur if you had a large neuronal assembly. It would be where the world seems gray and remote, where you feel cutoff from other people, where, instead of the senses imploding in on you, as they do in dreaming or fast-paced sports or childhood or in schizophrenia, you feel numb and remote, and your emotions are turned down—you perhaps feel nothing at all or you do not think you feel anything. That, of course, you might recognize as the features of clinical depression: the outside world is remote, the senses are understimulated, and a continuity of thought exists, even a persistent thought. In such conditions people do not feel pleasure. It is not that they feel desperately sad; they just feel nothing. They suffer from something clinically called anhedonia, meaning literally "not enjoying yourself." A depressed person may have the sun on her face or the grass between her bare toes but she does not feel that sensual pleasure that I would like to think we all feel to some measure and certainly children feel considerably. They are completely cutoff from it. In clinical depression, then, we have an imbalance of the fountains of the modulating chemicals and therefore a lack of pleasure and a lack of emotion. I would like to suggest, because of that, the greater the neuronal assembly, the fewer emotions you have. High emotional states, like childhood, dreaming, or schizophrenia, are associated with small assemblies and the emotions therefore must be the basic form of consciousness, not learning and memory.

This has all been a rather long-winded way to get round to the question: How we are going to model this on a computer if, indeed, we wish to? Let us go the other way round and say: What kind of consciousness could we have? How would we interpret that in terms of this model? Sadly, something everyone has experienced is pain. Most people think of pain as rather boring, as something that surely we would all feel the same if, for example, we put our hands over a flame. But nothing could be further from the truth.

First, we know pain is expressed as other associations: pricking, stabbing, burning, chilling. We know that it can vary, interestingly enough, throughout the day. There are some particularly sadistic experiments where volunteers had electrical shocks through their teeth and had to report when they felt the pain. Amazingly, if that happens, you find that throughout the day your so-called pain threshold (when you report that the pain is particularly intense) varies. But the conduction velocity of your pain fibers has not changed, so something in the brain is changing, something in its chemical landscape; something transient is changing if you as the same individual do not experience the same pain depending on what time of day it is. We know that the more people anticipate pain, the more they will perceive it as painful, and I would suggest that this is because there is a buildup of the connections. If you are anticipating pain that is because more and more assemblies are being recruited before you feel it. And, incidentally, the diurnal threshold occurs because throughout the day those chemical

fountains are changing. We know that phantom limb pain is felt by people who do not have the limb but feel as though they do. That is because a so-called neuronal matrix—which I would call "assembly"—corresponds to the severed limb that would be stimulated by the lack of input from signals resulting from it. Pain is absent in dreams—which, we have seen, would be a small assembly state. Similarly, morphine, which is a strong analgesic or painkiller, creates a dreamlike euphoria that works through a natural opiate that makes the brain cell assemblies less efficient at being corralled. People will therefore often say they feel the pain but it no longer "matters," it is no longer significant to them. With schizophrenia, which I have suggested is a small assembly state, people have a higher threshold for pain. For people who are depressed, it is the opposite: they feel pain more. Finally, anesthetics—which have always proved a puzzle to understand how they work because there are many different types of anesthetics chemically—could work by depressing the activity, so that in the end gradually it reduced the size of your assembly to such a small one that you did not have appreciable consciousness. If that were the case, you would expect, as the assembly was shrinking, you would go through the small assembly state and have some form of delirium, some madness, or some kind of euphoria or pleasure—a rather odd idea if you are going under an anesthetic. Nowadays it is not possible because anesthetics are so efficient that they work very quickly, but in the old days people would actually have "ether frolics" or inhale nitrous oxide at fun fairs to have the pleasure of taking the anesthetic. (Even Ketamine, which is an anesthetic in high doses, is a drug of abuse in low doses.) So, paradoxically, a link exists just as you are going under: because it is less efficient, you go through that period of euphoria where suddenly you are experiencing a sensual time.

One can actually work out the different factors that will determine the size of a brain cell assembly, and they can be expressed bilingually, in neuroscientific or phenomenological terms, so we can talk about the "intensity"' of our senses, and that is the degree to which your neurons are active. We can talk about "significance," and that can be the existence of preexisting associations. We can talk about how "aroused" you are, and that is the availability of those chemical fountains that are called amines. I have not talked about predisposition or mood but they can be modified by other chemicals that also put cells on red alert, such as hormones. And, finally, we can talk about "distraction," which bilingually one could refer to as the formation of competing assemblies.

What I have done in this paper is relate that which you feel to that which could be happening in the brain so you can build up some kind of match. I think in the future we could image these brain cell assemblies and manipulate those factors differentially and make predictions as to the type of consciousness someone might have according to how big their assembly was or vice versa. I am not suggesting this model is right, but its strength is that it can be tested one day.

Finally, we must remember—and this is another problem for computer modeling—that the brain is an integral part of the body, that your central nervous system, your hormones, and your immune systems are all interlinked; otherwise you would have biological anarchy. So these brain cell assemblies that I am suggesting are related to consciousness are merely an index of consciousness. If you put one in a dish, you would not have consciousness. Somehow that causes a readout to the rest of the body and somehow the rest of the body signals back through chemicals that will influence the size of the assembly and hence the consciousness. One candidate group of chemicals is the peptides, which can also function as hormones and could coordinate the immune, endocrine, and nervous systems.

In conclusion, we will never be able to get inside someone else's brain. Yet science is starting to make a contribution by being a little more modest, by actually saying, "Well, let's match up physical brain states with what people are feeling and then perhaps we will have some insight into why people take drugs, what happiness is, and, perhaps most important of all, why people go bungee jumping or to raves."

Susan Greenfield is Professor of Pharmacology at the University of Oxford and Director of the Royal Institution of Great Britain. She is also cofounder of a spin-off company specializing in novel approaches to neurodegeneration, Synaptica Ltd. Her books include *Journey to the Centres of the Mind* (1995) and *The Private Life of the Brain* (2000).

From *Social Research*, Fall 2001, pp. 609-618. © 2001 by Social Research. Reprinted by permission.

Brain-Based Learning

The wave of the brain

By Ruth Palombo Weiss

It's a jungle out there! We have all heard and probably uttered that phrase. Well, the Nobel Prize winning neurobiologist Gerald Edelman postulates that it's a jungle inside there as well. Edelman, director of the Neuroscience Institute at the Scripps Research Institute, compares our brains to a dense web of interconnecting synapses. His metaphor gives us insight into current, sometimes confusing, research on how the brain works and its connection to learning theory.

Many of us use the Internet daily and are astounded by the vast and seemingly endless connections we can make. The brain's interconnections exceed the Internet's by an astronomical number. The typical brain has approximately 100 billion neurons, and each neuron has one to 10,000 synaptic connections to other neurons. Says Edelman, "The intricacy and numerosity of brain connections are extraordinary."

Our brains are suffused with a vast number of interdependent networks. We process all incoming information through those networks, and any information already stored influences how and what we learn.

"The human brain is the best-organized, most functional three pounds of matter in the known universe," says educator Robert Sylwester in his book, *A Celebration of Neurons: An Educator's Guide to the Human Brain*. "It's responsible for Beethoven's Ninth Symphony, computers, the Sistine Chapel, automobiles, the Second World War, *Hamlet*, apple pie, and a whole lot more."

Increasingly, educators such as Sylwester are relying on brain-based learning theory to take advantage of the growing body of evidence that neurologists are uncovering about how humans learn. He says, "To learn more about the brain, scientists had to discover how to perform intricate studies that would provide solid information on its most basic operations—the normal and abnormal actions of a single neuron, the synchronized actions of networks of neurons, and the factors that trigger neuronal activity."

It's clear that no two human brains are alike. Every nerve cell (neuron) serves as a relay station. Neurons not only receive signals from other cells, but they also process the signals and send them on to other cells across tiny gaps called synapses. Chemicals called neurotransmitters (there may be as many as 100) cause the signals to flow from one neuron to another. That electrochemical process is the basis of all human behavior. Every time we speak, move, or think, electrical and chemical communication are taking place between tens of thousands of neurons.

"As a nerve cell is stimulated by new experiences and exposure to incoming information from the senses, it grows branches called dendrites. Dendrites are the major receptive surface of the nerve cell. One nerve cell can receive input from as many as 20,000 other nerve cells. If you have 100 billion cells in your brain, think of the complexity! With use, you grow branches; with impoverishment, you lose them.

"The ability to change the structure and chemistry of the brain in response to the

The Gist
❏ The human brain's interconnections exceed the Internet's by an astronomical number.
❏ Educators are increasingly relying on brain-based learning theory.
❏ Imaging technologies such as MRIs are helping scientists understand memory, recall, and how the brain manages information and information overload.

environment is what we call plasticity," says Marian Diamond, a neuroscientist and professor of neuroanatomy at the University of California at Berkeley.

As we might imagine, for a subject as vast and complicated as brain research and learning theory there are a variety of views. Some scientists feel that there are fundamental differences between learning and education. They insist that brain-based research on learning isn't the same as research done on education theory. They also note that many of the initial neurological inquiries into learning have been done on animals and that it's an iffy proposition to extrapolate from animals to humans.

But during the past 10 years, known as the Decade of the Brain, a number of scientists have been using new technologies such as Magnetic Resonance Imaging (MRI), Functional MRI (fMRI), and Positron Emission Topography (PET) scans. Those tests help scientists explore how human brains process memory, emotion, attention, patterning, and context—

A Few Brain Facts

❑ Weight: 3 pounds
❑ Shape: walnut
❑ Color: uncooked liver

The brain is divided into two hemispheres called the *cerebral cortex* (commonly known as the conscious thinking center), covered in a thin skin of deeply wrinkled gray tissue, and separated by the *corpus callosum*. That curved band of white tissue acts as a bridge between the two halves, shuttling information back and forth at such a rate of speed that for all practical purposes the two hemispheres act as one. With the exception of the *pineal gland*, every brain module is duplicated in each hemisphere—another of nature's creative duplication systems.

The areas lying beneath the corpus callosum make up the *limbic system*, the area that relates to the unconscious and yet profoundly affects our experience. Its job is to feed information upward to the conscious cortex. Emotions are generated in the limbic system along with many urges that direct our behavior and usually help in survival. Within this limbic system, are the
❑ *thalamus*. Directs incoming information to the appropriate part of the brain for further processing.

❑ *hypothalamus*. and *pituitary*
❑ *thalamus*. Directs incoming information to the appropriate part of the brain for further processing.
❑ *hypothalamus*. and *pituitary glands*. Adapt the body to environment by constantly adjusting hormones.
❑ *amygdala*. Registers and generates fear.

Last, the *brainstem* carries information from the body into the brain and establishes general levels of alertness and such automatic tasks as breathing, blood pressure, and heartbeat.

A few additional terms are needed to understand the brain's physiology:
❑ *neuron*. The primary building block of the brain. Neurons carry electrical charges and make chemical connections to other neurons.
❑ *axons*. Long fibers (extending from the cell body) that receive messages.
❑ *dendrites*. Short fibers (surrounding the cell body) that receive messages.
❑ *synapses*. Tiny gaps between axons and dendrites (with chemical bridges) that transmit messages.
❑ *myelin* A sheath that serves as insulation and allows electricity to flow between the axons and dendrites.

The definitions come from Mapping the Mind *by Rita Carter.*

among other areas in this vast area of inquiry.

Renate Numella Caine and Geoffrey Caine, in their book *Unleashing the Power of Perceptual Change: The Potential of Brain-Based Teaching*, confirm the idea that our brains are whole and interconnected. "Even though there are a multitude of specific modules with specific functions, thought, emotion, physical health, the nature of our interactions with others, even the time and environment in which we learn, are not separated in the brain. They are not dealt with one thing at a time."

Says Edelman: "The nervous system behavior is to some extent self-generated in loops: Brain activity leads to movement, which leads to further sensation and perception and still further movement. The layers and loops between them are the most intricate of any object we know, and they are dynamic. They continually change. Parts of the brain (indeed, the major portion of its tissues) receive input only from other parts of the brain, and they give outputs to other parts without intervention from the outside world. The brain might be said to be in touch more with itself than with anything else."

There are several areas/topics that brain-based learning theories are examining. As we will see, they are intercon-

nected in much the same way as our own complex neuronal groups.

Attention

It appears that the thalamus, in the center of the brain, plays an especially important role in attention. According to Sylwester, the thalamus is the "relay center between our sense organs and the cortex…. This process holds the important information within our attentional and short-term memory systems by ignoring the less important information, and thus seems to create the visual awareness we experience." Eric Jensen, author of *Teaching With the Brain in Mind*, points out that our bodies have high-low cycles of about 90 to 110 minutes. When students are at the top of those cycles, they're more attentive. At the bottom of the cycle, people's energy drops along with their level of attention. Jensen suggests that if educators and trainers "learn to ride with the cycles," they'll have fewer problems.

Renate Caine talks about the different types of motivators and what happens in our brains depending on the source of motivation. "When we encounter high stress in learning, there is a psychophysiological response to the threat, accompanied by a feeling of helplessness or fatigue. This type of response keeps people from using

their higher order, more complex thinking, and creativity."

During high-stress situations, physiologically the information takes the primary pathway through the thalamus and amygdala and then moves into the cerebellum. Memorization of isolated facts can be accomplished under high-stress conditions, but higher order and creative thinking may be lost. We tend to respond with either a primitive mode of behaving or to rely solely on early programmed behavior.

In situations that may involve stress but in which we have a sense of control or choice, the physiology shifts. The primary path is no longer directly through the amygdala but through other paths of the cortex, the parts that are involved in higher-order functioning. Thus, we avoid a "knee jerk response."

Learning situations that are low stress favor reflection and analytic thinking. Says Renate Caine, "The thalamus, hippocampus, and cortex (where stored memories are housed and higher-level thinking takes place) are involved. With this system, you can translate factual elements and make connections. Furthermore, you can make inferences based on other things you know. That higher-order thinking includes synthesizing information and integrating it to come up with new ideas."

Context and patterns

"Without context, emotions, or patterns, information is considered meaningless. There's a tendency to try to form some kind of meaningful pattern out of our learning—this process seems innate," says Jensen.

He adds, "While the brain is a consummate pattern maker, intellectual maturity often enriches the process. PET scans indicate that a novice chess player burns more glucose (has to work harder) and uses the step-by-step sequential left side of the brain. A master chess player uses less glucose and engages larger patterns from the right side of the brain."

A lot of recent memory research involves pattern-making abilities. One study that has been replicated several times involves reading a long list of words to a subject. When the subject is asked to remember certain words on the list, an interesting thing happens. Let's say the list has 25 words strung together, including cake, cookie, sugar, train, candy, tree, car, dog. If asked whether the word *sweet* is on the list (it wasn't), most subjects say *yes* because of the words *cake, cookies,* and *sugar*. Interestingly, the same area of the brain that registered other words on the list lights up on an MRI.

That clearly illustrates the economy of brain-processing mechanisms. The brain makes a connection and generalizes even though the generalization might be wrong. One conclusion is that detail isn't efficient and generalization is, though not always correct. The brain doesn't have values; it's an information organ. It isn't an arbiter of values, of right and wrong. What we do have is a system that puts related events together in hierarchies and categories.

Geoffrey Caine states: "The brain-mind naturally organizes information into categories. We can generically call that 'patterning.' These patterns always involve interpreting information in context. There's a great deal of research to show that we learn from focused attention as well as from peripheral perception. When people are forming patterns, a lot of the information that brings the pattern together is peripheral or contextual information."

Emotion

The amygdala, an almond-shaped structure in the brain's center, seems most involved with emotions. According to Jensen, it has 12 to 15 distinct emotive regions and often exerts a tremendous influence on the cortex. "Information flows both ways between the amygdala and the cortex, but many other areas are involved in subtle emotions," he says.

"Making daily decisions based on emotions is not an exception; it's the rule," says professor Antonio Damasio, a neurologist at the University of Iowa, in his book *Descartes's Error: Emotion, Reason, and the Human Brain.* "While extremes of emotion are usually harmful to our best thinking, a middle ground makes sense. Appropriate emotions speed up decision making enormously."

Brain research shows that emotions and thought are deeply interconnected. In *Molecules of Emotion*, Candace Pert wrote that on the surface of every cell in the body are receptors that respond to molecules such as various peptides and neurotransmitters. Scientists used to think that those neurotransmitters were found only in neurons in the brain, but it turns out they're in every part of the body. When we have a thought, many of the peptides and neurotransmitters interact with cells throughout the body, and those interactions trigger what we call "the experience of emotions."

"Good learning engages feelings. Rather than viewing them as an add-on, emotions are a form of learning. Emotions also engage meaning and predict future learning because they involve our goals, beliefs, biases, and expectancies. Emotions drive the threesome of attention, meaning, and memory," says Renate Caine.

According to Daniel Schacter of Harvard University, author of *Searching for Memory*, there are two possible explanations for the way emotionally charged events are emblazoned in our memories. One is that stress hormones and chemical messengers, or neurotransmitters, are released at such times, which "tag" the event with special significance and give it prominence in the memory pathways. The other explanation for what are commonly known as flashbulb memories is that even though they don't need to be rehearsed or reiterated, they usually are. "People tend to discuss and go over the things in their lives that are important to them, and that strengthens the memory," says Schacter.

Renate Caine points out that the climate of the workplace is critical to the kind of product you're going to get. If we feel supported in that environment, the physiological effect is a slight increase in dopamine, which releases the right amount of acetylcholine (another neurotransmitter) that stimulates the hippocampus. People with increased dopamine show improved episodic memory, working memory, verbal functioning, flexibility in thinking, creative problem solving, decision making, and social interactions.

Memory and recall

One of the most spectacular uses of recently improved imaging technologies such as CAT scans, MRIs, and fMRIs is to show the brain at work—thereby helping scientists understand memory, recall, and how we manage information and information overload.

"Memory is the ability to repeat a performance. In the nervous system, it is a dynamic property of populations of neuronal groups. Unlike computer-based memory, brain-based memory is inexact. But it's also capable of great degrees of generalization. Memory would be useless if it couldn't in some way take into account the temporal succession of events—of sensory events as well as patterns of movement," says Edelman.

Rita Carter, who wrote *Mapping the Mind*, says that new neural connections are made with every incoming sensation and old ones disappear as memories fade.

"Each fleeting impression is recorded for a while in some new configuration, but if it's not laid down in memory, the pattern degenerates and the impression disappears like the buttocks-shaped hollow in a foam rubber cushion after you stand up. Patterns that linger may in turn connect with, and spark off, activity in other groups—forming associations (memories) or combining to create new concepts.

"Little explosions and waves of new activity, each with a characteristic pattern, are produced moment by moment as the brain reacts to outside stimuli. That activity creates a constantly changing internal environment, which the brain then reacts to as well. That creates a feedback loop that ensures constant change. The loop-back process, sometimes referred to as neural Darwinism, ensures that patterns that produce thoughts (and thus behavior) and that help the organism thrive are laid down permanently while those that are useless fade. It's not a rigid system."

According to Carter, it seems that incoming information is split into several parallel paths within the brain, each of which is given a slightly different treatment depending on the route it takes. Information that's of particular interest to one side of the brain will activate that side more strongly than the other. You can see that happen in a brain scan: The side that's in charge of a particular task will light up while the matching area on the other side will glow more dully.

For More About the Brain and Learning

❏ ascd.org
❏ brainconnection.com
❏ cainelearning.com
❏ dana.org
❏ 21learn.org
❏ lern.org
❏ newhorizons.org/blab.html
❏ thebrainstore.com

Geoffrey Caine reminds us that when we can connect rote memory with ordinary experience, we understand and make sense of things and remember more easily. To transfer information effectively, we need to see the relevance of what we're learning.

Motivation

Richard Restak, a neurobiologist, writes in his book *The Brain:* "Learning is not primarily dependent on a reward. In fact, rats—as well as humans—will consistently seek new experiences and behaviors with no perceivable reward or impetus. Experimental rats respond positively to simple novelty. Studies confirm that the mere pursuit of information can be valuable by itself and that humans are just as happy to seek novelty."

Robert Aitken at the Vancouver British Columbia Community College points out that we choose to stay motivated. "One of the things becoming clear is that our brains have been built for survival. That hasn't changed in 30,000 years. If something helps us survive, we're motivated to learn.

"Trainers have to find ways to convince learners that this is vital to their survival. If we get an emotional buy-in then learning takes place."

We can approach motivation from several different points of view, says Geoffrey Caine. "The distinction is between intrin-sic and extrinsic motivation. Intrinsic motivation has to do with what we want, need, and desire. It's deeply grounded in our values and feelings. Extrinsic motivation is often an attempt by someone else trying to make us want to do something. In terms of learning and creativity, we know there's a positive correlation between creativity and intrinsic motivation. When we're organizing information in our minds, the way we form patterns is deeply motivated by what we're interested in."

We have all heard the phrase *Use it or lose it.* That's the ultimate truth of the healthy brain's capability to learn, change, and grow as long as we're alive.

"The most exciting discovery about all of this work is that education should continue for a lifetime. With enrichment, we grow dendrites; with impoverishment, we lose them at any age," concludes Diamond.

Ruth Palombo Weiss *is a freelance writer based in Potomac, Maryland; pivotal@ erols.com*

From *Training & Development,* July 2000, pp. 20-24. © 2000 by ASTD Magazines. Reprinted by permission.

Resolved: No More Dumb Resolutions

Jennifer Huget
Special to The Washington Post

It's the day after New Year's, and you know the drill: You vow to lose 15 pounds by the end of the year.

Again.

Chances are, you're not going to make it this year, either. Research shows that half of those seriously committed to New Year's resolutions will peter out by April 1.

But if the 15 pounds you resolve to lose this year are the same ones you pledged to shed a year ago, maybe the problem isn't you or the strength of your resolve. Maybe what you need is a whole new kind of resolution—one that focuses on the process of reaching your goal rather than the goal itself.

It's not that losing 15 pounds isn't a good idea. But experts in a variety of fields, from nutrition and fitness to business management and Eastern philosophy, agree that when it comes to making changes, attending to the individual steps leading to your goal can be at least as important as getting there in the end.

Of course, such an approach runs afoul of some of our most deeply rooted values. Setting goals—whether making partner by 30, marriage by 40 or mastering Greek by 70— and then doing our damnedest to achieve them is insinuated into the American DNA.

This does not mean, of course, that it's either wise or effective.

John Norcross, professor of psychology at the University of Scranton and co-author of the 1996 book "Changing for Good" (Avon), is something of an authority on New Year's resolutions. Having conducted three academic studies on these annual promises we make to ourselves, Norcross claims to have a pretty good handle on what works—and what doesn't.

He contends that one of the right ways to plan a personal change is to—don't cringe, please—think positively. "There is strong scientific evidence that focusing on a positively stated goal is superior to either a vague or a negatively stated goal," he says.

In other words, ditch the pledge to "lose 15 pounds." Instead, vow to "exercise three times a week, for at least 15 minutes." True, this might lead you to lose 15 pounds over the course of the year. But if it doesn't, you're still fitter and trimmer and healthier—and you've accomplished a goal.

Explains Norcross: "It is intuitively easier to implement a new behavior than to root out an old one. It's better to say, 'I'm going to eat more servings of vegetables, or fish, or chicken, per week' than to say, 'I'm going to stop eating junk.'"

Norcross's screening test for a good resolution: "A positively phrased behavioral goal that is measurable, short-term, easy to self-monitor, and reinforces the progress as it is made."

Break Big Goals Into Little Goals

Bethesda-based nutritionist Pamela Peeke, assistant professor of medicine at the University of Maryland School of Medicine in Baltimore and author of "Fight Fat After 40" (Viking), is all for small, measurable changes.

"One of the biggest mistakes people make is to set a yearly goal," she says. "Big goals are achieved by achieving little goals."

Peeke counsels her patients to break their annual goals into 12 monthly goals, and from there into 52 weekly goals. "There's no way you can make a grand leap and lose 50 pounds," she says. "You need to look at your day planner and break that goal down into smaller commitments you can make every day."

Peeke's path to better eating habits is laid out in baby steps. If you've been eating a pint of ice cream every night, she doesn't recommend going cold turkey. Instead, you could start by reducing to half a pint a night, and then, eventually, substituting frozen yogurt. While "it might take three months" to get to the point where you're satisfied with fresh fruit instead of a frozen treat, Peeke says, "relax. You've got 12 months to phase it in."

Make It Count

The process-oriented, small-step approach that Norcross and Peeke espouse is supported more by anecdotal evidence than by clinical studies, but it does have roots in hard science. David Johnson, executive director of the Federation of Behavioral, Psychological and Cognitive Sciences, a Washington-based coalition of research organizations, cites what he calls the "classic" experiment demonstrating the value of setting achievable mini-goals. Its central feature is "the finger-press task."

Experiment subjects, says Johnson, repeatedly press a lever under two different circumstances: In the first instance, they are asked simply to keep pressing again and again until they grow tired. In the second instance, subjects are asked to count the number of times they press. Invariably, the counters press the lever more times than the non-counters.

The experiment, which Johnson describes as "testing the difference between not attending to specifics versus attending to them," suggests that "you do better if you focus your attention rather than just being global," he says.

The finger-press task's "real-world analog," says Johnson, is that the more you focus your attention through the devices of daily behavior modification, the greater the likelihood that you will accomplish your goal. The "counting" makes your progress toward the goal concrete.

In other words, breaking your 15-pound weight-loss goal down into daily tasks—exercising for 30 minutes, say, and eating five servings of fruit and vegetables daily—gives you something to count, and therefore helps you stay focused on your goal.

Johnson adds that businesses and the federal government have increasingly based their planning approaches on the same principle: "Setting a goal, listing objectives that support that goal, and designating milestones along the way has become the common model."

Well, Well, Well

The process-over-result approach really isn't new at all: It's what the wellness folks have been doing for decades. Drawing from Eastern philosophies and from Native American beliefs, the wellness movement emerged in the United States in the 1970s. The National Wellness Institute defines wellness as "an active process of becoming aware of and making choices toward a more successful existence."

While the wellness movement emphasizes physical health, its tenets of positive, realistic goals and step-by-step progression apply to other areas of personal development, including the social, occupational, spiritual, intellectual and emotional.

A worksheet available on the National Wellness Institute Web site (www.nationalwellness.org) breaks big goals down into tiny steps. "I want to have more time to relax and enjoy life," for instance, boils down to mini-goals such as creating a prioritized, "do-able" to-do list every day.

The process involves selecting behaviors to change, identifying the benefits of the change, identifying specific goals and strategies for accomplishing them,

creating an atmosphere in which you can achieve those goals, rewarding yourself for your successes and making adjustments.

Now and Zen

Then there's the possibility of rethinking the very idea of what goals really are. Sports psychologist Jerry Lynch applies to fitness the notion that goals should be viewed not as ends in themselves but as tools, "as beacons or lanterns that will lead the way, help keep your soul and spirit on track and give you access to a deeper passion."

Lynch, a consultant to several women's sports teams at the University of Maryland, is an athlete himself and coach to world-class performers in several sports. He also has doctorates in psychology and comparative religion. His interest in Eastern philosophy, particularly Zen Buddhism, informs his 1998 book (with Chungliang Al Huang) "Working Out, Working Within: The Tao of Inner Fitness Through Sports and Exercise" (now out in Penguin Putnam paperback).

"I make a distinction between setting goals as beacons instead of something to arrive at so that we can actually enjoy the process because we have set the goal," Lynch says. "I know that if I set the goal to run a marathon [something he has repeatedly accomplished], I guarantee myself three incredible months of living" as he works to achieve that goal.

Quoting Miguel de Cervantes, the Spanish writer best known for "Don Quixote," Lynch reminds us that "the journey is better than the inn." To set up a fulfilling journey, he says, you should "set goals that are aligned with things you love, then enjoy the process of following where they take you."

If all of this sounds a bit abstract, Lynch offers practical advice, too. Like others who have pondered this whole goal-setting thing, he advocates small, accomplishable measures.

"Rather than refrain from drinking beer, simply limit yourself to having just one or two once a week," he has written. "Realize that it often takes more time to achieve your objectives than expected."

In fitness as in life, he says, "failures and setbacks are our teachers. Don't beat yourself up for your failures." But don't give up pursuing the goals, large or small, just because you've had a misstep along the way. "Perhaps the act of 'sticking with it' "—even in the face of failure—"could be your new goal."

Enjoying the Results

So does this stuff work? Peeke's weight-loss patients think it does. Take 32-year-old Becky York, a quality assurance engineer in Silver Spring, who says she's always been overweight. She's tried lots of weight-loss programs, but she "usually loses focus after a few months, when the regimen gets too hard." She found that the programs required her to "artificially put my life on hold."

Peeke, whom York began seeing in May, encouraged a different perspective. She suggested York view her weight-loss efforts the same way she views brushing her teeth, as manageable and important daily tasks. "Now I don't think of it as optional," says York, who has lost 45 pounds from her May weight of 270. "I just have to do it."

York, who still wants to lose around 50 more pounds, credits Peeke with helping her see that her initial 100-pound weight-loss goal was "too huge" and that she "had to break it down into smaller pieces."

"I asked myself, 'What's the routine I have to establish?' Then I did it for a month, looked at it, and refined it," York says. "The first month, I did fine on my diet, eating about the right number of calories," she says. "But it wasn't right nutritionally, not the right content. So after a couple of weeks, once I got the caloric part down, then I started working on the content. A big part of it has been establishing little routines that help me stay with it."

For instance, York shops and cooks for a whole week's worth of meals on the weekends; by Sunday night, she says, she has enough marinated lean meat and vegetables prepared to get her through the week. That way she never finds herself hungry without a well-planned meal at the ready, and thus cuts down on damaging impulse eating.

In October, recognizing that it might be tough for her to stick with her new routines through the winter, she decided to walk a marathon in New Orleans this February. "I knew I needed a goal that was imminent enough to spur me on," she says. "Now I train every day for the long walk."

Adam Abramowitz is another convert. The Potomac college student returned from a semester abroad in 1999 with a vague notion that he'd like to make improvements to his life. While he was, in his words, "grossly overweight," he didn't have a clear weight-loss goal in mind when he first consulted Peeke a year ago.

With that meeting, he says, "everything turned upside down." Abramowitz, now a senior at Skidmore College in Saratoga Springs, N.Y., decided he "wanted to be a healthy person."

Under Peeke's guidance, Abramowitz started what he calls his "journey" with a single lifestyle change: He committed to a daily 45-minute cardiovascular workout, which he now supplements with regular weight-training sessions. "The big thing for me to realize was that workouts aren't fun. I enjoy the results, but it's not an intrinsically fun activity for me on a day-to-day basis. Of course, at 6 a.m., it's hard to be fun." Getting it out of the way early is his way to cope.

Only after establishing that routine did he tackle his food habits, following Peeke's suggestions for limiting carbohydrates and loading protein. Slowly his menu got more healthful.

Eventually, Abramowitz says, "the workout became part of my day, almost perfunctory, and the food became just second nature." None of it happened immediately. The steps were small. Sustaining the new habits and choices was more important than the specific goals. But along the way he has lost almost 90 pounds and "countless pants sizes."

"I don't think I'm ever going back," he says.

Resource

Check out a document created by the National Institutes of Health, "Go! How to Change Your Eating Habits & Be More Physically Active" (http://www.nhlbi.nih.gov/health/public/heart/chol/sbs-chol/chapter3.htm), which breaks the big, daunting goals of eating better and getting moving into bite-sized chunks. If you're looking to make reasonable, doable New Year's resolutions, this might be a good place to start.

From *Washington Post*, January 2, 2002. © 2002 by The Washington Post Writer Group. Reprinted by permission.

UNIT 3
Problems Influencing Personal Growth

Unit Selections

Key Points to Consider

- Individuals face challenges at every phase of development. What are some of the phases or stages of development? What age-related changes are typical of each stage, as mentioned in this unit?

- What are the various factors that can influence fetal development?

- What are four myths about infancy? How can we conduct research with infants who cannot always respond to us?

- How has childhood changed in modern society? Do you believe children are pressured to achieve? Explain. What suggestions could you offer to a parent who wants "childhood to be for children"?

 **Links: www.dushkin.com/online/**
These sites are annotated in the World Wide Web pages.

Adolescence: Changes and Continuity
http://www.personal.psu.edu/faculty/n/x/nxd10/adolesce.htm

Ask NOAH About: Mental Health
http://www.noah-health.org/english/illness/mentalhealth/mental.html

Facts for Families
http://www.aacap.org/info_families/index.htm

Mental Health Infosource: Disorders
http://www.mhsource.com/disorders/

Mental Health Risk Factors for Adolescents
http://education.indiana.edu/cas/adol/mental.html

Suicide Awareness: Voices of Education
http://www.save.org

At each stage of development from infancy to old age, humans are faced with new challenges. The infant has the rudimentary sensory apparatus for seeing, hearing, and touching but needs to begin coordinating stimuli into meaningful information. For example, early in life the baby begins to recognize familiar and unfamiliar people and usually becomes attached to the primary caregivers. As a toddler, the same child must master the difficult skills of walking, talking, and toilet training at almost the same time. This energetic, mobile, and sociable child also needs to learn the boundaries set by others on his or her behavior.

As the child matures, not only do physical changes continue to take place, but the family composition may change when siblings are added, parents divorce, or mother and father start to work outside the home. Playmates become more influential, and others in the community, such as day-care workers and teachers, have an increasing influence on the child. The child eventually may spend more time at school than at home. The demands in this new environment require that the child sit still, pay attention, learn, and cooperate with others for long periods of time—behaviors perhaps never before extensively demanded of him or her.

In adolescence the body changes noticeably while at the same time the teenager may search for his or her unique identity. Some teenagers may face an identity crisis when they must choose among career, education, and marriage. Peers may pressure the individual to indulge in new behaviors such as using illicit drugs or engaging in premarital sex. The pressures of work and family life exact a toll on less mature youths, while others are satisfied with the workplace, school, or home.

Adulthood, middle age, and old age may bring contentment or turmoil as individuals face career peaks and troughs, empty nests, advancing age, and perhaps the death of loved ones, such as parents or spouses. Again, some individuals cope more effectively with these events than do others.

At any step in the developmental sequence, unexpected stressors challenge individuals. These stressors include major illnesses, accidents, natural disasters, economic recessions, and family or personal crises. It is important to remember, however, that an event need not be negative to be stressful. Any major life change may cause stress. As welcome as weddings, new babies, and job promotions may be, they, too, can be stressful because of the changes in daily life that they demand. Each challenge and each change must be met and adjusted to if the individual is going to move successfully to the next stage of development. Some individuals continue along their paths unscathed; others do not fare as well.

This unit of the book examines problems in various stages of life from before birth to death. The first article commences with and forecasts our chronological look at issues of development. In "The Biology of Aging," Geoffrey Cowley offers an overview of what can go right or wrong for both males and females in various life eras.

We next look at several developmental stages in more detail. In "Fetal Psychology," Janet Hopson reveals why fetal life is so important and so delicate. Drugs, alcohol, and other substances can adversely affect the fetus. As the article suggests, problems for our development exist even before birth.

We next turn to early childhood. In "Four Things You Need to Know About Raising Baby," Joanna Lipari explains that babies are not passive recipients of sensory information. Babies, in fact, are far more capable than we first believed. Lipari tackles myths about infancy by enlisting scientific evidence to refute them.

In the next article, author Johann Arnold questions what has happened to childhood in America. Children used to have lots of free time to play. Today, parents seem to involve their children in too many planned activities and exert pressure on children to achieve; play, which is natural and normal, has fallen by the wayside. Arnold concludes that "childhood is for children."

Continuing our developmental theme with another article, this one by Kay Hymowitz, we next focus on the parents, rather than the children. Parenting apparently is a "lost art." Hymowitz claims that parents today would rather be friends or peers of their children than parents who discipline, set boundaries, and act as adults around their children. Hymowitz suggests that this is why schools and parents are often at odds about a child's behavior.

We move next to adolescence. A timely issue of great importance is school violence committed by American adolescents. Recent studies have linked violence to students who are isolated and bullied by their peers. The article "Disarming the Rage" reveals why bullying occurs and what the sad consequences are. Schools and parents are provided with tips to help reduce or prevent bullying and therefore the violent aftermath.

A companion article about adolescents and about their search for identity explains that teens search for the answers to "Who am I. What will I be?" The article provides tips for parents who want to guide their children in their search for self.

Middle age is the next developmental milestone undertaken in this unit. As the baby boomers swell the ranks of the middle aged, some are bound to be disappointed in midlife while others will be content. In "The Funmasters," Priscilla Grant discusses the issues facing boomers and how the masses of boomers can remain active and find happiness at midlife. A large survey on the topics of happiness and favorite activities reveals the answers of middle-aged individuals as well as those at other life stages.

Old age is the central issue in "Living to 100: What's the Secret?" How do people who live to 100 find the fountain of youth? That is, what contributes to healthy longevity? Some of the answers—a good diet, for example—won't surprise you but will serve as reminders about the benefits of healthy living.

The ultimate developmental stage is death. Death is a topic that both fascinates and frightens most of us. In "Start the Conversation," the veil of stigma that surrounds the issue of death is lifted. The article is designed to help people come to grips with their own fears and thus accept their own or another person's death more comfortably.

The Biology of Aging

Why, after being so exquisitely assembled, do we fall apart so predictably? Why do we outlive dogs, only to be outlived by turtles? Could we catch up with them? Living to 200 is not a realistic goal for this generation, but a clearer picture of how we grow old is already within our reach.

By Geoffrey Cowley

IF ONLY GOD HAD FOUND A more reliable messenger. Back around the beginning of time, according to east African legend, he dispatched a scavenging bird known as the halawaka to give us the instructions for endless self-renewal. The secret was simple. Whenever age or infirmity started creeping up on us, we were to shed our skins like tattered shirts. We would emerge with our youth and our health intact. Unfortunately, the halawaka got hungry during his journey, and happened upon a snake who was eating a freshly killed wildebeest. In the bartering that ensued, the bird got a satisfying meal, the snake learned to molt and humankind lost its shot at immortality. People have been growing old and dying ever since.

The mystery of aging runs almost as deep as the mystery of life. During the past century, life expectancy has nearly doubled in developed countries, thanks to improvements in nutrition, sanitation and medical science. Yet the potential life span of a human being has not changed significantly since the halawaka met the snake. By the age of 50 every one of us, no matter how fit, will begin a slow decline in organ function and sensory acuity. And though some will enjoy another half century of robust health, our odds of living past 120 are virtually zero. Why, after being so exquisitely assembled, do we fall apart so predictably? Why do we outlive dogs, only to be outlived by turtles? And what are our prospects for catching up with them?

Until recently, all we could do was guess. But as the developed world's population grows grayer, scientists are bearing down on the dynamics of aging, and they're amassing crucial insights. Much of the new understanding has come from the study of worms, flies, mice and monkeys—species whose life cycles can be manipulated and observed in a laboratory. How exactly the findings apply to people is still a matter of conjecture. Could calorie restriction extend our lives by half? It would take generations to find out for sure. But the big questions of why we age—and which parts of the experience we can change—are already coming into focus.

The starkest way to see how time changes us (aside from hauling out an old photo album) is to compare death rates for people of different ages. In Europe and North America the annual rate among 15-year-olds is roughly .05 percent, or one death for every 2,000 kids. Fifty-year-olds are far less likely to ride their skateboards down banisters, yet they die at 30 times that rate (1.5 percent annually). The yearly death rate among 105-year-olds is 50 percent, 1,000 times that of the adolescents. The rise in mortality is due mainly to heart disease, cancer and stroke—diseases that anyone over 50 is right to worry about. But here's the rub. Eradicating these scourges would add only 15 years to U.S. life expectancy (half the gain we achieved during the 20th century), for unlike children spared of smallpox, octogenarians without cancer soon die of something else. As the biologist Leonard Hayflick observes, what ultimately does us in is not disease per se, but our declining ability to resist it.

Biologists once regarded senescence as nature's way of pushing one generation aside to make way for the next. But under natural conditions, virtually no creature lives long enough to experience decrepitude. Our own ancestors typically starved, froze or got eaten long before they reached old age. As a result, the genes that leave us vulnerable to chronic illness in later life rarely had adverse consequences. As long as they didn't hinder reproduction, natural selection had no occasion to weed them out. Natural selection may even *favor* a gene that causes cancer late in life if it makes young adults more fertile.

But why should "later life" mean 50 instead of 150? Try thinking of the body as a vehicle, designed by a group of genes to transport them through time. You might expect durable bodies to have an inherent advantage. But if a mouse is sure to become a cat's dinner within five years, a body that could last twice that long is a waste of resources. A 5-year-old mouse that can produce eight litters annually will leave twice the legacy of a 10-year-old mouse that delivers only four each year. Under those conditions, mice will evolve to live roughly five years. A sudden disappearance of cats may improve their odds of completing that life cycle, but it won't change their basic genetic makeup.

That is the predicament we face. Our bodies are nicely adapted to the harsh conditions our Stone Age ancestors faced, but often poorly adapted to the cushy ones we've created. There is no question that we can age better by exercising, eating healthfully, avoiding cigarettes and staying socially and mentally active. But can we realistically expect to extend our maximum life spans?

The First Years of Growth

In childhood the body is wonderfully resilient, and **sound sleep** supports the growth of tissues and bones. During the teenage years, **hormonal changes** trigger the development of sexual organs. Boys add **muscle mass**. Even the muscles in their voice box lengthen, causing voices to deepen. In girls, fat is redistributed to hips and breasts.

Researchers have already accomplished that feat in lab experiments. In the species studied so far, the surest way to increase life span has been to cut back on calories—way back. In studies dating back to the 1930s, researchers have found that species as varied as rats, monkeys and baker's yeast age more slowly if they're given 30 to 60 percent fewer calories than they would normally consume. No one has attempted such a trial among humans, but some researchers have already embraced the regimen themselves. Dr. Roy Walford, a 77-year-old pathologist at the University of California, Los Angeles, has survived for years on 1,200 calories a day and expects to be doing the same when he's 120. That may be optimistic, but he looks as spry as any 60-year-old in the photo he posts on the Web, and the animal studies suggest at least a partial explanation. Besides delaying death, caloric restriction seems to preserve bone mass, skin thickness, brain function and immune function, while providing superior resistance to heat, toxic chemicals and traumatic injury.

How could something so perverse be so good for you? Scientists once theorized that caloric restriction extended life by delaying development, or by reducing body fat, or by slowing metabolic rate. None of these explanations survived scrutiny, but studies have identified several likely mechanisms. The first involves oxidation. As mitochondria (the power plants in our cells) release the energy in food, they generate corrosive, unpaired electrons known as free radicals. By reacting with nearby fats, proteins and nucleic acids, these tiny terrorists foster everything from cataracts to vascular disease. It appears that caloric restriction not only slows the production of free radicals but helps the body counter them more efficiently.

Food restriction may also shield tissues from the damaging effects of glucose, the sugar that enters our bloodstreams when we eat carbohydrates. Ideally, our bodies respond to any rise in blood glucose by releasing insulin, which shuttles the sugar into fat and muscle cells for storage. But age or obesity can make our

cells resistant to insulin. And when glucose molecules linger in the bloodstream, they link up with collagen and other proteins to wreak havoc on nerves, organs and blood vessels. When rats or monkeys are allowed to eat at will, their cells become less sensitive to insulin over time, just as ours do. But according to Dr. Mark Lane of the National Institute on Aging, older animals on calorie-restricted diets exhibit the high insulin sensitivity, low blood glucose and robust health of youngsters. No one knows whether people's bodies will respond the same way. But the finding suggests that life extension could prove as simple, or rather as complicated, as preserving the insulin response.

Another possible approach is to manipulate hormones. No one has shown conclusively that any of these substances can alter life span, but there are plenty of tantalizing hints. Consider human growth hormone, a pituitary protein that helps drive our physical development. Enthusiasts tout the prescription-only synthetic version as an antidote to all aspects of aging, but mounting evidence suggests that it could make the clock tick faster. The first indication came in the mid-1980s, when physiologist Andrzej Bartke outfitted lab mice with human or bovine genes for growth hormone. These mighty mice grew to twice the size of normal ones, but they aged early and died young. Bartke, now based at Southern Illinois University, witnessed something very different in 1996, when he began studying a strain of rodents called Ames dwarf mice. Due to a congenital lack of growth hormone, these creatures reach only a third the size of normal mice. But they live 50 to 60 percent longer.

As it happens, the mini-mice aren't the only ones carrying this auspicious gene. The island of Krk, a Croatian outpost in the eastern Adriatic, is home to a group of people who harbor essentially the same mutation. The "little people of Krk" reach an adult height of just 4 feet 5 inches. But like the mini-mice, they're exceptionally long-lived. Bartke's mouse studies suggest that besides stifling growth hormone, the gene that causes this stunting may also improve sensitivity to—you guessed it—insulin. If so, the mini-mice, the Croatian dwarfs and the half-starved rats and monkeys have more than their longevity in common. No one is suggesting that we stunt people's growth in the hope of extending their lives. But if you've been pestering your doctor for a vial of growth hormone, you may want to reconsider.

The Early Years of Adulthood

In many ways, the 20s are the prime of life. We're blessed with an efficient metabolism, **strong bones** and **good flexibility**. As early as the 30s, however, metabolism begins to slow and women's **hormone levels** start to dip. Bones may start to lose density in people who don't exercise or who don't get the vitamin D required for calcium absorption.

Growth hormone is just one of several that decline as we age. The sex hormones estrogen and testosterone follow the same pattern, and replacing them can rejuvenate skin, bone and muscle. But like growth hormone, these tonics can have costs as well as benefits. They evolved not to make us more durable but to make us more fertile. As the British biologist Roger Gosden observed in his 1996 book, "Cheating Time," "sex hormones are required for fertility and for making biological gender distinctions, but they do not prolong life. On the contrary, a price may have to be paid for living as a sexual being." Anyone suffering from breast or prostate cancer would surely agree.

The Joys of Middle Age

Around 40, people often start noticing gray hairs, mild **memory lapses** and difficulty focusing their eyes on small type. Around 51, most women will experience **menopause**. Estrogen levels plummet, making the skin thinner and bones less dense. Men suffer more **heart disease** than women at this age. Metabolism slows down in both sexes.

In most of the species biologists have studied, fertility and longevity have a seesaw relationship, each rising as the other declines. Bodies designed for maximum fertility have fewer resources for self-repair, some perishing as soon as they reproduce (think of spawning salmon). By contrast, those with extraordinary life spans are typically slow to bear offspring. Do these rules apply to people? The evidence is sketchy but provocative. In a 1998 study, researchers at the University of Manchester analyzed genealogical records of 32,000 British aristocrats born during the 1,135-year period between 740 and 1875 (long before modern contraceptives). Among men and women who made it to 60, the least fertile were the most likely to survive beyond that age. A whopping 50 percent of the women who reached 81 were childless.

Eunuchs seem to enjoy (if that's the word) a similar advantage in longevity. During the 1940s and '50s, anatomist James Hamilton studied a group of mentally handicapped men who had been castrated at a state institution in Kansas. Life expectancy was just 56 in this institution, but the neutered men lived to an average age of 69—a 23 percent advantage—and not one of them went bald. No one knows exactly how testosterone speeds aging, but athletes who abuse it are prone to ailments ranging from hypertension to kidney failure.

All of this research holds a fairly obvious lesson. Life itself is lethal, and the things that make it sweet make it *more* lethal. Chances are that by starving and castrating ourselves, we really could secure some extra years. But most of us would gladly trade a lonely decade of stubborn survival for a richer middle age. Our bodies are designed to last only so long. But with care and maintenance, they'll live out their warranties in style.

With RACHEL DAVIS

From *Newsweek*, Special Issue, Fall/Winter 2001, pp. 12-19. © 2001 by Newsweek, Inc. All rights reserved. Reprinted by permission.

FETAL PSYCHOLOGY

Behaviorally
speaking, there's little
difference between a newborn
baby and a 32-week-old fetus.
A new wave of research suggests
that the fetus can feel, dream, even
enjoy *The Cat in the Hat*. **The
abortion debate may never
be the same.**

By Janet L. Hopson

T he scene never fails to give goose bumps: the baby, just seconds old and still dewy from the womb, is lifted into the arms of its exhausted but blissful parents. They gaze adoringly as their new child stretches and squirms, scrunches its mouth and opens its eyes. To anyone watching this tender vignette, the message is unmistakable. Birth is the beginning of it all, ground zero, the moment from which the clock starts ticking. Not so, declares Janet DiPietro. Birth may be a grand occasion, says the Johns Hopkins University psychologist, but "it is a trivial event in development. Nothing neurologically interesting happens."

Armed with highly sensitive and sophisticated monitoring gear, DiPietro and other researchers today are discovering that the real action starts weeks earlier. At 32 weeks of gestation—two months before a baby is considered fully prepared for the world, or "at term"—a fetus is behaving almost exactly as a newborn. And it continues to do so for the next 12 weeks.

A fetus spends hours in the rapid eye movement sleep of dreams.

As if overturning the common conception of infancy weren't enough, scientists are creating a startling new picture of intelligent life in the womb. Among the revelations:

• By nine weeks, a developing fetus can hiccup and react to loud noises. By the end of the second trimester it can hear.

• Just as adults do, the fetus experiences the rapid eye movement (REM) sleep of dreams.

• The fetus savors its mother's meals, first picking up the food tastes of a culture in the womb.

• Among other mental feats, the fetus can distinguish between the voice of Mom and that of a stranger, and respond to a familiar story read to it.

• Even a premature baby is aware, feels, responds, and adapts to its environment.

• Just because the fetus is responsive to certain stimuli doesn't mean that it should be the target of efforts to enhance development. Sensory stimulation of the fetus can in fact lead to bizarre patterns of adaptation later on.

The roots of human behavior, researchers now know, begin to develop early—just weeks after conception, in fact. Well before a woman typically knows she is pregnant, her embryo's brain has already begun to bulge. By five weeks, the organ that looks like a lumpy inchworm has already embarked on the most spectacular feat of human development: the creation of the deeply creased and convoluted cerebral cortex, the part of the brain that will eventually allow the growing person to move, think, speak, plan, and create in a human way.

At nine weeks, the embryo's ballooning brain allows it to bend its body, hiccup, and react to loud sounds. At week ten, it moves its arms, "breathes" amniotic fluid in and out, opens its jaw, and stretches. Before the first trimester is over, it yawns, sucks, and swallows as well as feels and smells. By the end of the second trimester, it can hear; toward the end of pregnancy, it can see.

FETAL ALERTNESS

Scientists who follow the fetus' daily life find that it spends most of its time not exercising these new abilities but sleeping. At 32 weeks, it drowses 90 to 95% of the day. Some of these hours are spent in deep sleep, some in REM sleep, and some in an indeterminate state, a product of the fetus' immature brain that is different from sleep in a baby, child, or adult. During REM sleep, the fetus' eyes move back and forth just as an adult's eyes do, and many researchers believe that it is dreaming. DiPietro speculates that fetuses dream about what they know—the sensations they feel in the womb.

Closer to birth, the fetus sleeps 85 to 90% of the time, the same as a newborn. Between its frequent naps, the fetus seems to have "something like an awake alert period," according to developmental psychologist William Fifer, Ph.D., who with his Columbia University colleagues is monitoring these sleep and wakefulness cycles in order to identify patterns of normal and abnormal brain development, including potential predictors of sudden infant death syndrome. Says Fifer, "We are, in effect, asking the fetus: 'Are you paying attention? Is your nervous system behaving in the appropriate way?'"

FETAL MOVEMENT

Awake or asleep, the human fetus moves 50 times or more each hour, flexing and extending its body, moving its head, face, and limbs and exploring its warm wet compartment by touch. Heidelise Als, Ph.D., a developmental psychologist at Harvard Medical School, is fascinated by the amount of tactile stimulation a fetus gives itself. "It touches a hand to the face, one hand to the other hand, clasps its feet, touches its foot to its leg, its hand to its umbilical cord," she reports.

Als believes there is a mismatch between the environment given to preemies in hospitals and the environment they would have had in the womb. She has been working for years to change the care given to preemies so that they can curl up, bring their knees together, and touch things with their hands as they would have for weeks in the womb.

By 15 weeks, a fetus has an adult's taste buds and may be able to savor its mother's meals.

Along with such common movements, DiPietro has also noted some odder fetal activities, including "licking the uterine wall and literally walking around the womb by pushing off with its feet." Laterborns may have more room in the womb for such maneuvers than first babies. After the initial pregnancy, a woman's uterus is bigger and the umbilical cord longer, allowing more freedom of movement. "Second and subsequent children may develop more motor experience in utero and so may become more active infants," DiPietro speculates.

Fetuses react sharply to their mother's actions. "When we're watching the fetus on ultrasound and the mother starts to laugh, we can see the fetus, floating upside down in the womb, bounce up and down on its head, bum-bum-bum, like it's bouncing on a trampoline," says DiPietro. "When mothers watch this on the screen, they laugh harder, and the fetus goes up and down even faster. We've wondered whether this is why people grow up liking roller coasters."

FETAL TASTE

Why people grow up liking hot chilies or spicy curries may also have something to do with the fetal environment. By 13 to 15 weeks a fetus' taste buds already look like a mature adult's, and doctors know that the amniotic fluid that surrounds it can smell strongly of curry, cumin, garlic, onion and other essences from a mother's diet. Whether fetuses can taste these flavors isn't yet known, but scientists have found that a 33-week-old preemie will suck harder on a sweetened nipple than on a plain rubber one.

"During the last trimester, the fetus is swallowing up to a liter a day" of amniotic fluid, notes Julie Mennella, Ph.D., a biopsychologist at the Monell Chemical Senses Center in Philadelphia. She thinks the fluid may act as a "flavor bridge" to breast milk, which also carries food flavors from the mother's diet.

FETAL HEARING

Whether or not a fetus can taste, there's little question that it can hear. A very premature baby entering the world at 24 to 25 weeks responds to the sounds around it, observes Als, so its auditory apparatus must already have been functioning in the womb. Many pregnant women report a fetal jerk or sudden kick just after a door slams or a car backfires.

Even without such intrusions, the womb is not a silent place. Researchers who have inserted a hydrophone into the uterus of a pregnant woman have picked up a noise level "akin to the background noise in an apartment," according to DiPietro. Sounds include the whooshing of blood in the mother's vessels, the gurgling and rumbling of her stomach and intestines, as well as the tones of her voice filtered through tissues, bones, and fluid, and the voices of other people coming through the amniotic wall. Fifer has found that fetal heart rate slows when the mother is speaking, suggesting that the fetus not only hears and recognizes the sound, but is calmed by it.

FETAL VISION

Vision is the last sense to develop. A very premature infant can see light and shape; researchers presume that a fetus has the same ability. Just as the womb isn't com-

What's the Impact on Abortion?

Though research in fetal psychology focuses on the last trimester, when most abortions are illegal, the thought of a fetus dreaming, listening and responding to its mother's voice is sure to add new complexity to the debate. The new findings undoubtedly will strengthen the convictions of right-to-lifers—and they may shake the certainty of pro-choice proponents who believe that mental life begins at birth.

Many of the scientists engaged in studying the fetus, however, remain detached from the abortion controversy, insisting that their work is completely irrelevant to the debate.

"I don't think that fetal research informs the issue at all," contends psychologist Janet DiPietro of Johns Hopkins University. "The essence of the abortion debate is: When does life begin? Some people believe it begins at conception, the other extreme believes that it begins after the baby is born, and there's a group in the middle that believes it begins at around 24 or 25 weeks, when a fetus can live outside of the womb, though it needs a lot of help to do so.

"Up to about 25 weeks, whether or not it's sucking its thumb or has personality or all that, the fetus cannot survive outside of its mother. So is that life, or not? That is a moral, ethical, and religious question, not one for science. Things can behave and not be alive. Right-to-lifers may say that this research proves that a fetus is alive, but it does not. It cannot."

"Fetal research only changes the abortion debate for people who think that life starts at some magical point," maintains Heidelise Als, a psychologist at Harvard University. "If you believe that life begins at conception, then you don't need the proof of fetal behavior." For others, however, abortion is a very complex issue and involves far more than whether research shows that a fetus hiccups. "Your circumstances and personal beliefs have much more impact on the decision," she observes.

Like DiPietro, Als realizes that "people may use this research as an emotional way to draw people to the pro-life side, but it should not be used by belligerent activists." Instead, she believes, it should be applied to helping mothers have the healthiest pregnancy possible and preparing them to best parent their child. Columbia University psychologist William Fifer, Ph.D., agrees. "The research is much more relevant for issues regarding viable fetuses—preemies."

Simply put, say the three, their work is intended to help the babies that live—not to decide whether fetuses should.—*Camille Chatterjee*

pletely quiet, it isn't utterly dark, either. Says Fifer: "There may be just enough visual stimulation filtered through the mother's tissues that a fetus can respond when the mother is in bright light," such as when she is sunbathing.

A fetus prefers hearing Mom's voice over a stranger's—speaking in her native, not a foreign tongue—and being read aloud familiar tales rather than new stories.

Japanese scientists have even reported a distinct fetal reaction to flashes of light shined on the mother's belly. However, other researchers warn that exposing fetuses (or premature infants) to bright light before they are ready can be dangerous. In fact, Harvard's Als believes that retinal damage in premature infants, which has long been ascribed to high concentrations of oxygen, may actually be due to overexposure to light at the wrong time in development.

A six-month fetus, born about 14 weeks too early, has a brain that is neither prepared for nor expecting signals from the eyes to be transmitted into the brain's visual cortex, and from there into the executive-branch frontal lobes, where information is integrated. When the fetus is forced to see too much too soon, says Als, the accelerated stimulation may lead to aberrations of brain development.

FETAL LEARNING

Along with the ability to feel, see, and hear comes the capacity to learn and remember. These activities can be rudimentary, automatic, even biochemical. For example, a fetus, after an initial reaction of alarm, eventually stops responding to a repeated loud noise. The fetus displays the same kind of primitive learning, known as habituation, in response to its mother's voice, Fifer has found.

But the fetus has shown itself capable of far more. In the 1980s, psychology professor Anthony James De-Casper, Ph.D., and colleagues at the University of North Carolina at Greensboro, devised a feeding contraption that allows a baby to suck faster to hear one set of sounds through headphones and to suck slower to hear a different set. With this technique, DeCasper discovered that within hours of birth, a baby already prefers its mother's voice to a stranger's, suggesting it must have learned and remembered the voice, albeit not necessarily consciously, from its last months in the womb. More recently, he's found that a newborn prefers a story read to it repeatedly in the womb—in this case, *The Cat in the Hat*—over a new story introduced soon after birth.

DeCasper and others have uncovered more mental feats. Newborns can not only distinguish their mother from a stranger speaking, but would rather hear Mom's voice, especially the way it sounds filtered through amniotic fluid rather than through air. They're xenophobes, too: they prefer to hear Mom speaking in her native language than to hear her or someone else speaking in a foreign tongue.

By monitoring changes in fetal heart rate, psychologist Jean-Pierre Lecanuet, Ph.D., and his colleagues in Paris have found that fetuses can even tell strangers' voices apart. They also seem to like certain stories more than others. The fetal heartbeat will slow down when a familiar French fairy tale such as *"La Poulette"* ("The Chick") or *"Le Petit Crapaud"* ("The Little Toad"), is read near the mother's belly. When the same reader delivers another unfamiliar story, the fetal heartbeat stays steady.

The fetus is likely responding to the cadence of voices and stories, not their actual words, observes Fifer, but the conclusion is the same: the fetus can listen, learn, and remember at some level, and, as with most babies and children, it likes the comfort and reassurance of the familiar.

FETAL PERSONALITY

It's no secret that babies are born with distinct differences and patterns of activity that suggest individual temperament. Just when and how the behavioral traits originate in the womb is now the subject of intense scrutiny.

In the first formal study of fetal temperament in 1996, DiPietro and her colleagues recorded the heart rate and movements of 31 fetuses six times before birth and compared them to readings taken twice after birth. (They've since extended their study to include 100 more fetuses.) Their findings: fetuses that are very active in the womb tend to be more irritable infants. Those with irregular sleep/wake patterns in the womb sleep more poorly as young infants. And fetuses with high heart rates become unpredictable, inactive babies.

"Behavior doesn't begin at birth," declares DiPietro. "It begins before and develops in predictable ways." One of the most important influences on development is the fetal environment. As Harvard's Als observes, "The fetus gets an enormous amount of 'hormonal bathing' through the mother, so its chronobiological rhythms are influenced by the mother's sleep/wake cycles, her eating patterns, her movements."

The hormones a mother puts out in response to stress also appear critical. DiPietro finds that highly pressured mothers-to-be tend to have more active fetuses—and more irritable infants. "The most stressed are working pregnant women," says DiPietro. "These days, women tend to work up to the day they deliver, even though the implications for pregnancy aren't entirely clear yet. That's our cultural norm, but I think it's insane."

Als agrees that working can be an enormous stress, but emphasizes that pregnancy hormones help to buffer both mother and fetus. Individual reactions to stress also matter. "The pregnant woman who chooses to work is a different woman already from the one who chooses not to work," she explains.

She's also different from the woman who has no choice but to work. DiPietro's studies show that the fetuses of poor women are distinct neurobehaviorally—less active, with a less variable heart rate—from the fetuses of middle-class women. Yet "poor women rate themselves as less stressed than do working middle-class women," she notes. DiPietro suspects that inadequate nutrition and exposure to pollutants may significantly affect the fetuses of poor women.

Stress, diet, and toxins may combine to have a harmful effect on intelligence. A recent study by biostatistician Bernie Devlin, Ph.D., of the University of Pittsburgh, suggests that genes may have less impact on IQ than previously thought and that the environment of the womb may account for much more. "Our old notion of nature influencing the fetus before birth and nurture after birth needs an update," DiPietro insists. "There is an antenatal environment, too, that is provided by the mother."

Parents-to-be who want to further their unborn child's mental development should start by assuring that the antenatal environment is well-nourished, low-stress, drug-free. Various authors and "experts" also have suggested poking the fetus at regular intervals, speaking to it through a paper tube or "pregaphone," piping in classical music, even flashing lights at the mother's abdomen.

Does such stimulation work? More importantly: Is it safe? Some who use these methods swear their children are smarter, more verbally and musically inclined, more physically coordinated and socially adept than average. Scientists, however, are skeptical.

"There has been no defended research anywhere that shows any enduring effect from these stimulations," asserts Fifer. "Since no one can even say for certain when a fetus is awake, poking them or sticking speakers on the mother's abdomen may be changing their natural sleep patterns. No one would consider poking or prodding a newborn baby in her bassinet or putting a speaker next to her ear, so why would you do such a thing with a fetus?"

Als is more emphatic: "My bet is that poking, shaking, or otherwise deliberately stimulating the fetus might alter its developmental sequence, and anything that affects the development of the brain comes at a cost."

Gently talking to the fetus, however, seems to pose little risk. Fifer suggests that this kind of activity may help parents as much as the fetus. "Thinking about your fetus, talking to it, having your spouse talk to it, will all help prepare you for this new creature that's going to jump into your life and turn it upside down," he says—once it finally makes its anti-climactic entrance.

Reprinted with permission from *Psychology Today*, September/October 1998, pp. 44-48, 76. © 1998 by Sussex Publishers, Inc.

FOUR THINGS YOU NEED TO KNOW ABOUT RAISING BABY

New thinking about the newborn's brain, feelings and behavior are changing the way we look at parenting

BY JOANNA LIPARI, M.A.

Bookstore shelves are crammed with titles purporting to help you make your baby smarter, happier, healthier, stronger, better-behaved and everything else you can imagine, in what I call a shopping-cart approach to infant development. But experts are now beginning to look more broadly, in an integrated fashion, at the first few months of a baby's life. And so should you.

Psychological theorists are moving away from focusing on single areas such as physical development, genetic inheritance, cognitive skills or emotional attachment, which give at best a limited view of how babies develop. Instead, they are attempting to synthesize and integrate all the separate pieces of the infant-development puzzle. The results so far have been enlightening, and are beginning to suggest new ways of parenting.

The most important of the emerging revelations is that the key to stimulating emotional and intellectual growth in your child is your own behavior—what you do, what you don't do, how you scold, how you reward and how you show affection. If the baby's brain is the hardware, then you, the parents, provide the software. When you understand the hardware (your baby's brain), you will be better able to design the software (your own behavior) to promote baby's well-being.

The first two years of life are critical in this regard because that's when your baby is building the mental foundation that will dictate his or her behavior through adulthood. In the first year alone, your baby's brain grows from about 400g to a stupendous 1000g. While this growth and development is in part predetermined by genetic force, exactly how the brain grows is dependent upon emotional interaction, and that in-

volves you. "The human cerebral cortex adds about 70% of its final DNA content after birth," reports Allan N. Schore, Ph.D., assistant clinical professor of psychiatry and biobehavioral sciences at UCLA Medical School, "and this expanding brain is directly influenced by early environmental enrichment and social experiences."

Failure to provide this enrichment during the first two years can lead to a lifetime of emotional disability, according to attachment theorists. We are talking about the need to create a relationship and environment that allows your child to grow up with an openness to learning and the ability to process, understand and experience emotion with compassion, intelligence and resilience. These are the basic building blocks of emotional success.

Following are comparisons of researchers' "old thinking" and "new thinking." They highlight the four new insights changing the way we view infant development. The sections on "What To Do" then explain how to apply that new information.

1FEELINGS TRUMP THOUGHTS

It is the emotional quality of the relationship you have with your baby that will stimulate his or her brain for optimum emotional and intellectual growth.
OLD THINKING: In this country, far too much emphasis is placed on developing babies' cognitive abilities. Some of this push came out of the promising results of the Head Start program. Middle-class families reasoned that if a little stimulation in an underendowed home environment is beneficial, wouldn't "more" be better? And the race to create the "superbaby" was on.

Gone are the days when parents just wished their child were "normal" and could "fit in" with other kids. Competition for selective schools and the social pressure it generates has made parents feel their child needs to be "gifted." Learning exercises, videos and educational toys are pushed on parents to use in play with their children. "Make it fun," the experts say. The emphasis is on developing baby's cognitive skills by using the emotional reward of parental attention as a behavior-training tool.
THE NEW THINKING: Flying in the face of all those "smarter" baby books are studies suggesting that pushing baby to learn words, numbers, colors and shapes too early forces the child to use lower-level thinking processes, rather than develop his or her learning ability. It's like a pony trick at the circus: When the pony paws the ground to "count" to three, it's really not counting; it's simply performing a stunt. Such "tricks" are not only not helpful to baby's learning process, they are potentially harmful. Tufts University child psychologist David Elkind, Ph.D., makes it clear that putting pressure on a child to learn information sends the message that he or she needs to "perform" to gain the parents' acceptance, and it can dampen natural curiosity.

Instead, focus on building baby's emotional skills. "Emotional development is not just the foundation for important capacities such as intimacy and trust," says Stanley Greenspan, M.D., clinical professor of psychiatry and pediatrics at George Washington University Medical School and author of the new comprehensive book *Building Healthy Minds.* "It is also the foundation of intelligence and a wide variety of cognitive skills. At each stage of development, emotions lead the way, and learning facts and skills follow. Even math skills, which appear [to be] strictly an impersonal cognition, are initially learned through the emotions: 'A lot' to a 2-year-old, for example, is more than he would expect, whereas 'a little' is less than he wants."

It makes sense: Consider how well you learn when you are passionate about a subject, compared to when you are simply required to learn it. That passion is the emotional fuel driving the cognitive process. So the question then becomes not "what toys and games should I use to make my baby smarter?" but "how should I interact with my baby to make him 'passionate' about the world around him?"

WHAT TO DO: When you read the baby "milestone" books or cognitive development guides, keep in mind that the central issue is your baby's *emotional* development. As Greenspan advises, "Synthesize this information about milestones and see them with emotional development as the central issue. This is like a basketball team, with the coach being our old friend, emotions. Because emotions tell the child what he wants to do—move his arm, make a sound, smile or frown. As you look at the various 'milestone components'—motor, social and cognitive skills—look to see how the whole mental team is working together."

Not only will this give you more concrete clues as to how to strengthen your emotional relationship, but it will also serve to alert you to any "players" on the team that are weak or injured, i.e., a muscle problem in the legs, or a sight and hearing difficulty.

2 NOT JUST A SCREAMING MEATLOAF: BIRTH TO TWO MONTHS It's still largely unknown how well infants understand their world at birth, but new theories are challenging the traditional perspectives.

OLD THINKING: Until now, development experts thought infants occupied some kind of presocial, precognitive, preorganized life phase that stretched from birth to two months. They viewed newborns' needs as mainly physiological—with sleep-wake, day-night and hunger-satiation cycles, even calling the first month of life "the normal autism" phase, or as a friend calls it, the "screaming meatloaf" phase. Certainly, the newborn has emotional needs, but researchers thought they were only in response to basic sensory drives like taste, touch, etc.

THE NEW THINKING: In his revolutionary book, *The Interpersonal World of the Infant*, psychiatrist Daniel Stern, Ph.D., challenged the conventional wisdom on infant development by proposing that babies come into this world as social beings. In research experiments, newborns consistently demonstrate that they actively seek sensory stimulation, have distinct preferences and, from birth, tend to form hypotheses about what is occurring in the world around them. Their preferences are emotional ones. In fact, parents would be unable to establish the physiological cycles like wake-sleep without the aid of such sensory, emotional activities as rocking, touching, soothing, talking and singing. In turn, these interactions stimulate the child's brain to make the neuronal connections she needs in order to process the sensory information provided.

WHAT TO DO: "Take note of your baby's own special biological makeup and interactive style," Greenspan advises. You need to see your baby for the special individual he is at birth. Then, "you can deliberately introduce the world to him in a way that maximizes his delight and minimizes his frustrations." This is also the time to learn how to help your baby regulate his emotions, for example, by offering an emotionally overloaded baby some soothing sounds or rocking to help him calm down.

3 THE LOVE LOOP: BEGINNING AT TWO MONTHS At approximately eight weeks, a miraculous thing occurs— your baby's vision improves and for the first time, she can fully see you and can make direct eye contact. These beginning visual experiences of your baby play an important role in social and emotional development. "In particular, the mother's emotionally expressive face is, by far, the most potent visual stimulus in the infant's environment," points out UCLA's Alan Schore, "and the child's intense interest in her face, especially in her eyes, leads him/her to track it in space to engage in periods of intense mutual gaze." The result: Endorphin levels rise in the baby's brain, causing pleasurable feelings of joy and excitement. But the key is for this joy to be interactive.

OLD THINKING: The mother pumps information and affection into the child, who participates only as an empty receptacle.

THE NEW THINKING: We now know that the baby's participation is crucial to creating a solid attachment bond. The loving gaze of parents to child is reciprocated by the baby with a loving gaze back to the

parents, causing their endorphin levels to rise, thus completing a closed emotional circuit, a sort of "love loop." Now, mother (or father) and baby are truly in a dynamic, interactive system. "In essence, we are talking less about what the mother is doing to the baby and more about how the mother is being with the baby and how the baby is learning to be with the mother," says Schore.

The final aspect of this developing interactive system between mother and child is the mother's development of an "emotional synchronization" with her child. Schore defines this as the mother's ability to tune into the baby's internal states and respond accordingly. For example: Your baby is quietly lying on the floor, happy to take in the sights and sounds of the environment. As you notice the baby looking for stimulation, you respond with a game of "peek-a-boo." As you play with your child and she responds with shrieks of glee, you escalate the emotion with bigger and bigger gestures and facial expressions. Shortly thereafter, you notice the baby turns away. The input has reached its maximum and you sense your child needs you to back off for awhile as she goes back to a state of calm and restful inactivity. "The synchronization between the two is more than between their behavior and thoughts; the synchronization is on a biological level—their brains and nervous systems are linked together," points out Schore. "In this process, the mother is teaching and learning at the same time. As a result of this moment-by-moment matching of emotion, both partners increase their emotional connection to one another. In addition, the more the mother fine-tunes her activity level to the infant during periods of play and interaction, the more she allows the baby to disengage and recover quietly during periods of nonplay, before initiating actively arousing play again."

Neuropsychological research now indicates that this attuned interaction—engaged play, disengagement and restful nonplay, followed by a return to play behavior—is especially helpful for brain growth and the development of cerebral circuits. This makes sense in light of the revelation that future cognitive development depends not on the cognitive stimulation of flashcards and videos, but on the attuned, dynamic and emotional interactions between parent and child. The play periods stimulate baby's central nervous system to excitation, followed by a restful period of alert inactivity in which the developing brain is able to process the stimulation and the interaction.

In this way, you, the parents, are the safety net under your baby's emotional highwire; the act of calming her down, or giving her the opportunity to calm down, will help her learn to handle ever-increasing intensity of stimulation and thus build emotional tolerance and resilience.

WHAT TO DO: There are two steps to maximizing your attunement ability: spontaneity and reflection. When in sync, you and baby will both experience positive emotion; when out of sync, you will see negative emotions. If much of your interactions seem to result in negative emotion, then it is time to reflect on your contribution to the equation.

In these instances, parents need to help one another discover what may be impeding the attunement process. Sometimes, on an unconscious level, it may be memories of our own childhood. For example, my friend sings nursery rhymes with a Boston accent, even though she grew up in New York, because her native Bostonian father sang them to her that way. While the "Fah-mah in the Dell" will probably not throw baby into a temper tantrum, it's a good example of how our actions or parenting style may be problematic without our realizing it.

But all parents have days when they are out of sync with baby, and the new perspective is that it's not such a bad thing. In fact, it's quite valuable. "Misattunement" is not a bioneurological disaster if you can become attuned again. The process of falling out of sync and then repairing the bond actually teaches children resilience, and a sense of confidence that the world will respond to them and repair any potential hurt.

Finally, let your baby take the lead. Schore suggests we "follow baby's own spontaneous expression of himself," which lets the child know that another person, i.e., mom or dad, can understand what he is feeling, doing, and even thinking. Such experiences, says Schore, assist in the development of the prefrontal area, which controls "empathy, and therefore that which makes us most 'human.'"

4 THE SHAME TRANSACTION Toward the end of the first year, as crawling turns to walking, a shift occurs in the com-munication between child and parents. "Observational studies show that 12-month-olds receive more positive responses from mothers, while 18-month-olds receive more instructions and directions," says Schore. In one study, mothers of toddlers expressed a prohibition—basically telling the child "no"—approximately every nine minutes! That's likely because a mobile toddler has an uncanny knack for finding the most dangerous things to explore!

Yesterday, for example, I walked into the living room to find my daughter scribbling on the wall with a purple marker. "NO!" shot out of my mouth. She looked up at me with stunned shock, then realized what she had done. Immediately, she hung her head, about to cry. I babbled on a bit about how markers are only for paper, yada-yada and then thought, "Heck, it's washable." As I put my arm around my daughter, I segued into a suggestion for another activity: washing the wall! She brightened and raced to get the sponge. We had just concluded a "shame transaction."

OLD THINKING: Researchers considered all these "no's" a necessary byproduct of child safety or the socialization process. After all, we must teach children to use the potty rather than wet the bed, not to hit another child when mad, to behave properly in public. Researchers did not consider the function of shame vis-à-vis brain development. Instead, they advised trying to limit situations in which the child would feel shame.

NEW THINKING: It's true that you want to limit the shame situations, but they are not simply a necessary evil in order to civilize your baby. Neurobiological studies indicate that episodes of shame like the one I described can actually stimulate the development of the right hemisphere, the brain's source of creativity, emotion and sensitivity, as long as the shame period is short and followed by a recovery. In essence, it's not the experience of shame that can be damaging, but rather the inability of the parent to help the child recover from that shame.

WHAT TO DO: It's important to understand "the growth-facilitating importance of small doses of shame in the socialization process of the infant," says Schore. Embarrassment (a component of shame) first emerges around 14 months, when mom's "no" results in the child lowering his head and looking down in obvious sadness. The child goes from excited (my daughter scribbling on the wall) to sudden deflation (my "NO!") back to excitement ("It's okay, let's wash the wall together"). During this rapid process, various parts of the brain get quite a workout and experience heightened connectivity, which strengthens these systems. The result is development of the orbitofrontal cortex (cognitive area) and limbic system (emotional area) and the ability for the two systems to interrelate emotional resiliency in the child and the ability to self-regulate emotions and impulse control.

What is important to remember about productive shame reactions is that there must be a quick recovery. Extended periods of shame result in a child learning to shut down, or worse, become hyperirritable, perhaps even violent. It's common sense: Just think how you feel when someone embarrasses you. If that embarrassment goes on without relief, don't you tend to either flee the situation or rail against it?

From these new research findings, it's clear that successful parenting isn't just about intuition, instinct and doing what your mother did. It's also not about pushing the alphabet, multiplication tables or violin lessons. We now believe that by seeing the newborn as a whole person—as a thinking, feeling creature who can and should participate in his own emotional and cognitive development—we can maximize the nurturing and stimulating potential of our relationship with a newborn baby.

Joanna Lipari is pursuing a Psy.D. at Pepperdine University in Los Angeles.

READ MORE ABOUT IT

The Irreducible Needs of Children: What Every Child Must Have to Grow, Learn and Flourish, T. Berry Brazelton, M.D., and Stanley Greenspan, M.D. (Perseus Books, 2000).

Building Healthy Minds, Stanley Greenspan, M.D. (Perseus Books, 1999).

Reprinted with permission from *Psychology Today,* July/August 2000, pp. 38-43. © 2000 by Sussex Publishers, Inc.

Childhood Is for Children

"More and more, it seems that we have lost sight of the 'child' in childhood and turned it into a joyless training camp for the adult world."

BY JOHANN CHRISTOPH ARNOLD

Photos courtesy of Plough Publishing House

DESPITE ALL THE TALK about putting children first, our society is becoming increasingly hostile to its young. How different schools and homes would be if parents and educators would defend youngsters' right to a childhood, instead of fixating on their progress and success.

The pressure to excel is undermining childhood as never before. Naturally, parents have always wanted their offspring to "do well," both academically and socially. No one wants his or her kid to be the slowest in the class or the last to be chosen in a pick-up game. Yet, what is it about the culture we live in that has made that natural worry into such an obsessive fear, and what is it doing to our children? Why are

we so keen to mold them into successful adults, instead of treasuring their carefree innocence?

Jonathan Kozol, a best-selling author and children's advocate, puts it bluntly: "Up to the age of 11 or maybe 12, the gentleness and honesty of children is so apparent. Our society has missed an opportunity to seize that moment. It's almost as though we view those qualities as useless, as though we don't value children for their gentleness, but only as future economic units, as future workers, as future assets and deficits."

Of all the ways in which we push kids to meet adult expectations, the trend toward high-pressure academics may be the

most widespread, and the worst. I say "worst" because of the age at which we begin to subject them to it and the fact that, for some of them, school quickly becomes a place they dread and a source of misery they cannot escape for months at a time.

In my book, *Endangered: Your Child in a Hostile World*, I quote Melinda, a veteran preschool teacher in California: "We have parents asking whether their two-and-a-half-year-olds are learning to read yet, and grumbling if they can't. I see kids literally shaking and crying because they don't want to go in to testing. I've even seen parents dragging their child into the room."

Childhood itself has come to be viewed as a suspect phase. Children of all ages and means are being squelched on the playground and in class, not because they are unmanageable or unruly, but simply because they are behaving as youngsters should. Diagnosed with "problems" that used to be recognized as normal childhood traits—impulsiveness and exuberance, spontaneity and daring—thousands of kids are being diagnosed as hyperactive and drugged into submission.

I am referring, of course, to the widespread use of Ritalin and to the public's fascination with medicine as the answer to any and every problem. Given the fivefold increase in Ritalin prescriptions in the last decade, one has to wonder if it isn't being misused to rein in lively children who may not even have attention deficit-hyperactivity disorder. After all, much of what is designated as ADHD is nothing more than a defense against overstructuring—a natural reflex that used to be called letting off steam or, alternately, a symptom of various unmet emotional needs.

More and more, it seems that we have lost sight of the "child" in childhood and turned it into a joyless training camp for the adult world. We have abandoned the idea of education as growth and decided to see it only as a ticket to the job market. Guided by charts and graphs, and cheered on by experts, we have turned our backs on the value of uniqueness and creativity and fallen instead for the lie that the only way to measure progress is a standardized test.

Children ought to be stretched and intellectually stimulated. They should be taught to articulate their feelings, to write, read, develop and defend an idea, and think critically. However, what is the purpose of the best academic education if it fails to prepare young people for the "real" world beyond the confines of the classroom? What about those life skills that can never be taught by putting kids on a bus and sending them to school?

As for the things that schools are supposed to teach, even they are not always passed on. Writer John Taylor Gatto points out that, even though American pupils sit through an average of 12,000 hours of compulsory academic instruction, there are plenty who leave the system as 18-year-olds who still can't read a book or calculate a batting average—let alone repair a faucet or change a flat.

It is not just schools that are pressuring kids into growing up too fast. The practice of rushing them into adulthood is so widely accepted and so thoroughly ingrained that people often go blank when you voice concern about the matter. Take, for example, the number of parents who tie up their children's afterschool hours in extracurricular activities. On the surface, the explosion of opportunities for "growth" in areas like music and sports looks like the perfect answer to the boredom faced by millions of latchkey kids, but the reality is not always so pretty.

It is one thing when a child picks up a hobby, a sport, or an instrument on his or her own steam, but quite another when the driving force is a parent with an overly competitive edge. In one family I know, their daughter showed a genuine talent for the piano in the second grade, but by the time she was in the sixth, she wouldn't touch a keyboard for any amount of coaxing. She was tired of the attention, sick of lessons (her father was always reminding her what a privilege they were), and virtually traumatized by the strain of having been pushed through one competition after another. The pattern is all too familiar: ambitious expectations are followed by the pressure to meet them, and what was once a perfectly happy part of a youngster's life becomes a burden that is impossible to bear.

As an author, I became aware, after completing my first book, of something I had never noticed previously—the importance of white space. I am referring to the room between the lines of type, the margins, extra space at the beginning of a chapter, and/or a page left blank at the beginning of a book. It allows the type to "breathe" and gives the eye a place to rest. White space is not something you are conscious of when you read a book. It is what isn't there.

Just as books require white space, so do children. That is, they need room to grow. Nevertheless, too many children aren't getting that. The ancient Chinese philosopher Lao-Tzu reminds us that "it is not the clay the potter throws that gives the jar its usefulness, but the space within."

Certainly, there is nothing wrong with giving kids chores and requiring them to carry out the tasks on a daily basis. However, the way many parents overbook their children, emotionally and time-wise, robs them of the space and flexibility they need to develop at their own pace. They need stimulation and guidance, but also need time to themselves. Hours spent alone in daydreams or quiet, unstructured activities instill a sense of security and independence and provide a necessary lull in the rhythm of the day.

It is a beautiful thing to see kids absorbed in play. In fact, it is hard to think of a purer, more spiritual activity. Play brings joy, contentment, and detachment from the troubles of the day. Especially nowadays, in our hectic, time- and money-driven culture, the importance of play cannot be emphasized enough. Educator Friedrich Froebel, the father of the modern kindergarten, goes so far as to say that "a child who plays thoroughly and perseveringly, until physical fatigue forbids, will be a determined adult, capable of self-sacrifice both for his own welfare and that of others." In an age when fears of playground injuries and the misguided idea that play interferes with "real" learning has led approximately 40% of the school districts across the country to do away with recess, one can only hope that the wisdom of these words will not go unheeded.

Allowing youngsters the room to grow at their own pace does not mean ignoring them. Clearly, the bedrock of their security from day to day is the knowledge that we who care for them are always at hand, ready to help them, talk with them, give them what they need, and simply be there for them. How often, though, are we swayed instead by our own ideas of what they want or need?

Isn't the parental desire to have superstar or genius offspring in the first place just another sign of our distorted vision—a reflection of the way we tend to view children as little adults, no matter how loudly we may protest such a "Victorian" idea? The answer, of course, is to drop our adult expectations entirely, to get down on the same level as our children and look them in the eye. Only when we lay aside our ambitions for them will we begin to hear what they are saying, find out what they are thinking, and see the goals we have set for them from their point of view.

Obviously, every child is different. Some seem to get all the lucky breaks, while others have a rough time simply coping with life. One child consistently brings home perfect scores, while another is always at the bottom of the class. One is gifted and popular, while still another, no matter how hard he or she tries, is always in trouble and often gets forgotten. As parents, we must refrain from comparing our offspring with others. Above all, we must refrain from pushing them to become something that their unique personal makeup may never allow them to be.

Raising a "good" child is a dubious goal in the first place. Getting into trouble can be a vital part of building character. As the Polish pediatrician Janusz Korczak pointed out, "The good child cries very little, he sleeps through the night, he is confident and good-natured. He is well-behaved, convenient, obedient, and good. Yet no consideration is given to the fact that he may grow up to be indolent and stagnant."

It is often hard for parents to see the benefits of having raised a difficult child, even when the outcome is positive. Strange as it may sound, I believe that the more challenging the youngster, the more grateful the parents should be. If anything, the parents of difficult children really ought to be envied, because it is they, more than any others, who are forced to learn the most wonderful secret of parenthood: the true meaning of unconditional love. It is a secret that remains hidden from those whose love is never tested.

When we welcome the prospect of raising a problematic child with these things in mind, we will begin to see our frustrations as moments that can awaken our best qualities. Instead of envying the ease with which our neighbors seem to raise perfect offspring, we will remember that rule-breakers and children who show their horns often make more self-reliant and independent adults than those whose limits are never tried. By helping us to discover the limitations of "goodness" and the boredom of conformity, they can teach us the necessity of genuineness, the wisdom of humility, and the reality that nothing good is won without struggle.

"Unlearning" our adult mindsets is never easy, especially at the end of a long day, when children sometimes seem more of a bother than a gift. When there are kids around, things just don't always go as planned. Furniture gets scratched, flower-beds trampled, new clothes torn or muddied, and toys lost and broken. Children want to have fun, to run in the aisles. They need space to be rambunctious, silly, and noisy. After all, they are not china dolls or little adults, but unpredictable rascals with sticky fingers and runny noses who sometimes cry at night. If we truly love them, we will welcome them as they are.

Johann Christoph Arnold is a children's advocate, family counselor, father of eight, and author of Endangered: Your Child in a Hostile World.

From *USA Today* magazine, July 2001. © 2001 by the Society for the Advancement of Education. Reprinted by permission.

PARENTING: THE LOST ART

BY KAY S. HYMOWITZ

LAST FALL the Federal Trade Commission released a report showing what most parents already knew from every trip down the aisle of Toys R Us and every look at prime time television: Entertainment companies routinely market R-rated movies, computer games, and music to children. The highly publicized report detailed many of the abuses of these companies—one particularly egregious example was the use of focus groups of 9- and 10-year-olds to test market violent films—and it unleashed a frenzied week of headlines and political grandstanding, all of it speaking to Americans' alarm over their children's exposure to an increasingly foul-mouthed, vicious, and tawdry media.

But are parents really so alarmed? A more careful reading of the FTC report considerably complicates the fairy tale picture of big, bad wolves tempting unsuspecting, innocent children with ads for *Scream* and *Doom* and inevitably raises the question: "Where were the parents?" As it turns out, many youngsters saw the offending ads not when they were reading *Nickelodeon Magazine* or watching *Seventh Heaven* but when they were leafing through *Cosmo Girl*, a junior version of Helen Gurley Brown's sex manual *Cosmopolitan*, or lounging in front of *Smackdown!*—a production of the World Wrestling Federation where wrestlers saunter out, grab their crotches, and bellow "Suck It!" to their "ho's" standing by. Other kids came across the ads when they were watching the WB's infamous teen sex soap opera *Dawson's Creek* or MTV, whose most recent hit, "Undressed," includes plots involving whipped cream, silk teddies, and a tutor who agrees to strip every time her student gets an answer right. All of these venues, the report noted without irony, are "especially popular among 11- to 18-year-olds." Oh, and those focus groups of 9- and 10-year-olds? It turns out that all of the children who attended the meetings had permission from their parents. To muddy the picture even further, only a short time before the FTC report, the Kaiser Family Foundation released a study entitled *Kids and Media: The New Millennium*

showing that half of all parents have no rules about what their kids watch on television, a number that is probably low given that the survey also found that two-thirds of American children between the ages of eight and eighteen have televisions in their bedrooms; and even more shocking, one-third of all under the age of seven.

In other words, one conclusion you could draw from the FTC report is that entertainment companies are willing to tempt children with the raunchiest, bloodiest, crudest media imaginable if it means expanding their audience and their profits. An additional conclusion, especially when considered alongside *Kids and the Media*, would be that there are a lot of parents out there who don't mind enough to do much about it. After all, protesting that your 10-year-old son was subjected to a trailer for the R-rated *Scream* while watching *Smackdown!* is a little like complaining that he was bitten by a rat while scavenging at the local dump.

Neither the FTC report nor *Kids and the Media* makes a big point of it, but their findings do begin to bring into focus a troubling sense felt by many Americans—and no one more than teachers—that parenting is becoming a lost art. This is not to accuse adults of being neglectful or abusive in any conventional sense. Like always, today's boomer parents love their children; they know their responsibility to provide for them and in fact, as *Kids and the Media* suggests, they are doing so more lavishly than ever before in human history. But throughout that history adults have understood something that perplexes many of today's parents: That they are not only obliged to feed and shelter the young, but to teach them self-control, civility, and a meaningful way of understanding the world. Of course, most parents care a great deal about their children's social and moral development. Most are doing their best to hang on to their sense of what really matters while they attempt to steer their children through a dizzyingly stressful, temptation-filled, and in many ways unfamiliar world. Yet these parents know they often cannot count on the support of their peers. The parents of their 10-year-old's friend let the girls watch an R-rated movie until 2 a.m. during a sleepover; other parents are nowhere to be found when beer is passed around at a party attended by their 14-year-old. These AWOL parents have redefined the meaning of the term. As their children gobble down their own microwaved dinners, then go on to watch their own televisions or surf the Internet on their own computers in wired bedrooms where they set their own bedtimes, these parents and their children seem more like housemates and friends than experienced adults guiding and shaping the young. Such parent-peers may be warm companions and in the short run effective advocates for their children, but they remain deeply uncertain about how to teach them to lead meaningful lives.

If anyone is familiar with the fallout from the lost art of parenting, it is educators. About a year ago, while researching an article about school discipline, I spoke to teachers, administrators, and school lawyers around the country and asked what is making their job more difficult today. Their top answer was almost always the same: parents. Sometimes they describe overworked, overburdened parents who have simply checked out: "I work 10 hours a day, and I can't come home and deal with this stuff. He's *your* problem," they might say. But more often teachers find parents who rather than accepting their role as partners with educators in an effort to civilize the next generation come in with a "my-child-right-or-wrong" attitude. These are parent-advocates.

Everyone's heard about the growing number of suspensions in middle and high schools around the country. Now the state of Connecticut has released a report on an alarming increase in the number of young children—first-graders, kindergartners, and *preschoolers*—suspended for persistent biting, kicking, hitting, and cursing. Is it any wonder? Parent-advocates have little patience for the shared rules of behavior required to turn a school into a civil community, not to mention those who would teach their own children the necessary limits to self-expression. "'You and your stupid rules.' I've heard that a hundred times," sighs Cathy Collins, counsel to the School Administrators of Iowa, speaking not, as it might sound, of 16-year-olds, but of their parents. Even 10 years ago when a child got into trouble, parents assumed the teacher or principal was in the right. "Now we're always being second-guessed," says a 25-year veteran of suburban New Jersey elementary schools. "I know my child, and he wouldn't do this," or, proudly, "He has a mind of his own," are lines many educators repeat hearing.

In the most extreme cases, parent-advocates show (and teach their children) their contempt for school rules by going to court. Several years ago, a St. Charles, Mo., high schooler running for student council was suspended for distributing condoms on the day of the election as a way of soliciting votes. His family promptly turned around and sued on the grounds that the boy's free speech rights were being violated because other candidates had handed out candy during student council elections without any repercussions. Sometimes principals are surprised to see a lawyer trailing behind an angry parent arriving for a conference over a minor infraction. Parents threaten teachers with lawsuits, and kids repeat after them: "I'll sue you," or "My mother's

going to get a lawyer." Surveys may show a large number of parents in favor of school uniforms, but for parent-advocates, dress codes that limit their child's self-expression are a particular source of outrage. In Northumberland County, Pa., parents threatened to sue their children's *elementary* school over its new dress code. "I have a little girl who likes to express herself with how she dresses," one mother of a fourth-grader said. "They ruined my daughter's first day of school," another mother of a kindergartner whined.

Parent-advocates may make life difficult for teachers and soccer coaches. But the truth is things aren't so great at home either. Educators report parents of second- and third-graders saying things like: "I can't control what she wears to school," or "I can't make him read." It's not surprising. At home, parent-advocates aspire to be friends and equals, hoping to maintain the happy affection they think of as a "good relationship." It rarely seems to happen that way. Unable to balance warmth with discipline and affirmation with limit-setting, these parents are puzzled to find their 4-year-old ordering them around like he's Louis XIV or their 8-year-old screaming, "I hate you!" when they balk at letting her go to a sleepover party for the second night in a row. These buddy adults are not only incapable of helping their children resist the siren call of a sensational, glamorous media; in a desperate effort to confirm their "good relationship" with their kids, they actively reinforce it. They buy them their own televisions, they give them "guilt money," as market researchers call it, to go shopping, and they plan endless entertainments. A recent article in *Time* magazine on the Britney Spears fad began by describing a party that parents in Westchester, N.Y., gave their 9-year-old complete with a Britney impersonator boogying in silver hip-huggers and tube top. Doubtless such peer-parents tell themselves they are making their children happy and, anyway, what's the harm. They shouldn't count on it. "When one of our teenagers comes in looking like Britney Spears, they carry with them an attitude," one school principal was quoted as saying. There's a reason that some of the clothing lines that sell the Britney look adopt names such as "Brat" or "No Boundaries."

Of course, dressing like a Las Vegas chorus girl at 8 years old does not automatically mean a child is headed for juvenile hall when she turns 14. But it's reasonable to assume that parent-friends who don't know how to get their third-graders to stop calling them names, never mind covering their midriffs before going to school, are going to be pretty helpless when faced with the more serious challenges of adolescence. Some parents simply give up. They've done all they can, they say to themselves; the kids have to figure it out for themselves. "I feel if [my son] hasn't learned the proper values by 16, then we haven't done our job," announces the mother of a 16-year-old in a fascinating 1999 *Time* magazine series, "Diary of a High School." Others continue the charade of peer friendship by endorsing their adolescent's risk-taking as if they were one of the in-crowd. In a recent article in *Education Week*, Anne W. Weeks, the director of college guidance at a Maryland high school, tells how when police broke up a party on the field of a nearby college, they discovered that most of the kids were actually local high schoolers. High school officials called parents to express their concern, but they were having none of it; it seems parents were the ones providing the alcohol and dropping their kids off at what they knew to be a popular (and unchaperoned) party spot. So great is the need of some parents to keep up the pretense of their equality that they refuse to heed their own children's cry for adult help. A while back, the *New York Times* ran a story on Wesleyan University's "naked dorm" where, as one 19-year-old male student told the reporter: "If I feel the need to take my pants off, I take my pants off," something he evidently felt the need to do during the interview. More striking than the dorm itself—after all, when kids are in charge, as they are in many colleges, what would we expect?—was the phone call a worried female student made to her parents when she first realized she had been assigned to a "naked dorm." She may have been alarmed, but her father, she reports, simply "laughed."

Perhaps more common than parents who laugh at naked dorms or who supply booze for their kids' parties, are those who dimly realize the failure of their experiment in peer-parenting. These parents reduce their role to exercising damage control over kids they assume "are going to do it anyway." For them, there is only one value left they are comfortable fighting for: safety. One mother in *Time*'s "Diary of a High School" replenishes a pile of condoms for her own child and his friends once a month, doubtless congratulating herself that she is protecting the young. Safety also appears to be the logic behind the new fad of co-ed sleepover parties as it was described recently in the *Washington Post*. "I just feel it's definitely better than going to hotels, and this way you know all the kids who are coming over, you know who they are with," explains the mother of one high schooler. Kids know exactly how to reach a generation of parents who, though they waffled on whether their 8-year-old could call them "idiot," suddenly became tyrants when it came to seat belts and helmets. The article describes how one boy talked his parents into allowing him to give a co-ed sleepover party. "It's too dangerous for us to be out late at night with all the drunk drivers. Better that we are home. It's better than us lying about where we are and renting some sleazy motel room." The father found the "parental logic," as the reporter puts it, so irresistible that he allowed the boy to have not one, but two co-ed sleepover parties.

NOTHING GIVES a better picture of the anemic principles of peer-parenting—and their sorry impact on kids—than a 1999 PBS *Frontline* show entitled "The Lost Children of Rockdale County." The occasion for the show was an outbreak of syphilis in an affluent Atlanta suburb that ultimately led health officials to treat 200 teenagers. What was so remarkable was not that 200 teenagers in a large suburban area were having sex and that they have overlapping partners. It was the way they were having sex. This was teen sex as *Lord of the Flies* author William Golding might have imagined it—a heart of darkness tribal rite of such degradation that it makes a collegiate "hook up" look like splendor in the grass. Group sex was commonplace, as were 13-year-old participants. Kids would gather together after school and watch the Playboy cable TV channel, making a game of imitating everything they saw. They tried almost every permutation of

sexual activity imaginable—vaginal, oral, anal, girl-on-girl, several boys with a single girl, or several girls with a boy. During some drunken parties, one boy or girl might be "passed around" in a game. A number of the kids had upwards of 50 partners.

To be sure, the Rockdale teens are the extreme case. The same could not be said of their parents. As the *Frontline* producers show them, these are ordinary, suburban soccer moms and dads, more affluent than most, perhaps, and in some cases overly caught up in their work. But a good number were doing everything the books tell you to do: coaching their children's teams, cooking dinner with them, going on vacations together. It wasn't enough. Devoid of strong beliefs, seemingly bereft of meaningful experience to pass on to their young, these parents project a bland emptiness that seems the exact inverse of the meticulous opulence of their homes and that lets the kids know there are no values worth fighting for. "They have to make decisions, whether to take drugs, to have sex," the mother of one of the boys intones expressionlessly when asked for her view of her son's after-school activity. "I can give them my opinion, tell them how I feel. But they have to decide for themselves." These lost adults of Rockdale County have abdicated the age-old distinction between parents and children, and the kids know it. "We're pretty much like best friends or something," one girl said of her parents. "I mean I can pretty much tell 'em how I feel, what I wanna do and they'll let me do it." Another girl pretty well sums up the persona of many contemporary parents when she says of her own mother. "I don't really consider her a mom all that much. She takes care of me and such, but I consider her a friend more."

So what happened to the lost art of parenting? Why is it that so many adults have reinvented their traditional role and turned themselves into advocates, friends, and copious providers of entertainment?

For one thing, this generation of parents has grown up in a culture that devotedly worships youth. It's true that America, a nation of immigrants fleeing the old world, has always been a youthful country with its eye on the future. But for the "I-hope-I-die-before-I-get-old" generation, aging, with its threat of sexual irrelevance and being out of the loop, has been especially painful. Boomers are the eternal teenagers—hip, sexy, and aware—and when their children suggest otherwise, they're paralyzed with confusion. In an op-ed published in the *New York Times* entitled "Am I a Cool Mother?" Susan Borowitz, co-creator of *Fresh Prince of Bel-Air*, describes her struggle with her role as parent-adult that one suspects is all too common. On a shopping expedition, she is shocked when her 10-year-old daughter rolls her eyes at the outfits she has chosen for her. "There is nothing more withering and crushing," she writes. "I stood there stunned. 'This can't be happening to me. I'm a cool mom.'" Determined to hang on to her youthful identity, she buys a pair of bell-bottom pants to take her daughter to DJ Disco Night at her school where she spots other "cool moms... pumping their fist and doing the Arsenio woof." Finally Borowitz comes to her senses. "This was a party for the kids. I am not a kid. I am a mom." No one could quarrel with her there, but the telling point is that it took 10 years for her to notice.

The Parent as Career Coach

There is one exception to today's parents' overall vagueness about their job description: They *know* they want their children to develop impressive résumés. This is what William Doherty, professor of family science at the University of Minnesota, calls "parenting as product development."

As early as the preschool years, parent-product developers begin a demanding schedule of gymnastics, soccer, language, and music lessons. In New York City, parents take their children to "Language for Tots," beginning at six months—that is, before they can even speak. Doherty cites the example of one Minnesota town where, until some cooler—or more sleep-deprived—heads prevailed, a team of 4-year-olds was scheduled for hockey practice the only time the rink was available—at 5 A.M. By the time children are ready for Little League, some parents hire hitting and pitching coaches from companies like Grand Slam USA. So many kids are training like professionals in a single sport instead of the more casual three or four activities of childhood past that doctors report a high rate of debilitating and sometimes even permanent sports injuries.

Of course, there's nothing wrong with wanting to enrich your children's experience by introducing them to sports and the arts. But as children's list-worthy achievements take on disproportionate and even frenzied significance, parents often lose sight of some of the other things they want to pass down—such as kindness, moral clarity, and a family identity. One Manhattan nursery school director reports that if a child receives a high score on the ERB (the IQ test required to get into private kindergarten), parents often conclude that the child's brilliance excuses him or her from social niceties. "If he can't pass the juice or look you in the eye, it's 'Oh, he's bored.'" Douglas Goetsch, a teacher at Stuyvesant High School, the ultra-competitive school in New York City, recently wrote an article in the school newspaper about the prevalence of cheating; in every case, he says, cheating is related to an "excessively demanding parent." Other educators are seeing even young children complaining about stress-related headaches and stomachaches.

Katherine Tarbox, a Fairfield, Conn., teen, describes all this from the point of view of the child-product in her recently published memoir *Katie.com*. At 13, Katie was an "A" student, an accomplished pianist who also sang with the school choir, and a nationally ranked swimmer. Impressive as they were, Katie's achievements loomed too large. "I always felt like my self-worth was determined by how well I placed. And I think my parents felt the same way—their status among the team parents depended on how well their child placed." Like many middle-class children today, the combination of school, extracurricular activities, and her parents' work schedule reduced family time so much that, "Home was a place I always felt alone." Aching to be loved for herself rather than her swim times and grade point average, she develops an intense relationship with a man on the Internet who very nearly rapes her when they arrange to meet at an out-of-town swim meet.

Even after their daughter's isolation stands revealed, Katie's parents are so hooked on achievement they still don't really notice their daughter. Katie complains to her therapist that her mother is always either at the office or working on papers at home. The woman has a helpful suggestion that epitomizes the overly schematized, hyper-efficient lives that come with parenting as product development: She suggests that Katie schedule appointments with her mother.

Related to this youth worship is the boomer parents' intense ambivalence about authority. The current generation of parents came of age at a time when parents, teachers, the police, and the army represented an authority to be questioned and resisted. Authority was associated with *Father Knows Best*, the Vietnam War, Bull Connor, and their own distant fathers. These associations linger in boomer parents' subconscious minds and make them squirm uncomfortably when their own children beg for firm guidance. Evelyn Bassoff, a Colorado therapist, reports that when she asks the women in her mothers' groups what happens when they discipline their daughters, they give answers such as "I feel mean," "I feel guilty," and "I quake all over; it's almost like having dry heaves inside." A survey by Public Agenda confirms that parents feel "tentative and uncertain in matters of discipline and authority." And no wonder. Notice the way *Time* describes the dilemma faced by parents of Britney Spears wannabes; these parents, the writers explain, are "trying to walk the line between fashion and fascism." The message is clear; the opposite of letting your child do what she wants is, well, becoming Hitler.

It would be difficult to overstate how deep this queasiness over authority runs in the boomer mind. Running so hard from outmoded models of authority that stressed absolute obedience, today's parents have slipped past all recognition of the child's longing for a structure he can believe in. In some cases, their fear not only inhibits them from disciplining their children, it can actually make them view the rebellious child as a figure to be respected. (Oddly enough, this is true even when, as is almost always the case these days, that rebellion takes the form of piercings and heavy metal music vigorously marketed by entertainment companies.) It's as if parents believe children learn individuality and self-respect in the act of defiance, or at the very least through aggressive self-assertion. Some experts reinforce their thinking. Take Barbara Mackoff, author of *Growing a Girl* (with a chapter tellingly entitled "Make Her the Authority"). Mackoff approvingly cites a father who encourages a child "to be comfortable arguing or being mad at me. I figure if she has lots of practice getting mad at a six-foot-one male, she'll be able to say what she thinks to anyone." The author agrees; the parent who tells the angry child "calm down, we don't hit people," she writes, "is engaging in silencing." In other words, to engage in civilization's oldest parental task—teaching children self-control—is to risk turning your child into an automaton ripe for abuse.

But the biggest problem for boomer peer-parents is that many of them are not really sure whether there are values important enough to pursue with any real conviction. In his book *One Nation After All*, the sociologist Alan Wolfe argues that although Americans are concerned about moral decline, they are also opposed to people who get too excited about it. This inherent contradiction—people simultaneously judge and refuse to judge—explains how it is that parents can both dislike their children watching *Smackdown!* on TV, talking back to them, drinking, or for that matter, engaging in group sex, but also fail to protest very loudly. Having absorbed an ethos of nonjudgmentalism, the parents' beliefs on these matters have been drained of all feeling and force. The Rockdale mother who blandly repeats "her opinion" about drugs and sex to her son is a perfect example; perhaps she is concerned about moral decline, but because her concern lacks all gravity or passion, it can't possibly have much effect. All in all, Wolfe seems to find the combination of concern and nonjudgmentalism a fairly hopeful state of affairs—and surely he is right that tolerance is a key value in a pluralistic society—but refusing to judge is one thing when it comes to your neighbor's divorce and quite another when it comes to your 13-year-old child's attitudes toward, say, cheating on a test or cursing out his soccer coach.

WHEN PARENTS fail to firmly define a moral universe for their children, it leaves them vulnerable to the amoral world evoked by their peers and a sensational media. As the Rockdale story makes clear, the saddest consequences appear in the sex lives of today's teenagers. Recently in an iVillage chat room, a distraught mother wrote to ask for advice after she learned that her 15-year-old daughter had sex with a boy. The responses she got rehearsed many of the principles of peer-parenting. Several mothers stressed safety and told the woman to get her daughter on the pill. Others acted out the usual boomer uneasiness over the power they have with their children. "Let your daughter know you trust her to make the 'right' decision when the time comes," wrote one. "Tell her that you are not 'giving your permission,'" another suggested, "but that you are also very aware that she will not 'ask for permission' either when the time comes." But it was the one teenager who joined in that showed how little these apparently hip mothers understood about the pressures on kids today; when she lost her virginity at 14, the girl writes: "it was because of a yearning to be loved, to be accepted." Indeed, the same need for acceptance appears to be driving the trend among middle-schoolers as young as seventh grade engaging in oral sex. According to the December 2000 *Family Planning Perspectives*, some middle school girls view fellatio as the unpleasant price they have to pay to hang on to a boyfriend or to seem hip and sophisticated among their friends. The awful irony is that in their reluctance to evoke meaningful values, parent advocates and peers have produced not the free-thinking, self-expressive, confident children they had hoped, but kids so conforming and obedient they'll follow their friends almost anywhere.

And so in the end, it is children who pay the price of the refusal of parents to seriously engage their predicament in a media-saturated and shadowy adult world. And what a price it is. When parenting becomes a lost art, children are not only deprived of the clarity and sound judgment they crave. They are deprived of childhood.

Kay S. Hymowitz, a senior fellow at the Manhattan Institute and contributing editor at City Journal, *is the author of* Ready or Not: What Happens When We Treat Children as Small Adults (Encounter Books, 2000).

From *American Educator,* Spring 2001, pp. 4-9. © 2001 by American Educator, the quarterly journal of the American Federation of Teachers. Reprinted by permission.

DISARMING THE RAGE

Across the country, thousands of students stay home from school each day, terrified of humiliation or worse at the hands of bullies. In the wake of school shootings—most recently in California and Pennsylvania—parents, teachers and lawmakers are demanding quick action

Richard Jerome

In the rigid social system of Bethel Regional High School in Bethel, a remote town in the tundra of southwest Alaska, Evan Ramsey was an outcast, a status earned by his slight frame, shy manner, poor grades and broken family. "Everybody had given me a nickname: Screech, the nerdy character on *Saved by the Bell*," he recalls. "I got stuff thrown at me, I got spit on, I got beat up. Sometimes I fought back, but I wasn't that good at fighting." Taunted throughout his years in school, he reported the incidents to his teachers, and at first his tormentors were punished. "After a while [the principal] told me to just start ignoring everybody. But then you can't take it anymore."

On the morning of Feb. 19, 1997, Ramsey, then 16, went to school with a 12-gauge shotgun, walked to a crowded common area and opened fire. As schoolmates fled screaming, he roamed the halls shooting randomly— mostly into the air. Ramsey would finally surrender to police, but not before killing basketball star Josh Palacios, 16, with a blast to the stomach, and principal Ron Ed-

wards, 50, who was shot in the back. Tried as an adult for murder, Ramsey was sentenced to 210 years in prison after a jury rejected a defense contention that he had been attempting "suicide by cop," hoping to be gunned down but not intending to kill anyone. Still, Ramsey now admits in his cell at Spring Creek Correctional Center in Seward, Alaska, "I felt a sense of power with a gun. It was the only way to get rid of the anger."

Unfortunately Ramsey is not alone. Children all over the country are feeling fear, hopelessness and rage, emotions that turn some of them into bullies and others into their victims. Some say that is how it has always been and always will be—that bullying, like other adolescent ills, is something to be endured and to grow out of. But that view is changing. At a time when many parents are afraid to send their children to school, the wake-up call sounded by the 13 killings and 2 suicides at Columbine High School in Colorado two years ago still reverberates. It is now clear that Columbine shooters Dylan Klebold and

Eric Harris felt bullied and alienated, and in their minds it was payback time.

In recent months there have been two other horrifying shooting incidents resulting, at least in part, from bullying. On March 5, 15-year-old Charles "Andy" Williams brought a .22-cal. pistol to Santana High School in Santee, Calif., and shot 15 students and adults, killing 2. He was recently certified to stand trial for murder as an adult. His apparent motive? Lethal revenge for the torment he had known at the hands of local kids. "We abused him pretty much, I mean verbally," concedes one of them. "I called him a skinny faggot one time."

Two days after the Williams shooting, Elizabeth Bush, 14, an eighth grader from Williamsport, Pa., who said she was often called "idiot, stupid, fat, ugly," brought her father's .22-cal. pistol to school and shot 13-year-old Kimberly Marchese, wounding her in the shoulder. Kimberly, one of her few friends, had earned Elizabeth's ire by allegedly turning on her and joining in with the taunters. Bush admitted her guilt and offered apologies. A ward of the court until after she turns 21, she is now in a juvenile psychiatric facility. Kimberly, meanwhile, still has bullet fragments in her shoulder and is undergoing physical therapy.

As school enrollment rises and youths cope with the mounting pressures of today's competitive and status-conscious culture, the numbers of bullied children have grown as rapidly as the consequences. According to the National Education Association, 160,000 children skip school each day because of intimidation by their peers. The U.S. Department of Education reports that 77 percent of middle and high school students in small midwestern towns have been bullied. And a National Institutes of Health study newly released in the *Journal of the American Medical Association* reveals that almost a third of 6th to 10th graders—5.7 million children nationwide—have experienced some kind of bullying. "We are talking about a significant problem," says Deborah Prothrow-Stith, professor of public health practice at Harvard, who cites emotional alienation at home as another factor in creating bullies. "A lot of kids have grief, loss, pain, and it's unresolved."

Some experts see bullying as an inevitable consequence of a culture that rewards perceived strength and dominance. "The concept of power we admire is power over someone else," says Jackson Katz, 41, whose Long Beach, Calif., consulting firm counsels schools and the military on violence prevention. "In corporate culture, in sports culture, in the media, we honor those who win at all costs. The bully is a kind of hero in our society." Perhaps not surprisingly, most bullies are male. "Our culture defines masculinity as connected to power, control and dominance," notes Katz, whose work was inspired in part by the shame he felt in high school when he once stood idly by while a bully beat up a smaller student.

As for the targets of bullying, alienation runs like a stitch through most of their lives. A study last fall by the U.S. Secret Service found that in two-thirds of the 37 school shootings since 1974, the attackers felt "persecuted, bullied, threatened, attacked or injured." In more than three-quarters of the cases, the attacker told a peer of his violent intentions. William Pollack, a clinical psychologist and author of *Real Boys' Voices*, who contributed to the Secret Service study, said that several boys from Columbine described bullying as part of the school fabric. Two admitted to mocking Klebold and Harris. "Why don't people get it that it drives you over the edge?" they told Pollack. "It isn't just Columbine. It is everywhere."

That sad fact is beginning to sink in, as the spate of disturbing incidents in recent years has set off desperate searches for answers. In response, parents have begun crusades to warn and educate other families, courts have seen drawn-out legal battles that try to determine who is ultimately responsible, and lawmakers in several states—including Texas, New York and Massachusetts—have struggled to shape anti-bullying legislation that would offer remedies ranging from early intervention and counseling to the automatic expulsion of offenders.

One of the most shocking cases of victimization by bullies took place near Atlanta on March 28, 1994. That day, 15-year-old Brian Head, a heavyset sophomore at suburban Etowah High School, walked into his economics class, pulled out his father's 9-mm handgun and pressed it to his temple. "I can't take this anymore," he said. Then he squeezed the trigger. Brian had been teased for years about his weight. "A lot of times the more popular or athletic kids would make him a target," his mother, Rita, 43, says of her only child, a sensitive boy with a gift for poetry [see box, next page]. "They would slap Brian in the back of the head or push him into a locker. It just broke him." Not a single student was disciplined in connection with his death. After his suicide, Rita, a magazine copy editor, and her husband, Bill, 47, counseled other parents and produced a video for elementary school students titled *But Names Will Never Hurt Me* about an overweight girl who suffers relentless teasing.

Georgia residents were stunned by a second child's death on Nov. 2, 1998. After stepping off a school bus, 13-year-old Josh Belluardo was fatally punched by his neighbor Jonathan Miller, 15, who had been suspended in the past for bullying and other infractions. In that tragedy's wake Georgia Gov. Roy Barnes in 1999 signed an anti-bullying law that allows schools to expel any student three times disciplined for picking on others.

On the other side of the continent, Washington Gov. Gary Locke is pressing for anti-bullying training in schools, following two high-profile cases there. Jenny Wieland of Seattle still cannot talk of her only child, Amy Ragan, shot dead at age 17 more than eight years ago, without tearing up. A soccer player and equestrian in her senior year at Marysville-Pilchuck High School, Amy was heading to the mall on the night of Nov. 20, 1992, when she stopped at a friend's apartment. There, three schoolmates had gathered by the time Trevor Oscar Turner

83

showed up. Then 19, Turner was showing off a .38-cal. revolver, holding it to kids' heads, and when he got to Amy, the weapon went off. Turner pleaded guilty to first-degree manslaughter and served 27 months of a 41-month sentence.

"I can't help but wonder what Amy's life would be like if she was still alive," says Wieland today. "I wonder about her career and if she'd be in love or have a baby." Wieland turned her grief into action. In 1994 she helped start Mothers Against Violence in America (MAVIA), an activist group patterned after Mothers Against Drunk Driving. She left her insurance job to become the program's director and speaks annually at 50 schools. In 1998 she became the first director of SAVE (Students Against Violence Everywhere), which continues to grow, now boasting 126 student chapters nationwide that offer schools anti-harassment and conflict-resolution programs. "People ask how I can stand to tell her story over and over," she says. "If I can save just one child, it's well worth the pain."

Not long after Amy Ragan's death, another bullying scenario unfolded 50 miles away in Stanwood, Wash. Confined to a wheelchair by cerebral palsy, Calcutta-born Taya Haugstad was a fifth grader in 1993, when a boy began calling her "bitch" and "retard." The daily verbal abuse led to terrible nightmares. By middle school, according to a lawsuit Taya later filed, her tormentor—a popular athlete—got physical, pushing her wheelchair into the wall and holding it while his friends kicked the wheels. Eventually Taya was diagnosed with posttraumatic stress disorder. "Imagine that you can't run away or scream," says her psychologist Judith McCarthy. "Not only was she traumatized, she's handicapped. She felt terribly unsafe in the world." Her adoptive parents, Karrie and Ken Haugstad, 48 and 55, complained to school authorities and went to court to get a restraining order against the bully, but it was never issued. Taya sued the school district and the boy in 1999. The judge awarded her $300,000 last year, ruling that the school was negligent in its supervision, thus inflicting emotional distress. (The ruling is under appeal.) Taya, now 19 and a high school junior, hopes to study writing in college. She says she holds no grudge against her nemesis, who received undisclosed punishment from the school. "I don't think about him," she says.

But Josh Sneed may never forgive the boys he refers to as the Skaters. It was in 1996, late in his freshman year at Powell High School in Powell, Tenn., when, he says, a group of skateboarders began to terrorize him. With chains clinking and baseball bats pounding the pavement, he claims, they chased him and threatened to beat him to death. Why Josh? He was small and "a country boy," says his homemaker mother, Karen Grady, 41. "They made fun of him for that. They told him he was poor and made fun of him for that."

Then on Oct. 17, 1996, "I just snapped," her son says. As Jason Pratt, known as one of the Skaters, passed him in the cafeteria, Sneed whacked him on the head with a tray. "I figured if I got lucky and took him out, all the other non-

Lost in the Shadows

BRIAN HEAD, 15

After years of being tormented at school, this Georgia teen who loved music and video games ended his life with a gunshot. Later, his parents found this poem among his belongings.

As I walk in the light, the shadow draws me closer,
with the ambition and curiosity of a small boy
and the determination of a man.
The shadow is sanctuary, a place to escape the light.
In the light they can see me,
in the light they can see all.
Although the light is wide in its spread,
they still cannot see the pain in my face.
The pain that their eyes bring to bear when
they look upon me.
They see me as an insignificant "thing,"
Something to be traded, mangled and mocked.
But in the shadows I know they would not,
nor could not, see such a lie.
In the shadows, their evil eyes cannot stare
my soul into oblivion.
In the dark, I am free to move without their
judgmental eyes on me.
In the shadows, I can sleep without dreams of
despair and deception.
In the shadows I am home.

sense would stop." But after a few punches, Josh slipped on a scrap of food, hit his head on the floor and lost consciousness as Pratt kneed him in the head several times. Finally a football player leapt over two tables and dragged Sneed away, likely saving his life. Four titanium plates were needed to secure his shattered skull, and he was so gravely injured that he had to relearn how to walk and talk. Homeschooled, Sneed eventually earned his GED, but he hasn't regained his short-term memory. Assault charges against both him and Pratt were dismissed, but Pratt (who declined to comment) was suspended from school for 133 days.

Grady sued the county, claiming that because the school knew Josh was being terrorized but never disciplined the tormentors, they effectively sanctioned the conditions that led to the fight. Her attorney James A. H. Bell hopes the suit will have national implications. "We tried to make a statement, holding the school system accountable for its failure to protect," he says. In February Sneed and Grady were awarded $49,807 by a judge who found the county partly at fault. A tractor buff who once aspired to own a John Deere shop, Josh now lives on his grandfather's farm, passing his days with cartoons, video games and light chores. "Everybody's hollering that they need to get rid of guns, but it's not that," he says. "You need to find out what's going on in school."

Around the country, officials are attempting to do precisely that, as many states now require a safe-school plan that specifically addresses bullying. Most experts agree that metal detectors and zero-tolerance expulsions ignore the root of the problem. Counseling and fostering teamwork seem most effective, as evidenced by successful programs in the Cherry Creek, Colo., school district and DeKalb County, Ga. "We create an atmosphere of caring—it's harder to be a bully when you care about someone," says John Monferdini, head counselor at the DeKalb Alternative School, which serves 400 county students, most of whom have been expelled for bullying and violent behavior. Apart from academics, the school offers conflict-resolution courses and team-oriented outdoor activities that demand cooperation. "Yeah, I'm a bully," says Chris Jones, 15. "If I'm with friends and we see someone coming along we can jump on, we do it. It's like, you know, an adrenaline rush." But a stint in DeKalb is having a transformative effect. "When I came here, it was because we beat up a kid so badly—sticking his head in the bleachers—and the only thing I wished was that we'd had a chance to hurt him worse before we got caught. That's not the way I am now."

One wonders if intervention might have restrained the bullies who tormented Evan Ramsey. Ineligible for parole until 2066, when he'll be 86, Ramsey, now 20, spends most days working out, playing cards, reading Stephen King novels and studying for his high school diploma. He also has plenty of time to reflect on the horrible error in judgment he made. "The worst thing is to resort to violence," he says. "I'd like to get letters from kids who are getting problems like I went through. I could write back and help them." His advice: "If they're being messed with, they have to tell someone. If nothing's done, then they have to go [to] higher and higher [authority] until it stops. If they don't get help, that's when they'll lose it and maybe do something bad—really bad. And the pain of doing that never really stops."

Ron Arias in Seward, **Mary Boone** in Seattle, **Lauren Comander** in Chicago, **Joanne Fowler** in New York City, **Maureen** Harrington in Stanwood, **Ellen Mazo** in Jersey Shore, Pa., **Jamie Reno** in Santee, **Don Sider** in West Palm Beach and **Gail Cameron Wescott** in Atlanta

BULLIES 101

How can parents tell when their child is being bullied—or bullying others?

In 1993 a panel of experts in the Cherry Creek School District in Englewood, Colo., published Bully-Proofing Your School, *a manifesto designed to stop bullying at an early age. One of its coauthors, Dr. William Porter, 55, a clinical psychologist, offers the following guidelines for parents.*

• **What is a bully?**
A bully is a child who takes repeated hostile actions against another child and has more power than the individual he targets. Bullies tend to be very glib and don't accept responsibility for their behavior.

• **How do I know if my child is being bullied?**
He or she may show an unwillingness to go to school and may have bruises or damage to belongings that can't be explained. Children who are being bullied tend to keep silent about it and may become withdrawn, depressed and feel no one can help.

• **What do I do if my child is being bullied?**
Listen to your child and express confidence that the problem can be solved. Keep trying until you find someone at the school to help. Practice with your child such protective skills as avoiding the confrontation or using humor to deflate a tense moment.

• **What if my child is a bully?**
Set clear and consistent expectations of behavior, and work with the school on follow-up. Don't let the child talk his or her way out of the behavior, and find positive ways for him or her to get attention.

From *People Weekly*, June 4, 2001, pp. 54-61. © 2001 by Richard Jerome. Reprinted by permission. All rights reserved.

You can help your adolescent in the search for identity

Their bodies kick into overdrive. They find themselves disoriented, scared and alone. They become moody, secretive and sarcastic. You don't recognize your own child. What happened to the child you used to know? The answer: adolescence.

In the teenage years, young people begin their quest for identity. To help you understand your child's adolescence, Les Parrott, Ph.D., a professor of psychology, offers the five most common ways in which teens demonstrate their struggles with identity.

Through status symbols.   Adolescents try to establish themselves through prestige—wearing the right clothes, having the right possessions, from stereos to sunglasses. These symbols help form teen identities by expressing affiliation with specific groups.

Through forbidden behaviors.   Teens often feel that appearing mature will bring recognition and acceptance. They begin engaging in practices they associate with adulthood—tabooed pleasures—such as smoking, drinking, drugs and sexual activity.

Through rebellion.   Rebellion demonstrates separation. Teens can show that they differentiate themselves from parents and authority figures, while maintaining the acceptance of their peers.

Through idols.   Celebrities may become "models" for teens who are looking for a way of experimenting with different roles. They may identify with a known figure, trying to become like that person, and in effect, losing hold of their own identity. This identification with a well-known personality gives teens a sense of belonging.

Through cliquish exclusion.   Teens often can be intolerant in their exclusion of their peers. Since they are constantly trying to define and redefine themselves in relation to others, they do not want to be associated with anyone having unacceptable or unattractive characteristics. They try to strengthen their own identities by excluding those who are not like themselves.

Offering help

Establishing an identity is not an easy process. There are difficult and confusing choices at every step of the way. You can help adolescents discover the most stable aspects of their identities by becoming aware of what they are going through, the ways in which they attempt to mold their identities and by being patient. Try these exercises with your adolescent as a way to open up discussion about identity-building and values.

- Draw a set of three concentric circles. Then have your teen list or describe the personal characteristics that are most important and resistant to change in the innermost circle; the aspects least important and least stable in the outermost circle; and the aspects of intermediate importance in the middle circle. Use this chart to talk about values and the threat that peer pressure poses to unpopular beliefs.
- Using some old magazines, have your adolescent create two collages: one entitled "Who I Am," and the other, "Who I Would Like to Be." After the collages are completed, discuss why the specific images were chosen in each collage. Ask how the collages compare to each other and how the images portrayed in each collage show satisfaction or confusion about identity.
- At the top of a sheet of paper, write the words, "Who Am I?" Then have your teen write down 20 responses to this question as quickly as possible, without self-censoring. Discuss the answers, as well as the process of choosing each answer.

From *The Brown University Child and Adolescent Behavior Letter*, January 1998, pp. S1-2. Published with information authorized for use by Manisses Communications Group, Inc., 208 Governor Street, Providence, RI 02906, 401-831-6020/800-333-7771, Fax 401-861-6370, email: manissescs@manisses.com. For more information visit www.manisses.com.

Meet the men and women who seem to have found life's sweet spot, a balance of work and play that experts say is the key to happiness. According to a new AARP MODERN MATURITY survey, three out of 10 Americans 55 and over say they're having more fun than ever before. And that's why we call them...

the funmasters

BY PRISCILLA GRANT

We see you out there. You're the two-career couple who still manage to slip away for ski weekends and canoe trips. The retired schoolteacher who regularly dons an apron for exotic cooking classes. The businesswoman who stars in community theater musicals.

How do you do it? You've got just as many problems and responsibilities as anyone else. And you're not getting any younger, either. Yet somewhere in midlife, you caught a wave of pleasure you've been riding ever since.

One of the most eye-opening findings of a recent AARP MODERN MATURITY survey on enjoyment in life was that nearly 30 percent of Americans 55 and over say that the older they get, the more fun they have. The survey of more than 2,000 adults, conducted by RoperASW in July 2001 and January 2002, also found that another three in 10 report having the same amount of fun as earlier in life, while 34 percent say growing older means that they're having less fun.

THE DOCTOR IS NOT IN
Weekdays Dr. Cathy Carron, 51, is the physician for the American Stock Exchange in New York. Weekends she's sailing in Florida. "In most ways, I'm better off than when I was younger," says Carron. "My outlook's better, too."

The good news is there's hope for those who aren't natural-born funmasters. Members of the more-fun group aren't just lucky: They share attitudes and habits that everyone can learn from.

People who find joy in the second phase of life experience a "second growth," says sociologist William A. Sadler, author of *The Third Age: Six Principles for Growth and Renewal After Forty* (Perseus, 2000). He developed the concept during a 12-year study of midlifers. The findings of his long-term study challenge the stereotype that "starting in one's 40s, people have midlife crises or give up on their dreams and accommodate to loss," Sadler says. He found that a significant number of midlifers consciously began to take risks, continued to be productive, and increasingly enjoyed their relationships with those closest to them. In short, as the years went by life just kept getting better and better. "The oldest among them showed me that it's possible to experience and sustain renewal well beyond the conventional boundaries of old age," he says.

Stepping Out

Charlie Meade, New York City

Age 71, Former professional dancer and bus driver
Fun Factor: Still dancing
"I was born in Jamaica and danced all over Europe with a group. I was even in the movie *Cleopatra*—I played a Watusi dancer and a witch doctor. I drove a bus for 26 years and it was an interesting job, but I always loved to dance. When I'd get to the end of the bus line and I'd need to stretch my legs, I used to dance right on the bus. Sometimes I would create a step right there. Ever since the New York Swing Dance Society began back in the 1980s, I've looked forward to every Sunday night. Now my time is mine. My girlfriend and I go to dances at Lincoln Center or down at the pier. I get a certain high from dancing. It's playing. I seem to forget all my problems when I'm dancing."

The AARP MODERN MATURITY survey confirmed that people who are having more fun also feel good about themselves, enjoy close relationships, are intellectually curious, and are physically active. Compared with those whose fun times are on the wane, the more-fun group is more likely to feel

- happy (81 percent versus 53 percent)
- peaceful (66 percent versus 46 percent)
- truly alive (67 percent versus 44 percent)
- capable and competent (72 percent versus 59 percent)

What Turns Us On Age 55–64	
Men	**Women**
19% FISHING	**22%** READING
17% TRAVEL	20% TRAVEL
14% TIME WITH FAMILY	**19%** TIME WITH GRANDCHILDREN
10% WORK	16% GARDENING
9% MUSIC	**13%** TIME WITH FAMILY

Source: AARP MODERN MATURITY Study

According to the survey, the more-fun group is also more likely than their less-fun counterparts to

- socialize with friends (67 percent versus 49 percent)
- spend a romantic evening with a spouse or partner (35 percent versus 25 percent)
- exercise or play sports (49 percent versus 33 percent)
- do something educational or cultural (45 percent versus 31 percent)
- make love (40 percent versus 29 percent)

Those percentages may be rising. Sadler believes that because people are living longer than ever before, this second growth will one day be seen as the norm. The men and women in his study, he says, do not think in terms of retiring—certainly not in the old-fashioned sense of disengaging. "We have the potential for a 'third age' that our parents and grandparents didn't have," says Sadler. "We get this 30-year life bonus. People ask, 'Where am I going to put those years—if I put them in the middle, isn't that better than putting them at the end?'"

The members of the more-fun group agree that enjoyment of life doesn't have to decline with age: Starting in their 40s and 50s, they developed or deepened interests that keep them productive and happy. Here's what makes them different:

They Make Fun a Priority Finding enjoyment in life takes time, and those most successful at it dedicate an average of 24 hours per week to "just having fun." Our survey shows they are also more likely than their wet-blanket counterparts to claim they "live for having fun."

What Turns Us On Age 65+	
Men	**Women**
17% TRAVEL	**19%** TRAVEL
17% FISHING	18% GARDENING
12% GARDENING	**17%** READING
11% TIME WITH GRANDCHILDREN	16% RELIGION
11% READING	**13%** NEEDLEWORK

Source: AARP MODERN MATURITY Study

They Think of Themselves as Fun People Fun lovers are more likely to describe themselves as "a fun person to be around." In fact, 22 percent say they're disappointed if they don't have some fun every day.

They Love to Learn Two-thirds of the fun-loving group say they're "always trying to learn new things." Plus, taking classes or joining learning groups helps prevent personal isolation, which is "a dream killer," according to Barbara Sher, author of *It's Only Too Late if You Don't Start Now* (Delacorte Press, 1998).

Brush With Life

Denis Clifford, Albany, CA

Age 62, Attorney, writes legal self-help books
Fun Factor: Painting, writing personal essays, traveling, shooting hoops
"I felt I didn't have enough money, that I had to crank out the books. But then, roughly at age 45, I realized that maybe I don't have to work so hard. At first I had real inner conflicts about painting, that it was a waste of time, that I should be making money. But I told that part of me to go sit on a stool in the corner, and I sat the part of me that wanted to paint in front of the easel. I just needed to get myself there. I took a two-year art class, and when it ended I said, 'I have to keep doing this.' So I formed a drawing group and hired a model. I think that laughing and having a good time is only one kind of fun. The other kind is a process, like painting, that resonates with my soul."

Best of all, it's possible to join the ranks of those who get the most fun out of life. All you need to do is give yourself a little kick-start, says Gail Cassidy, author of *Discover Your Passion* (Tomlyn Publications, 2000).

Hidden Yearnings

Results for all respondents, 18 and up

43% of women and **38%** of men wish they were incredibly good-looking

69% of men and women wish they were very wealthy

59% of women and **61%** of men want to express emotions better.

41% of women and **56%** of men want a more satisfying sex life.

83% of people surveyed hope to do good deeds for others.

Source: AARP MODERN MATURITY Study

"Notice, for instance, what part of the newspaper you read first. Then make a list of your skills, work experiences, knowledge areas, and talents. Finally, use that information to draw a road map of your interests. I used to be a teacher, and I thought I was done with education. But I still found myself reading the education section of the newspaper, so now I'm offering a course on self-confidence for battered women."

You can combine skills and interests in different ways. Cassidy had a client who, after visiting Appalachia, developed a new type of quilting. She also loved genealogy. So she started to help people design quilts based on their family trees.

Ironically, other people can be the best route to self-discovery. "Your friends know you and may have some good advice," adds Geoffrey C. Godbey, professor of leisure studies at Pennsylvania State University.

And while you're trying new things, Godbey adds, give yourself permission to fail or be embarrassed in your pursuit.

Convince yourself that not trying is the greater failure, and take the leap.

Driving Force

Marjorie Thomas, Norman, OK

Age 72, Former admissions officer at University of Oklahoma

Fun Factor: Traveling with husband Bill, weight training, writing family histories

"First of all, I like being with my husband, We've been married 20 years and he's my major source of enjoyment. We have many likes in common, and what we don't have in common we tolerate. We're on the road much of the time—we've been to all the states. We just get up and go when we want. I've always been interested in genealogy, and I recently wrote a book about our family. Sure, I have chores that I'm not too fond of—laundry and cooking. But when we travel I have a wonderful feeling of space and happiness. And when I'm writing I get this sense of elation. It's, 'Oh, boy, euphoria, here I come!'"

Having fun can clearly be a lot of work. But the payoff can be substantial. Studies show that people who take time to play are healthier physically and emotionally. In fact, the AARP MODERN MATURITY survey found that members of the more-fun group are far more likely than their less-fun counterparts to rate their physical health as "excellent." As they get older, they also feel more balanced emotionally.

Play has also been shown to increase creativity, one of the hallmarks of successful living. "It's well-known that many Nobel Prizes have been won by people who were just playing in their minds and having fun," says Lenore Terr, professor of psychiatry and the author of *Beyond Love and Work: Why Adults Need to Play* (Touchstone Books, 1999). "We used to think that if we could just work hard and be good people, then that would be enough. But if we play throughout our lives, it's a better way to live. Playing gets your mind working. It gives you a reason to get up in the morning."

Priscilla Grant last wrote for AARP MODERN MATURITY *about cosmetic surgery (March–April 2001).*

From *AARP Modern Maturity*, July/August 2002, pp. 47-53. © 2002 by Priscilla Grant.

Aging

Living to 100: What's the Secret?

Forget about Generation X and Generation Y. Today, the nation's most intriguing demographic is Generation Roman numeral C—folks age 100 and over. In the United States, the number of centenarians doubled in the 1980s and did so again in the 1990s. The total now exceeds 70,000. By 2050, according to midrange projections, there could be over 800,000 Americans who celebrate the century mark. Studies show the same trend in other industrialized countries and recently in China. Indeed, demographers are now counting the number of *supercentenarians,* people age 110 and over.

The swelling population of people age 100 and over has given researchers an opportunity to answer some of the most fundamental questions about human health and longevity: What does it take to live a long life? How much do diet, exercise, and other lifestyle factors matter compared with "good" genes? And, perhaps most importantly, what is the quality of life among the "old old"? Does getting older inevitably mean getting sicker, or can people remain productive, social, and independent on their 100th birthday and beyond?

Centenarian studies

There are a dozen or so centenarian studies. The Harvard-based New England Centenarian Study started with 46 people age 100 and over in the Boston area but is now recruiting people from throughout the United States. A health-advice book has been recently published based on findings from the centenarian study in Okinawa, where the average life expectancy, 81.2 years, is the highest in the world. There are active centenarian studies in Italy, Sweden, and Denmark. For the most part, results from these studies belie the myth that the oldest old are doddering and dependent. Some harsh demographic selection may come into play. Frail individuals die sooner, leaving only a relatively robust group still alive. In fact, one of the rewards of living a long life is that, for the most part, the "extra" years are healthy years.

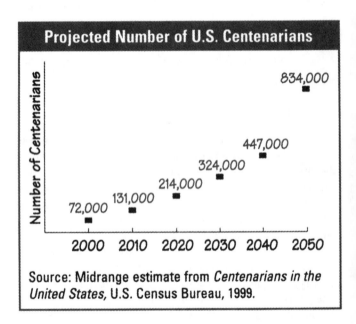

Projected Number of U.S. Centenarians

Number of Centenarians

72,000 (2000)
131,000 (2010)
214,000 (2020)
324,000 (2030)
447,000 (2040)
834,000 (2050)

Source: Midrange estimate from *Centenarians in the United States,* U.S. Census Bureau, 1999.

Physical activity is a recurring them: the people in these studies are walkers, bikers, and golfers. In Okinawa, centenarians do tai chi and karate. People who live to 100 and beyond exercise their brains, too, by reading, painting, and playing musical instruments. Some continue to work, an indication that our love affair with retirement may be a mixed blessing.

100 is still old

This isn't to say that centenarians escape unscathed. Although 75% of the people in the New England study were well enough to live at home and take care of themselves at age 95, this number dropped to 30% by age 102. About two-thirds of centenarians suffer from some form of dementia. Danish investigators, who have taken a decidedly less sunny view of extremely old age than their New England counterparts, published a study earlier this year reporting that many of the centenarians in their study had cardiovascular disease (72%), urinary incontinence (60%), osteoarthritis of a major joint (54%), and dementia (51%). And life expectancy is short at 100. On average, centenarians will only live another year or two, although that might change as the size of the age group increases.

It is notable, however, that the period of serious illness and disability for the exceptionally long-lived tends to be brief. Aging experts say that *compressing morbidity* in this way should be our goal. The Stanford researcher who coined the term, James F. Fries, has compared the ultimate in compressed morbidity to the "wonderful one-hoss shay" described in Oliver Wendell Holmes's poem "The Deacon's Masterpiece." The shay in the poem is a carriage built so carefully by the deacon that no single part breaks down for 100 years. Then it collapses "all at once, and nothing first/Just as bubbles do when they burst." Notwithstanding the Danish study, centenarians approach this ideal, as they tend to live well into their nineties free of serious diseases such as cancer and Alzheimer's.

Good genes

Traits that run in families are not necessarily genetic. After all, families often share the same eating habits, activity levels, and other so-called environmental factors that influence health. Still, similarities within families are often a good clue of a strong genetic influence, and longevity does seem to run in families. The New England Centenarian Study, for example, has found that its subjects were four times more likely to have a sibling who lived past age 90 than people with an average life span.

Now the search is on for genetic attributes. Researchers have previously identified some forms of a gene called apolipoprotein E that increase the risk for cardiovascular disease and Alzheimer's disease. Studies have shown that those dangerous variants are rare among centenarians. Scientists have had success building long life into some animals. They've genetically engineered a strain of fruit fly to live 35% longer than normal strains. Certain mice genes have been mutated so the animals live 30% longer than normal.

No one has found such a mutation in people. But last year, Thomas Perls, director of the New England study, and Louis Kunkel, a molecular geneticist at Children's Hospital in Boston, believe they got closer by identifying a section of chromosome 4 that may predispose people to long life. They made their discovery by scanning the genes of 137 sets of very old siblings—one person age 98 or older with a brother who was at least age 91 or a sister who was at least age 95. The siblings shared this distinctive section of chromosome 4.

Health conditions

But genes aren't the whole story. Public health advances like sanitation and routine vaccination have greatly improved the odds for long life. Indeed, it may be the intersection of genes

with ever-changing health conditions that really determines how long we live. Today's centenarians may have survived so long partly because they had genes that protected them against infectious diseases prevalent in the early 20th century. Tomorrow's centenarians may need to have a different kind of genetic advantage attuned to 21st century circumstances.

The Gender Gap

Female centenarians outnumber males by a 9:1 ratio. The longest documented life was that of a French woman, Jeanne Calment, who died in 1997 at age 122. And throughout most of the world, women, on average, live longer than men. Some researchers say it is estrogen that gives women the longevity edge. Others theorize that menstruation and systems related to childbirth better equip women to rid their bodies of toxins. Women also tend to be more social than men, and social connections are believed to be critical to weathering old age.

Yet the men who reach their 100th birthday are, on the whole, healthier than the women. They are far less likely to have dementia or other serious medical problems. Thomas Perls, head of the New England Centenarian Study, calls these men "aging superstars."

Longevity statistics favoring women suggest that there may be some protective genes lurking on the X chromosome, the sex chromosome that women have two copies of and men only one. Another possibility: genetics are relatively neutral but social conditions favor long life for women. But healthy, odds-defying 100-year-old gentlemen hint of healthy aging genes somewhere else in the genome.

Medical interventions are starting to make a demographic difference, particularly with respect to mortality from cardiovascular disease. Most centenarians still die from heart disease, but they might have died much sooner without the medicines we now have to control cholesterol levels and hypertension.

Diet and other choices

Diet and other health habits play a role, too. Okinawans lose their actuarial edge when they move to Western countries and, presumably, adopt a more Western lifestyle. Italian researchers reported last year that healthy centenarians had exceptionally high blood levels of vitamins A and E compared with healthy younger adults. The study didn't address, however, what causes high levels. Still, the authors theorized that vitamin-rich blood may both strengthen the immune system of these centenarians and defend them against damage done by *oxygen free radicals,* the reactive molecules that some researchers believe is the principal cause of aging.

It's not a centenarian study, but a large, long-term study of Seventh-Day Adventists in California has produced some valuable information about longevity because the Adventists, on average, live several years longer than their fellow Californians. By some reckonings, they even outlive the Okinawans. There is no reason to believe the Adventists have any special genes, so other factors probably explain their longevity. Researchers broke down their health habits in a statistical analysis published in the July 9, 2001, *Archives of Internal Medicine*. A great deal of physical activity, frequent consumption of nuts, not eating meat, and medium body weight each was found to add about 1.5–2.5 years of life.

Centenarians may well have a genetic head start on most of us, but in his 1999 book *Living to 100,* Perls argues that we can make choices that may help us catch up. Of course, we don't have complete free will over these choices; behavior of almost all kinds has a genetic component. Still, there are some lessons to be learned from the do's and don'ts of centenarians:

- *They don't smoke or drink heavily.*
- *Those who had smoked didn't do so for long.*
- *They gained little or no weight during adulthood.* Being overweight makes people more vulnerable to many life-threatening illnesses, including heart disease, diabetes, cancer, and stroke.
- *They don't overeat.* Okinawan centenarians consume 10%–20% fewer calories per day than typical Americans. And in animal studies, calorie-restricted diets have consistently increased the life span. The old Okinawans consume less fat, too. About 26% of their energy intake comes from fat, compared with 30% or more for Americans. And more of that fat is beneficial—omega-3 fatty acids and the unsaturated fats found in vegetable oils.
- *They eat many fruits and vegetables.* The Okinawans have an average of seven servings a day.
- *They get regular physical activity for as long as they are able.* Strength-building activities, such as climbing stairs or lifting small weights, are especially beneficial because they help slow the age-related loss of muscle mass.
- *They challenge their minds.* Stimulating mental activity may help prevent age-related thinking and memory problems by stimulating communication between brain cells. Particularly among elderly men, decreased cognitive performance is strongly associated with mortality.
- *They have a positive outlook.* Perls says centenarians seem to have personalities that shed stress easily. An inability to control emotional stress has been linked to memory loss and heart disease.
- *They are friendly and maintain close ties with family and friends.* Not surprisingly, positive relationships are associated with lower rates of depression. And lower rates of depression may result in lower rates of heart disease.

Many researchers think that people could add up to a decade to their lives if they emulated the centenarians. And, from what we know so far, they aren't doing anything mysterious. They're simply following the standard health commandments: don't smoke, keep trim, get exercise, manage stress, and avoid social isolation.

All easier said than done, but after all, what are New Year's resolutions for?

From *Harvard Health Letter,* January 2002, pp. 1-3. © 2002 by President and Fellows of Harvard College. Reprinted by permission.

Start the Conversation

The MODERN MATURITY guide to end-of-life care

The Body Speaks

Physically, dying means that "the body's various physiological systems, such as the circulatory, respiratory, and digestive systems, are no longer able to support the demands required to stay alive," says Barney Spivack, M.D., director of Geriatric Medicine for the Stamford (Connecticut) Health System. "When there is no meaningful chance for recovery, the physician should discuss realistic goals of care with the patient and family, which may include letting nature take its course. Lacking that direction," he says, "physicians differ in their perception of when enough is enough. We use our best judgment, taking into account the situation, the information available at the time, consultation with another doctor, or guidance from an ethics committee."

Without instructions from the patient or family, a doctor's obligation to a terminally ill person is to provide life-sustaining treatment. When a decision to "let nature take its course" has been made, the doctor will remove the treatment, based on the patient's needs. Early on, the patient or surrogate may choose to stop interventions such as antibiotics, dialysis, resuscitation, and defibrillation. Caregivers may want to offer food and fluids, but those can cause choking and the pooling of dangerous fluids in the lungs. A dying patient does not desire or need nourishment; without it he or she goes into a deep sleep and dies in days to weeks. A breathing machine would be the last support: It is uncomfortable for the patient, and may be disconnected when the patient or family finds that it is merely prolonging the dying process.

The Best Defense Against Pain

Pain-management activists are fervently trying to reeducate physicians about the importance and safety of making patients comfortable. "In medical school 30 years ago, we worried a lot about creating addicts," says Philadelphia internist Nicholas Scharff. "Now we know that addiction is not a problem: People who are in pain take

pain medication as long as they need it, and then they stop." Spivack says, "We have new formulations and delivery systems, so a dying patient should never have unmet pain needs."

In Search of a Good Death

If we think about death at all, we say that we want to go quickly, in our sleep, or, perhaps, while flyfishing. But in fact only 10 percent of us die suddenly. The more common process is a slow decline with episodes of organ or system failure. Most of us want to die at home; most of us won't. All of us hope to die without pain; many of us will be kept alive, in pain, beyond a time when we would choose to call a halt. Yet very few of us take steps ahead of time to spell out what kind of physical and emotional care we will want at the end.

The new movement to improve the end of life is pioneering ways to make available to each of us a good death—as we each define it. One goal of the movement is to bring death through the cultural process that childbirth has achieved; from an unconscious, solitary act in a cold hospital room to a situation in which one is buffered by pillows, pictures, music, loved ones, and the solaces of home. But as in the childbirth movement, the real goal is choice— here, to have the death you want. Much of death's sting can be averted by planning in advance, knowing the facts, and knowing what options we all have. Here, we have gathered new and relevant information to help us all make a difference for the people we are taking care of, and ultimately, for ourselves.

In 1999, the Joint Commission on Accreditation of Healthcare Organizations issued stern new guidelines about easing pain in both terminal and nonterminal patients. The movement intends to take pain seriously:

to measure and treat it as the fifth vital sign in hospitals, along with blood pressure, pulse, temperature, and respiration.

The best defense against pain, says Spivack, is a combination of education and assertiveness. "Don't be afraid to speak up," he says. "If your doctor isn't listening, talk to the nurses. They see more and usually have a good sense of what's happening." Hospice workers, too, are experts on physical comfort, and a good doctor will respond to a hospice worker's recommendations. "The best situation for pain management," says Scharff, "is at home with a family caregiver being guided by a hospice program."

The downsides to pain medication are, first, that narcotics given to a fragile body may have a double effect: The drug may ease the pain, but it may cause respiratory depression and possibly death. Second, pain medication may induce grogginess or unconsciousness when a patient wants to be alert. "Most people seem to be much more willing to tolerate pain than mental confusion," says senior research scientist M. Powell Lawton, Ph.D., of the Philadelphia Geriatric Center. Dying patients may choose to be alert one day for visitors, and asleep the next to cope with pain. Studies show that when patients control their own pain medication, they use less.

Final Symptoms

Depression This condition is not an inevitable part of dying but can and should be treated. In fact, untreated depression can prevent pain medications from working effectively, and antidepressant medication can help relieve pain. A dying patient should be kept in the best possible emotional state for the final stage of life. A combination of medications and psychotherapy works best to treat depression.

Anorexia In the last few days of life, anorexia—an unwillingness or inability to eat—often sets in. "It has a protective effect, releasing endorphins in the system and contributing to a greater feeling of well-being," says Spivack. "Force-feeding a dying patient could make him uncomfortable and cause choking."

Dehydration Most people want to drink little or nothing in their last days. Again, this is a protective mechanism, triggering a release of helpful endorphins.

Drowsiness and Unarousable Sleep In spite of a coma-like state, says Spivack, "presume that the patient hears everything that is being said in the room."

Agitation and Restlessness, Moaning and Groaning The features of "terminal delirium" occur when the patient's level of consciousness is markedly decreased; there is no significant likelihood that any pain sensation can reach consciousness. Family members and other caregivers may interpret what they see as "the patient is in pain" but as these signs arise at a point very close to death, terminal delirium should be suspected.

Hospice: The Comfort Team

Hospice is really a bundle of services. It organizes a team of people to help patients and their families, most often in the patient's home but also in hospice residences, nursing homes, and hospitals:

•Registered nurses who check medication and the patient's condition, communicate with the patient's doctor, and educate caregivers.
•Medical services by the patient's physician and a hospice's medical director, limited to pain medication and other comfort care.
•Medical supplies and equipment.
•Drugs for pain relief and symptom control.
•Home-care aides for personal care, homemakers for light housekeeping.
•Continuous care in the home as needed on a short-term basis.
•Trained volunteers for support services.
•Physical, occupational, and speech therapists to help patients adapt to new disabilities.
•Temporary hospitalization during a crisis.
•Counselors and social workers who provide emotional and spiritual support to the patient and family.
•Respite care—brief noncrisis hospitalization to provide relief for family caregivers for up to five days.
•Bereavement support for the family, including counseling, referral to support groups, and periodic check-ins during the first year after the death.

Hospice Residences Still rare, but a growing phenomenon. They provide all these services on-site. They're for patients without family caregivers; with frail, elderly spouses; and for families who cannot provide at-home care because of other commitments. At the moment, Medicare covers only hospice services; the patient must pay for room and board. In many states Medicaid also covers hospice services (see How Much Will It Cost?). Keep in mind that not all residences are certified, bonded, or licensed; and not all are covered by Medicare.

Getting In A physician can recommend hospice for a patient who is terminally ill and probably has less than six months to live. The aim of hospice is to help people cope with an illness, not to cure it. All patients entering hospice waive their rights to curative treatments, though only for conditions relating to their terminal illness. "If you break a leg, of course you'll be treated for that," says Karen Woods, executive director of the Hospice Association of America. No one is forced to accept a hospice referral, and patients may leave and opt for curative care at any time. Hospice programs are listed in the Yellow Pages. For more information, see Resources.

The Ultimate Emotional Challenge

Adying person is grieving the loss of control over life, of body image, of normal physical functions, mobility and strength, freedom and independence, security, and the illusion of immortality. He is also grieving the loss of an earthly future, and reorienting himself to an unknowable destiny.

At the same time, an emotionally healthy dying person will be trying to satisfy his survival drive by adapting to this new phase, making the most of life at the moment, calling in loved ones, examining and appreciating his own joys and accomplishments. Not all dying people are depressed; many embrace death easily.

Facing the Fact

Doctors are usually the ones to inform a patient that he or she is dying, and the end-of-life movement is training physicians to bring empathy to that conversation in place of medspeak and time estimates. The more sensitive doctor will first ask how the patient feels things are going. "The patient may say, 'Well, I don't think I'm getting better,' and I would say, 'I think you're right,' " says internist Nicholas Scharff.

At this point, a doctor might ask if the patient wants to hear more now or later, in broad strokes or in detail. Some people will need to first process the emotional blow with tears and anger before learning about the course of their disease in the future.

"Accept and understand whatever reaction the patient has," says Roni Lang, director of the Geriatric Assessment Program for the Stamford (Connecticut) Health System, and a social worker who is a longtime veteran of such conversations. "Don't be too quick with the tissue. That sends a message that it's not okay to be upset. It's okay for the patient to be however she is."

Getting to Acceptance

Some patients keep hoping that they will get better. Denial is one of the mind's miracles, a way to ward off painful realities until consciousness can deal with them. Denial may not be a problem for the dying person, but it can create difficulties for the family. The dying person could be leaving a lot of tough decisions, stress, and confusion behind. The classic stages of grief outlined by Elisabeth Kübler-Ross—denial, anger, bargaining, depression, and acceptance—are often used to describe post-death grieving, but were in fact delineated for the process of accepting impending loss. We now know that these states may not progress in order. "Most people oscillate between anger and sadness, embracing the prospect of death and unrealistic episodes of optimism," says Lang. Still, she says, "don't place demands on them

Survival Kit for Caregivers

A study published in the March 21, 2000, issue of **Annals of Internal Medicine** shows that caregivers of the dying are twice as likely to have depressive symptoms as the dying themselves.

No wonder. Caring for a dying parent, says social worker Roni Lang, "brings a fierce tangle of emotions. That part of us that is a child must grow up." Parallel struggles occur when caring for a spouse, a child, another relative, or a friend. Caregivers may also experience sibling rivalry, income loss, isolation, fatigue, burnout, and resentment.

To deal with these difficult stresses, Lang suggests that caregivers:

•Set limits in advance. How far am I willing to go? What level of care is needed? Who can I get to help? Resist the temptation to let the illness always take center stage, or to be drawn into guilt-inducing conversations with people who think you should be doing more.
•Join a caregiver support group, either disease-related like the Alzheimer's Association or Gilda's Club, or a more general support group like The Well Spouse Foundation. Ask the social services department at your hospital for advice. Telephone support and online chat rooms also exist (see Resources).
•Acknowledge anger and express it constructively by keeping a journal or talking to an understanding friend or family member. Anger is a normal reaction to powerlessness.
•When people offer to help, give them a specific assignment. And then, take time to do what energizes you and make a point of rewarding yourself.
•Remember that people who are critically ill are self-absorbed. If your empathy fails you and you lose patience, make amends and forgive yourself.

to accept their death. This is not a time to proselytize." It is enough for the family to accept the coming loss, and if necessary, introduce the idea of an advance directive and health-care proxy, approaching it as a "just in case" idea. When one member of the family cannot accept death, and insists that doctors do more, says Lang, "that's the worst nightmare. I would call a meeting, hear all views without interrupting, and get the conversation around to what the patient would want. You may need another person to come in, perhaps the doctor, to help 'hear' the voice of the patient."

What Are You Afraid Of?

The most important question for doctors and caregivers to ask a dying person is, What are you afraid of? "Fear aggravates pain," says Lang, "and pain aggravates fear." Fear of pain, says Spivack, is one of the most common problems, and can be dealt with rationally. Many people do not know, for example, that pain in dying is not inevitable. Other typical fears are of being separated from loved ones, from home, from work; fear of being a burden, losing control, being dependent, and leaving things undone. Voicing fear helps lessen it, and pinpointing fear helps a caregiver know how to respond.

How to Be With a Dying Person

Our usual instinct is to avoid everything about death, including the people moving most rapidly toward it. But, Spivack says, "In all my years of working with dying people, I've never heard one say 'I want to die alone.' " Dying people are greatly comforted by company; the benefit far outweighs the awkwardness of the visit. Lang offers these suggestions for visitors:

•Be close. Sit at eye level, and don't be afraid to touch. Let the dying person set the pace for the conversation. Allow for silence. Your presence alone is valuable.

•Don't contradict a patient who says he's going to die. Acceptance is okay. Allow for anger, guilt, and fear, without trying to "fix" it. Just listen and empathize.

•Give the patient as much decision-making power as possible, as long as possible. Allow for talk about unfinished business. Ask: "Who can I contact for you?"

•Encourage happy reminiscences. It's okay to laugh.

•Never pass up the chance to express love or say goodbye. But if you don't get the chance, remember that not everything is worked through. Do the best you can.

Taking Control Now

Sixty years ago, before the invention of dialysis, defibrillators, and ventilators, the failure of vital organs automatically meant death. There were few choices to be made to end suffering, and when there were—the fatal dose of morphine, for example—these decisions were made privately by family and doctors who knew each other well. Since the 1950s, medical technology has been capable of extending lives, but also of prolonging dying. In 1967, an organization called Choice in Dying (now the Partnership for Caring: America's Voices for the Dying; see Resources) designed the first advance directive—a document that allows you to designate under what conditions you would want life-sustaining treatment to be continued or terminated. But the idea did not gain popular understanding until 1976, when the parents of Karen Ann Quinlan won a long legal battle to disconnect her from respiratory support as she lay for months in a vegetative state. Some 75 percent of Americans are in favor of advance directives, although only 30–35 percent actually write them.

Designing the Care You Want

There are two kinds of advance directives, and you may use one or both. A Living Will details what kind of life-sustaining treatment you want or don't want, in the event of an illness when death is imminent. A durable power of attorney for health care appoints someone to be your decision-maker if you can't speak for yourself. This person is also called a surrogate, attorney-in-fact, or health-care proxy. An advance directive such as Five Wishes covers both.

Most experts agree that a Living Will alone is not sufficient. "You don't need to write specific instructions about different kinds of life support, as you don't yet know any of the facts of your situation, and they may change," says Charles Sabatino, assistant director of the American Bar Association's Commission on Legal Problems of the Elderly.

The proxy, Sabatino says, is far more important. "It means someone you trust will find out all the options and make a decision consistent with what you would want." In most states, you may write your own advance directive, though some states require a specific form, available at hospital admitting offices or at the state department of health.

When Should You Draw Up a Directive?

Without an advance directive, a hospital staff is legally bound to do everything to keep you alive as long as possible, until you or a family member decides otherwise. So advance directives are best written before emergency status or a terminal diagnosis. Some people write them at the same time they make a will. The process begins with discussions between you and your family and doctor. If anybody is reluctant to discuss the subject, Sabatino suggests starting the conversation with a story. "Remember what happened to Bob Jones and what his family went through? I want us to be different...." You can use existing tools—a booklet or questionnaire (see Resources)—to keep the conversation moving. Get your doctor's commitment to support your wishes. "If you're asking for something that is against your doctor's conscience" (such as prescribing a lethal dose of pain medication or removing life support at a time he considers premature), Sabatino says, "he may have an obligation to transfer you to another doctor." And make sure the person you name as surrogate agrees to act for you and understands your wishes.

Filing, Storing, Safekeeping...

An estimated 35 percent of advance directives cannot be found when needed.

•Give a copy to your surrogate, your doctor, your hospital, and other family members. Tell them where to find the original in the house—not in a safe deposit box where it might not be found until after death.

Five Wishes

Five Wishes is a questionnaire that guides people in making essential decisions about the care they want at the end of their life. About a million people have filled out the eight-page form in the past two years. This advance directive is legally valid in 34 states and the District of Columbia. (The other 16 require a specific state-mandated form.)

The document was designed by lawyer Jim Towey, founder of Aging With Dignity, a nonprofit organization that advocates for the needs of elders and their caregivers. Towey, who was legal counsel to Mother Teresa, visited her Home for the Dying in Calcutta in the 1980s. He was struck that in that haven in the Third World, "the dying people's hands were held, their pain was managed, and they weren't alone. In the First World, you see a lot of medical technology, but people die in pain, and alone." Towey talked to MODERN MATURITY about his directive and what it means.

What are the five wishes? Who do I want to make care decisions for me when I can't? What kind of medical treatment do I want toward the end? What would help me feel comfortable while I am dying? How do I want people to treat me? What do I want my loved ones to know about me and my feelings after I'm gone?

Why is it so vital to make advance decisions now? Medical technology has extended longevity, which is good, but it can prolong the dying process in ways that are almost cruel. Medical schools are still concentrating on curing, not caring for the dying. We can have a dignified season in our life, or die alone in pain with futile interventions. Most people only discover they have options when checking into the hospital, and often they no longer have the capacity to choose. This leaves the family members with a guessing game and, frequently, guilt.

What's the ideal way to use this document? First you do a little soul searching about what you want. Then discuss it with people you trust, in the livingroom instead of the waiting room—before a crisis. Just say, "I want a choice about how I spend my last days," talk about your choices, and pick someone to be your health-care surrogate.

What makes the Five Wishes directive unique? It's easy to use and understand, not written in the language of doctors or lawyers. It also allows people to discuss comfort dignity, and forgiveness, not just medical concerns. When my father filled it out, he said he wanted his favorite afghan blanket in his bed. It made a huge difference to me that, as he was dying, he had his wishes fulfilled.

For a copy of Five Wishes in English or Spanish, send a $5 check or money order to Aging With Dignity, PO Box 1661, Tallahassee, FL 32302. For more information, visit www.agingwithdignity. org.

• Some people carry a copy in their wallet or glove compartment of their car.
• Be aware that if you have more than one home and you split your time in several regions of the country, you should be registering your wishes with a hospital in each region, and consider naming more than one proxy.
• You may register your Living Will and health-care proxy online at uslivingwillregistry.com (or call 800-548-9455). The free, privately funded confidential service will instantly fax a copy to a hospital when the hospital requests one. It will also remind you to update it: You may want to choose a new surrogate, accommodate medical advances, or change your idea of when "enough is enough." M. Powell Lawton, who is doing a study on how people anticipate the terminal life stages, has discovered that "people adapt relatively well to states of poor health. The idea that life is still worth living continues to readjust itself."

Assisted Suicide: The Reality

While advance directives allow for the termination of life-sustaining treatment, assisted suicide means supplying the patient with a prescription for life-ending medication. A doctor writes the prescription for the medication; the patient takes the fatal dose him- or herself. Physician-assisted suicide is legal only in Oregon (and under consideration in Maine) but only with rigorous preconditions. Of the approximately 30,000 people who died in Oregon in 1999, only 33 received permission to have a lethal dose of medication and only 26 of those actually died of the medication. Surrogates may request an end to life support, but to assist in a suicide puts one at risk for charges of homicide.

Good Care: Can You Afford It?

The ordinary person is only one serious illness away from poverty," says Joanne Lynn, M.D., director of the Arlington, Virginia, Center to Improve Care of the Dying. An ethicist, hospice physician, and health-services researcher, she is one of the founding members of the end-of-life-care movement. "On the whole, hospitalization and the cost of suppressing symptoms is very easy to afford," says Lynn. Medicare and Medicaid will help cover that kind of acute medical care. But what is harder to afford is at-home medication, monitoring, daily help with eating and walking, and all the care that will go on for the rest of the patient's life.

"When people are dying," Lynn says, "an increasing proportion of their overall care does not need to be done by doctors. But when policymakers say the care is nonmedical, then it's second class, it's not important, and nobody will pay for it."

Bottom line, Medicare pays for about 57 percent of the cost of medical care for Medicare beneficiaries.

Another 11 percent is paid by Medicaid, 20 percent by the patient, 10 percent from private insurance, and the rest from other sources, such as charitable organizations.

Medi-what?

This public-plus-private network of funding sources for end-of-life care is complex, and who pays for how much of what is determined by diagnosis, age, site of care, and income. Besides the private health insurance that many of us have from our employers, other sources of funding may enter the picture when patients are terminally ill.

•**Medicare** A federal insurance program that covers health-care services for people 65 and over, some disabled people, and those with end-stage kidney disease. Medicare Part A covers inpatient care in hospitals, nursing homes, hospice, and some home health care. For most people, the Part A premium is free. Part B covers doctor fees, tests, and other outpatient medical services. Although Part B is optional, most people choose to enroll through their local Social Security office and pay the monthly premium ($45.50). Medicare beneficiaries share in the cost of care through deductibles and co-insurance. What Medicare does not cover at all is outpatient medication, long-term nonacute care, and support services.

•**Medicaid** A state and federally funded program that covers health-care services for people with income or assets below certain levels, which vary from state to state.

•**Medigap** Private insurance policies covering the gaps in Medicare, such as deductibles and co-payments, and in some cases additional health-care services, medical supplies, and outpatient prescription drugs.

Many of the services not paid for by Medicare can be covered by private long-term-care insurance. About 50 percent of us over the age of 65 will need long-term care at home or in a nursing home, and this insurance is an extra bit of protection for people with major assets to protect. It pays for skilled nursing care as well as non-health services, such as help with dressing, eating, and bathing. You select a dollar amount of coverage per day (for example, $100 in a nursing home, or $50 for at-home care), and a coverage period (for example, three years—the average nursing-home stay is 2.7 years). Depending on your age and the benefits you choose, the insurance can cost anywhere from around $500 to more than $8,000 a year. People with pre-existing conditions such as Alzheimer's or MS are usually not eligible.

How Much Will It Cost?

Where you get end-of-life care will affect the cost and who pays for it.

•**Hospital** Dying in a hospital costs about $1,000 a day. After a $766 deductible (per benefit period), Medicare reimburses the hospital a fixed rate per day, which varies by region and diagnosis. After the first 60 days in a hospital, a patient will pay a daily deductible ($194) that goes up (to $388) after 90 days. The patient is responsible for all costs for each day beyond 150 days. Medicaid and some private insurance, either through an employer or a Medigap plan, often help cover these costs.

•**Nursing home** About $1,000 a week. Medicare covers up to 100 days of skilled nursing care after a three-day hospitalization, and most medication costs during that time. For days 21–100, your daily co-insurance of $97 is usually covered by private insurance—if you have it. For nursing-home care not covered by Medicare, you must use your private assets, or Medicaid if your assets run out, which happens to approximately one-third of nursing-home residents. Long-term-care insurance may also cover some of the costs.

•**Hospice care** About $100 a day for in-home care. Medicare covers hospice care to patients who have a life expectancy of less than six months. (See Hospice: The Comfort Team.) Such care may be provided at home, in a hospice facility, a hospital, or a nursing-home. Patients may be asked to pay up to $5 for each prescription and a 5 percent co-pay for in-patient respite care, which is a short hospital stay to relieve caregivers. Medicaid covers hospice care in all but six states, even for those without Medicare.

About 60 percent of full-time employees of medium and large firms also have coverage for hospice services, but the benefits vary widely.

•**Home care without hospice services** Medicare Part A pays the full cost of medical home health care for up to 100 visits following a hospital stay of at least three days. Medicare Part B covers home health-care visits beyond those 100 visits or without a hospital stay. To qualify, the patient must be homebound, require skilled nursing care or physical or speech therapy, be under a physician's care, and use services from a Medicare-participating home-health agency. Note that this coverage is for medical care only; hired help for personal nonmedical services, such as that often required by Alzheimer's patients, is not covered by Medicare. It is covered by Medicaid in some states.

A major financial disadvantage of dying at home without hospice is that Medicare does not cover out-patient prescription drugs, even those for pain. Medicaid does cover these drugs, but often with restrictions on their price and quantity. Private insurance can fill the gap to some extent. Long-term-care insurance may cover payments to family caregivers who have to stop work to care for a dying patient, but this type of coverage is very rare.

Resources

MEDICAL CARE

For information about pain relief and symptom management: **Supportive Care of the Dying** (503-215-5053; careofdying.org).

For a comprehensive guide to living with the medical, emotional, and spiritual aspects of dying:

Handbook for Mortals by Joanne Lynn and Joan Harrold, Oxford University Press.

For a 24-hour hotline offering counseling, pain management, downloadable advance directives, and more:

The Partnership for Caring (800-989-9455; www.partnershipforcaring.org).

EMOTIONAL CARE

To find mental-health counselors with an emphasis on lifespan human development and spiritual discussion:
American Counseling Association (800-347-6647; counseling.org).

For disease-related support groups and general resources for caregivers:
Caregiver Survival Resources (caregiver911.com).

For AARP's online caregiver support chatroom, access **America Online** every Wednesday night, 8:30–9:30 EST (keyword: AARP).

Education and advocacy for family caregivers:
National Family Caregivers Association (800-896-3650; nfcacares.org).

For the booklet,
Understanding the Grief Process (D16832, EEO143C), e-mail order with title and numbers to member@aarp.org or send postcard to AARP Fulfillment, 601 E St NW, Washington DC 20049. Please allow two to four weeks for delivery.

To find a volunteer to help with supportive services to the frail and their caregivers:
National Federation of Interfaith Volunteer Caregivers (816-931-5442; nfivc.org).

For information on support to partners of the chronically ill and/or the disabled:
The Well Spouse Foundation (800-838-0879; www.wellspouse.org).

LEGAL HELP

AARP members are entitled to a free half-hour of legal advice with a lawyer from **AARP's Legal Services Network**. (800-424-3410; www.aarp.org/lsn).

For **Planning for Incapacity**, a guide to advance directives in your state, send $5 to Legal Counsel for the Elderly, Inc., PO Box 96474, Washington DC 20090-6474. Make out check to LCE Inc.

For a **Caring Conversations** booklet on advance-directive discussion:
Midwest Bioethics Center (816-221-1100; midbio.org).

For information on care at the end of life, online discussion groups, conferences:
Last Acts Campaign (800-844-7616; lastacts.org).

HOSPICE

To learn about end-of-life care options and grief issues through videotapes, books, newsletters, and brochures:
Hospice Foundation of America (800-854-3402; hospice-foundation.org).

For information on hospice programs, FAQs, and general facts about hospice:
National Hospice and Palliative Care Organization (800-658-8898; nhpco.org).

For **All About Hospice: A Consumer's Guide** (202-546-4759; www.hospice-america.org).

FINANCIAL HELP

For **Organizing Your Future**, a simple guide to end-of-life financial decisions, send $5 to Legal Counsel for the Elderly, Inc., PO Box 96474, Washington DC 20090-6474. Make out check to LCE Inc.

For **Medicare and You 2000** and a **2000 Guide to Health Insurance for People With Medicare** (800-MEDICARE [633-4227]; medicare.gov).

To find your State Agency on Aging: **Administration on Aging, U.S. Department of Health and Human Services** (800-677-1116; aoa.dhhs.gov).

GENERAL

For information on end-of-life planning and bereavement: (www.aarp.org/endoflife/).

For health professionals and others who want to start conversations on end-of-life issues in their community:
Discussion Guide: On Our Own Terms: Moyers on Dying, based on the PBS series, airing September 10–13. The guide provides essays, instructions, and contacts. From PBS, www.pbs.org/onourownterms Or send a postcard request to On Our Own Terms Discussion Guide, Thirteen/WNET New York, PO Box 245, Little Falls, NJ 07424-9766.

Funded with a grant from The Robert Wood Johnson Foundation, Princeton, N.J. *Editor* Amy Gross; *Writer* Louise Lague; *Designer* David Herbick

Reprinted from *AARP Modern Maturity*, September/October 2000. © 2000 by American Association for Retired Persons (AARP).

UNIT 4

Relating to Others

Unit Selections

Key Points to Consider

- What is a friend? Do friendships change as we mature? How so? What kinds of people attract us to them? How is mental health related to friendship? What is happening to today's adult friendships?

- What is emotional intelligence? How does it develop? How can we tell if we possess it? How do people with EQ differ from people without it? Do you have EQ? If not, can you do anything to cultivate it? Explain.

- What is empathy? Why is it important? Can empathy be nurtured in children? How? Is empathy the same as EQ?

- Why is the face important to emotional expression and social interactions? Does face perception occur the same way object perception does? How do researchers study the face and emotionality? Why is it important for lay persons to understand the emotions and moods of others?

- How do you feel when you know that someone has lied to or deceived you? Can you spot a liar? How? Are faces the best key to detecting a deceit? Are humans the only creatures who use deception? How do other organisms use and detect deception?

 **Links: www.dushkin.com/online/**
These sites are annotated in the World Wide Web pages.

CYFERNET-Youth Development
http://www.cyfernet.mes.umn.edu/youthdev.html

Hypermedia, Literature, and Cognitive Dissonance
http://www.engr.ncsu.edu/TDE_Workshop/1997/abstracts/gingher.html

Emotional Intelligence Discovery
http://www.cwrl.utexas.edu/~bump/Hu305/3/3/3/

The Personality Project
http://www.personality-project.org/personality.html

P eople can be seen everywhere in groups: couples in love, parents and their children, teachers and students, gatherings of friends, church groups, theatergoers. People have much influence on one another when they congregate in groups.

Groups spend a great deal of time communicating with members and nonmembers. The communication can be intentional and forceful, such as when protesters demonstrate against a totalitarian regime in a far-off land. Or communication can be more subtle, for example, when fraternity brothers secretly reject a prospective brother who does not "fit in" as well as they feel he should.

In some groups, the reason a leader emerges is clear—perhaps the most skilled individual in the group is elected by the group members. In other groups, for example, during a spontaneous nightclub fire, the qualities of the rapidly emerging, perhaps self-appointed, leader are less apparent. Nonetheless, the followers flee unquestioningly in the leader's direction. Even in dating couples, one person may seem to lead or be dominant over the other.

Some groups, such as formalized business corporations, issue official rules; discipline for rule breaking is also formalized. Other groups, families or trios of friends, for example, possess fewer and less formalized rules and disciplinary codes, but their rules are still quickly learned by and are important to all unit members.

Some groups are large but seek more members, such as nationwide labor unions. Other groups seek to keep their groups small and somewhat exclusive, such as teenage cliques. Groups exist that are almost completely adversarial with other groups. Conflict between youth gangs is a good example. Other groups pride themselves on their ability to remain cooperative, such as neighbors who band together in a community crime watch.

Psychologists are so convinced that interpersonal relationships are important to the human experience that they have intensively studied them. There is ample evidence that contact with other people is a necessary part of human existence. Research has shown that most individuals do not like being isolated from other people. In fact, in laboratory experiments in which participants experience total isolation for extended periods, they begin to hallucinate the presence of others. In prisons, solitary confinement is often used as a form of punishment because of its aversive effect. Other research has shown that people who must wait under stressful circumstances prefer to wait with others, even if the others are total strangers, rather than wait alone.

This unit examines smaller and therefore fairly interpersonal relationships, such as those among friends, dating partners, and married couples. The next unit examines the effects of larger groups, specifically, society at large.

The first article provides a general introduction to the unit. In "Got Time for Friends?" Andy Steiner discusses why friendship is vitally important and how childhood friendships differ from adult friendships. Steiner says that too many adults neglect friendships when friendships are so beneficial to our emotional and physical health.

In the next two articles various factors that color our relationships are discussed. The first reviews a fairly new and important concept—emotional intelligence or EQ. Emotional intelligence relates to our ability to get along with and be sensitive to other people's needs and emotions. In fact, there exists research that indicates that EQ may be more predictive of our life trajectory than IQ, or intelligence.

A related article concerns empathy, the ability to vicariously experience someone else's emotions. Parents who wish to promote empathy in their children may want to read "Nurturing Empathy."

An important avenue to understanding others' emotions, moods, and behaviors is to watch their faces. In "Faces of Perception," author Bruce Bower discusses how to "read" faces and therefore know more about others. He explains the science behind face perception.

Another concept related to the importance of the face is the ability to detect deception on the part of others. In "How to Spot a Liar," James Geary examines how nature has provided various species with a way for members to deceive others. Similarly, nature usually also provides clues that point to these very same deceptions in order to help the deceived detect the delusion. In the human, the face is one of the best lie detectors.

While those with EQ, empathy, and the ability to read others thrive in social situations, others are not so fortunate. Shyness overwhelms them and sometimes prevents them from making and keeping friends. The research of psychologist Bernardo Carducci on shyness or social anxiety and how to overcome it is explained in "Shy Squared."

The next few articles are about special types of interpersonal relationships, especially romantic ones. In "Revealing Personal Secrets" the author discloses why and when we tell others our secrets. The article would not be complete, though, without reference to the secrets we decide to keep to ourselves and why. We then cover some very close and intimate interpersonal relationships. "Welcome to the Love Lab" is an article that discusses research by renowned expert John Gottman (with coauthor Sybil Carrere). Gottman contends that he can detect which romantic relationships are headed for trouble even at their beginning.

In a companion piece, "Prescription for Passion," the author discusses jealousy, an emotion that can signal problems in a romantic relationship. David Buss takes the approach that jealousy is normal and, interestingly, might in fact hold couples together rather than drive them apart.

Finally, when jealousy, deception, or some other negative aspect of a relationship has turned it sour, forgiveness may be the solution. Michael McCullough, the author of "Forgiveness: Who Does It and How Do They Do It?" presents research on forgiveness. He tells us which people easily forgive others and which people cannot and why.

Got time for Friends?

Sure, you're busy. But are you paying attention to what's really important?
Why finding—and keeping—friends is the key to a happy life.

BY ANDY STEINER

It's not the last time my daughter will make me look foolish, but it was one of the first. Maybe it was silly to take a toddler to an art opening, but there we were, the effervescent Astrid and her uptight mama. As I hovered near her, hoping to intercept toppling *objets d'art*, Astrid spotted Claire across the room.

Maybe their attraction was predestined, since Claire and Astrid, 18 and 16 months respectively, were the only under-three-footers in what to them must have looked like a sea of kneecaps. Still, Astrid's eyes lit up when she saw young Claire, and she turned on the charm, hopping and squealing and running in some strange kiddie ritual. Claire squealed back, Astrid flashed her tummy, and that was it: They were fast friends.

The culture-at-large tells us that once school is over or we hit 30, friendship ought to take a backseat to more pressing concerns.

It wasn't so easy for Claire's mother and me. When our kids started making nice, we smiled politely, and as the junior friendship heated up, we attempted shy (on my part at least) and distracted attempts at conversation. "How old is she?" I asked. "What's her name?" she countered. I'd like to say that today Claire's mommy is a good friend, but that's not the case. We continued to exchange pleasantries while our daughters pranced around together, but when our partners appeared, we picked up our squirmy squirts and said good-bye. We haven't seen each other since. Too bad, because I could have used a new friend. Who couldn't?

In college, and for several years after, I was immersed in a warm circle of friends, the kind of exciting and exotic people I'd spent my small-town youth dreaming about. These friends came to my college from around the world, and after graduation, many of them stayed. We had a great time. We went to movies—and for a bit created our own monthly film group. We gathered at each other's apartments to cook big dinners and stay up late, sharing our opinions on music, sex, and dreams. We even took a few trips together—to a friend's wedding in the mountains of Colorado and to a cabin on the edge of a loon-covered lake. But time passes, and as these friends moved on, got married, or found great jobs, my gang of compatriots began to dwindle.

"We cannot tell the precise moment when friendship is formed. As in filling a vessel drop by drop, there is at last a drop which makes it run over; so in a series of kindnesses there is at last one which makes the heart run over."

Samuel Johnson

Now many of them have moved to other states—other countries, even. Though a precious core group still lives within shouting distance, I worry that grown-up life will soon scatter them all and I'll be left, lonely and missing them.

So it goes for many of us as we leave our youth behind and face "real" life. While generations of young adults have probably felt the same way, the yearning for close friends takes on a greater sense of urgency now as modern life makes our lives busier and more fragmented. "It's not that it's so hard to make friends when you're older," says sociologist Jan Yager, author of *Friendshifts*, "but making friends—and finding time to maintain and nurture old friendships as well as new ones—is just one of the many concerns that occupy your time."

Astrid's encounter with Claire (and my parallel one with her mother) cast a spotlight on one reality: Kids see potential friends everywhere. Adults, on the other hand, have a harder time of it, especially as we (and our potential friends) enter the realm of romantic commitments, full-time jobs, motherhood and fatherhood. While we may wish to add to our collection of friends, we feel too busy, too consumed by other obligations, too caught up in everyday bustle to make time to help a friendship blossom and grow.

> *"Be a friend to thyself, and others will befriend thee."*
>
> **English proverb**

And we may be following subtle clues from the culture-at-large telling us that, once school is over or we near 30, friendship ought to take a back seat to more pressing concerns. Despite the central role that idealized gangs of pals play on sitcoms, our primary sources of information—self-help books, magazines, and personal interest TV shows—rarely talk about how to get—or keep—friends. Instead they barrage us with detailed advice on how to attract a lover, get ahead in a career, rekindle a marriage, or keep peace in the family. Friendships, unlike these other kinds of relationships, are supposed to just happen, with little effort on your part. But what if they don't?

"Friends can get relegated to secondary status," says Aurora Sherman, assistant professor of psychology at Brandeis University. "Even if you don't have children or a partner or aging parents, the pressures of adult responsibility can force people to place friendship in the background."

> *"All I can do is to urge you to put friendship ahead of all other human concerns, for there is nothing so suited to man's nature, nothing that can mean so much to him, whether in good times or in bad... I am inclined to think that with the exception of wisdom, the gods have given nothing finer to men than this."*
>
> **Marcus Tullius Cicero**

Children's full-scale focus on friendship may have to do with more than just their carefree attitude about life. Sherman cites the research theorizing that kids' interest in making friends serves a larger developmental purpose.

"A young person's primary motivation for social interaction is to get information and to learn about the world," Sherman explains. "When you're a kid, practically everybody that you meet has the potential to help you learn about something that you didn't know." Grown-ups already know most things (or at least they think they do), so as you get older, you may feel less of a drive to make new friends.

So, if you're someone who embraces the goal of lifelong learning, it's important not to write off friendship as a thing of the past. Meeting new people is a lot less work than going back to college for another degree, and more fun, too. Want to learn yoga or steep yourself in South American culture? How about sharpening your skills as an entrepreneur or activist? Think outside the classroom by finding someone eager to show what they know. An added benefit is that you, too, can share your passion about knitting or bocce ball or radical history. If the people you currently hang out with don't know much about the things you want to know, maybe it's time to break into some new circles.

> *"The proper office of a friend is to side with you when you are in the wrong. Nearly anybody will side with you when you are in the right."*
>
> **Mark Twain**

The tangible rewards of friendship go far beyond exchanges of information. In 1970 Lenny Dee left New York and moved across the country to Portland, Oregon, where he knew barely a soul. "The first week I was there I met probably half the people who became my lifelong friends," says Dee. "It was like I walked through this magic door and a whole world opened up for me." Within a day of his arrival, he had moved into a house that was an epicenter of the city's alternative culture. He could barely step out of the house without running into one of his new friends.

"At one point in my life all of the people I knew were footloose and fancy free," Dee says, "but over the years that changed. A certain segment of my friends in Portland became more settled while I remained less settled. People got families and jobs, and they started disappearing. Now you have to make an appointment to get together."

Still, Dee has been vigilant in nurturing old friendships; people all across the country can count on a birthday phone call from Portland. "I have always thought you could invest your energies in making money or making friends," Dee says, "and they achieve much the same ends—security, new experiences, personal options, travel, and so forth. I have always found it more fulfilling to make friends."

And Dee's life has been shaped in many ways by the enduring connections he's maintained, including a key position at the start-up of a now successful educational software company and a recent vacation in Corsica at the summer home of an old Portland friend who now lives in Paris.

A slew of recent research supports Dee's example that friends make life complete.

"As hard as it is with everyone so busy and consumed with the day-to-day workings of their lives, it's important to understand that making and maintaining friendships is really pivotal to social, emotional, and physical well-being," says Yager. She ticks off research that touts the value of building strong nonfamilial bonds, including: an in-depth study of thousands of Northern California residents that revealed that having ties to at least one close friend extends a person's life, and another study of 257 human resource managers that discovered adults who have friends at work report not only higher productivity but also higher workplace satisfaction.

When you know who his friend is, you know who he is.
Senegal proverb

For New York psychotherapist Kathlyn Conway, a three-time cancer survivor and author of the memoir *An Ordinary Life*, friends provided an anchor during times when she felt her life was drifting off course.

"I had friends I could talk to at any time," Conway says of her 1993 battle with breast cancer. "If I was upset, it was easy for me to call someone and expect them to listen—no matter what."

And when the busy mother of two needed physical help, friends came to her aid. "One friend went to the hospital after my mastectomy and helped me wash my hair," Conway recalled in an article she wrote for the women's cancer magazine *Mamm*. "Another, who herself had had breast cancer, visited and stealthily, humorously, kindly opened her blouse to show me her implanted breast in order to reassure me. Yet another left her very busy job in the middle of the week to go shopping with me for a wig."

One time when adults tend to make new friends is during major life changes, like a move, a new job, or the birth of a child. Ellen Goodman and Patricia O'Brien, authors of *I Know Just What You Mean*, a book chronicling their quarter-century friendship, met in 1973 when both were completing Neiman fellowships at Harvard. At the time, Goodman, now a nationally syndicated newspaper columnist, and O'Brien, a novelist and former editorial writer for the *Chicago Sun-Times*, were both newly divorced mothers in their 30s.

"We were both broke and busy and we were not at all alike—at least on the surface," Goodman recalls, "but we bonded, maybe out of some sense of great urgency, and during that year we spent an enormous amount of time in Harvard Square, drinking coffee and talking. We missed a lot of classes, but those times together were some of the best seminars either of us ever attended."

"Life shifts—like a divorce or an illness or another unexpected change—can occur at any time, and when that happens, there's always this powerful draw to another person who's going through the same thing," O'Brien says. "For Ellen and me there was this wonderful opportunity to talk to another woman who was hitting the same bumps in the road as we were. We could talk for hours and always understand what the other person was saying." After the short spell at Harvard, they never again lived in the same place but kept the friendship going with letters, phone calls, and frequent visits.

Three is the magic number

When it comes to making friends, there's much we can learn from kids about flashing a wide grin and harboring a playful spirit. But Stanford University psychology professor Laura Carstensen emphasizes that an important lesson also comes from the over-65 set. In studying senior citizens' social networks, she has found that "it is the *quality* of their relationships that matters—not the *quantity*. In our work we find that three is the critical friend number. If you have three people in your life that you can really count on, then you are doing as well as someone who has 10 friends. Or 20, for that matter. If you have fewer than three friends, then you could be a little precarious."

So sit down, get out a piece of paper, and start listing your friends. Got three folks you're always excited about seeing and feel certain you can trust? Then put down the pencil. Who says you can't put a number on success?

—Andy Steiner

Awhile back—inspired by my daughter's happy, open face and ready giggle—I resolved that making new friends might be just the cure for the post-baby blahs I was experiencing.

So I set my sights on one particular woman. Even though I have wonderful old friends, people I wouldn't trade for a billion dollars, this particular woman caught my eye. She seemed smart and funny. We were both writers. I'd heard that she lived in my neighborhood. Then, the kicker: Someone we both knew suggested that we would hit it off. So I called her—out of the blue—and invited her to coffee. Sure, she said. So we met.

Just the other day, this woman told me that at the time she wondered about my motivation, this strange, nervously enthusiastic young woman who peppered her with questions about writing and reading and her impressions of the university we'd both attended, she as an undergraduate, I as a master's student. Still, a few weeks later she took me up on my invitation to go for a walk, and our conversation soon became natural and fun. Suddenly, she became my new friend.

Astrid, riding in her stroller, witnessed it all. Besides babbling and napping, she was watching closely as my new friend and I laughed and told the stories of our lives. Taking a risk and extending yourself is one way to form a bond with someone. We weren't squealing or flashing our tummies, but it was close.

Andy Steiner, mother of gregarious Astrid, is a senior editor of Utne Reader.

Reprinted with permission from *Utne Reader*, September/October 2001, pp. 67-71. © 2001 by Utne Reader. To subscribe, call 800-736-UTNE or visit our website at www.utne.com.

What's your emotional IQ?

Emotional intelligence can affect your mental and physical health,
as well as those around you.

Melissa Abramovitz

On March 5, 2001, 15-year-old Andy Williams brought a 22-caliber pistol to school at Santana High School in Santee, California. With a smile on his face, he used the gun to kill two students and injure 13 other people. When later asked why he did it, Williams revealed that he'd had enough of his schoolmates' teasing, taunting, and ostracism because he was small and scrawny.

Some of Williams' friends reported that, prior to the shooting, the boy frequently drank alcohol and used illegal drugs. He also made repeated threats to shoot students at the school, but no one took these threats seriously. "I didn't think he was like that," said one boy who had laughed off Williams' promises to kill others.

Both Andy Williams' horrific act and his friends' lack of insight into his true intentions and feelings are frightening examples of how the lack of emotional intelligence can have disastrous consequences. Williams' inability to cope productively with his feelings of anger and rejection led him to endanger himself and others with drugs and violence. In a similar manner, his friends' unwillingness or inability to detect the desperation in his threats prevented them from stopping him from carrying out his deadly plans.

WHAT IS EI?

Emotional intelligence, or EI, is similar to cerebral intelligence, except that it involves awareness and insight into emotions rather than into other mental functions. Emotional IQ, also known as EQ (emotional quotient), refers to measurements of an individual's ability to understand and manage his or her emotions and interpersonal relationships.

Although many of the ideas related to EI and EQ were originally applied to business and leadership skills, these concepts are also relevant to everyday living and health. EI and EQ affect many aspects of an individual's mental and physical well-being, as well as the ability to get along with others, to make wise lifestyle choices, and to succeed in school, athletics, careers, and other areas.

Recent studies indicate that programs which seek to prevent violence, teen smoking, drug abuse, pregnancy, and dropping out of school are most effective when they address the elements of emotional intelligence. Indeed, according to the Center for the Advancement of Health in Washington, D.C., "Nearly half of the nation's premature deaths are attributable to controllable behavioral factors, such as using tobacco, alcohol, and illegal substances and engaging in risky sex." The center concludes that to be effective, a program must integrate behavioral and psychological perspectives with biomedical interventions.

Experts say that developing emotional intelligence can help you avoid both short-term injury risks and long-term illnesses such as heart disease, liver disease, and some cancers. These hazards are often a result of substance abuse and other dangerous lifestyle choices that go along with out-of-control emotional stress. Says Jan Wallender, Ph.D., "The way we feel and think and relate to others definitely has an impact on our biology, our health, and our disease experience."

THE ELEMENTS OF EI

Daniel Goleman, Ph.D., a well-known psychologist, has written extensively on the subject of EI and has identified five basic elements: self-awareness, managing emotions, motivating oneself, empathy, and social skills. Goleman and other EI experts point out that these elements are not automatically set in stone at birth, but instead can be learned and improved upon throughout a person's lifetime. Accordingly, many schools and businesses now offer EI training programs to help students and employees learn about and master these five aspects of dealing effectively with everyday challenges to emotional stability.

1. Self-awareness refers to the ability to recognize and identify your feelings. The EI experts emphasize that it's important to be able to recognize emotions such as anger or love in order to act appropriately. Bullies, for example, generally do not recognize their own feelings of insecurity or unhappiness and behave aggressively toward others as a result. One way that everyone can improve self-awareness is to verbalize emotions rather than ignore them. If you're angry, say "I'm angry" and explain why. If you're frightened, admit it, at least to yourself. Trying to appear tough and invincible at all times is OK only for legendary superheroes who don't have to live with their emotions the way real people do.

2. Managing your emotions involves using techniques for handling all sorts of feelings in a productive and appropriate manner. If your best friend suddenly informs you she has a new best friend, for example, most likely you will feel hurt, angry, and jealous. If you don't manage these emotions wisely, you might do something that you would probably regret. By effectively managing your emotions, though, hopefully you could take a deep breath, count to 10, control your desire to tell her off, and muster the strength to say something like, "I'm sorry you made that choice. I value our friendship and hope we can discuss this sometime."

3. Motivating oneself builds on managing your emotions to the extent that you can delay the immediate gratification of an impulse and can maintain a positive outlook. Studies show that individuals who are able to restrain themselves from immediately fulfilling a desire are more optimistic and successful in school, athletics, careers, and interpersonal relationships. This is due in part to using self-restraint, which is an important indicator of how someone responds to challenges. If you flunk a math test and say, "I'll never pass math, so I'm going to quit going to class," you will definitely not improve your math skills. If, however, you realize that going for tutoring can help you do better in the future, you have a good chance of passing the course and of applying these perseverance skills to other areas of your life.

4. Empathy is being sensitive to and understanding other people's feelings. Some individuals seem to have a natural ability to empathize, but this, like the other elements of EI, can be learned. To hone your empathy skills, try "putting yourself in someone else's shoes" and asking yourself how you would feel in his or her situation. Another useful technique is to focus on "reading" people's facial expressions and other body cues to gauge their true feelings. For example, observing the face and body language of a guy who says "I'm not scared"—yet exhibits wide-eyed terror and hunches his shoulders forward—will help you realize that this guy is definitely scared.

5. Social skills refers to an individuals's ability to interact with others in a positive and productive manner. Actually, if you do your homework on the other four elements of EI and master those concepts, you should be in pretty good shape in the social skills department. People who are self-aware, successfully manage their emotions, are motivated, and are able to empathize are generally quite adept in social situations.

TEST YOUR EMOTIONAL IQ

How would you deal with these emotional intelligence issues?

1. After a classmate dies in a car accident, you
   a. tell yourself it couldn't happen to you.
   b. realize you are feeling intense fear and sadness.
2. You've just been offered a beer at a party. Your friend Jamie says you're a wuss if you don't chug it. You don't want to be a wuss, so you
   a. drink the beer.
   b. politely refuse since you promised your parents there would be no alcohol at the party.
3. When you feel depressed, you
   a. cry and feel sorry for yourself.
   b. try to find a positive distraction like volunteering at a homeless shelter.
4. Your best friend just got dumped by his girlfriend. You
   a. tell him it doesn't matter.
   b. understand he's feeling depressed and encourage him to talk about it.
5. You hardly know anyone on your new hockey team. You
   a. request a transfer to a team where you know more people.
   b. look forward to getting to know the new people.

How did you do?
If you answered with a's, your emotional IQ needs some work. You are having trouble recognizing and managing your own emotions and recognizing other people's emotions. If you chose mostly b's, it means your emotional IQ is way up there! You are most likely successfully recognizing and managing your emotions and have good interpersonal relationships skills.

HOW EI AFFECTS THE WORLD

While emotional intelligence is certainly not a cure-all for the ills that exist in the world, it is an important factor in many global and personal issues. Road rage, child and spousal abuse, and school shootings are just a few of the serious problems in our society that raising people's EI can address. Experts point out that children and teens are especially vulnerable to the dangers of what psychologists call "emotional malaise." To combat this problem, many schools are including emotional-awareness training in their programs.

You alone have the power to improve your emotional intelligence with practice and effort. And becoming aware of your emotional intelligence can be beneficial not only to your own health and happiness, but it can also help make the world a more civilized and peaceful place.

FOR REVIEW

1. Define emotional intelligence. (It is similar to cerebral intelligence, except it involves awareness and insight into emotions rather than other mental functions. EQ is a measure of an individual's ability to understand and manage his or her emotions and interpersonal relationships.)

2. Summarize the five elements of emotional intelligence. (They include self-awareness—the ability to recognize and identify your feelings; managing emotions—using techniques for handling all sorts of feelings in a productive and appropriate manner; motivating oneself—ability to manage your emotions well enough to be able to delay immediate gratification of an impulse and to maintain a positive outlook; empathy—being sensitive to and understanding other people's feelings; and having social skills—the ability to interact with others in a positive, productive manner.)

ACTIVITY

Based on the five elements of emotional intelligence in the article, have students work in groups of three or four to write a skit in which a fellow student demonstrates a fairly low emotional intelligence. Have them act out the skits for the class and allow them to critique and make observations on the EI of the characters as they saw it. Then allow the authors of each skit to rewrite it to demonstrate improved EI skills.

From *Current Health 2,* December 2001, p. 1. © 2001 by Weekly Reader Corporation. Reprinted by permission.

nurturing
empathy

How seeing the world through another's eyes not only makes a child compassionate but helps him learn right from wrong

BY JULIA GLASS

On mellow summer evenings, my neighbor Holly Lance and I used to get our 2-year-old sons together outside for "run them bone tired" playdates. One evening, as they were sprinting and cavorting with typical pinball momentum, Holly's son, Stefan, burst into tears. Holding his elbow in obvious pain, he collapsed in his mother's arms. My son approached his inconsolable playmate with a look of alarm. He watched Stefan cry for a few seconds, then walked to a nearby wall, bumped his head against it, and erupted into sobs to rival Stefan's.

I had never seen Alec do anything so peculiar. Was he trying to upstage his friend? It was Holly who said, "What a sweet thing to do!" And then I saw that Alec had clearly been attempting—if somewhat clownishly—to comfort someone he loved. I'd long since begun to encourage Alec's verbal, physical, and musical abilities, but what about his emotional abilities? Should I be nurturing this flair for compassion? I wondered.

"At its simplest, empathy means feeling the same thing another person's feeling; at its most sophisticated, it's understanding his entire life situation," says Martin Hoffman, Ph.D., professor of psychology at New York University and author of *Empathy and Moral Development: Implications for Caring and Justice.*

It's empathy that leads us, as adults, not just to help out friends and family but also to stop for a driver stranded by the side of the road, point a bewildered tourist in the right direction, even water a thirsty tree. Without it, our species would probably be extinct, says Hoffman. It is also a key to moral internalization—our children's increasing ability, as they grow, to make decisions by themselves that weigh others' needs and desires against their own.

The root of empathy is linking what an emotion feels like for you with what it feels like for others.

Given the importance of this attribute, here's how to recognize empathy's earliest signs and encourage it to blossom.

Born to Connect

There you are squeezing melons in the produce aisle, your 1-year-old babbling blissfully away, when a baby over in the snack-foods section starts to wail. All too predictably, so does yours. Experts believe that such copycat grief may be an emotional reflex that helps "train" our nature toward a more genuine form of compassion.

"The root of empathy is being able to recognize a link between what it feels like for you to be in a particular emotional state and what that feels like for another person, and it looks as if we're born with a primitive form of that kind of identification," says Alison Gopnik, Ph.D., a psychology professor at the University of California at Berkeley and coauthor of *The Scientist in the Crib.* "Even within an hour of birth, babies will try to make the same facial expression they see someone else making." Over the next few months, infants strive to coordinate their gestures and vocalizations as well as their expressions with those of adults around them.

At about 9 months, a baby begins to pay attention to how others feel about things. Confronted with an unfamiliar object—a toy robot or pureed squash—he'll instantly look at Mom to read her take. If she looks apprehensive, he'll hold back; if she looks pleased, he'll probably dive right in. While this reveals a new depth of perception, it also shows that babies have yet to grasp the most fundamental principle of civilized society: Each of us is a separate being with individual proclivities and feelings. You can't comprehend the feelings of another person until you grasp the concept that there is such a thing as another person.

You Are You, I Am I: Discovering Others

"For most of the first year, babies are pretty confused about what's going on around them," says Hoffman. "If they see another baby fall down and need comfort from his mother, they'll cry and need comfort too."

About midway through the second year, most toddlers begin to recognize themselves in a mirror— seeing themselves as unique, distinct objects. They now see other people as separate—but only physically. They have yet to learn that different people have different inner states as well. So when one toddler sees another in distress, her instinct is to fetch her own mother rather than her playmate's, to placate the child with her own favorite toy. She'll recognize the suffering as belonging to someone else but can't imagine any appropriate remedy other than the one that would suit her. This impulse is one of the most common early signs of what we recognize as genuine empathy, and it may continue even after kids gain a greater sense of what makes other people tick.

When 4-year-old Shai Karp's mother was rushed to the hospital for an appendectomy, he went along and sat with her as she was being checked in for surgery. "He'd brought his favorite stuffed animal, Tumby—short for the 'tumble dry low' on its label," says his mother, Judy

Wilner. "As I sat there, feeling miserable, Shai insisted I keep Tumby with me that night."

---

3 empathy busters

"Empathy is innate, but you can stunt its development," says psychologist Martin Hoffman, Ph.D. Try not to:

Overindulge. Just as an authoritative, "because I said so" style of parenting may prevent children from understanding the whys and wherefores of considerate behavior, so may overly permissive parenting. Kids raised without enough limits may come to feel very entitled—and entitlement, which focuses on the self, is anything but empathic.

Smother. Empathizing with another's strong feelings sometimes requires keeping a respectful distance, especially when a child needs to retreat for a time with a difficult emotion, such as shame or guilt. Resist the urge to try to protect kids from such strong emotions.

Stress competition. "In middle-class America, consideration of others is valued very highly," says Hoffman, "but so is individual achievement." For the first few years of life, those two values rarely collide; mothers may compare kids' developmental milestones, for instance, but such competition takes place mainly between parents. Come the school years, that changes.

"If a kid does excel, it's normal to feel some empathic distress for friends who don't do as well," says Hoffman, but many parents just want their kids to feel good about succeeding and don't acknowledge their empathy. Likewise, students who perform poorly need a more compassionate response than a dose of tutoring and a well-meant "You'll do better next time." The competition won't go away; what's important is to recognize its dark side and discuss how it affects your child's feelings toward peers.

Somewhat ironically, the age at which this type of generosity arises is exactly when, behaviorally speaking, the Tubby custard hits the fan. Because just as toddlers are trying to learn how to make other people feel better, they're also learning how to make other people—most notably, their parents—feel decidedly worse. And it's not just, as I used to think, that Mother Nature throws in these random adorable moments to pacify our rage; the two tendencies are closely intertwined.

The Altruistic Twos?

Toward the end of the second year, children begin to understand that other people have thoughts, feelings, and wants different from their own—often through a process of trial and error. When a toddler trying to comfort his friend sees that his own favorite toy doesn't do the trick, he'll try the friend's favorite toy instead or he'll fetch the friend's mom.

Preschoolers begin to perceive subtler feelings, such as that a classmate may be sad because he misses his parents.

This stage marks a primitive but true form of empathy, says Hoffman, one when children not only start to recognize the different experiences of other people but also, when necessary, reach out to them. "Empathy isn't just a feeling; it's a motive," he stresses. Whether we're throwing a bridal shower or helping a friend cope with a death in the family, empathy spurs us to partake in someone else's experience. We don't always act on the urge, but when we do, it often makes us feel good.

This eventful early age is also a period of intensive experimenting to find out what makes people different from one another. "It's around age two that we begin to see children perform these lovely altruistic acts—and do things precisely because we don't want them to," says Gopnik. "The same impulse that leads a child to think, 'Mom's crying, I'm not; I can comfort her,' also leads to 'Mom doesn't want me to touch that lamp; I can touch that lamp, I'm going to touch it.' If you think about what we want to encourage—understanding how other people feel—the 'terrible twos' is a part of that." (For more on promoting this understanding, see "Encouraging Compassion.")

Toward a More Mature Compassion

From this point on, children refine and enlarge their perspective on other people's inner lives. In the preschool years, says Hoffman, they begin to perceive more subtle, removed feelings—such as that a classmate may be sad because he misses his parents. They also learn that a single event can lead to different reactions from different people. Sometime between ages 5 and 8—having grasped their own gender and ethnic identity—they begin to look at each person around them as having a distinct personal history and to consider its influences on that person's experiences and feelings. "They also start to see how having different personalities makes people react differently, and they begin to take that into account when dealing with people," adds Gopnik.

Children are now on the threshold of what Hoffman says is a highly sophisticated form of empathy—empathy for another's experience beyond the immediate situation, a skill that we work on for the rest of our lives. They can

encouraging compassion

"Showing affection to kids helps them feel secure and loved," says psychologist Hoffman, "and that contributes to their ability to feel consideration for others. Being a model of empathy—actively helping others—is also important." Beyond these fairly obvious gestures, you can encourage compassion if you:

•**Discipline in ways that invoke natural empathy.** By the end of the second year, scoldings constitute some two-thirds of all parent-child interactions, says Hoffman. And much of the offending behavior involves situations in which the child hurts or upsets someone else.

When your child is the transgressor, it's important not just to let him know he was wrong but also to be specific about the consequences of his actions. Saying, "You made me angry when you poured your milk on the table because now I have to mop it up and we don't have any more" or "You hurt his feelings when you grabbed that airplane—how would you feel if he grabbed it from you?" is an essential step toward making a child feel both guilt for the behavior and responsibility for how other people feel. In time, the ability to anticipate that guilt can motivate kids to "do the right thing."

•**Encourage conciliatory gestures.** Ask your child to apologize or give the person he hurt a hug, pat, or kiss.

•**Don't stifle his emotions.** Adults may try too quickly to "fix" a child's bad feelings—to distract him from sadness with treats, negotiate to thwart his anger, or otherwise derail an emotion that may help teach him the less pleasant aspect of human nature. This doesn't mean you have to accept misbehavior in the name of letting your child "feel"; part of learning to be empathic is learning that we can't act on every emotion we have.

•**Make feelings a topic of discussion.** When you see other people in different situations, ask your child to imagine what those people might be feeling. And don't limit yourself to real life. Talk about your child's emotional response to books, TV shows, and videos.

•**Revel in role-playing games.** "They let kids feel what it's like to be somebody else—a daddy, a baby," says psychologist Alison Gopnik, Ph.D. "That's important to empathy. When my son was three, I'd say, 'I'm going to be Alexei, and you be Mommy.' I'd be difficult and carry on, and he'd say things like 'You can't do that! It's going to be a big mess and I'm going to have to clean it up!' It was a great way to work out some of our conflicts."—J.G.

see that some people have generally happy or sad lives, and they can begin to empathize with entire groups of people (the homeless, earthquake victims, firefighters battling an inferno).

Last Thanksgiving a friend's 4-year-old daughter had a poignant moment. "AnnaBess walked into the kitchen when her father was dressing the turkey," recalls her mother, Wendy Greenspun. "She started crying and said, 'Daddy, that turkey doesn't want to be dead! He wants to be alive! He wants to be with his friends.' She was extremely upset for almost an hour." Whether or not AnnaBess was expressing an unusually precocious empathy, this much is clear: She was saddened by another creature's hardship, and her outrage occurred spontaneously—without prompting by anyone else.

For when it comes to raising empathic children, says Hoffman, parents need not fret about following some rule book or missing a narrow window of opportunity. "The beauty of empathy," he says, "is that it comes naturally. It doesn't have to be forced. You need only nourish it."

JULIA GLASS *recently won her third Nelson Algren Fiction Award and a fellowship in writing from the New York Foundation for the Arts.*

From *Parenting* magazine, June/July 2001, p. 72. © 2001 by The Parenting Group. Reprinted by permission.

Faces of Perception

It's tough to explain how people so easily tell one face from another

By Bruce Bower

Newborn babies are wrinkled, wide-eyed strangers in a strange land of light, shadow, and color. Nonetheless, these little bundles of visual innocence take an immediate shine to faces.

Just a few hours after birth, infants begin to imitate adults' smiles, frowns, and other expressions. Given a choice, the same babies gaze longer at a picture of their mother's face than at an image of the face of a female stranger. They also boast a budding aptitude for telling strangers' faces apart and give particular notice to faces rated as attractive by adults.

The magnetic pull that faces exert on babies' attention has stimulated much research by psychologists over the past 30 years. In related work, neuroscientists are pursuing the brain areas that enable most adults to say with confidence, "I never forget a face." Debate over the meaning of all this research has now come to a head.

Some scientists suspect that newborns possess an innate ability to spot basic facial features, such as two eyes situated above a mouth. As a result of humanity's extended evolution in small groups, where it's critical to discern friends from foes, genes now give human brains a head start in decoding faces, according to these researchers.

Consequently, they add, a few brain areas—in particular, a small patch of right-brain tissue just behind the ear—specialize in per-

ceiving and recognizing faces. People who incur damage to these regions neither recognize the faces of those they know nor remember new faces.

An alternate explanation of face recognition, however, is gaining momentum. Its adherents argue that infants come equipped not with a special face-recognition capability but only with preferences for general perceptual features, such as curved contours. Babies use these visual inclinations as a launching pad for learning to recognize faces, say researchers in this camp.

A propensity for looking at faces may coexist with preferences for several other visual categories in newborns, none of which is predetermined by genes, these researchers argue. By 3 to 4 months of age, infants usually prefer pictures of cats over horses, tigers over cats, chairs over tables, and mammals over birds. Such curious predilections probably exist even in newborns, these scientists propose.

Moreover, they point out, the behind-the-ear brain area most directly implicated in face recognition actually coordinates all sorts of expert visual judgments. It's just as crucial for making deft distinctions among classic cars, bird species, and imaginary creatures with no faces as it is for recognizing pictures of one's high school classmates. Damage to this part of the brain hinders object recognition to a lesser extent than it does face recognition, but the effect

is still noticeable, add supporters of this view.

The theoretical division runs deep among face researchers. "Debate about the nature of face recognition is unbelievably heated right now," says neuroscientist Charles A. Nelson of the University of Minnesota in Minneapolis. "It has polarized groups of researchers."

In the long run, this dispute will yield major scientific insights, holds neuroscientist Nancy Kanwisher of the Massachusetts Institute of Technology. "It will take a while to figure out how the brain carves up visual perception," she says. "This is how science works."

It's hard to know precisely what a baby sees when he or she looks at a face looming overhead. Studies indicate that newborns perceive a fuzzy world, devoid of sharp delineations among objects and the nuances of noses, cheeks, and other parts of the facial landscape.

Despite their vague take on the world, infants have an innate preference for gazing at facelike sights, such as a pair of round blobs over a horizontal line, contends psychologist Mark H. Johnson of Birkbeck College in London.

"Newborns possess a simple, blurred representation of facial structure," Johnson says.

His view derives from several findings. First, newborns see well enough to imitate adults' facial

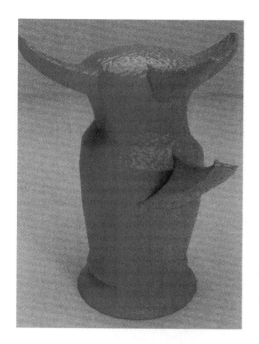

Participants in one set of visual-discrimination studies learn to discern differences among imaginary creatures called greebies, shown here in versions designated as male (left) and female (right) by researchers

M. TARR AND I. GAUTHIER

expressions. Second, babies so quickly start to distinguish among faces and recognize their mother's face that there is virtually no time for learning these tricks. Third, within days of birth, infants know enough about facial features that they prefer attractive over unattractive faces.

Finally, as with adults, babies show no partiality to good-looking faces if the images of the faces are turned upside down.

To do all this, babies must begin life knowing how the human face is organized, contends psychologist Alan Slater of the University of Exeter, England. Newborns thus naturally look toward facelike configurations, with two eyes above a nose and mouth, he theorizes.

Other scientists see more merit in visual simplicity. Newborns probably focus on general elements of faces, contends psychologist Paul C. Quinn of Washington and Jefferson College in Washington, Pa. The contour, or shape, of the head may represent a particularly compelling component of the face for babies, he says.

For instance, in the January JOURNAL OF EXPERIMENTAL CHILD PSYCHOLOGY, Quinn and his coworkers reported that 3- and 4-month-old

infants distinguish among cats and dogs based on silhouettes of the animals' heads.

Consider babies who first spent time looking at a cat's head silhouette. In a later trial, these infants looked longer at a head silhouette of either a new cat or a dog than at the silhouette of the previously seen cat, revealing a preference for visual novelty. Along the same line, babies who viewed a series of head silhouettes of either cats or dogs later preferred to look at head silhouettes of the other species.

In contrast, no such signs of appreciating novel figures appeared among infants shown body silhouettes of either cats or dogs.

In earlier work, Quinn had found that 3-and 4-month-olds also distinguish among familiar and novel silhouettes of human heads. At that age, babies favor head shapes of people over those of cats, dogs, and other animals, he says.

Babies soak up the subtleties of the faces they encounter with surprising ease, Quinn adds. In one stark example, he finds that 7-month-old infants of both sexes raised by single mothers prefer to look at pictures of female faces,

whereas those raised by single fathers opt for male faces.

In fact, constant exposure to faces in the first few years of life generates the brain's face-recognition system, argues Nelson in the March-June INFANT AND CHILD DEVELOPMENT. He suggests that babies only need to start out with a capacity for discerning general properties of figures, much as Quinn proposes.

Experience in looking at faces during the first year of life focuses infants' perceptual spotlight, Nelson contends. For instance, he and his coworkers find that infants do better than adults at noticing facial differences in monkeys and also in people from racial backgrounds other than their own. These advantages illuminate babies' reliance on broad visual cues that, in Nelson's opinion, eventually get replaced by a system for rapidly recognizing familiar human faces.

Faces contain two structural elements that are big-time baby pleasers but are by no means unique to faces, according to studies directed by psychologist Francesca Simion of the University of Padova, in Italy. First, newborns prefer to look at pat-

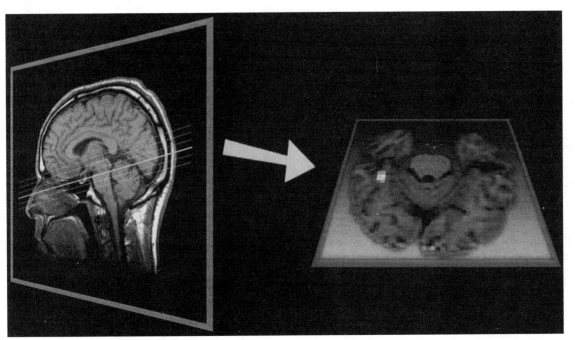

Taken at the solid line in whole-brain image (left), a computer-generated slice (right) highlights areas, including the fusiform gyrus, that participate in face recognition.

M. TARR AND I. GAUTHIER

terns with a greater number of elements in the top half of the visual field. They gaze longer at a T-shape pattern composed of squares than at an upside-down T shape, as well as at head shapes with more squares randomly positioned in the top than in the bottom half.

Second, in the days after birth, babies fixate more readily on curved rather than straight contours. Infants shown face drawings without head contours exhibit none of their usual preference for an upright face, Simion's team finds.

Babies aren't the only ones who can use such basic visual cues to grasp faces. A computer network programmed to respond to simple visual features and to modify its output after getting feedback on errors learns to recognize faces with considerable accuracy. This system, devised by Herve Abdi of the University of Texas at Dallas and his colleagues, captures increasingly fine visual details as it encounters a greater number of faces.

"The bulk of the evidence suggests that the ability to recognize faces is learned," Nelson argues.

Controversy also surrounds efforts, conducted mainly with adults, to track down brain areas devoted to face recognition.

Evidence that faces enjoy special status in the brain comes from individuals with a condition called prosopagnosia. After suffering damage to the brain's right temporal lobe, these people have lost the ability to recognize familiar faces. Moreover, a different pattern of temporal lobe brain damage blocks the capability to identify inanimate objects, while sparing face recognition.

A 16-year-old boy named Adam presents a particularly intriguing case of prosopagnosia. Adam's temporal-brain damage occurred when he contracted meningitis at 1 day of age. He now exhibits "impressively bad" face recognition and mild difficulty at detecting various objects, says psychologist Martha J. Farah of the University of Pennsylvania in Philadelphia. Adam draws a blank even for pictures of his mother.

Uninjured parts of Adam's young brain apparently had no way to regroup and assume responsibility for face recognition, Farah proposes. "This indicates that the genome

encodes for a specific face-processing area in the brain that can't be replaced," she says.

Several brain-imaging studies suggest that face recognition depends on a few regions of the temporal lobes, particularly the area just behind the right ear known as the fusiform gyrus. Kanwisher and other investigators find that neural activity in the fusiform gyrus surges at least twice as strongly when healthy adults view faces as when they look at assorted objects, letter strings, or the backs of human heads.

The findings from brain-damaged patients and healthy volunteers justify renaming the fusiform gyrus as "the fusiform face area," Kanwisher says.

You could just as easily dub this patch of tissue "the fusiform greeble area," according to Isabel Gauthier of Vanderbilt University in Nashville, who has directed a series of brain-imaging studies on object recognition. After a little training, most volunteers easily classify imaginary, faceless, plantlike creatures called greebles according to their sex and family. These participants display elevated fusiform gyrus activity as they identify pairs of matching greebles.

Comparable brain responses occur as people peruse real-world objects or animals that they know much about, Gauthier and her coworkers find. For instance, the fusiform gyrus lights up in car buffs as they examine pictures of different makes and models of classic automobiles and in bird authorities as they inspect images of various avian species (SN: 2/5/00, p. 91).

Rather than specializing solely in faces, the fusiform gyrus fosters proficiency at visually analyzing any class of items that a person strives to master, Gauthier asserts. "The brain doesn't need to care about different categories of things in the world, such as faces," she remarks. Instead, neural tissue solves computational problems, such as assembling visual elements into meaningful wholes.

Kanwisher remains skeptical of Gauthier's findings until the data on greebles, cars, and birds are confirmed by independent researchers. Gauthier, who did postdoctoral work in Kanwisher's lab, responds that she looks forward to such attempts.

It's unclear whether infants and children learn to identify faces in the same way that adults gain visual expertise with whatever strikes their fancy, Gauthier adds. In a recent study, she and her colleagues tested young adults with autism, a disorder that includes difficulty with face recognition but involves no apparent temporal lobe damage. Nevertheless, the participants exhibited unusually low fusiform gyrus activity while trying to tell faces apart.

Whatever mechanisms enable neurologically healthy kids to develop face expertise in the fusiform gyrus may be unavailable to their peers with autism, Gauthier theorizes.

She now wants a closer examination of brain-damaged patients, such as Adam. Having been told that their injury should cause problems with recognizing faces, prosopagnosics usually give up quickly on tests of this ability, she says. In contrast, the same individuals assume they should routinely conquer object-recognition tasks, so they spend a lot of time poring over such tests. As a result, the relative superiority of object recognition among prosopagnosics has been exaggerated, in Gauthier's view.

Investigators have yet to assess whether Adam looks longer at objects than at faces on recognition tests, she notes.

Intriguing leads from other research groups seem unlikely to break the theoretical stalemate over face recognition.

Distinct, overlapping patterns of temporal lobe activity occur when volunteers look at faces, chairs, shoes, cats, and other remarkably specific categories of objects, according to brain-imaging studies directed by James V. Haxby of the National Institute of Mental Health in Bethesda, Md.

"We can tell if a person is looking at a shoe, a chair, or a face, based on the pattern of their brain activity," Haxby remarks. He described such findings in March at the annual meeting of the Cognitive Neuroscience Society in New York City.

Specific neural-activity patterns serve as maps of the visual features that characterize each category, Haxby proposes. Overlapping maps occur because categories often share some visual elements.

It's unclear how the brain generates maps for different categories. There's clearly not a genetic capacity for distinguishing chairs from shoes, although one might exist for telling faces apart, says Haxby.

Whatever the case, the first few months of life appear to be critical for forming the neural framework of face recognition. A team of McMaster University psychologists in Hamilton, Ont., examined 14 young people, 9 to 21 years old, who were born with cataracts in both eyes and were blind until they had eye surgery at 2 to 6 months of age. They now have great difficulty in seeing faces as unified entities, the team reports in the April 19 NATURE.

When shown a pair of face pictures that differ only in the configuration of the same features—say, one face with closely set eyes and little space between the nose and upper lip and another face with eyes wide apart and more space above the upper lip—the former cataract patients usually couldn't distinguish one picture from the other. Volunteers of the same age but with no previous vision problems did far better at this task.

Further testing of these people suggests that adults who were deprived of vision early in life manage to recognize faces by focusing on the shape of the nose and other isolated features, says study coauthor Richard Le Grand.

Early visual input to the right brain, which arrives via the left eye, proves vital for perceiving faces as integrated units, Le Grand adds. People born only with left-eye cataracts that were later removed do just as poorly on face-configuration tasks as those who needed two cataracts removed, he and his coworkers find.

LeGrand's team plans to use brain-scan technology to identify right-brain areas activated in these individuals during face recognition. The researchers will also see if early-cataract patients can learn to make expert visual distinctions of objects other than faces, such as Gauthier's greebles.

If such studies don't change the face of the face-recognition debate, they'll certainly feed into its body of hotly contested data.

From *Science News*, July 7, 2001, pp. 10–12. © 2001 by the Science Service, 1719 N Street, N.W., Washington, D.C. 20036; www.sciserv.org. Reprinted by permission.

How to Spot a Liar

With some careful observation— and a little help from new software—anyone can learn to be a lie detector

By JAMES GEARY/London
With reporting by Eric Silver/Jerusalem

"You can tell a lie but you will give yourself away. Your heart will race. Your skin will sweat... I will know. I am the lie detector." Thus began each episode of Lie Detector, a strange cross between a relationship counseling session and an episode of the Jerry Springer Show that ran on British daytime television last year. Against a backdrop of flashing computer screens and eerie blue light, participants—usually feuding couples but sometimes warring neighbors or aggrieved business partners—sat on a couch and were quizzed by the program's host. A frequent topic of discussion was one guest's suspicion that his or her partner had been unfaithful. The person suspected of infidelity denied it, of course, and the object of the show was to find out—through cross-examination and computer analysis—whether that person was telling the truth.

However much we may abhor it, deception comes naturally to all living things. Birds do it by feigning injury to lead hungry predators away from nesting young. Spider crabs do it by disguise: adorning themselves with strips of kelp and other debris, they pretend to be something they are not—and so escape their enemies. Nature amply rewards successful deceivers by allowing them to survive long enough to mate and reproduce. So it may come as no surprise to learn that human beings—who, according to psychologist Gerald Jellison of the University of South California, are lied to about 200 times a day, roughly one untruth every five minutes—often deceive for exactly the same reasons: to save their own skins or to get something they can't get by other means.

But knowing how to catch deceit can be just as important a survival skill as knowing how to tell a lie and get away with it. A person able to spot falsehood quickly is unlikely to be swindled by an unscrupulous business associate or hoodwinked by a devious spouse. Luckily, nature provides more than enough clues to trap dissemblers in their own tangled webs—if you know where to look. By closely observing facial expressions, body language and tone of voice, practically anyone can recognize the telltale signs of lying. Researchers are even programming computers—like those used on Lie Detector—to get at the truth by analyzing the same physical cues available to the naked eye and ear. "With the proper training, many people can learn to reliably detect lies," says Paul Ekman, professor of psychology at the University of California, San Francisco, who has spent the past 15 years studying the secret art of deception.

In order to know what kind of lies work best, successful liars need to accurately assess other people's emotional states. Ekman's research shows that this same emotional intelligence is essential for good lie detectors, too. The emotional state to watch out for is stress, the conflict most liars feel between the truth and what they actually say and do.

Even high-tech lie detectors don't detect lies as such; they merely detect the physical cues of emotions, which may or may not correspond to what the person being tested is saying. Polygraphs, for instance, measure respiration, heart rate and skin conductivity, which tend to increase when people are nervous—as they usually are when lying. Nervous people typically perspire, and the salts contained in perspiration conduct electricity. That's why a sudden leap in skin conductivity indicates nervousness—about getting caught, perhaps?—which might, in turn, suggest that someone is being economical with the truth. On the other hand, it might also mean that the lights in the television studio are too hot—which is one reason polygraph tests are inadmissible in court. "Good lie detectors don't rely on a single sign," Ekman says, "but interpret clusters of verbal and nonverbal clues that suggest someone might be lying."

Those clues are written all over the face. Because the musculature of the face is directly connected to the areas of the brain that process emotion, the countenance can be a window to the soul. Neurological studies even suggest that genuine emotions travel different pathways through the brain than insincere ones. If a patient paralyzed by stroke on one side of the face, for example, is asked to smile deliberately, only the mobile side of the mouth is raised. But tell that same person a funny joke, and the patient breaks into a full and spontaneous smile. Very few people—most notably, actors and politicians—are able to consciously control all of their facial expressions. Lies can often be caught when the liar's true feelings briefly leak through the mask of deception. "We don't think before we feel," Ekman says. "Expressions tend to show up on the face before we're even conscious of experiencing an emotion."

One of the most difficult facial expressions to fake—or conceal, if it is genuinely felt—is sadness. When someone is truly sad, the forehead wrinkles with grief and the inner corners of the eyebrows are pulled up. Fewer than 15% of the people Ekman tested were able to produce this eyebrow movement voluntarily. By contrast, the lowering of the eyebrows associated with an angry scowl can be replicated at will by almost everybody. "If someone claims they are sad and the inner corners of their eyebrows don't go up," Ekman says, "the sadness is probably false."

The smile, on the other hand, is one of the easiest facial expressions to counterfeit. It takes just two muscles—the zygomaticus major muscles that extend from the cheekbones to the corners of the lips—to produce a grin. But there's a catch. A genuine smile affects not only the corners of the lips but also the orbicularis oculi, the muscle around the eye that produces the distinctive "crow's-feet" associated with people who laugh a lot. A counterfeit grin can be unmasked if the lip corners go up, the eyes crinkle but the inner corners of the eyebrows are not lowered, a movement controlled by the orbicularis oculi that is difficult to fake. The absence of lowered eyebrows is one reason why false smiles look so strained and stiff.

Ekman and his colleagues have classified all the muscle movements—ranging from the thin, taut lips of fury to the arched eyebrows of surprise—that underlie the complete repertoire of human facial expressions. In addition to the nervous tics and jitters that can give liars away, Ekman discovered that fibbers often allow the truth to slip through in brief, unguarded facial expressions. Lasting no more than a quarter of a second, these fleeting glimpses of a person's true emotional state—or "microexpressions," as Ekman calls them—are reliable guides to veracity.

In a series of tests, Ekman interviewed and videotaped a group of male American college students about their opinions regarding capital punishment. Some participants were instructed to tell the truth—whether they were for or against the death penalty—and some were instructed to lie. Liars who successfully fooled the interviewer received $50. Ekman then studied the tapes to map the microexpressions of mendacity.

One student, for example, appeared calm and reasonable as he listed the reasons why the death penalty was

wrong. But every time he expressed these opinions, he swiftly, almost imperceptibly, shook his head. But the movement is so subtle and quick many people don't even see it until it's pointed out to them. While his words explained the arguments against capital punishment, the quick, involuntary shudder of his head was saying loud and clear, "No, I don't believe this!" He was, in fact, lying, having been for many years a firm supporter of the death penalty.

THE LYIN' KING

Four signs that may indicate deception

1. AN EMBLEM is a gesture with a specific meaning, like shrugging the shoulders to say, "I don't know." An emblem may be a sign of deceit if only part of the gesture is performed (a one-shoulder shrug, for example) or if it is performed in a concealed manner.

2. MANIPULATORS are repetitive touching motions like scratching the nose, tapping the foot or twisting the hair. They tend to increase when people are nervous, and may be an attempt to conceal incriminating facial expressions.

3. AN ILLUSTRATOR is a movement that emphasizes speech. Illustrators increase with emotion, so too few may indicate false feelings while too many may be an attempt to distract attention from signs of deceit on the face.

4. MICROEXPRESSIONS flash across the face in less than a quarter of a second—a frown, for example, that is quickly covered up by a grin. Though fleeting, they can reveal subtle clues about the true feelings that a person may wish to repress or conceal.

"With proper training, many people can learn to reliably detect lies."

"It would be an impossible world if no one lied."

James Geary/London
With reporting by Eric Silver/Jerusalem.

Another student also said that he was against the death penalty. But during the interview, he spoke very slowly, paused often, and rarely looked the interrogator in the eye, instead fixing his gaze on some vague point on the floor. Speech that is too slow (or too fast), frequent hesitations, lack of direct eye contact: these are all classic symptoms of lying. But this man was telling the truth. He paused and hesitated because he was shy. After all, even honest and normally composed individuals can become flustered if they believe others suspect them of lying. His lack of eye contact could be explained by the fact that he came from Asia, where an averted gaze is often a sign of deference and respect, not deception. This scenario highlights Ekman's admonition that before branding someone a liar, you must first know that person's normal behavior patterns and discount other explanations, such as cultural differences.

Ekman has used this tape to test hundreds of subjects. His conclusion: most people are lousy lie detectors, with few individuals able to spot duplicity more than 50% of the time. But Ekman's most recent study, published last year in Psychological Science, found that four groups of people did significantly better than chance: members of the U.S. Central Intelligence Agency, other U.S. federal law enforcement officers, a handful of Los Angeles County sheriffs and a group of clinical psychologists. Reassuringly, perhaps, the federal officials performed best, accurately detecting liars 73% of the time. What makes these groups so good at lie catching? According to Ekman, it's training, experience and motivation. The jobs—and in some cases, the lives—of everyone in these groups depend on their ability to pick up deceit.

Ekman has used his findings to assist law enforcement agents—including members of the U.S. Secret Service and Federal Bureau of Investigation, Britain's Scotland Yard and the Israeli police force—in criminal investigations and antiterrorist activities. He refuses to work with politicians. "It is unlikely that judging deception from demeanor alone will ever be admissible in court," Ekman says. "But the research shows that it's possible for some people to make highly accurate judgments about lying without any special aids, such as computers."

But for those who still prefer a bit of technological assistance, there's the Verdicator—a device that, according to its 27-year-old inventor Amir Liberman, enables anyone equipped with a personal computer and a phone or microphone to catch a liar. A person's tone of voice can be just as revealing as the expression on his face. A low tone, for example, can suggest a person is lying or is stressed, while a higher pitch can mean excitement. Liberman claims the Verdicator, a $2,500 piece of software produced by Integritek Technologies in Petah Tikvah near Tel Aviv, is between 85% and 95% accurate in determining whether the person on the other end of the line is lying, an accuracy rate better than that for traditional polygraphs. "Our software knows how to size you up," Liberman boasts.

The Verdicator delivers its results by analyzing voice fluctuations that are usually inaudible to the human ear. When a person is under stress, anxiety may cause muscle tension and reduce blood flow to the vocal cords, producing a distinctive pattern of sound waves. Liberman has catalogued these patterns and programmed the Verdicator to distinguish among tones that indicate excitement, cognitive stress—the difference between what you think and what you say—and outright deceit. Once linked to a communications device and computer, the Verdicator monitors the subtle vocal tremors of your conversational partner and displays an assessment of that person's veracity on the screen. "The system can tell how nervous you are," Liberman explains. "It builds a psychological profile of what you feel and compares it to patterns associated with deception." And the Verdicator has one great advantage over the polygraph: the suspect doesn't need to know he's being tested. To be accurate, though, the Verdicator must pick up changes—which might indicate deceit—in a person's normal voice.

During the Monica Lewinsky scandal, Liberman demonstrated the system on President Clinton's famous disclaimer, "I did not have sexual relations with that woman." After analyzing an audio tape of the statement 100 times, the Verdicator showed that Clinton "was telling the truth," Liberman says, "but he had very high levels of cognitive stress, or 'guilt knowledge.' He didn't have sexual relations, but he did have something else."

Integritek will not name the law enforcement agencies, banks or financial institutions that are using the Verdicator. But company president Naaman Boury says that last year more than 500 Verdicators were sold in North and South America, Australia, Asia and Europe. The Japanese firm Atlus is marketing a consumer version of the Verdicator in Asia. "We get the best results—close to 95% accuracy—in Japan," Liberman reports. "The Japanese feel very uncomfortable when lying. We get the poorest results—nearer 85% accuracy—in Russia, where people seldom seem to say what they really feel."

In moderation, lying is a normal—even necessary—part of life. "It would be an impossible world if no one lied," Ekman says. But by the same token, it would be an intolerable world if we could never tell when someone was lying. For those lies that are morally wrong and potentially harmful, would-be lie detectors can learn a lot from looking and listening very carefully. Cheating partners, snake oil salesmen and scheming politicians, beware! The truth is out there.

James Geary/London
With reporting by Eric Silver/Jerusalem

From *Time Europe*, March 13, 2000, pp. 44–49. © 2000 by Time Inc. Reprinted by permission.

Shy Squared

America's 'in-your-face' culture and isolating technologies are making it harder for shy kids to overcome their inhibitions.

By Karen Goldberg Goff

Lori Ruhl says she noticed how her daughter, Kiersti, would react to strangers and unfamiliar situations even when the child was 9 months old. A picture of baby Kiersti on Santa Claus' lap shows her mouth cuffed in a tense expression. "You could see how nervous she was" says Ruhl, of Sedro Wooley, Wash.

Things didn't change dramatically through the years. Kiersti, now 7, does not like loud noises and prefers to watch the other children on the playground rather than join in boisterous play. While Ruhl tries to encourage her daughter to warm up to social situations, she also reassures the child that it is all right to be shy.

"I try and tell her nothing is wrong with it" Ruhl says. "She is artistic. She is sensitive. She is a good friend. I just worry about the future. It might get to the point where people think she is a weird kid who does not talk at school."

Kiersti is not alone. Bernardo J. Carducci, director of the Shyness Research Institute at Indiana University Southeast in New Albany, Ind., says about 40 to 45 percent of Americans consider themselves shy. Researchers are debating whether shyness can be a learned behavior or is a natural disposition. "We have found there are almost as many reasons for shyness as there are shy people" Carducci says. "It is a myth that shyness is due to low self-esteem."

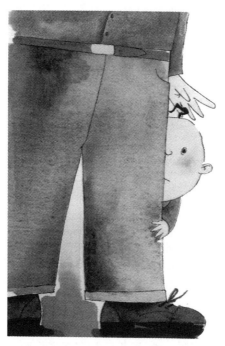

FRANCIS BLAKE

While some researchers say shyness is inherited, that concept remains open for debate. Jerome Kagan, a Harvard University psychology professor who has studied shyness and children for decades, estimates that 20 percent of infants are born with what he calls "inhibited temperament." By about 8 weeks of age, these babies show signs of sensitivity toward strangers and loud noises. Their anxiety is manifested in a faster heart rate and louder crying. "These children have an inherent chem-istry that makes them sensitive to anything unfamiliar," Kagan says.

Biology is not necessarily destiny, however. Life experiences will condition many with an inhibited temperament "to grow out of it." Shyness needn't be a lifelong condition. "Just like you get over a fear of the ocean by dipping your toe in, you gradually get involved in new situations until you get accustomed to them," Kagan says. "By adolescence, many shy children are not shy anymore"

On the other hand, Carducci does not believe that a tendency to shyness is inherent. "There is no way that you can be born shy" he argues. "Shyness involves an excessive sense of self-consciousness, a negative self-evaluation. Your sense of self does not even develop until you are 18 months old."

Deborah C. Beidel, a University of Maryland psychologist and codirector of the university's Childhood Shyness Program, stands somewhere between, ascribing shyness to a little bit of nature and nurture. "I do agree that there is some biological underpinning for shyness" she says. "A large part of it has to do with environmental situations, such as a specific response to an embarrassing situation. We had one patient who had to sing 'Rudolph the Red-Nosed Reindeer' in a school play. She sang out, 'Then one froggy Christmas Eve' instead of 'foggy Christmas Eve.' She was mortified in those situations ever since."

Don't Be Shy... Get More Info

Books

The Shy child: Helping Children Triumph Over Shyness, by Ward K. Swallow (Warner Books, $9.95, 288 pp). Walks parents through shyness at different stages of a child's life and suggests ways to cope with situations.

Shyness: A Bold New Approach, by Bernardo J. Carducci (HarperCollins, $15, 400 pp). A shyness researcher explains ways to help overcome shyness.

Shy Children, Phobic Adults: Nature and Treatment of Social Phobias, by Deborah C. Beidel and Samuel M. Turner (American Psychological Association, $39.95, 324 pp). Explains the difference between shyness and the anxiety disorder known as social phobia.

Beyond Shyness: How to Conquer Social Anxieties, by Jonathan Berent (Fireside Books, $12, 285 pp). A social worker helps children and adults cope.

How Kids Make Friends: Secrets for Making Lots of Friends, No Matter How Shy You Are, by Lonnie Michelle (Freedom Publishing, $9.95, 64 pp).

Associations

American Psychological Association, 750 First St. N.E., Washington, D.C. 20002. Phone: (202) 336-5500; Website: *www.apa.org*. This professional association has psychological referrals as well as fact sheets and research on shyness.

Online

At Shyness.com, a Website started by the mother of two shy children, parents can get tips on helping their children and teens connect with others with the same concerns.

Expert opinions and bulletin boards for the parents of shy children can be found at the following general parenting sites: Babycenter Inc. (*www.babycenter.com*), iVillage's Parentsplace (*www.parentsplace.com*) and iVillage's ParentSoup (*www.parentsoup.com*).

In most cases, having a shy child is nothing for parents to worry about. Children such as Kiersti Ruhl tend to be quite talkative at home and have a few close friends. A child with social anxiety, however, will refuse to attend parties, join teams or even go to school. "They might have physical symptoms over these situations, such as stomachaches and a racing heart" Beidel says. "A lot of kids who are just a little shy may outgrow it, but a child who exhibits signs of social phobia before about age 8 may need intervention."

Intervention could involve play therapy or behavior therapy. Beidel's clinic concentrates on social-skills training, in which children learn how to respond in group situations. "It is exposure therapy" she says. "We give children a chance to practice what they are afraid of."

Technology, regarded as the catalyst for bringing people together in places such as the Internet, is not helping shy children, Carducci says. As parents get money from an ATM and shop for shoes online, children miss opportunities to see social interaction.

"Think about it," Carducci says. "Children don't see people interacting as much. Children come home and get on their computers. That means social isolation and a loss in negotiation. They play games where the computer decides. They play organized sports where the parents make decisions. The culture has changed. We are losing the spontaneity of social interactions." Technology also has made society faster (think instant messaging, drive-through dinners), making it difficult for those who need more time to adjust to situations.

This also is an era of brash, attention-getting behavior, one that makes it easy for a shy child to get left behind. "In our society, you have to be more extreme to get noticed," Carducci says. "You have to have the brand-name clothes. It is all about self-image. The way shy children, particularly teens, cope with that is by acting out or withdrawing."

Dorothy Venditto, mother of a 7-year-old and a 10-year-old in Mount Kisco, N.Y., worries about how the culture will affect her girls as they mature. "I believe that an 'in-your-face' style is considered the fashionable way to behave today, so overcoming fears and gaining confidence is now more difficult than ever for shy children," says Venditto, editor of Shykids.com, a support Website for parents and teens. "It makes it particularly difficult for them to find a way to fit in."

Reprinted with permission of *Insight*, June 11, 2001, pp. 32-33. © 2001 by News World Communications, Inc. All rights reserved.

Revealing Personal Secrets

Abstract
Both the health benefits and the potential drawbacks of revealing personal secrets (i.e., those that directly involve the secret keeper) are reviewed. Making the decision to reveal personal secrets to others involves a trade-off. On the one hand, secret keepers can feel better by revealing their secrets and gaining new insights into them. On the other hand, secret keepers can avoid looking bad before important audiences (such as their bosses or therapists) by not revealing their secrets. Making a wise decision to reveal a personal secret hinges on finding an appropriate confidant—someone who is discreet, who is perceived by the secret keeper to be nonjudgmental, and who is able to offer new insights into the secret.

Keywords
revealing secrets; new insights; confidants

Anita E. Kelly[1]
Department of Psychology, University of Notre Dame, Notre Dame, Indiana

Psychologists and lay persons have long believed that keeping personal secrets is stressful and that unburdening oneself of such secrets offers emotional relief and physiological benefits. Supporting this notion is recent experimental research that has demonstrated the health benefits of revealing personal secrets (i.e., ones that directly involve the secret keeper). These findings lead to several key questions: Why do these health benefits occur? When does revealing personal secrets to various confidants backfire? And, finally, when should someone reveal his or her personal secrets?

SECRECY

Secrecy involves actively hiding private information from others. The most painful or traumatic personal experiences are often concealed, and most secrets are likely to involve negative or stigmatizing information that pertains to the secret keepers themselves. For example, people may keep secret the fact that they have AIDS, are alcoholic, or have been raped. Secrecy has also been called self-concealment and active inhibition of disclosure.

HEALTH BENEFITS OF REVEALING SECRETS

The belief that secrecy is problematic is supported by studies showing that, on average, people who tend to conceal personal information have more physical problems, such as headaches, nausea, and back pains, and are more anxious, shy, and depressed than people who do not tend to conceal personal information. Recent research has also shown that gay men who tend to conceal their sexual orientation from others are at a greater risk for cancers and infectious diseases than those who do not conceal their orientation.

Moreover, research has shown that talking or writing about private traumatic experiences is associated with health benefits, such as improved immunological functioning and fewer visits to the doctor. For example, a survey of spouses of suicide and accidental-death victims demonstrated that participants who had talked about the loss of their spouses with family and friends suffered fewer health problems the year after the loss than participants who did not speak with others about their loss (Pennebaker & O'Heeron, 1984). These correlations remained even in an analysis that statistically adjusted for the number of friends these individuals had before and after the loss of the spouse.

Particularly compelling evidence concerning the benefits of revealing secrets has emerged from a series of in-the-field and laboratory experiments. One experiment showed that advanced-breast-cancer patients who were randomly assigned to a group that was designed to encourage them to talk about their emotions survived twice as long as patients assigned to a routine oncological-care group (Spiegel, Bloom, Kraemer, & Gottheil, 1989). In another experiment, medical students were randomly assigned to write about either private traumatic events or control topics for four consecutive days and then were vaccinated against hepatitis B (Petrie, Booth, Pennebaker, Davison, & Thomas, 1995). The group that wrote about traumatic events had significantly higher antibody levels against hepatitis B at the 4- and 6-month follow-ups than did the control group, suggesting that emotional expression of traumatic experiences can lead to improved immune functioning.

WHAT IS IT ABOUT REVEALING SECRETS THAT IS BENEFICIAL?

It is believed that revealing secrets offers these health benefits because the revealer gains new insights into the trauma and no longer has to expend cognitive and emotional resources actively hiding the trauma (Pennebaker, 1997). It has also been suggested that gaining catharsis (i.e., expressing pent-up emotions behaviorally) may play an important role in reducing one's level of emotional arousal surrounding a troubling event (Polivy, 1998), even though some studies have raise the questions of whether catharsis actually purges or provokes emotions (Polivy, 1998).

Because of the controversy surrounding the benefits of catharsis, my colleagues and I recently conducted an experiment that directly compared the effect of gaining catharsis with the effects of gaining new insights into one's troubling secrets (Kelly, Klusas, von Weiss, & Kenny, 1999, Study 2). Undergraduates ($N = 85$) were randomly assigned to one of three groups, which differed as to whether they were asked (a) to try to gain new insights through writing about their secrets, (b) to try to gain catharsis by writing about their secrets, or (c) to write about their previous day. The results revealed that the new-insights

group felt significantly better about their secrets after their writing than did the other groups, and thus the findings support the idea that the key to recovery from troubling secrets is gaining new insights. Correlational analyses of the content of the writing showed that participants' coming to terms with their secrets mediated the relation between their gaining new insights and feeling better about their secrets. In other words, it was only through coming to terms with their secrets that participants seemed to benefit from gaining new insights into them. These findings are consistent with the results from a series of writing-about-trauma studies which showed that when participants increased their use of words associated with insightful and causal thinking, they tended to experience improved physical health (Pennebaker, Mayne, & Francis, 1997, Study 1).

The reason why gaining new insights is likely to be curative is that people may be able to find closure on the secrets and avoid what has been termed the Zeigarnik effect, wherein people actively seek to attain a goal when they have failed to attain the goal or failed to disengage from it. Zeigarnik (1927) showed that people continue to think about and remember interrupted tasks more than finished ones, suggesting that they may have a need for completion or resolution of events. Revealing a secret with the explicit intention of gaining a new perspective on it may help people feel a sense of resolution about the secret.

SELF-PRESENTATION AND THE ROLE OF THE CONFIDANT

The findings from the experiments described so far clearly suggest that it is healthy to reveal one's secrets. However, almost all of the experiments conducted to date have involved revealing secrets in an anonymous setting, and the health benefits observed in those experiments may not generalize to circumstances in which people reveal unfavorable or stigmatizing information

about themselves to important audiences (e.g., their coworkers or friends) in their everyday interactions. In such circumstances, the revealers may perceive that they are being rejected by and alienated from the listeners.

Supporting this concern are the results from a 9-year longitudinal study of initially healthy, HIV-positive gay men who were sensitive to social rejection. Those who tended to conceal their sexual orientation from others experienced a slower progression of HIV-related symptoms than did those who tended to reveal their sexual orientation to others (Cole, Kemeny, & Taylor, 1997). These results qualify these same researchers' finding, referred to earlier, that gay men who tended to conceal their sexual orientation were at a greater risk for cancers and infectious diseases.

The essence of the problem with revealing personal, undesirable information is that revealers may come to see themselves in undesirable ways if others know their stigmatizing secrets. A number of experiments from the self-presentation literature have demonstrated that describing oneself as having undesirable qualities, such as being depressed or introverted, to various audiences leads to negative shifts in one's self-beliefs and behaviors (e.g., Schlenker, Dlugolecki, & Doherty, 1994; Tice, 1992). Moreover, a recent in-the-field study showed that among a sample of therapy outpatients who had received an average of 11 therapy sessions, the clients (40.5%) who reported that they were keeping a relevant secret from their counselors actually had a greater reduction in their symptomatology than did those who were not keeping a relevant secret (Kelly, 1998). These results were obtained after adjusting for clients' social-desirability scores (i.e., scores indicating their tendency to try to "look good" to other people) and their tendency to keep secrets in general. It is possible that clients hid negative aspects of themselves in an effort to provide desirable views of themselves for their therapists.

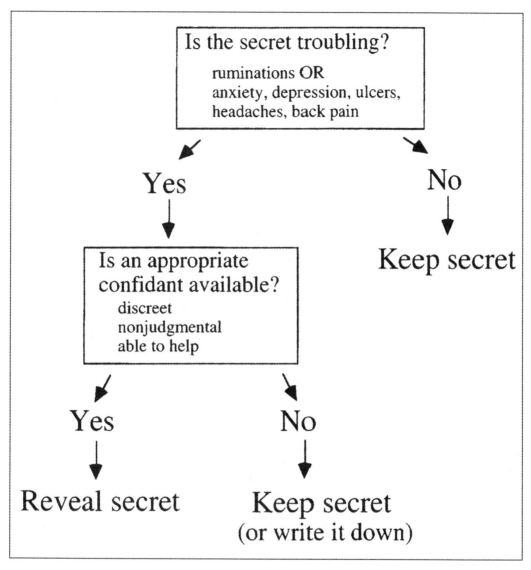

FIGURE 1. DECISION-MAKING MODEL FOR REVEALING SECRETS (FROM KELLY & MCKILLOP, 1996).

Another problem associated with revealing one's secrets is that confidants often cannot be trusted to keep the secrets or to protect one's identity. For example, in a study of college students' self-reports, the students indicated that when someone disclosed an emotional event to them, they in turn revealed the emotional disclosure to other people in 66% to 78% of the cases—despite the fact that these students were intimates of the original revealers in 85% of the cases (Christophe & Rime, 1997). Moreover, original disclo-

sures that were of a high emotional intensity were more likely to be shared with others and were told to more people (specifically, to more than two people, on average) than disclosures that were low or moderate in emotional intensity. In addition, another study showed that in 78% of the cases in which the original event was disclosed to others, the name of the original revealer was explicitly mentioned. Christophe and Rime recommended that if people do not want others to learn about their emotional experiences, then

they should avoid sharing the experiences with others altogether. It is important to note, however, that these researchers did not specifically ask the confidants if they had been sworn to secrecy.

In sum, two sets of findings qualify the conclusion that revealing secrets leads to health benefits. First, the findings from the self-presentation literature suggest that revealing undesirable personal information to important audiences can have negative implications for one's self-image. Second, studies have shown that confidants often cannot be trusted to keep a secret or to protect the revealer's identity; therefore, revealing secrets may damage one's reputation.

WHEN TO REVEAL SECRETS

The findings just discussed, taken together, call attention to the trade-offs involved in revealing personal secrets. Revealing secrets can help a person feel better if he or she gains new insights into them, and yet not revealing secrets may help a person look good before important audiences (such as one's boss and therapist). A way to avoid the negative side of revealing personal secrets is to carefully select a confidant. There is empirical support for the idea that if a troubled secret keeper has a confidant who can be trusted not to reveal a secret, is perceived by the secret keeper to be nonjudgmental, and is able to offer the secret helper new insights into the secret, then the secret keeper should reveal the secret to that person (see the model in Fig. 1; Kelly & McKillop, 1996). At the same time, however, because there are risks to one's identity associated with revealing secrets to others, people should reveal their personal secrets only if keeping the secrets seems to be troubling. Specifically, if a secret keeper is experiencing the symptoms that have been found to be associated with self-concealment, such as depression, ulcers, and headaches, then he or she should consider the possibility that the symptoms are the result of the secret keeping and should reveal the secret to an appropriate confidant. The rationale for taking such a risk is that even if the secret is not actually causing the symptoms, the secret helper is still unlikely to be harmed as a result of having revealed personal information to a discreet, nonjudgmental, and insightful confidant.

A limitation to the model for when to reveal secrets is the finding (Kelly, 1998), discussed earlier, that even with trained therapists who presumably fit all of the positive qualities of confidants, clients who were keeping a relevant secret experienced greater symptom reduction than those who were not keeping one. The seeming contradiction between this finding and the model can be resolved by the fact that the model emphasizes the revealer's perception of the confidant as nonjudgmental. It is likely that, at times, clients may imagine, or even accurately perceive, that their therapists are judgmental, particularly when the clients have committed unusually heinous acts, such as savagely beating their children. In such instances, the clients' decision to avoid revealing some of the details of their secrets to their therapists may not be problematic. It is possible that the clients may instead benefit from either discussing the themes of their secrets (e.g., experiencing uncontrollable anger) with the therapists or, as the model suggests, privately writing about the secrets in an effort to gain new insights into them.

CONCLUSION

Even though there is some exciting experimental evidence that revealing one's secrets leads to health benefits, these findings must be viewed with caution because the experiments have involved anonymous revealing of secrets and the findings may not generalize to everyday interactions with confidants. Researchers have not paid sufficient attention to the role of the confidant, and there is some preliminary evidence pointing to the possibility that revealing secrets, even to one's therapist, might backfire. Future research will need to examine the trade-offs between revealing and not revealing secrets to confidants who offer varying degrees of support. There is also a need for research assessing how a person's perceptions of such support can affect his or her self-images.

Recommended Reading

Derlega, V. J., Metts, S., Petronio, S., & Margulis, S. T. (1993). Self-disclosure. Newbury Park, CA: Sage.

Kelly, A. E., & McKillop, K. J. (1996). (See References)

Lane, J. D., & Wegner, D. M. (1995). The cognitive consequences of secrecy. Journal of Personality and Social Psychology, 69, 237–253.

Pennebaker, J. W. (1995). Emotion, disclosure, and health. Washington, DC: American Psychological Association.

Pennebaker, J. W. (1997). (See References)

Acknowledgments—I thank Thomas V. Merluzzi for his thoughtful feedback on a draft of this article.

Notes

1. Address correspondence to Anita E. Kelly, Department of Psychology, University of Notre Dame, Notre Dame, IN 46556; e-mail: kelly.79@nd.edu.

References

Christophe, V., & Rime, B. (1997). Exposure to the social sharing of emotion: Emotional impact, listener responses and secondary social sharing. European Journal of Social Psychology, 27, 37–54.

Cole, S. W., Kemeny, M. E., & Taylor, S. E. (1997). Social identity and physical health: Accelerated HIV progression in rejection-sensitive gay men. Journal of Personality and Social Psychology, 72, 320–335.

Kelly, A. E. (1998). Clients' secret keeping in outpatient therapy. Journal of Counseling Psychology, 45, 50–57.

Kelly, A. E., Klusas, J., von Weiss, R., & Kenny, C. (1999). What is it about revealing secrets that leads to health benefits? Unpublished manuscript, University of Notre Dame, Notre Dame, IN.

Kelly, A. E., & McKillop, K. J. (1996). Consequences of revealing personal secrets. Psychological Bulletin, 120, 450–465.

Pennebaker, J. W. (1997). Opening up: The healing power of expressing emotions. New York: Guilford Press.

Pennebaker, J. W., Mayne, T. J., & Francis, M. E. (1997). Linguistic predictors of adaptive bereavement. Journal of Personality and Social Psychology, 72, 863–871.

Pennebaker, J. W., & O'Heeron, R. C. (1984). Confiding in others and illness rate among spouses of suicide and accidental-death victims. Journal of Abnormal Psychology, 93, 473–476.

Petrie, K. J., Booth, R. J., Pennebaker, J. W., Davison, K. P., & Thomas, M. G. (1995). Disclosure of trauma and immune response to a hepatitis B vaccination program. *Journal of Consulting and Clinical Psychology, 63*, 787–792.

Policy, J. (1998). The effects of behavioral inhibition: Integrating internal cues, cognition, behavior, and affect. *Psychological Inquiry, 9*, 181–204.

Schlenker, B. R., Dlugolecki, D. W., & Doherty, K. (1994). The impact of self-presentations on self-appraisals and behavior: The power of public commitment. *Personality and Social Psychology Bulletin, 20*, 20–33.

Spiegel, D., Bloom, J. H., Kraemer, H. C., & Gottheil, E. (1989). Effects of psychosocial treatment of patients with metastatic breast cancer. *Lancet, 2*, 888–891.

Tice, D. M. (1992). Self-concept change and self-presentation: The looking glass self is also a magnifying glass. *Journal of Personality and Social Psychology, 63*, 435–451.

Zeigarnik, B. (1927). Uber das behalten von erledigten und unerledigten handlungen. *Psychologische Forschung, 9*, 1–85.

From *Current Directions in Psychological Science*, August 1999, pp. 105–109. © 1999 by Anita E. Kelly and the American Psychological Society. Reprinted by permission of Blackwell Publishers.

Welcome to the Love Lab

Words can heal an ailing relationship—or seal its negative fate.

By John Gottman, Ph.D. and Sybil Carrere, Ph.D.

The way a couple argues can tell you a lot about the future of their relationship. In fact, just three minutes of fighting can indicate whether the pair will flourish with time or end in ruin.

The 10-year study that led to this discovery was one of many we've conducted over the years. John Gottman began his groundbreaking research on married couples 28 years ago. Since then, his University of Washington laboratory—dubbed the "Love Lab"—has focused on determining exactly what makes marriages thrive or fail. With the help of a remarkable team and hundreds of couples, we can now predict a relationship's outcome with 88% to 94% accuracy.

To do this, we watch couples during spats and analyze partners' communication patterns and physiology, as well as their oral descriptions of their relationship histories. We then follow the pairs over time to see whether their patterns and descriptions lead to happy outcomes or breakups. We have learned that some negative emotions used in arguments are more toxic than others: Criticism, contempt, defensiveness and stonewalling (withdrawing from a discussion, most frequently seen among men) are all particularly corrosive. On the other hand, we have repeatedly found that happy couples use five times more positive behaviors in their arguments than negative behaviors. One way they do this is by using humor to break the tension in an argument. This is a kind of a "repair" effort to mend conflict. We find that happy couples also use expressions of affection for their partner and acknowledge their partner's point of view ("I'm sorry I hurt your feelings") in order to keep quarrels from getting too heated.

We have learned much from our couples over the last 11 years that we try to bring to our own marriages. Two things: One is the importance of building and maintaining a friendship in your marriage so that you give your partner the benefit of the doubt when times are tough. This takes constant work. The second thing is that you have a choice every time you say something to your partner. You can say something that will either nurture the relationship or tear it down. You may win a particular fight with your spouse, but you could lose the marriage in the long run.

In this article, we show just how we diagnose the health of a marriage. Using three examples of dialogue from real couples discussing their problems, we will illustrate how reading between the lines of people's arguments can predict where some marriages have gone wrong—and why others have stayed strong. Welcome to the "Love Lab!"

Susan, 45, and Bob, 47, have been married for 23 years.

Bob: Um, communication. The question is…

Susan: How we disagree.

B: On communication?

S: You don't see a need for it.

B: Oh yeah.

S: You just said you kept to yourself.

B: Well, yeah, I just…. I dunno. Idle chitchat, I guess.

Defensiveness; Tension

S: You what?

B: Idle chitchat, I guess, if that is what you refer to as communication.

S: What do you mean, chitchat?

B: General run-of-the-mill bull.

S: There's nonverbal communication if you're tuned in.

B: (Nods head)

S: Like that man said in that canoeing class, as they went over the rapids, that they were still communicating.

B: That's true. What do you think we need to talk about more then? Huh?

S: Well, I think when there's a problem, or I'm trying to tell you something, sometimes I shouldn't have to say anything. You can know when I'm in a hurry or tired.

B: I just take communication as being, uh, should we sit down and discuss things more fully.

S: We don't sit down and discuss anything unless it's a problem, or if somebody gets mad. You know lots of families have what they call, which is kinda silly, but a weekly meeting or some time when they just sit down and talk about everything that has been going on there all week, what they like and don't like.

B: We used to have those at home.

S: That's a little far-fetched, maybe, but I'm just saying.

B: I know. I just…

S: It makes sense.

B: …you know what major problem we have at work is communication.

S: It's a problem everywhere.

B: Yeah. Yeah.

S: People don't say what they mean.

B: Or assume that people know what they mean or want.

S: Well, how many times have I asked you what's wrong, and you say nothing. And then a month later you say what was wrong and I couldn't have guessed it in a million years.

B: I don't know why that is. Why, you know, you can ask almost anybody at work what's bothering them.

S: But you never ask me what's wrong.

B: Maybe I know.

Expressing Hidden Life Dream: Wants Husband to take Active Interest

S: No, I don't think you do.

B: Maybe I just enjoy the quietness of it. I don't know.

S: Well, seriously, I think that as long as we've been married that you don't know very much about me at all.

B: No, I think it's true, about both of us maybe.

GOTTMAN SAYS: This couple rates quite low in marital satisfaction. They are also emotionally disengaged, with high depression in addition to marital distress. The marriage has generally low conflict, but also low positivity (shared romance, humor, affection)—the best marker of emotional disengagement. Our findings suggest that, in general, emotionally disengaged couples divorce later in life than those who have a "hotter," more explosive pattern of unhappiness, although this couple did not break up.

This couple is also in a state of gridlocked conflict. Susan and Bob keep coming close to resolving their issue, which is that Bob would rather keep to himself than communicate. But they don't—they keep recycling it over and over again. Emotional disengagement is often a later stage of continued gridlock. After a while, a "hot" couple begins polarizing their positions, digging in and becoming more stubborn, vilifying one another, then trying to isolate the problem. Unfortunately, most gridlocked conflict cannot be permanently enclaved, and negotiations to fix a problem reach a stalemate.

The reason gridlocked conflicts don't get resolved is because there is an underlying life dream within each person that isn't being fulfilled. Susan's dream is expressed when she says, "You never ask me what's wrong." Bob responds that "maybe I just enjoy the quietness"—that he prefers emotional distance to fighting—but she sadly replies that he doesn't know her at all. They are lacking in what we call "love maps," which spouses construct by being interested in each other and tracking each other's stresses, hopes, dreams, concerns, etc. Her latent wish for love maps keeps them from agreeing to the weekly meeting plan.

This couple is still married, but unhappily so.

Valerie, 24, and Mark, 25, have a young baby. They have recently moved, and both have new jobs.

Valerie: (Laughter) We don't go that long without talking.

Mark: I know, I just start going stir-crazy.

V: The problem…

M: Huh?

Despite Initial Humor, The Problem Surfaces

V: …is, you told me that when you took the job as manager at Commonwealth that you'd come home in the afternoons and spend some time with us.

M: That's right, but I did not say that it would start in the first week when I'm trying to do two different jobs. I gotta get myself replaced. Right now, I'm not just a manager.

V: It's been three weeks.

M: Well, I just don't go out on the street and say "Hey you. Want to sell insurance?" It's not that easy. There's two people in the program. One of them is probably gonna be hired within the next couple weeks. But in the meantime it's tough. It's just the way it's gotta be.

V: I realize that.

M: Okay.

V: But.

M: At midnight when you get off work and you're all keyed up, I'm all worn out. I haven't been stimulated for two hours.

V: I realize that. That doesn't bother me that much, you going to sleep at night.

M: I'll just be starting to go to sleep and you'll go "Are you listening to me?" I'll be trying to stay awake…

V: I'm laughing about it usually. I'm not upset about it.

M: I don't know by then. I'm half out.

V: But now with me having a car, you'll be able to go to sleep early and get up with Stephanie a little bit. That's one of my big problems. I'm not getting any sleep. I don't get to sleep until two.

M: I've been getting up with her.

V: You've been real good about that.

M: Okay.

V: I guess I just wish that you didn't have to go in early.

M: Yeah, we don't get a whole lot of time together.

V: When I have the car, I can get out and get stuff then. I feel like I'm stuck at home and here you are…

M: I'll be able to meet you for lunch and stuff. I guess that wasn't any big problem.

V: It is a problem. It seems like we talk about it every day.

M: Yeah, we do.

V: That's about the only thing we really complain about.

M: Yeah. The last couple nights I tried to take you out to the lake and look at the stars and stuff, so…

V: I know.

M: We just need to get used to our schedules.

V: That first week I was so, I was real upset cause it seemed like all I did was stay home with Stephanie all morning till three and just work all evening. I wasn't doing anything. It didn't seem like we had family gatherings every weekend. We never had time to go out, just the two of us.

M: I got a little surprise for ya next weekend.

Criticism; Conflict Renewed

V: Yeah, it's always next weekend. It's never this weekend.

M: Eight weekends in a row.

V: I just went from not working at all and being home. We've both been through major job changes and all.

M: And I can't breathe.

V: But we're getting used to it and I feel so much better about going to work at three

(o'clock), three-thirty now than I did that first week.

M: Um.

V: I just wish I had more time to do what I wanted to do. I, it's just being…

M: I'll, I'll be able to stay…

V: …a wife and mother.

M: …to stay at home during the days a little bit more or I'll have to go in early but then I can take a couple of hours off in the afternoons.

Retaliation with Anger

V: Do you have to go in early every day?

M: I'm going to go in early every day.

V: Why?

M: 'Cause there are things I need to do every morning.

V: I think you just like going in to your office.

M: You don't know a thing about it then. Randy was in there early every day, tell me why?

V: Yeah, but he was home at a decent hour too.

M: He stays out late.

V: Eight to eight or eight to nine every day.

M: Every day.

V: Now, then, I don't want you taking that job. You forget it.

M: No.

GOTTMAN SAYS: This couple also has low levels of marital satisfaction. Unlike the previous couple, they have the "hot," corrosive kind of marital conflict characterized by what I call the "Four Horsemen of the Apocalypse": criticism, contempt, defensiveness and stonewalling. This type of conflict tends to lead to early divorce.

However, also unlike the previous couple, there is still a lot of strength in their relationship. Their friendship is intact. There is humor and affection, and they are confident that they can resolve their conflict.

Though the couple begins their discussion very well, by laughing, Valerie soon expresses anger because Mark's new job is demanding so much of his time. She then repairs this with humor and more affection. This shows that there is still quite a bit of strength in this marriage. The respite is only temporary; Valerie raises the family issue again. But Mark agrees affectionately, showing another strength: He makes her problems "their" problems.

They are doing very well discussing the problem until Valerie's angry line about going in early every day. This leads to a pattern of her anger and his defensiveness in response. So there is still a lot of strength in their interaction, but something is keeping him from fully understanding how hard it is for her to have him gone so much. Something is deteriorating in this relationship and it's exemplified by her ultimatums and his resistance.

When we were doing this research, we didn't intervene to help couples, and this one, unfortunately, divorced after seven years of marriage. Now I think we can prevent this type of marital meltdown. The secrets are in keeping fathers involved with their babies so they make the same kind of philosophical transformation in meaning that their wives are probably making; in teaching couples what to expect during this transition to parenthood; and in helping them with the inevitable marital conflict, sleepless irritability and depression that often follow a new baby.

Wilma, 31, and Harris, 35, have been married 11 years.

Wilma: The communication problem. Tell me your feelings. (Both laughing)

Harris: A lot of times I don't know. I've always been quiet.

W: Is it just because you have nothing to talk about, or is it because you don't want to talk about it?

H: A lot of times I don't know.

W: Okay. Example: when we went to Lake Bariessa. I mean, I can understand that you couldn't find your way around and everything, that was fine. But it still doesn't hurt to open your lips, you know?

H: I was kind of burned out that day…

W: Well, you suggested we go…

H: I was trying to take you out somewhere, then I was trying to figure out my money in the bank and I end up coming short…

W: You did all that driving up there…

H: Yeah. And I was trying to figure out my bank account and how I was going to, you know, have the gas money for the week.

W: But, like, when we got there, you didn't want to talk. We got off the truck, we got set up and you ate your sandwich. Your little bologna sandwich. (Both laughing)

H: Yeah. I was starving. (Laughing}

W: I didn't know you were. And then it was like, you still didn't want to talk, so Dominique and me started playing tennis.

H: It was almost time to go then and I had to drive back. I didn't want to check it out.

W: Yeah. I thought it was such a nice drive.

H: I didn't know it was going to be that far.

W: And I really appreciate that.

H: Thank you very much.

Playful Acceptance of Differences

W: You're welcome. I don't mind you talking about bills all the time, but we can only pay what we can pay, so why worry?

H: 'Cause that's how I am.

W: You shouldn't do that.

H: Well, I can't help it. I'm always trying to be preventive.

W: Okay, "Preventive." (Laughter)

H: I can't help it. I have learned from my mistakes. Have you ever heard of people worried about bills?

W: I've heard of those people. I'm one of those people.

H: And I'm one of those people, whether you know it or not.

W: The thing is, I just pay what I can. You can't give everybody money at the same time when you don't have it to give.

H: The only thing I can do is have life insurance for me and you. I paid the kids'. Now I can't pay ours.

W: So you haven't paid the insurance in a month and a half?

H: I paid the kids, but I haven't been able to pay ours.

W: You see, you don't say anything, so I've been thinking that everything is okay.

H: Yeah, I gathered that. (Laughter)

W: (Laughter) Honestly. We need to figure out how we can pay that before it's due. I mean, the same thing with the phone bill.

H: But you haven't been trying to keep that down. Yappity yappity yap!

W: Well, we'll try to figure it out. We'll both of us try to take something out.

H: Right. That's what I'd like.

W: All right. Work with me baby. And now maybe you'll start talking more. See, now you're sitting up here talking about this. And like that day at the park. We could have talked about that. It was a nice relaxing moment to discuss things.

H: I don't know what happened then. When I got there, I was blown out.

W: If you sit and talk with me like this…

H: When do we have a chance to sit down?

W: On weekends.

H: I don't think we have enough time on weekends to sit down.

W: See, that's why I said we need to take a day for ourselves. Momma would keep Dominique for a day. We've got to start focusing on ourselves more.

H: Mmm-hmm.

W: Just every now and then so we can do something for ourselves, even if it isn't anything more than taking in a movie.

H: Yeah.

W: Or go have dinner. When was the last time we had dinner in a restaurant?

H: That would be nice. Or go to a movie. How do you do it? First you go have dinner, then you go to a movie. (Laughter)

W: Or if you go to a movie early enough, you can go have dinner afterwards.

H: Right.

W: Right.

GOTTMAN SAYS: Wilma and Harris have a long-term, stable and happy marriage. They easily discuss two long-standing marital issues: the fact that he doesn't talk very much and she wants him to, and their financial differences. These issues are never going to change fundamentally. Our research has revealed that 69% of couples experience "perpetual problems"—issues with no resolution that couples struggle with for many years. Our data now lead us to believe that whenever you marry someone, your personality differences ensure that you and your partner will grapple with these issues forever. Marriages are only successful to the degree that the problems you have are ones you can cope with.

For most perpetual conflicts in marriages, what matters is not conflict resolution, but the attitudes that surround discussion of the conflict. Wilma and Harris both basically accept that there will always be differences between them, and they essentially accept one another as they are. Still, it is their ability to exchange viewpoints, making each other feel comfortable and supported all the while, that keeps them from getting gridlocked.

This couple, which is typical of our long-term couples, are real pros at being married and at using positive affect—like humor and gentle teasing—to de-escalate conflict. This is likely a sign that they are keeping their arousal levels low. Notice the wide array of strategies used to alleviate potential tension, such as expressing appreciation, softening complaints, responding nondefensively, backing down and using humor. The two of them do this together.

What these middle-aged spouses do is exactly what newlyweds who wind up stable and happy do, and this process moves them toward some semblance of problem-solving. What this master couple has effectively accomplished is to actualize the great marital paradox: that people can only change if they don't feel they have to.

Harris and Wilma make it look easy, just like a high-wire act makes it look easy. They are "athletes" at marriage, and that is one reason we study long-term marriages. There is a marital magic in what they do. The only function of my research is to make this marital magic clear so therapists can teach it to other couples.

READ MORE ABOUT IT

The Seven Principles for Making Marriage Work, John Gottman, Ph.D. (Crown, 1999)
The Marriage Clinic, John Gottman, Ph.D. (W. W. Norton, 1999)

John Gottman, Ph.D., is William Mifflin Professor of Psychology at the University of Washington in Seattle. Sybil Carrere, Ph.D., is a research scientist at the University of Washington in Seattle.

Reprinted with permission from *Psychology Today*, October 2000, pp. 42–47, 87. © 2000 by Sussex Publishers, Inc.

PRESCRIPTION FOR PASSION

Jealousy ignites rage, shame, even life-threatening violence.
But it is just as necessary as love. In fact, it preserves and protects that fragile emotion. Consider it a kind of old-fashioned mate insurance, an evolutionary glue that holds modern couples together.

BY DAVID M. BUSS, PH.D.

Every human alive is an evolutionary success story. If any of our ancestors had failed to survive an ice age, drought, predator or plague, the previously inviolate chain of descent would have been irreparably broken, and we would not be alive to tell the tale. Each of us owes our existence to thousands of generations of successful ancestors. As their descendants, we have inherited the passions that led to their success—passions that drive us, often blindly, through a lifelong journey in the struggle for survival, the pursuit of position and the search for relationships.

These passions have many sides. They inspire us to achieve life's goals. They impel us to satisfy our desire for sex, our yearning for prestige and our quest for love. But passions also have a darker, more sinister side. The same passions that inspire us to love can lead to the disastrous choice of a mate, the desperation of unrequited obsession or the terror of stalking. Jealousy can keep a couple committed or drive a man to savagely beat his wife.

Jealousy's Two Faces

Jealousy poses a paradox. Consider that in a sample of 651 university students who were actively dating, more than 33% reported that jealousy posed a significant problem in their current relationship. The problems ranged from loss of self-esteem to verbal abuse, from rage-ridden arguments to the terror of being stalked. But the irony of jealousy, which can shatter the most harmonious relationships, is that it flows from deep and abiding love. The paradox was reflected in O.J. Simpson's statement: "Let's say I committed this crime [the slaying of ex-wife Nicole Brown Simpson]. Even if I did, it would have to have been because I loved her very much, right?"

Consider these findings: 46% of a community sample said jealousy was an inevitable consequence of true love. St. Augustine noted this link when he declared, "He that is not jealous is not in love." Shakespeare's tormented Othello "dotes, yet doubts, suspects, yet strongly loves." Women and men typically interpret a partner's jealousy as a sign of the depth of their love; a partner's absence of jealousy as a lack of love. The psychologist Eugene Mathes of Western Illinois University asked a sample of unmarried but romantically involved men and women to complete a jealousy test. Seven years later, he contacted the participants again and asked them about the current status of their relationship. Roughly 25% had married, while 75% had broken up. The jealousy scores from seven years earlier for those who married averaged 168, whereas the scores for those who broke up registered significantly lower at 142. These results must be interpreted cautiously; it's just one study with a small sample. But it points to the idea that jealousy might be inexorably linked with long-term love. In fact, it may be integral to it.

Evolution of an Alarm

Jealousy is an adaptive emotion, forged over millions of years, symbiotic with long-term love. It evolved as a primary defense against threats of infidelity and abandonment. Coevolution tells us that reciprocal changes occur sequentially in interacting species or between the sexes in one species. As a result, women have become excellent detectors of deception, as indicated by their superiority in decoding nonverbal signals. Men, in turn, can be notoriously skilled at deceiving women.

Jealousy is activated when one perceives signs of defection—a strange scent, a sudden change in sexual behavior, a suspicious absence. It gets triggered when a partner holds eye contact with someone else for a split second too long, or when a rival stands too close to your loved one or is suddenly fascinated by the minutia of his or her life. These signals alert us to the possibility of infidelity, since they have been statistically linked with relationship loss over the long course of human evolutionary history.

Margaret Mead called jealousy 'a festering spot in every personality...'

Obviously, episodes of extreme irrational or pathological jealousy can destroy an otherwise solid marriage. In most instances, however, it's not the experience of jealousy per se that's the problem. Rather, it's the real threat of defection by a partner interested in a real rival. In 1931, Margaret Mead disparaged jealousy as "undesirable, a festering spot in every personality so afflicted, an ineffective negativistic attitude which is more likely to lose than to gain any goal." Her view has been shared by many, from advocates of polyamory, a modern form of open marriage, to religious treatises. But properly used, jealousy can enrich relationships, spark passion and amplify commitment. The total absence of jealousy, rather than its presence, is a more ominous sign for romantic partners, for it portends emotional bankruptcy.

This was certainly true for one wife, who, noting her husband's lack of jealousy, grew to feel unloved and began acting out. She raged at him, harassing him on the telephone at work, causing him great embarrassment. When the husband sought help from a therapist, he was advised to act the part of the jealous husband. Having learned over many years how a jealous person behaves, he was able to perform the role so skillfully and subtly that his wife of 21 years didn't realize he was role-playing. While he had seldom called home in the past, he now called his wife frequently to check on her, to see whether she was home and to ask exactly what she was doing. He made suspicious and critical remarks about any new clothes she wore, and expressed displeasure when she showed the slightest interest in another man. The result was dramatic. The wife, flattered by her husband's attentiveness and newfound interest, stopped her jealous behavior completely. She became pleasant and loving toward

her husband and expressed remorse over her earlier behavior. At an eight-month follow-up, she was still behaving more lovingly toward her husband, but as a precaution he still played the jealous one from time to time.

Evoking Jealousy

Once jealousy evolved in the human repertoire, it became fair game for partners to exploit for their own purposes. Eliciting jealousy intentionally emerged as an assessment device to gauge the strength of a mate's commitment. Both sexes do it, but not equally. In one study, 31% of women, but only 17% of men, reported that they had intentionally elicited jealousy in their romantic partner. Women and men also employ different tactics. In our study of newlyweds, we found that women more than men report flirting with others in front of a partner, showing interest in others, going out with others and talking to another man at a party, all to make their partner jealous or angry.

William Tooke, Ph.D., and his colleagues at the State University of New York at Plattsburgh have found strong sex differences in several clusters of acts designed to induce jealousy. First, women intentionally socialize with other people. One woman said that she purposefully neglected to invite her partner along when she went out with friends. Another said she made a point of talking with members of the opposite sex when she and her boyfriend went out to a bar. A third indicated that she made sure to casually mention to her boyfriend how much fun she had when she was out partying without him.

The second jealousy-inducing strategy centered on intentionally ignoring a partner. One woman reported acting distant and uninterested in her partner to make him think she didn't care about him that much. Another said she deliberately failed to answer her phone when she knew her boyfriend was calling so he would think she was out with someone else. Yet another told her boyfriend she did not have time to see him, even though it was the weekend.

The third mode of strategic jealousy induction was especially effective at pushing men's jealousy buttons—direct flirtation with other men. One woman reported dancing closely and seductively with someone her partner didn't like while he stood on the sidelines. Several reported going out to bars with members of the opposite sex and coming back to the boyfriend

a bit intoxicated. Others reported that they dressed in especially sexy outfits while going out without their boyfriends, a sure method of fanning a man's jealous flames.

A more subtle and ingenious tactic for evoking jealousy involves merely smiling at other men while out with a partner. Antonia Abbey, Ph.D., of Wayne State University, discovered a fascinating difference in how men and women interpret a woman's smiles. When women smile, men often erroneously read into it sexual interest, mistaking friendliness for romantic intent. Martie Haselton, Ph.D., of the University of Texas at Austin, and I have labeled men's sexual inference as "adaptive bias" in mind reading because it's part of men's unconscious strategy of casual sex. By inferring sexual interest from a woman's smile, men are more likely to make sexual overtures.

So when a woman smiles at another man while at a party with her partner, she deftly exploits the evolved psychology of two different men. The smile causes its target to think she's sexually interested in him, so he makes advances. Simultaneously, it evokes her partner's jealousy, so he gets angry both about the rival and about his perception that she's encouraging the other man. The upshot might be a confrontation between the two rivals or a lovers' quarrel. But who can blame a woman just for being friendly? No other method for strategically inducing jealousy is as effective, for it makes two men dance to a woman's tune with merely a well-timed glance.

Who Needs Jealousy?

Why do women walk such a dangerous tightrope, trifling with a mechanism known to unleash male violence? Gregory White, Ph.D., of Southern Oregon University, conducted an in-depth study of 150 heterosexual couples in California to find out. He first asked each of the 300 participants whether they had ever intentionally tried to make their partner jealous and why. Only a few women reported that they induced jealousy to punish their partner. Eight percent reported doing it to bolster their self-esteem. Ten percent admitted doing it to act out feelings of revenge on a partner for a previous wrong. Increasing a partner's commitment, however, was cited by 38% of women. By evoking jealousy, a woman causes her partner to believe that she has attractive alternatives available, so that if he does not display greater commitment she might depart for greener mating pastures. Women who successfully use this tactic are more likely to keep the commitment of their mates. Fully 40% of women, the largest group, reported using jealousy to test the strength of the bond. By evoking jealousy, a woman gains valuable information about the depth and consistency of her partner's commitment.

By evoking jealousy, a woman is telling her partner she could leave for greener mating pastures.

Women reap this benefit most when the need to test the bond is especially strong: Women whose partners have been away for a while, those whose partners experience a sudden surge in status, and women who feel they might be perceived as less desirable than their partner, all need vital appraisals of a man's commitment.

For both sexes, the key to understanding who needs jealousy is determining who has the most to lose. White asked all 300 participants to rate whether they were more, equally or less involved in the relationship than their partner. Relative involvement is a powerful clue as to which partner is more desirable on the mating market, according to the principle of least interest—the less interested partner has the upper hand on the scale of desirability. Although 61% of the couples were well matched in their level of involvement, 39% showed a mismatch. Does this index of relative involvement predict who will deploy the jealousy-induction strategy? The effect for men was modest: 15% of those who were less involved intentionally induced jealousy; 17% of those equally involved did, as did 22% of the men more involved. So there is a slight tendency for the less desirable men to attempt to evoke more jealousy.

The results for women were more dramatic. Whereas only 28% of the women who were less involved reported intentionally inspiring jealousy, fully 50% of the women who were more involved than their partner reported doing so. Since women who fall below their partners in overall desirability confront commitment problems more poignantly than other women, they induce jealousy to correct the imbalance.

Strategically inducing jealousy serves several key functions for women. It can bolster self-esteem because of the attention it attracts from other men. It can increase a

partner's commitment by making him realize how desirable she really is. And it can test the strength of the bond: If he reacts to her flirtations with emotional indifference, she knows he lacks commitment; if he gets jealous, she knows he's in love. Evoking jealousy, although it inflicts a cost on the partner, provides valuable information that's difficult to secure otherwise. And it often works.

Jealousy can also spark or rekindle sexual passion

Virgil Sheets, Ph.D., and his colleagues at Indiana State University confirmed that one of the most common reactions in men whose jealousy is aroused is to increase the attention they pay to their partners. After becoming jealous, men report that they are more likely to "try to keep track of what my partner is doing," "do something special for my partner" and "try to show my partner more attention."

Although evoking jealousy can serve a useful function, it must be used with skill and intelligence to avoid unleashing unintended consequences.

Igniting Sexual Passion

Jealousy can also spark or rekindle sexual passion in a relationship. Consider the case of Ben and Stacy, a couple attending an intensive five-day jealousy workshop conducted by the Israeli psychologist Ayala Pines, Ph.D. Ben, 15 years older than Stacy, had been married before, but had been divorced for five years when he first got involved with Stacy.

Although Stacy had had a few romantic relationships, she was still a virgin when they met. Ben was flattered at the attentions of a woman as young and attractive as Stacy, but soon became bored with their sex life, and yearned for sex with other women. This unleashed intense jealousy in Stacy, which brought them into the workshop to solve what Ben described as "her problem." He saw no reason that he should not sleep with other women. During the early days of the workshop, Ben brought up Stacy's insecurity and jealousy, indicated his disapproval and proceeded to flirt with the other women in the group. During one session, Stacy was berated by the group for being so jealous. Tears streamed down her cheeks and others in the group responded with hugs and affection. The most attractive man in the group was espe-

cially supportive. He continued to comfort her, even after the session ended and Ben and the others had left the room. Hugging turned to kissing and eventually they had passionate sex right on the floor.

When Ben discovered the infidelity, he was furious, saying, "You hurt me more than any woman has done, and I trusted you to protect my feelings." Over the next two days the therapy group focused on Ben's jealousy. But when asked by the therapist whether any good had come of the event, he replied, "When we made love afterward, it was the most passionate sex we had ever had. It was unbelievably intense and exciting." Stacy agreed.

Ben's jealousy revived the sexual passion in their relationship. Why? Astute readers already have clues to the most probable explanations: The other man's attention reaffirmed Stacy's attractiveness in Ben's eyes. When it penetrates men's minds that other desirable men are interested in their partner, they perceive their partner as more sexually radiant.

There is also an evolutionary reason that Ben's jealousy reignited his passion for Stacy. A man whose partner has just been inseminated by another man is most at risk for genetic cuckoldry. By having sex with Stacy immediately following her infidelity, he reduced the odds that she would become pregnant with another man's child, although he obviously didn't think about it in those terms. The passionate nature of the sex implies that she had an orgasm, which causes the woman to retain more sperm. Increased sperm retention, in ancestral times, would have meant an increased likelihood of conception. Ben was merely a modern player in an ancient ritual in which men competed with one another in the battle for successful fertilization.

Emotional Wisdom

In my studies, I have discovered that some signs of jealousy are accurately interpreted as acts of love. When a man drops by unexpectedly to see what his partner is doing, this mode of jealous vigilance functions to preserve the safe haven of exclusivity while simultaneously communicating love. When a woman loses sleep thinking about her partner and wondering whether he's with someone else, it indicates simultaneously the depth of her love and the intensity of her jealousy. When a man tells his friends he is madly in love with a woman, it serves the dual purpose of conveying love and warning potential rivals to keep their hands off.

It is unlikely that love, with its tremendous psychological investment, could have evolved without a defense to shield it from the constant threat of rivals and the possibility of betrayal from a partner.

Jealousy evolved to fill that void, motivating vigilance as the first line of defense, and violence as the last. In its extreme forms, this vital shield has been called delusional, morbid and pathological, a symptom of neurosis and a syndrome of psychosis. Therapists try to expunge it from patients and individuals try to suppress it in themselves.

The experience of jealousy can be psychologically painful. But it alerts us to real threats from real rivals. It tells us when a partner's sexual indifference might not merely mean he or she is distracted by work. It causes us to remember subtle signals that, when properly assembled, portend a real defection.

Evolution has equipped all of us with a rich menu of emotions, including jealousy, envy, fear, rage, joy, humiliation, passion and love. The knowledge that comes with a deeper understanding of our dangerous passions will not eliminate conflicts between lovers, between rivals or between lovers who become rivals. But it may, in some small measure, give us the emotional wisdom to deal with them.

READ MORE ABOUT IT

The Red Queen: Sex and the Evolution of Human Nature, Matt Ridley (Penguin, 1995)

Romantic Jealousy: Causes, Symptoms, Cures, Ayala M. Pines, Ph.D. (Routledge, 1998)

This article is from Dangerous Passion *by David Buss, Ph.D. (Free Press, 2000). He is a professor of psychology at the University of Texas at Austin.*

Reprinted from *Psychology Today*, May/June 2000, pp. 54–61. Excerpted from *Dangerous Passion: Why Jealousy Is as Necessary as Love and Sex,* by David M. Buss. © 2000 by David M. Buss, by permission of The Free Press, a division of Simon & Schuster, Inc.

Forgiveness: Who Does It and How Do They Do It?

Abstract

Forgiveness is a suite of prosocial motivational changes that occurs after a person has incurred a transgression. People who are inclined to forgive their transgressors tend to be more agreeable, more emotionally stable, and, some research suggests, more spiritually or religiously inclined than people who do not tend to forgive their transgressors. Several psychological processes appear to foster or inhibit forgiveness. These processes include empathy for the transgressor, generous attributions and appraisals regarding the transgression and transgressor, and rumination about the transgression. Interpreting these findings in light of modern trait theory would help to create a more unified understanding of how personality might influence forgiveness.

Keywords

forgiveness; research; review; personality; theory

Michael E. McCullough[1]
Department of Psychology, Southern Methodist University, Dallas, Texas

Relating to others—whether strangers, friends, or family—inevitably exposes people to the risk of being offended or harmed by those other people. Throughout history and across cultures, people have developed many strategies for responding to such transgressions. Two classic responses are avoidance and revenge—seeking distance from the transgressor or opportunities to harm the transgressor in kind. These responses are normal and common, but can have negative consequences for individuals, relationships, and perhaps society as a whole.

Psychologists have been investigating interpersonal transgressions and their aftermath for years. However, although many of the world's religions have advocated the concept of forgiveness as a productive response to such transgressions (McCullough & Worthington, 1999), scientists have begun only recently to devote sustained attention to forgiveness. Nevertheless, researchers have made substantial progress in illuminating forgiveness during this short amount of time.

WHAT IS FORGIVENESS?

Most psychologists concur with Enright, Gassin, and Wu (1992) that forgiveness is distinct from pardon (which is more apposite to the legal realm), condonation (which implies justifying the transgression), and excusing (which implies recognition that the transgressor had a good reason for committing the transgression). Most scholars also concur that forgiveness is distinct from reconciliation—a term implying restoration of a relationship. But what is forgiveness foundationally? The first definition for "forgive" in *Webster's New Universal Unabridged Dictionary* (1983) is "to give up resentment against or the desire to punish; to stop being angry with; to pardon" (p. 720). Although this definition conflates the concepts of forgiveness and pardon, it nearly suffices as an adequate psychological definition because it points to what is perhaps the essence of forgiveness: prosocial motivational change on the victim's part. By using the term "prosocial," I am suggesting that when people forgive, they become less motivated to harm their transgressor (or their relationship with the transgressor) and, simultaneously, become more motivated to act in ways that will benefit the transgressor (or their relationship with the transgressor).

My colleagues and I have assumed that most people are motivated (at least initially) to respond to transgressions with other forms of negative behavior—particularly, to avoid contact with the transgressor and to seek revenge. When people forgive, they counteract or modulate these motivations to avoid or seek revenge so that the probability of restoring benevolent and harmonious interpersonal relations with their transgressors is increased (McCullough, Bellah, Kilpatrick, & Johnson, 2001; McCullough et al., 1998; McCullough, Worthington, & Rachal, 1997). When people indicate that they have forgiven a transgressor, we believe they are indicating that their perceptions of the transgression and transgressor no longer stimulate motivations for avoidance and revenge. Instead, a forgiver experiences the return of benevolent, constructive motivations regarding the transgressor. In this conceptualization, forgiveness is not a motivation per se, but rather, a complex of prosocial changes in one's motivations.

Locating forgiveness at the motivational level, rather than at the level of overt behaviors, accommodates the fact that many people who would claim to have forgiven someone who has harmed them might not behave in any particularly new and benevolent way toward their transgressors. Forgiveness might not cause an employee who forgives her boss for an insult to behave any less negatively toward the boss: Avoidance and revenge in the workplace can put one's job at risk, so most people are probably careful to inhibit the expression of such negative motivations in the first place, regardless of how strong they might have been as

a result of the transgression. The motivational definition does imply, however, that the employee would experience a reduced *potential* for avoidant and vengeful behavior (and an increased potential for benevolent behavior) toward the boss, which might or might not be expressed overtly. A motivational definition also accommodates the fact that someone can make public gestures of forgiveness toward his or her transgressor even in the absence of such prosocial motivational changes.

How would one describe the sorts of people who tend to engage in the motivational transformations collectively called forgiveness? What psychological processes appear to help people forgive? Several research teams have been investigating these questions in detail. In this article, I describe what psychological science has revealed about who tends to forgive and the psychological processes that may foster or hinder forgiveness for specific transgressions.

THE FORGIVING PERSONALITY

Researchers have found that the disposition to forgive is correlated (positively or negatively) with a broad array of variables, including several personality traits, psychological symptoms, moral emotions, hope, and self-esteem (e.g., see Berry, Worthington, Parrott, O'Connor, & Wade, in press; Tangney, Fee, Reinsmith, Boone, & Lee, 1999). For simplicity, it is useful to reduce this potentially bewildering array of correlates to a smaller set of higher-order personality factors, such as those in the Five Factor (or Big Five) personality taxonomy (McCrae & Costa, 1999). Several recent research efforts suggest that the disposition to forgive may be related most strongly to two of these higher-order dimensions: agreeableness and emotional stability (Ashton, Paunonen, Helmes, & Jackson, 1998; Berry et al., in press; Mc-

Cullough et al., 2001; McCullough & Hoyt, 1999). Some evidence also suggests that the disposition to forgive is related positively to religiousness and spirituality.

Agreeableness

Agreeableness is a personality dimension that incorporates traits such as altruism, empathy, care, and generosity. Highly agreeable people tend to thrive in the interpersonal realm and experience less conflict in relationships than less agreeable people do. Trait theorists and researchers have long been aware that agreeable people typically are rated highly on descriptors such as "forgiving" and low on descriptors such as "vengeful." Research specifically on the disposition to forgive has also confirmed the agreeableness-forgiveness association (Ashton et al., 1998; McCullough & Hoyt, 1999).

People who appear dispositionally inclined to forgive also possess many of the lower-order traits that agreeableness subsumes. For instance, compared with people who are not inclined to forgive, they tend to be less exploitative of and more empathic toward others (Tangney et al., 1999). They also report higher levels of moral responsibility and demonstrate a greater tendency to share resources with people who have been rude and inconsiderate to them (Ashton et al., 1998).

Emotional Stability

Emotional stability is a personality dimension that involves low vulnerability to experiences of negative emotion. Emotionally stable people also tend not to be moody or overly sensitive. Several studies demonstrate that people who are high in emotional stability score higher on measures of the disposition to forgive than do their less emotionally stable counterparts (Ashton et al., 1998; Berry et al., in press; McCullough & Hoyt, 1999).

Religiousness and Spirituality

A third personality trait that might be related to the disposition to forgive—and one that recent research suggests is empirically distinct from the Big Five personality factors—is religiousness or spirituality. A review of results from seven studies suggested that people who consider themselves to be highly religious or spiritual tend to value forgiveness more highly and see themselves as more forgiving than do people who consider themselves less religious or spiritual (McCullough & Worthington, 1999).

Despite the consistency of the existing evidence on this point, few studies have addressed whether religiousness and spirituality are associated with forgiving specific transgressors for specific, real-life transgressions. Indeed, studies addressing this issue hint that religiousness-spirituality and forgiveness of individual transgressions may be essentially unrelated (e.g., McCullough & Worthington, 1999). Therefore, it is possible that religious and spiritual people are no more forgiving than are less religious and spiritual people in real life, but only believe themselves (or aspire) to be highly forgiving. The connection of religiousness and spirituality to forgiveness of actual transgressions remains to be investigated more fully (McCullough & Worthington, 1999).

WHAT DO PEOPLE DO WHEN THEY FORGIVE?

Recent research has also helped to illuminate the psychological processes that people employ when they forgive. The processes that have been studied to date include empathy, attributions and appraisals, and rumination.

Empathy for the Transgressor

Empathy has been defined by some scholars as the vicarious experience of another person's emotional state, and by others as a specific emotion characterized by compassion, tenderness, and sympathy. Empathy (defined as a specific emotional state) for a particular transgressor correlates strongly with the extent to which a victim forgives the transgressor for a particular transgression. In several correlational studies (McCullough et al., 1997, 1998; Worthington et al., 2000), people's reports of the extent to which they had forgiven a specific transgressor were highly correlated with the extent to which they experienced empathy for the transgressor.

Empathy also helps explain why some social-psychological variables influence forgiveness. The well-known effect of transgressors' apologies on victims' likelihood of forgiving apparently is almost totally mediated by the effects of the apologies on victims' empathy for the transgressors (McCullough et al., 1997, 1998). When transgressors apologize, they implicitly express some degree of fallibility and vulnerability, which might cause victims to feel empathic, thereby motivating them to forgive the transgressors. Also, research on psychological interventions designed to help people forgive specific transgressors has revealed that empathy fosters forgiveness. Indeed, empathy for the transgressor is the only psychological variable that has, to date, been shown to facilitate forgiveness when induced experimentally (McCullough et al., 1997; Worthington et al., 2000), although experimental research on this issue is still in its infancy.

Generous Attributions and Appraisals

Another factor associated with the extent to which someone forgives a specific transgressor is the extent to which the victim makes generous attributions and appraisals about the transgression and transgressor. Compared with people who have not forgiven their transgressors, people who have forgiven their transgressors appraise the transgressors as more likable (Bradfield & Aquino, 1999), and the transgressors' explanations for the transgressions as more adequate and honest (Shapiro, 1991). In such situations, forgiveness is also related to the victim's appraisal of the severity of the transgression (Shapiro, 1991). People who tend to forgive their spouses also tend to attribute less responsibility to their spouses for their negative behavior than do people who do not tend to forgive their spouses (Fincham, 2000). Thus, forgivers apparently are inclined to give their transgressors "the benefit of the doubt." Whether the correlations between appraisals-attributions and forgiveness reflect the causal effects of attributional and appraisal processes, or simply reflect victims' accurate perceptions of the actual qualities of transgressors and transgressions that cause them to be more or less forgivable, remains to be explored more fully in the future.

Rumination About the Transgression

A third factor associated with the extent to which someone forgives a specific transgressor is the extent to which the victim ruminates about the transgression. Rumination, or the tendency to experience intrusive thoughts, affects, and images about past events, appears to hinder forgiveness. The more people brood about a transgression, the higher are their levels of revenge and avoidance motivation (McCullough et all., 1998, 2001). In a recent longitudinal study, my colleagues and I also found that victims who continued to ruminate about a particular transgression made considerably less progress in forgiving the transgressor during an 8-week follow-up period (McCullough et al., 2001). This longitudinal evidence indicates that the degree to which people reduce their ruminations about a particular transgression over time is a good predictor of how much progress they will make in forgiving their transgressor.

FUTURE RESEARCH AND THEORY

So far, research has shown that people who are more agreeable, more emotionally stable, and (possibly) more spiritual or religious have a stronger disposition to forgive than do their less agreeable, less emotionally stable, and less spiritually and religiously inclined counterparts. Moreover, research has shown that empathizing with the transgressor, making generous attributions and appraisals regarding the transgressor and transgression, and refraining from rumination about the transgression are associated with the extent to which a victim forgives a specific transgressor.

An interesting step for future research on the personality factors and psychological mechanisms associated with forgiveness would be to explore the specific cognitive and emotional habits of agreeable, emotionally stable, and (perhaps) religiously or spiritually inclined people that predispose them to forgive. For example, agreeableness reflects a tendency toward kindness and prosociality, so perhaps agreeable people are particularly inclined to experience empathy for their transgressors. They might also be inclined to perceive the transgressions they have incurred as less intentional and less severe, and their transgressors as more likable and contrite, than do less agreeable people.

Likewise, emotionally stable people might find forgiveness easier than people who are less emotionally stable because of perceptual processes: Emotionally stable people perceive many environmental factors—including physical pain and negative life events—less negatively than do less emotionally stable people. Emotionally stable people also ruminate less about negative life events. Research addressing such potential links between personality traits and psychological processes would enrich psychology's understanding of how personality might influence the extent to which people forgive particular transgressors.

Such empirical advances should be coupled with theoretical refinements. It might prove particularly useful to frame such investigations in the context of modern trait theory. Trait theorists such as McCrae and Costa (1999) have advocated for conceptualizing the empirical links between traits and real-life behavioral proclivities as causal connections that reflect how *basic tendencies* (i.e., traits) are "channelized" into *characteristic adaptations,* or approaches to negotiating life within one's own cultural and environmental context. Using McCrae and Costa's framework to theorize about forgiveness might explain how the basic, biologically based tendencies that are reflected in measures of higher-order personality dimensions lead people to use forgiveness to address certain problems encountered in daily life—namely, interpersonal transgressions.

Such a theoretical framework could lead to other interesting questions: Insofar as forgiveness can be viewed as a characteristic adaptation of agreeable and emotionally stable people, why might agreeable and emotionally stable people be predisposed to use forgiveness for navigating their social worlds? Is forgiveness a by-product of other characteristic adaptations resulting from agreeableness and emotional stability (such as a capacity for empathy, a tendency to make generous attributions regarding the negative behavior of other people, or an ability to refrain from rumination about negative events? Or is it more accurate to view forgiveness as a goal to which agreeable and emotionally stable people actively strive, using the other characteristic psychological adaptations (e.g., capacity for empathy, tendency to form generous attributions, disinclination to ruminate) associated with agreeableness and emotional stability as footholds on the climb toward that goal? Answers to these questions would raise even more interesting questions. In any case, more sophisticated theorizing would transform this new area of research from simply a search for the correlates of forgiveness to a quest to truly understand forgiveness and its place in human personality and social functioning.

Note

1. Address correspondence to Michael McCullough, Department of Psychology, Southern Methodist University, PO Box 750442, Dallas, TX 75275-0442; e-mail: mikem@at@;smu.edu.

References

Ashton, M. C., Paunonen, S. V., Helmes, E., & Jackson, D. N. (1998). Kin altruism, reciprocal altruism, and the Big Five personality factors. *Evolution and Human Behavior,* 243–255.

Berry, J. W., Worthington, E. L., Parrott, L., O'Connor, L. E., & Wade, N. G. (in press). Dispositional forgivingness: Development and construct validity of the Transgression Narrative Test of Forgivingness (TNTF). *Personality and Social Psychology Bulletin.*

Bradfield, M., & Aquino, K. (1999). The effects of blame attributions and offender likeableness on forgiveness and revenge in the workplace. *Journal of Management, 25,* 607–631.

Enright, R. D., Gassin, E. A., & Wu, C. (1992). Forgiveness: A developmental view. *Journal of Moral Education, 21,* 99–114.

Fincham, F. D. (2000). The kiss of the porcupines: From attributing responsibility to forgiving. *Personal Relationships, 7,* 1–23.

McCrae, R. R., & Costa, P. T., Jr. (1999). A five-factor theory of personality. In L. A. Pervin & O. P. John (Eds.), *Handbook of personality: Theory and research* (pp. 139–153). New York: Guilford.

McCullough, M. E., Bellah, C. G., Kilpatrick, S. D., & Johnson, J. L. (2001). Vengefulness: Relationships with forgiveness, rumination, well-being, and the Big Five. *Personality and Social Psychology Bulletin, 27,* 601–610.

McCullough, M. E., & Hoyt, W. T. (1999, August). *Recovering the person from interpersonal forgiving.* Paper presented at the annual meeting of the American Psychological Association, Boston.

McCullough, M. E., Rachal, K. D., Sandage, S. J., Worthington, E. L., Brown, S. W., & Hight, T. L. (1998). Interpersonal forgiving in close relationships: II. Theoretical elaboration and measurement. *Journal of Personality and Social Psychology, 75,* 1586–1603.

McCullough, M. E., & Worthington, E. L. (1999). Religion and the forgiving personality. *Journal of Personality, 67,* 1141–1164.

McCullough, M. E., Worthington, E. L., & Rachal, K. C. (1997). Interpersonal forgiving in close relationships. *Journal of Personality and Social Psychology, 73,* 321–336.

Shapiro, D. L. (1991). The effects of explanations on negative reactions to deceit. *Administrative Science Quarterly, 36,* 614–630.

Tangney, J., Fee, R., Reinsmith, C., Boone, A. L., & Lee, N. (1999, August). *Assessing individual differences in the propensity to forgive.* Paper presented at the annual meeting of the American Psychological Association, Boston.

Webster's new universal unabridged dictionary. (1983). New York: Dorset and Baker.

Worthington, E. L., Kurusu, T. A., Collins, W., Berry, J. W., Ripley, J. S., & Baier, S. N. (2000). Forgiving usually takes time: A lesson learned by studying interventions to promote forgiveness. *Journal of Psychology and Theology, 28,* 3–20.

Recommended Reading

McCrae, R. R., & Costa, P. T., Jr. (1999). (See References)

McCullough, M. E., Bellah, C. G. Kilpatrick, S. D., & Johnson, J. L. (2001). (See References)

McCullough, M. E., Pargament, K. I., & Thoresen, C. T. (Eds.). (2000). *Forgiveness: Theory, research, and practice.* New York: Guilford

McCullough, M. E., Rachal, K. C., Sandage, S. J., Worthington, E. L., Brown, S. W., & Hight, T. L. (1998). (See References)

McCullough, M. E., & Worthington, E. L. (1999). (See References)

From *Current Directions in Psychological Science,* December 2001, pp. 194-197. © 2001 by New Perspectives Quarterly. Reprinted by permission of Blackwell Publishers, Inc.

UNIT 5

Dynamics of Personal Adjustment: The Individual and Society

Unit Selections

Key Points to Consider

- Is America becoming a teen-centered society? If you believe the answer is yes, why do you think this is happening?

- In her article, Susan Faludi maintains that the American man has been betrayed. What does she mean by this?

- What is crowding? How does crowding differ from other concepts such as density? Is crowding more negative than positive?

- What is the definition of prejudice? Describe the jigsaw classroom and how it functions.

- What is trauma? What are the effects of terror and disaster on the human psyche?

- Are American families drifting apart? Defend your answer.

- Why are Americans working more today than ever before?

 **Links: www.dushkin.com/online/**
These sites are annotated in the World Wide Web pages.

AFF Cult Group Information
http://www.csj.org/index.html
Explanations of Criminal Behavior
http://www.uaa.alaska.edu/just/just110/crime2.html
National Clearinghouse for Alcohol and Drug Information
http://www.health.org
Schools Health Education Unit (SHEU)
http://www.sheu.org.uk/sheu.htm

The passing of each decade brings changes to society. Some historians have suggested that changes are occurring more rapidly than ever before. In other words, history appears to take less time to occur. How has American society changed historically? The inventory is long. Technological advances can be found everywhere. Not long ago, few people knew what the terms palm pilot and zip drive signified. Today these terms are readily identified with the rapidly changing computer industry. Twenty-five years ago, Americans felt fortunate to own a 13-inch television that received 3 local stations. Now people feel deprived if they cannot select from 250 different worldwide channels on their big, rear-screen projection sets. Today we can e-mail a message to the other side of the world faster than we can propel a missile to the same place.

In the Middle Ages, Londoners worried about the bubonic plague. Before vaccines were available, people feared polio and other diseases. Today much concern is focused on the transmission and cure of AIDS, the discovery of more carcinogenic substances, and the greenhouse effect. In terms of mental health, psychologists see few hysterics, the type of patient seen by Sigmund Freud in the 1800s. Psychosomatic ulcers and alcohol and drug addiction are more common today. In other words, lifestyle, more than disease, is killing Americans.

Issues concerning the changing American family continue to grab headlines. Nearly every popular magazine carries a story or two bemoaning the passing of the traditional, nuclear family and the decline in "family values."

And as if these spontaneous or unplanned changes are not enough to cope with, some individuals are intentionally trying to change the world. Witness, for example, the continuing dramatic changes in eastern Europe and the Middle East.

This list of societal transformations, while not exhaustive, reflects society's continual demand for adaptation by each of its members. It is not just society at large, however, that places stress on us. Smaller units within society, such as our work group, demand constant adaptation by individuals. Work groups expand and contract with every economic fluctuation. Even when group size remains stable, new members come and go as turnover takes place; hence, changes in the dynamics of the group occur in response to the new personalities. Each change, whether welcome or not, increases the stress of society on its individual members. This unit addresses the interplay between the individual and society (or culture) in producing the problems each creates for the other.

The feminist movement has created continuing changes in American society. In the first article, Susan Faludi, who first wrote about the feminist movement, excerpts her latest book on masculinity. Faludi contends that American men have no idea today what their role should be and how the ideal man should behave.

The next article, "Coping With Crowding," discusses early as well as recent research on the effects of crowding. Crowding is an important issue because the world population continues to grow. The early research, which showed that crowding was probably detrimental, is criticized. Newer research suggests that we are

much better at coping with environmental changes (such as an increase in number of people present) than believed earlier.

In the following article, "Nobody Left to Hate," another common social issue is discussed—prejudice. Social psychologists believe that prejudice is learned and can be overcome by new ways of thinking. In this article, Elliott Aronson shares with the reader his technique, known as the jigsaw classroom, for overcoming racial and ethnic bigotry in schools. Aronson also claims that this technique can alter the whole school climate and make schools more harmonious.

A more recent societal stressor in the United States is the reality and prospect of terrorism. The federal government expects terrorism to continue, and the government's continued warnings do little to assuage fears. The article "Disaster and Trauma" reviews various aspects of disastrous and traumatic events. Specifically, the article reviews the effects of trauma, which can last much longer than the event itself, as well as ways to cope with disaster. The next article tells how individuals who feel terrorized and traumatized can be helped.

Families often provide comfort and support for their members during difficult times. American families, however, seem to be drifting apart, at least says Barbara LeBey in her essay, "American Familier Are Drifting Apart." What this decline means for American society and why it has occurred are the focus of this article.

Our busy but normal day-to-day lives also take a toll on us. Americans seem more rushed and busier than ever. In "How to Multitask," Catherine Bush explores how we can motivate ourselves to keep up this pace and forgive ourselves when we cannot. She also explains the role of the nervous system in our ability to concentrate on several tasks at once. Finally, in "Work, Work, Work, Work!" Mark Hunter discusses how the boundaries between work and home and leisure have blurred. Hunter shares tips for coping with the increased pressure to work endless hours.

The Betrayal Of The American Man

BOOK EXCERPT: **Her groundbreaking 'Backlash' looked at the 'undeclared war on women.' Now in 'Stiffed,' the author explores the unseen war on men—the pressure to be masculine in a culture that no longer honors traditional codes of manhood.**

By Susan Faludi

When I listen to the sons born after World War II, born to the fathers who won that war, I sometimes find myself in a reverie. I imagine a boy, in bed pretending to sleep, waiting for his father. The door opens, and the hall light streams in, casting a cutout shadow man across the bedroom floor. A minute later, the boy, wearing his coonskin cap and clutching his flashlight, races after his father along the shadowy upper hallway, down the stairs and out the screen door. The man and the boy kneel on the scratchy wool of the father's old navy peacoat, and the father snaps off the boy's flashlight. The father directs the boy's vision to a faraway glimmer. Its name is Echo. The boy looks up, knowing that the satellite his father is pointing out is more than just an object; it is a paternal gift rocketing him into his future, a miraculous inheritance encased in the transit of an artificial star, infinitesimally tiny, impossibly bright.

I knew this boy. Like everyone else who grew up in the late 1950s and early 1960s, I knew dozens of him. He was Bobby on the corner, who roamed the neighborhood with his cap gun and holster, terrorizing girls and household pets. He was Frankie, who blew off part of his pinkie while trying to ignite a miniature rocket in the schoolyard. Even if he wasn't brought out into the backyard and shown a satellite glinting in the sky, he was introduced to the same promise and the same vision, and by such a father. Many of these fathers were veterans of World War II or Korea, but their bloody paths to virility were not ones they sought to pass on, or usually even discuss. This was to be the era of manhood after victory, when the pilgrimage to masculinity would be guided not by the god of war Mars, but by the dream of a pioneering trip to the planet Mars. The satellite; here was a visible patrimony, a visual marker of vaulting technological power and progress to be

claimed in the future by every baby-boom boy. The men of the fathers' generation had "won" the world and now they were giving it to their sons.

Four decades later, as the nation wobbled toward the millennium, its pulse-takers all seemed to agree that a domestic apocalypse was underway: American manhood was under siege. Newspaper editors, legislators, preachers, marketers, no matter where they perched on the political spectrum, had a contribution to make to the chronicles of the "masculinity crisis." Right-wing talk-radio hosts and left-wing men's-movement spokesmen found themselves uncomfortably on common ground. MEN ON TRIAL, the headlines cried, THE TROUBLE WITH BOYS. Journalists—myself included—raced to report on one young-male hot spot after another: Tailhook, the Citadel, the Spur Posse, South Central gangsters, militiamen blowing up federal buildings and abortion clinics, schoolyard shooters across the country.

CLOSING OF THE AMERICAN JOB

In the new economy, work moved from vital production
and job security to paper pushing and massive layoffs

The Broken Promise

On the surface, said Richard Foster, who came to McDonnell Douglas in the late '60s to work in the NASA space lab, life as an aerospace man seemed to offer the ultimate in masculine freedom. "It was idyllic," he told me. "All these little green lawns and houses all in a row. You could drive the freeways and plan your life out." But as time went on, he came to feel that it had all been planned without him, that he was expected to take the initiative in a game in which he was not even a player. "You began to feel so isolated," he said. Like the rest of the managers, he "belonged" to the company in only the most tenuous way. In the end, he would become a casualty of various corporate "cost-reduction" programs five times, his salary plunging from $80,000 to $28,000 to zero. Which was why he was sitting in a vinyl banquette in a chain restaurant in the shadow of McDonnell Douglas's blueglass tower in the middle of the afternoon, talking to me. "The next thing you know," he said, "you're standing outside, looking in. And you begin to ask, as a man, what is my role? What is it, really, that I do?"

About 11 miles up the road, a starkly different kind of leave-taking was unfolding at the Long Beach Naval Shipyard, one of the military bases slated for closure in 1995. If McDonnell Douglas had been the emblematic postwar corporation—full of functionaries whose jobs were unclear, even to themselves—the shipyard represented a particular vintage of American masculinity, monumental in its pooled effort, indefatigable in its industry and built on a sense of useful productivity. Ike Burr, one of the first black men to break into upper management, was a shipfitter who climbed steadily to project

superintendent. "Everything you ever dreamed of is here," Burr said. Unlike the McDonnell Douglas men, he wasn't referring to his dream house in the suburbs. He was talking about the work itself. "The shipyard is like a world within itself. Most items are one-of-a-type items, done once and not to be repeated. There's satisfaction in it, because you start and complete something. You *see* what you've created. The world of custom-made is finished—except here." After the shipyard's closing was announced, Burr postponed his official signing-out. He had found a temporary job at another military installation and was always "too busy" to get back to Long Beach to turn in his badge. But one morning he arrived to pay his last respects. He dressed sharply for the occasion: double-breasted gray suit, paisley tie and matching pocket hankie, even a hint of cologne. The morning management meeting was underway and he had been asked to stop by. He offered a few pointers, and then the shipyard commander gave an impromptu speech—about how Burr was the kind of guy "you could rely on to get the job done." Then he handed Burr a homemade plaque with a lengthy inscription.

Burr tucked it under his arm, embarrassed by the attention. "I better go get the signing-out business over," he said, his voice bumping over choppy seas. He headed out to make the rounds and get his termination physical. By late afternoon, Ike Burr had arrived at a small office, to sign a form surrendering the code word that gave him access to the yard. Though he burst out laughing as he signed, his words belied the laughter. "I have nothing in my possession," he said. "I have lost everything."

S.F.

In the meantime, the media's softer lifestyle outlets happily turned their attention to male-crisis lite: the retreat to cigar clubs and lap-dancing emporiums, the boom in male cosmetic surgery and the abuse of steroids, the brisk sales of Viagra. Social scientists pontificated on "endangered" young black men in the inner cities, Ritalin-addicted white "bad boys" in the suburbs, "deadbeat dads" everywhere and, less frequently, the anguish of downsized male workers. Social psychologists issued reports on a troubling rise in male-distress signals—from depressive disorders to suicides to certain criminal behaviors.

Pollsters investigated the electoral habits of a new voting bloc they called "the Angry White Male." Marketers hastened to turn the crisis into entertainment and profits from TV shows like "The Man Show" to T shirts that proclaimed DESTROY ALL GIRLS or WIFE BEATER. And by the hundreds of thousands, men without portfolio confirmed the male-crisis diagnosis, convening in

Washington for both the black Nation of Islam-led Million Man March and a largely white, evangelical-led Promise Keepers rally entitled, hopefully, "Stand in the Gap."

If so many concurred in the existence of a male crisis, consensus collapsed as soon as anyone asked the question Why. Everyone proposed a favorite whipping boy or, more often, whipping girl, and blame-seekers on all sides went after their selected culprits with righteous and bitter relish. Feminist mothers, indulgent liberals, videogame makers or testosterone itself all came under attack.

At Ground Zero of the Masculinity Crisis

THE SEARCH FOR AN ANSWER TO that question took me on a six-year odyssey, with stops along the way at a shuttered shipyard in Long Beach, a suburban living room where a Promise Keepers

group met, a Cleveland football stadium where fans grieved the loss of their team, a Florida horse farm where a Vietnam vet finally found peace, a grassy field in Waco where militiamen searched for an enemy and a slick magazine office where young male editors contended with a commodified manhood. But I began investigating this crisis where you might expect a feminist journalist to begin: at the weekly meetings of a domestic-violence group. Wednesday evenings in a beige stucco building a few blocks from the freeway in Long Beach, Calif., I attended a gathering of men under court order to repent the commission of an act that stands as the emblematic masculine sin of our age. What did I expect to divine about the broader male condition by monitoring a weekly counseling session for batterers? That men are by nature brutes? Or, more optimistically, that the efforts of such a group might point to methods of "curing" such beastliness?

GHETTO STAR

In a South-Central gang, Kody Scott finally felt useful as a man. But the biggest part of the 'work' was promoting the gangster image.

Glamour in the 'Hood

My father's generation was the last responsible generation," said Sanyika Shakur (now Kody Scott's legally adopted name) as he welcomed me in August 1997 to his girlfriend's two-bedroom house in California's San Fernando Valley. Four years had passed since the publication of Shakur's best-selling memoir, "Monster: The Autobiography of an L.A. Gang Member," written while he was serving a four-year sentence for robbery at Pelican Bay State Prison. The book's cover photo of the pumped-up, bare-chested author clutching a semiautomatic MAC-10, combined with the much-advertised news of his six-figure advance, turned the former member of the Eight-Tray Gangsters (a Crips set in South-Central L.A.) into what he rightly called a "ghetto star."

Shakur had just been released from jail three days earlier, after a year's sentence for a parole violation, his second such since the publication of what was supposed to be his transformational autobiography. He had fled after his first violation, and the police eventually found him on a neighborhood porch, receiving a long line of autograph seekers. The dictates of a celebrity culture demanded a manhood forged by being glamorous, not responsible.

Getting a rep:
'If the media knows about you,
damn, that's the top,' says Scott

As a young man, he had still hoped that he could demonstrate a workmanlike "usefulness" within his gang set. "You put in work and you feel needed in a gang. People would call on me because they needed me. You feel useful, and you're useful in your capacity as a man. You know, 'Don't send me no boys. Send me a man!'" But he

was beginning to see his former life in a different light. What he once perceived as "work" now seemed more like PR. "What the work was," he said, "was anything you did in *promotion* for the gang." He found it amusing how the media viewed gangs as clannish and occult. "We're not a secret society. Our whole thing is writing on walls, tattoos on necks, maintaining visibility. Getting media coverage is the s—t! If the media knows about you, damn, that's the top. We don't recognize ourselves unless we're recognized on the news."

Kody Scott's image-enhancement strategies were not homegrown. "I got all these ideas from watching movies and watching television. I was really just out there acting from what I saw on TV." And he wasn't referring to "Superfly" or "Shaft." "Growing up, I didn't see one blaxploitation movie. Not one." His inspiration came from shows like "Mission: Impossible" and "Rat Patrol" and films like "The Godfather." "I would study the guys in those movies," he recalled, "how they moved, how they stood, the way they dressed, that whole winning way of dressing. Their tactics became my tactics. I went from watching "Rat Patrol" to being in it. His prime model was Arthur Penn's 1967 movie "Bonnie and Clyde." "I watched how in 'Bonnie and Clyde' they'd walk in and say their whole names. They were getting their reps. I took that and applied it to my situation." Cinematic gangsterism was his objective, and it didn't seem like much of a reach. "It's like there's a thin line in this country now between criminality and celebrity. Someone has to be the star of the 'hood. Someone has to do the advertising for the 'hood. And it's like agencies that pick a good-looking guy model. So it became, 'Monster Kody! Let's push him out there!'" He grinned as he said this, an aw-shucks smile that was, doubtless, part of his "campaign."

S.F.

Either way, I can see now that I was operating from an assumption both underexamined and dubious: that the male crisis in America was caused by something men were doing unrelated to something being done to them. I had my own favorite whipping boy, suspecting that the crisis of masculinity was caused by masculinity on the rampage. If male violence was the quintessential expression of masculinity run amok, then a domestic-violence therapy group must be at the very heart of this particular darkness.

I wasn't alone in such circular reasoning. I was besieged with suggestions along similar lines from journalists, feminists, antifeminists and other willing advisers. Women's rights advocates mailed me news clips about male office stalkers and computer harassers. That I was not ensconced in the courtroom for O. J. Simp-

son's murder trial struck many of my volunteer helpers as an appalling lapse of judgment. "The perfect case study of an American man who thinks he's entitled to just control everything and everybody," one of them suggested.

But then, I had already been attending the domestic-violence group for several months—the very group O. J. Simpson was, by coincidence, supposed to have attended but avoided with the promise that he would speak by phone to a psychiatrist—and it was already apparent to me that these men's crises did not stem from a preening sense of entitlement and control. Each new member in the group, called Alternatives to Violence, would be asked to describe what he had done to a woman, a request that was met invariably with the disclaimer "I was out of control." The counselors would then expend much en-

ergy showing him how he had, in fact, been in control the entire time. He had chosen his fists, not a knife; he had hit her in the stomach, not the face. No doubt the moment of physical contact for these men had grown out of a desire for supreme control fueled by a need to dominate. I cannot conceive of a circumstance that would exonerate such violence. By making the abusive spouse take responsibility for his actions, the counselors were pursuing a worthy goal. But the logic behind the violence still remained elusive.

A serviceman who had turned to nightclub-bouncer jobs and pastry catering after his military base shut down seemed to confirm the counselors' position one evening shortly before his "graduation" from the group. "I denied it before," he said of the night he pummeled his girlfriend. "I thought I'd blacked out. But looking back at that night, I didn't black out. I was feeling good. I was in power, I was strong, I was in control. I felt like a man." But what struck me most strongly was what he said next: that moment of control had been the only one in his recent life. "That feeling of power," he said, "didn't last long. Only until they put the cuffs on. Then I was feeling again like I was no man at all."

He was typical in this regard. The men I got to know in the group had, without exception, lost their compass in the world. They had lost or were losing jobs, homes, cars, families. They had been labeled outlaws but felt like castoffs. There was something almost absurd about these men struggling, week after week, to recognize themselves as dominators when they were so clearly dominated, done in by the world.

Underlying all the disagreement over what is confusing and unnerving to men runs a constant line of thinking that blinds us—whatever our political beliefs—to the nature of the male predicament. Ask feminists to diagnose men's problems and you will often get a very clear explanation: men are in crisis because women are properly challenging male dominance. Ask antifeminists and you will get a diagnosis that is, in one respect, similar. Men are troubled, many conservative pundits say, because women have gone far beyond their demands for equal treatment and now are trying to take power away from men.

The veterans of World War II were eager to embrace a manly ideal that revolved around providing rather than dominating. Ultimately, society double-crossed them.

Both the feminist and antifeminist views are rooted in a peculiarly modern American perception that to be a man means you are at the controls at all times. The popular feminist joke that men are to blame for everything is the flip side of the "family values" reactionary expectation that men should be in charge of everything.

The man controlling his environment is today the prevailing American image of masculinity. He is to be in the driver's seat, the king of the road, forever charging down the open highway, along that masculine Möbius strip that cycles endlessly through a numbing stream of movies, TV shows, novels, advertisements and pop tunes. He's a man because he won't be stopped. He'll fight attempts to tamp him down; if he has to, he'll use his gun. But we forget the true Daniel Boone frontiersmanship was only incidentally violent, and was based on creating, out of wilderness, a communal context to which a man could moor himself through work and family.

Modern debates about how men are exercising or abusing their control and power neglect to raise whether a lack of mooring, a lack of context, is causing men's anguish. If men are the masters of their fate, what do they do about the unspoken sense that they are being mastered, in the marketplace and at home, by forces that seem to be sweeping away the soil beneath their feet? If men are mythologized as the ones who make things happen, then how can they begin to analyze what is happening to them?

More than a quarter century ago, women began to free themselves from the box in which they were trapped by feeling their way along its contours, figuring out how it was shaped and how it shaped them. Women were able to take action, paradoxically, by understanding how they were acted upon. Men feel the contours of a box, too, but they are told that box is of their own manufacture, designed to their specifications. Who are they to complain? For men to say they feel boxed in is regarded not as laudable political protest but as childish whining. How dare the kings complain about their castles?

What happened to so disturb the sons of the World War II GIs? The prevailing narrative that the sons inherited—fashioned from the battlefronts of Europe and the Pacific, laid out in countless newspapers, newsreels and movies—was a tale of successful fatherhood and masculine transformation: boys whose Depression-era fathers could neither provide for them nor guide them into manhood were placed under the benevolent wing of a vast male-run orphanage called the army and sent into battle. There, firm but kindly senior officers acting as surrogate fathers watched over them as they were tempered into men in the heat of a heroic struggle against malevolent enemies. The boys, molded into men, would return to find wives, form their families and take their places as adults in the community of a nation taking its place as a grown-up power in the world.

This was the story America told itself in dozens of war movies in which tough but tenderhearted commanding officers prepared their appreciative "boys" to assume their responsibilities in male society. It was the theme behind the 1949 film "Sands of Iwo Jima," with John Wayne as Sergeant Stryker, a stern papa molding his wet-behind-the-ears charges into a capable fraternity. "Before I'm through with you, you're gonna move like one man and think like one man," he tells them. "If I can't teach you one way, I'll teach you another, but I'm gonna get the job done." And he gets the job done, fathering a whole squad of youngsters into communal adulthood.

The veterans of World War II were eager to embrace a masculine ideal that revolved around providing rather than dominating. Their most important experiences had centered on the support they had given one another in the war, and it was this that they wished to replicate. As artilleryman Win Stracke told oral historian Studs Terkel in "The Good War," he came home bearing this most cherished memory: "You had 15 guys who for the first time in their lives could help each other without cutting each other's throat or trying to put down somebody else through a boss or whatever. I had realized it was the absence of competition and all those phony standards that created the thing I loved about the army."

The fathers who would sire the baby-boom generation would try to pass that experience of manhood on intact to their sons. The grunts who went overseas and liberated the world came home to the expectation that they would liberate the country by quiet industry and caretaking. The vets threw themselves into their federally funded educations, and later their defense-funded corporate and production-line jobs, and their domestic lives in Veterans Administration-financed tract homes. They hoped their dedication would be in the service of a higher national aim.

For their children, the period of soaring expectations that followed the war was truly the era of the boy. It was the culture of "Father Knows Best" and "Leave It to Beaver," of Pop Warner rituals and Westinghouse science scholarships, of BB guns and rocket clubs, of football practice and lettered jackets, of magazine ads where "Dad" seemed always to be beaming down at his scampy, cowboy-suited younger son or proudly handing his older son the keys to a brand-new convertible. It was a world where, regardless of the truth that lay behind each garden gate, popular culture led us to believe that fathers were spending every leisure moment in roughhouse play and model-air-plane construction with their beloved boys.

GONE TO SOLDIERS EVERY ONE

Michael Bernhardt went to Vietnam to honor his sense of justice. But the war destroyed his idea of manhood.

The Dogs of War

As far back as Michael Bernhardt could remember watching World War II movies, he could remember wanting to serve. The summers of his boyhood in the backyards of Long Island were one long idyll of war play on an imagined European front. "We had leaders," he said. "We attacked things with dirt bombs. We thought war was where we'd all go in together like D-Day and be part of this big coordinated army that would *do* something. And then you'd come back and have war stories to tell."

At his father's urging, Bernhardt headed off to college. But his mind was still on a military career. He joined not only Army ROTC but a special elite unit run by the Green Berets. Then in 1967, in the middle of his sophomore year, he dropped out and enlisted in the Army. He had only the haziest sense of what was going on in Vietnam: "It appeared to be about a small country that was having communism shoved down its throat, while we were trying, at least *ostensibly*, to give people a chance to do what they wanted to do. If I didn't go, somebody'd have to go in my place, which went against everything I'd grown up with."

Bernhardt ended up in Vietnam with Charlie Company, on the ground as a horrified witness to the My Lai massacre. He was the first soldier to break the silence and talk in public about what had happened in the face of the Army's cover-up. That decision caused great tension with the father he loved. "He believed that dissent and opposition to the government were uncalled for," said Bernhardt. "He never doubted authority. Nor did I. Up until Vietnam, it never occurred to me that I'd be opposed to the authorities, not in a million years."

After Bernhardt left the Army, he found himself sinking into another quagmire, the collapsing American economy of the 1970s. He bounced around Florida, working on a land surveyor's crew, then at a sign shop that made billboards for Sheraton and Kmart. He lived in a trailer, parked in a vacationer's lot on the Gulf of Mexico. But it wasn't really the recession that threw his peacetime life into disarray. Vietnam had changed forever his idea of a code of masculinity. "For years, I had been asking myself, did I do the right stuff? And I had thought that you just added it all up and you could say, This is my manliness score. You get points for going through the service, and bonus points for extra military stuff, and points for a job and a marriage and kids. But it didn't add up. There were all these people walking around with a high score who weren't much of a man in my estimation." Finally, he stopped keeping score, went back to college and got a degree in biology. He married and bought 10 acres of land in the Florida panhandle where he and his wife keep horses and a dozen stray dogs and cats. "In Charlie Company, cowardice and courage was all turned around. If you showed any sign of caring, it was seen as a sign of weakness. If you were the least bit concerned about the civilians, you were considered pathetic, definitely not a man." Now he's turned that experience around once more. "If you can define your manhood in terms of caring," he said, "then maybe we can come back from all that."

S.F.

In the aspiring middle-class suburb where I came of age, there was no mistaking the belief in the boy's pre-eminence; it was evident in the solicitous attentions of parents and schoolteachers, in the centrality of Cub Scouts and Little League, in the community life that revolved around boys' championships and boys' scores—as if these outposts of tract-home America had been built mainly as exhibition rings for junior-male achievement, which perhaps they had.

The "New Frontier" of space turned out to be a void no man could conquer, let alone colonize. The astronaut was no Daniel Boone, just a flattened image for TV viewers to watch.

The speech that inaugurated the shiny new era of the 1960s was the youthful John F. Kennedy's address to the Democratic National Convention, a month before the launch of Echo. The words would become, along with his Inaugural oration, a haunting refrain in adolescent male consciousness. What Kennedy implicitly presented was a new rite of passage for an untested male generation. "The New Frontier of which I speak is not a set of promises," he told them. "It is a set of challenges." Kennedy understood that it was not enough for the fathers to win the world for their sons; the sons had to feel they had won it for themselves. If the fathers had their Nazis and "Nips," then Kennedy would see to it that the sons had an enemy, too. He promised as much on Inauguration Day in 1961, when he spoke vaguely but unremittingly of communism's threat, of a country that would be defined by its readiness to "pay any price" and "oppose any foe." The fight was the thing, the only thing, if America was to retain its masculinity.

The drumrolls promised a dawning era of superpower manhood to the boy born on the New Frontier, a masculine honor and pride in exchange for his loyalty. Ultimately, the boy was double-crossed. The fix was in from the start: corporate and cold-war America's promise to continue the World War II GI's wartime experience of belonging, of meaningful engagement in a mission, was never authentic. "The New Frontier" of space turned out to be a void that no man could conquer, let along colonize. The astronaut was no Daniel Boone; he was just a flattened image for TV viewers to watch—and eventually, to be bored by. Instead of sending its sons to Normandy, the government dispatched them to Vietnam, where the enemy was unclear and the mission remained a tragic mystery. The massive managerial bureaucracies of postwar "white collar" employment, especially the defense contractors fat on government largesse, produced "organization men" who often didn't even know what they were managing—and who suspected they weren't really needed at all. What these corporations offered was a secure job, not a vital role—and not even that secure. The postwar fathers' submission to the national-security state would, after a prosperous period of historically brief duration, be rewarded with pink slips, with massive downsizing, union-breaking and outsourcing. The boy who had been told he was going to be the master of the universe and all that was in it found himself master of nothing.

As early as 1957, the boy's diminished future was foreshadowed in a classic sci-fi film. In "The Incredible Shrinking Man," Scott Carey has a good job, a suburban home, a pleasure boat, a pretty wife. And yet, after he passes through a mist of atomic radiation while on a boating vacation in the Pacific, something happens. As he tells his wife in horror, "I'm getting smaller, Lou, every day."

As Carey quite literally shrinks, the promises made to him are broken one by one. The employer who was to give him lifetime economic security fires him. He is left with only feminine defenses, to hide in a doll house, to fight a giant spider with a sewing pin. And it turns out that the very source of his diminishment is implicitly an atomic test by his own government. His only hope is to turn himself into a celebrated freak and sell his story to the media. "I'm a big man!" Carey says with bitter sarcasm. "I'm famous! One more joke for the world to laugh at."

The more Carey shrinks, the more he strikes out at those around him. "Every day I became more tyrannical," he comments, "more monstrous in my domination of my wife." It's a line that would ring a bell for any visitor to the Alternatives to Violence group and for any observer of the current male scene. As the male role has diminished amid a sea of betrayed promises, many men have been driven to more domineering and some even "monstrous" displays in their frantic quest for a meaningful showdown.

The Ornamental Culture

IF FEW MEN WOULD DO WHAT Shawn Nelson did one evening in the spring of 1995, many could relate. A former serviceman whose career in an army tank unit had gone nowhere, a plumber who had lost his job, a former husband whose wife had left him, the 35-year-old Nelson broke into the National Guard armory, commandeered an M-60 army tank and drove it through the streets of San Diego, flattening fire hy-

drants, crushing 40 cars, downing enough utility poles to cut off electricity to 5,000 people. He was at war with the domestic world that he once thought he was meant to build and defend. He was going to drive that tank he had been meant to command if it killed him. And it did. The police shot Shawn Nelson to death through the turret hatch.

If a man could not get the infrastructure to work for him, he could at least tear it down. If the nation would not provide an enemy to fight, he could go to war at home. If there was to be no brotherhood, he would take his stand alone. A handful of men would attempt to gun down enemies they imagined they saw in family court, employee parking lots, McDonald's restaurants, a Colorado schoolhouse and, most notoriously, a federal office building in Oklahoma. A far greater number would move their destruction of the elusive enemy to the fantasy realm to a clear-cut and controllable world of action movies and video combat, televised athletic tournaments and pay-per-view ultimate-fighting bouts.

But none of it would satisfy, because the world and the fight had changed.

What is left out of the nostalgia of baby-boom men for their heroic World War II fathers is how devastatingly unfathered and unprepared for manhood some of those sons were

A few glamorous men understood intuitively that in the coming media and entertainment age the team of men at work would be replaced by the individual man on display. Elevated onto the new pedestal of mass media and entertainment, they were unreachable. Like the astronauts who were their forebears, the new celebrated men—media stars, moussed models, telegenic baby moguls—existed in a realm from which all lines to their brothers had been cut. Where we once lived in a society in which men participated by being useful in public life, we now are surrounded by a culture that encourages people to play almost no functional public roles, only decorative or consumer ones.

Ornamental culture has proved the ultimate expression of the century, sweeping away institutions in which men felt some

sense of belonging and replacing them with visual spectacles that they can only watch and that benefit global commercial forces they cannot fathom. Celebrity culture's effects on men go far beyond the obvious showcasing of action heroes and rock musicians. The ordinary man is no fool: he knows he can't be Arnold Schwarzenegger. Nonetheless, the culture re-shapes his most basic sense of manhood by telling him that masculinity is something to drape over the body, not draw from inner resources; that it is personal, not societal; that manhood is displayed, not demonstrated. The internal qualities once said to embody manhood—surefootedness, inner strength, confidence of purpose—are merchandised to men to enhance their manliness. What passes for the essence of masculinity is being extracted and bottled and sold back to men. Literally, in the case of Viagra.

The culture that '90s men are stranded in was birthed by their fathers' generation—by men who, weary of Depression and wartime deprivation, embraced the new commercialized American dream. What gets left out of the contemporary nostalgia of baby-boom men for their World War II fathers—evidenced in the huge appetite for the film "Saving Private Ryan" and books like Tom Brokaw's "The Greatest Generation"—is what those fathers did after the war. When "Dateline NBC" produced a documentary based on Brokaw's book, celebrating the World War II "tougher than tough" heroes, especially relative to their pampered sons, the troubling subtext was how devastatingly unfathered those sons were, how inadequately they'd been prepared for manhood by their "heroic" fathers.

The men I came to know in the course of researching this book talked about their father's failures in the most private and personal terms, pointing inevitably to the small daily letdowns: "My father didn't teach me how to throw a ball" or "My father was always at work." That their fathers had emotionally or even literally abandoned the family circle was painful enough. But these men suspected, in some way hard to grasp, that their fathers had deserted them in the public realm, too. "My father never taught me how to be a man" was the refrain I heard over and over again. Down the generations, the father wasn't simply a good sport who bought his son a car for graduation. He was a human bridge connecting the boy to an adult life of public engagement and responsibility.

WHAT'S TROUBLING TROUBLED BOYS

As old measures of masculinity faded, the swaggering boys of the Spur Posse made a game of sexual conquest

Who's Keeping Score

The **Spur Posse burst out of the orderly suburb of Lakewood,** Calif., as America's dreaded nightmare—teenage boys run amok, a microcosm of a misogynistic and violent male culture. In March 1993 police arrested nine Spurs, ages 15 to 19, on suspicion of nearly 20 counts of sexual crimes. In the end, prosecutors concluded that the sex was consensual and all but one count were dropped. But for a time that spring, it was difficult to flip the channels without running into one Spur or another, strutting and bragging their way through the TV talk shows. "You gotta get your image out there," explained Billy Shehan, then 19, a Spur who was not among those arrested but who, despite honor grades and a promising future, felt compelled to hit the media circuit. "It all about building that image on a worldwide basis." Tirelessly, the Spurs repeated the details of their sex-for-points intramural contest, in which each time you had sex with a girl you racked up a point. And for four years running, the winner was Billy Shehan—with a final score of 67.

The media-paid trip that Billy took to New York City with two fellow Spurs started out with many promises. "First they said to us, 'New York! For free!'" Billy recalled. "'We'll give you $1,000, and you'll have limos every day, and elegant meals, and elegant this and elegant that.'" On the ride from the airport to the hotel, Billy felt like a long-exiled prince come to claim his kingdom. "Here I was in this limo in this giant-ass city, and it was like I owned the taxis and the cars, I owned the buildings and all the girls in the windows in the buildings. I felt like I could do whatever I wanted. I had instant exposure."

For the next week and a half, the shows vied for the Spurs' attention. "For 11 days, these guys were our best friends," Billy said

of the TV producers. "They showered admiration on us." One night, Billy said, a senior staffer from "Night Talk With Jane Whitney" took them in a limo to a strip bar, a club in Queens called Goldfingers. "The Maury Povich Show" wooed the boys by sending them our for the evening with four young women from the program's staff. Afterward, the Spurs took a cab to Times Square. "Everything was a fantasy," Billy recalled, "like I was in Mauryland. Like the whole city was a talk show." Billy had his tape recorder out, and he was talking into it as he walked. Suddenly, two hands reached out from the darkness and yanked him between two buildings. "He was holding something against me that felt like a gun," Billy said. The man ripped the tape recorder out of his hands, extracted his wallet and fled. Billy lay in his hotel room all night listening to his heart pound. The next morning he phoned the staff of "The Maury Povich Show" and demanded that they reimburse him for the robbery. When they declined, he refused to go on the program. "I felt they owed me something."

Billy did, however, make an appearance on "Night Talk With Jane Whitney," where he would be much vilified for his boast about scoring his 67th point that week with a girl he lured back to his hotel room. And then he'd return home, poorer and without taped memories. "For a while when I got back," Billy said, "everybody recognized me because of the shows. But now…" His voice trailed off. "Uh, you know something sort of funny?" he said. "I didn't get that [final sex] point. The producer said, 'Act like you got a point on the show.' So I did." He gave a short, bitter laugh. "I even wrote a song about it later. 'Everyone thought I was a 67, when I was just a 66.'"

S.F.

The guiding standards of the fathers, the approving paternal eye, has nearly vanished in this barren new landscape, to be replaced by the market-share standards of a commercial culture, the ogling, ever-restless eye of the camera. By the end of the century, every outlet of the consumer world—magazines, ads, movies, sports, music videos—would deliver the message that manhood had become a performance game to be won in the marketplace, not the workplace, and that male anger was now part of the show. An ornamental culture encouraged young men to see surliness, hostility and violence as expressions of glamour. Whether in Maxim magazine or in Brut's new "Neanderthal" ads, boorishness became a way for men to showcase themselves without being feminized before a potentially girlish mirror. But if celebrity masculinity enshrined the pose of the "bad boy," his rebellion was largely

cosmetic. There was nowhere for him to take a grievance because there was no society to take it to. In a celebrity culture, earnestness about social and political change was replaced by a pose of "irony" that was really just a sullen and helpless paralysis.

In a culture of ornament, manhood is defined by appearance, by youth and attractiveness, by money and aggression, by posture and swagger and "props," by the curled lip and flexed biceps, by the glamour of the cover boy and by the market-bartered "individuality" that sets one astronaut or athlete or gangster above another. These are the same traits that have long been designated as the essence of feminine vanity—the objectification and mirror-gazing that women have denounced as trivializing and humiliating qualities imposed on them by a misogynist culture. No wonder men are in such agony. At the

close of the century, men find themselves in an unfamiliar world where male worth is measured only by participation in a celebrity-driven consumer culture and awarded by lady luck.

The more I consider what men have lost—a useful role in public life, a way of earning a decent living, respectful treatment in the culture—the more it seems that men are falling into a status oddly similar to that of women at midcentury. The '50s housewife, stripped of her connections to a wider world and invited to fill the void with shopping and the ornamental display of her ultrafemininity, could be said to have morphed into the '90s man, stripped of his connections to a wider world and invited to fill the void with consumption and a gym-bred display of his ultramasculinity. The empty compensations of a "feminine mystique" are transforming into the empty compensations of a masculine mystique, with a gentlemen's cigar club no more satisfying than a ladies' bake-off.

But women have rebelled against this mystique. Of all the bedeviling questions my travels and research raised, none struck me more than this: why don't contemporary men rise up in protest against their betrayal? If they have experienced so many of the same injuries as women, the same humiliations, why don't they challenge the culture as women did? Why can't men seem to act?

The stock answers don't suffice. Men aren't simply refusing to "give up the reins of power," as some feminists have argued. The reins have already slipped from most of their hands. Nor are men merely chary of expressing pain and neediness, particularly in an era where emoting is the coin of the commercial realm. While the pressures on men to imagine themselves in control of their emotions are impediments to male revolt, a more fundamental obstacle overshadows them. If men have feared to tread where women have rushed in, then maybe women have had it easier in one very simple regard: women could frame their struggle as a battle against men.

For the many women who embraced feminism in one way or another in the 1970s, that consumer culture was not some intangible force; they saw it as a cudgel wielded by men against women. The mass culture's portfolio of sexist images was propaganda to prop up the myth of male superiority, the argument went. Men, not the marketplace, many women believed, were the root problem and so, as one feminist activist put it in 1969, "the task of the women's liberation movement is to collectively combat male domination in the home, in bed, on the job." And indeed, there were virulent, sexist attitudes to confront. But the 1970s model of confrontation could get feminism only halfway to its goal.

The women who engaged in the feminist campaigns of the '70s were able to take advantage of a ready-made model for revolt. Ironically, it was a male strategy. Feminists had a clearly defined oppressive enemy: the "patriarchy." They had a real frontier to conquer: all those patriarchal institutions, both the old ones that still rebuffed women, like the U.S. Congress or U.S. Steel, and the new ones that tried to remold women, like Madison Avenue or the glamour and media-pimp kingdoms of Bert Parks and Hugh Hefner. Feminists also had their own army of "brothers": sisterhood. Each GI Jane who participated in this struggle felt useful. Whether she was

working in a women's-health clinic or tossing her bottles of Clairol in a "freedom trash can," she was part of a greater glory, the advancement of her entire sex. Many women whose lives were touched by feminism felt in some way that they had reclaimed an essential usefulness; together, they had charged the barricades that kept each of them from a fruitful, thriving life.

The male paradigm of confrontation, in which an enemy could be identified, contested and defeated, proved useful to activists in the civil-rights movement, the antiwar movement, the gay-rights movement. It was, in fact, the fundamental organizing principle of virtually every concerted countercultural campaign of the last half century. Yet it could launch no "men's movement." Herein lies the critical paradox, and the source of male inaction: the model women have used to revolt is the exact one men not only can't use but are trapped in.

Men have no clearly defined enemy who is oppressing them. How can men be oppressed when the culture has already identified them as the oppressors, and when even they see themselves that way? As one man wrote plaintively to Promise Keepers, "I'm like a kite with a broken string, but I'm also holding the tail." Men have invented antagonists to make their problems visible, but with the passage of time, these culprits—scheming feminists, affirmative-action proponents, job-grabbing illegal aliens—have come to seem increasingly unconvincing as explanations for their situation. Nor do men have a clear frontier on which to challenge their intangible enemies. What new realms should they be gaining—the media, entertainment and image-making institutions of corporate America? But these are institutions already run by men; how can men invade their own territory? Is technological progress the frontier? Why then does it seem to be pushing men into obsolescence, socially and occupationally? And if the American man crushes the machine, whose machine has he vanquished?

The male paradigm of confrontation has proved worthless to men. Yet maybe that's not so unfortunate. The usefulness of that model has reached a point of exhaustion anyway. The women's movement and the other social movements have discovered its limits. Their most obvious enemies have been sent into retreat, yet the problems persist. While women are still outnumbered in the executive suites, many have risen in the ranks and some have

achieved authoritative positions often only to perpetuate the same transgressions as their male predecessors. Women in power in the media, advertising and Hollywood have for the most part continued to generate the same sorts of demeaning images as their male counterparts. Blaming a cabal of men has taken feminism about as far as it can go. That's why women have a great deal at stake in the liberation of the one population uniquely poised to discover and employ a new paradigm—men.

Beyond the Politics of Confrontation

THERE ARE SIGNS THAT MEN ARE seeking such a breakthrough. When the Million Man March and Promise Keepers attracted record numbers of men, pundits scratched their heads—why would so many men want to attend events that offered no battle plan, no culprit to confront? No wonder critics who were having trouble placing the gatherings in the usual frame of political conflict found it easier to focus their attentions on the reactionary and hate-mongering attitudes of the "leaders" of these movements, concluding that the real "agenda" must be the anti-Semitism of the Nation of Islam's Louis Farrakhan or the homophobia and sexism of Promise Keepers founder Bill McCartney. But maybe the men who attended these mass gatherings weren't looking for answers that involved an enemy. As Farrakhan's speech, chock-full of conspiracy theories and numerological codes, dragged on, men in droves hastened for the exits. "What was really fantastic about the day was just being together with all these men, and thinking about what I might do differently," George Henderson, a 48-year-old social worker, told me as he headed out early. The amassing of huge numbers of men was a summoning of courage for the unmapped journey ahead.

American men have generally responded well as caretakers in times of crisis, whether that be in wars, depressions or natural disasters. The pre-eminent contemporary example of such a male mobilization also comes on the heels of a crisis: gay men's response to AIDS. Virtually overnight, just as the Depression-era Civilian Conservation Corps built dams and parks and salvaged farmland, so have gay men built a network of clinics, legal and psychological services, fund-raising and political-action brigades, meals on wheels, even laundry assistance. The courage of these caregivers has generated, even in this homophobic nation, a wellspring of admiration and respect. They had a job to do and they did it.

Social responsibility is not the special province of masculinity; it's the lifelong work of all citizens in a community where people are knit together by meaningful and mutual concerns. But if husbanding a society is not the exclusive calling of "husbands," all the better for men's future. Because as men struggle to free them-selves from their crisis, their task is not, in the end, to figure out how to be mascu-line—rather, their masculinity lies in figur-ing out how to be human. The men who worked at the Long Beach Naval Shipyard, where I spent many months, didn't go there and learn their crafts as riggers, weld-ers and boilermakers to be masculine; they were seeking something worthwhile to do. Their sense of their own manhood flowed out of their utility in a society, not the other way around.

And so with the mystery of men's non-rebellion comes the glimmer of an open-ing, a chance for men to forge a rebellion commensurate with women's and, in the course of it, to create a new paradigm for human progress that will open doors for both sexes. That was, and continues to be, feminism's dream, to create a freer, more humane world. It will remain a dream without the strength and courage of men who are today faced with a historic oppor-tunity: to learn to wage a battle against no enemy, to own a frontier of human liberty, to act in the service of a brotherhood that includes us all.

Reprinted from *Newsweek*, September 13, 1999, pp. 48-58. Excerpted from *Stiffed: The Betrayal of the American Man*, © 1999 by Susan Faludi. Reprinted by permission of William Morrow/HarperCollins Publishers, Inc.

Coping with CROWDING

A persistent and popular view holds that high population density inevitably leads to violence. This myth, which is based on rat research, applies neither to us nor to other primates

by Frans B. M. de Waal, Filippo Aureli and Peter G. Judge

In 1962 this magazine published a seminal paper by experimental psychologist John B. Calhoun entitled "Population Density and Social Pathology." The article opened dramatically with an observation by the late 18th-century English demographer Thomas Malthus that human population growth is automatically followed by increased vice and misery. Calhoun went on to note that although we know overpopulation causes disease and food shortage, we understand virtually nothing about its behavioral impact.

This reflection had inspired Calhoun to conduct a nightmarish experiment. He placed an expanding rat population in a crammed room and observed that the rats soon set about killing, sexually assaulting and, eventually, cannibalizing one another. Much of this activity happened among the occupants of a central feeding section. Despite the presence of food elsewhere in the room, the rats were irresistibly drawn to the social stimulation—even though many of them could not reach the central food dispensers. This pathological togetherness, as Calhoun described it, as well as the attendant chaos and behavioral deviancy, led him to coin the phrase "behavioral sink."

In no time, popularizers were comparing politically motivated street riots to rat packs, inner cities to behavioral sinks and urban areas to zoos. Warning that society was heading for either anarchy or dictatorship, Robert Ardrey, an American science journalist, remarked in 1970 on the voluntary nature of human crowding: "Just as Calhoun's rats freely chose to eat in the middle pens, we freely enter the city." Calhoun's views soon became a central tenet of the voluminous literature on aggression.

In extrapolating from rodents to people, however, these thinkers and writers were making a gigantic leap of faith. A look at human populations suggests why such a simple extrapolation is so problematic. Compare, for instance, per capita murder rates with the number of people per square kilometer in different nations—as we did, using data from the United Nations' *1996 Demographic Yearbook*. If things were straightforward, the two ought to vary in tandem. Instead there is no statistically meaningful relation.

But, one could argue, perhaps such a relation is obscured by variation in national income level, political organization or some other variable. Apparently not, at least for income. We divided the nations into three categories—free-market, former East Block and Third World—and did the analysis again. This time we did find one significant correlation, but it was in the other direction: it showed more violent crime in the least crowded countries of the former East Block. A similar trend existed for free-market nations, among which the U.S. had by far the highest homicide rate despite its low overall population density. The Netherlands had a population density 13 times as high, but its homicide rate was eight times lower.

Knowing that crime is generally more common in urban areas than it is in the countryside, we factored in the proportion of each nation's population that lives in large cities and controlled for it. But this correction did nothing to bring about a positive correlation between population density and homicide. Perhaps because of the overriding effects of history and culture, the link between available space and human aggression—if it exists at all—is decidedly not clearcut.

Even if we look at small-scale human experiments, we find no supporting evidence. Crowding of children and college students, for instance, sometimes produced irritation and mild aggression, but in general, people seemed adept at avoiding conflict. Andrew S. Baum and his co-workers in the psychiatry department at the Uniformed Services University found that dormitory residents who shared facilities with many people spent less time socializing and kept the doors to their rooms closed more often than did students who had more space. Baum concluded that the effects of crowding are not nearly as overwhelming as originally presumed. Published in the 1980s, these and other findings began to undermine, at least in the scientific community, the idea that people and rats react in the same ways to being packed together. In modern society, people commonly assemble in large masses—during their daily commute to work or during holiday-season shopping expeditions—and most of the time they control their behavior extraordinarily well.

RHESUS MONKEYS from three different settings show different rates of grooming—that is, of calming one another. The monkeys seem to adapt to crowded conditions by grooming more frequently. Among the males, grooming of each other and of females was more common when they lived in crowded conditions than when they lived in more spacious quarters. Among female non-kin, aggression was common and increased further with crowding but was accompanied by increased grooming, which served to reduce conflicts.

Calhoun's model, we must conclude, does not generally apply to human behavior. Is this because our culture and intelligence makes us unique, or is the management of crowding part of an older heritage? To answer this question, we turn to the primates.

PRIMATES ARE NOT RATS

Primate research initially appeared to support the harrowing scenario that had been presented for rats. In the 1960s scientists reported that city-dwelling monkeys in India were more aggressive than were those living in forests. Others claimed that monkeys in zoos were excessively violent. Those monkeys were apparently ruled by terrifying bullies who dominated a social hierarchy that was considered an artifact of captivity—in other words, in the wild, peace and egalitarianism prevailed. Borrowing from the hyperbole of popularizers, one study of crowding in small captive groups of baboons even went so far as to report a "ghetto riot."

As research progressed, however, conflicting evidence accumulated. Higher population density seemed to increase aggression occasionally—but the opposite was also true. One report, for instance, described intense fighting and killing when a group of macaques were released into a corral 73 times *larger* than their previous quarters had been. Then, after two and a half years in the corral, a similar increase in aggression occurred when the monkeys were crowded back into a small pen.

Whereas the macaque study manipulated population density through environmental change, other early research did so by adding new monkeys to existing groups. Given the xenophobic nature of monkeys, these tests mainly measured their hostile attitude toward strangers, which is quite different from the effect of density. The better controlled the studies became, the less clear-cut the picture turned out to be. Increased population density led to increased aggression in only 11 of the 17 best-designed studies of the past few decades.

In the meantime, the view of wild primates was changing. They were no longer the purely peaceful, egalitarian creatures people had presumed them to be. In the 1970s field-workers began reporting sporadic but lethal violence in a wide range of species—from macaques to chimpanzees—as well as strict and well-defined hierarchies that remained stable for decades. This view of an often anxiety-filled existence was confirmed when researchers found high levels of the stress hormone cortisol in the blood of wild monkeys [see "Stress in the Wild," by Robert M. Sapolsky; SCIENTIFIC AMERICAN, JANUARY1990].

As the view of primates became more complex, and as the rat scenario was weakened by counterexamples, researchers began to wonder whether primates had developed a means to reduce conflict in crowded situations. We saw the first hint of this possibility in a study of the world's largest zoo colony of chimpanzees in Arnhem, the Netherlands. The apes lived on a spacious, forested island in the summer but were packed together in a heated building during the winter. Despite a 20-fold reduction in space, aggression increased only slightly. In fact, the effect of crowding was not entirely negative: friendly grooming and greetings, such as kissing and submissive bowing, increased as well.

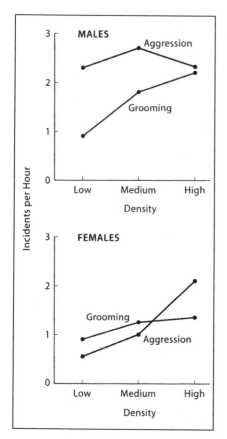

BRYAN CHRISTIE

SOURCE: Peter G. Judge and Frans B.M. de Waal

We wondered if this conciliatory behavior mitigated tension and proposed a way to test this possibility. Without ignoring the fact that crowding increases the potential for conflict, we predicted that primates employ counterstrategies—including avoiding potential aggressors and offering appeasement or reassuring body contact. Because some of the skills involved are probably acquired, the most effective coping responses would be expected in animals who have experienced high density for a long time. Perhaps they develop a different "social culture" in the same way that people in different places have varying standards of privacy and interpersonal comfort zones. For example, studies show that white North Americans and the British keep greater distances from others during conversations than Latin Americans and Arabs do.

FRANS B. M. DE WAAL

CHIMPANZEES IN THE WILD have hostile territorial relations with other groups, and in captivity they are bothered by the presence of noisy neighboring chimps. By examining apes under three conditions—those living in a crowded space and able to hear their neighbors, those living in a crowded space without such worrisome sounds, and those living in isolated large compounds (photograph right)—we were able to measure the association between aggression, space and stress. Aggression (photograph above) remained the same, but stress varied with neighbors' noise. Chimpanzees in small spaces exposed to vocalizations from other groups showed the highest levels of the stress hormone cortisol.

COPING CULTURE

We set about finding several populations of monkeys that were of the same species but that had been living in different conditions to see if their behavior varied in discernible ways. We collected detailed data on 122 individual rhesus monkeys at three different sites in the U.S.: in relatively cramped outdoor pens at the Wisconsin primate center in Madison, in large open corrals at the Yerkes primate center in Atlanta and on Morgan Island off the coast of South Carolina. These last monkeys had approximately 2,000 times more space per individual than the highest-density groups. All three groups had lived together for many years, often for generations, and included individuals of both sexes. All the groups had also been in human care, receiving food and veterinary treatment, making them comparable in that regard as well.

Rhesus society typically consists of a number of subgroups, known as matrilines, of related females and their offspring. Females remain together for life, whereas males leave their natal group at puberty. Rhesus monkeys make a sharp distinction between kin and non-kin: by far the most friendly contact, such as groom-

FRANS B.M. DE WAAL

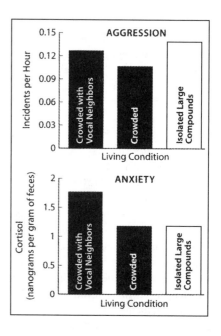

BRYAN CHRISTIE

ing, takes place within the matrilines. Females of one matriline also fiercely support one another in fights against other matrilines. Because of their strict hierarchy and pugnacious temperament, rhesus seemed to be ideal subjects. We figured that if this aggressive primate showed coping responses, our hypothesis would have withstood its most rigorous test.

Our first finding was, surprisingly, that density did not affect male aggressiveness. Adult males increasingly engaged in friendly contact under crowded conditions. They groomed females more, and likewise the females groomed the males more frequently. (Grooming is a calming behavior. In another study, we demonstrated that a monkey's heart rate slows down when it is being groomed.) Females also bared their teeth more often to the males—the rhesus way of communicating low status and appeasing potentially aggressive dominant monkeys.

Females showed a different response with other females, however. Within their own matrilines they fought more but did not change the already high level of friendly interaction. In their dealings with other matrilines, they also showed more aggression—but here it was coupled with more grooming and submissive grinning.

These findings make sense in light of the differences between kin and non-kin relationships. Related females—such as sisters and mothers and daughters—are so strongly bonded that their relationships are unlikely to be disrupted by antagonism. Rhesus monkeys are used to managing intrafamilial conflict, cycling through fights and reconciliations, followed by comforting contact. Crowding does little to change this, except that they may have to repair frayed family ties more often. Between matrilines, on the other hand, crowding poses a serious challenge. Normally, friendly contact between matrilines is rare and antagonism common. But reduced escape opportunities make the risk of escalated conflict greater in a confined space. And our data indicated that female rhesus monkeys make a concerted effort at improving these potentially volatile relationships.

EMOTIONS IN CHECK

In a second project, we turned our attention to chimpanzees. As our closest animal relatives, chimpanzees resemble us in appearance, psychology and cognition. Their social organization is also humanlike, with well-developed male bonding—which is rare in nature—reciprocal exchange and a long dependency of offspring on the mother. In the wild, male chimpanzees are extremely territorial, sometimes invading neighboring territories and killing enemy males. In captivity such encounters are, of course, prevented.

We collected data on more than 100 chimpanzees in various groups at the Yerkes primate center. Although some groups had only a tenth the space of others, cramped quarters had no measurable impact on aggression. In contrast to the monkeys, chimpanzees maintained their grooming and appeasement behavior—no matter the situation. If crowding did induce social tensions, our chimpanzees seemed to control them directly.

We usually do not think of animals as holding in their emotions, but chimpanzees may be different. These apes are known for deceptive behavior—for instance, they will hide hostile intentions behind a friendly face until an adversary has come within reach. In our study, emotional control was reflected in the way chimpanzees responded to the vocalizations of neighboring groups. Such noises commonly provoke hooting and charging displays, which in wild chimpanzees serve to ward off territorial intrusion.

In a confined space, however, excited reactions trigger turmoil within the group. We found that chimpanzees in the most crowded situations had a three times *lower* tendency to react to neighbors' vocalizations than chimpanzees with more space did. Chimpanzees may be smart enough to suppress responses to external stimuli if those tend to get them into trouble. Indeed, field-workers report that chimpanzee males on territorial patrol suppress all noise if being detected by their neighbors is to their disadvantage.

The inhibition of natural responses is not without cost. We know that continuous stress has the potential to suppress the immune system and therefore has important implications for health and longevity. We developed two noninvasive techniques to measure stress in our chimpanzees. One was to record the rate of self-scratching. Just as with college students who scratch their heads when faced with a tough exam question, self-scratching indicates anxiety in other primates. Our second technique was to collect fecal samples and analyze them for cortisol.

Both measures showed that groups of chimpanzees who had little space and heard neighbors' vocalizations experienced more stress. Space by itself was not a negative factor, because in the absence of noisy neighbors, chimpanzees in small spaces showed the same stress level as those with a good deal of space.

So even though chimpanzees fail to show a rise in aggression when crowded, this does not necessarily mean that they are happy and relaxed. They may be working hard to maintain the peace. Given a choice, they would prefer more room. Every spring, when the chimpanzees at the Arnhem zoo hear the door to their outdoor island being opened for the first time, they fill the building with a chorus of ecstasy. They then rush outside to engage in a pandemonium in which all of the apes, young and old, embrace and kiss and thump one another excitedly on the back.

The picture is even more complex if we also consider short periods of acute crowding. This is a daily experience in human society, whether we find ourselves on a city bus or in a movie theater. During acute crowding, rhesus monkeys show a rise in mild aggression, such as threats, but not violence. Threats serve to keep others at a distance, forestalling unwanted contact. The monkeys also avoid one another and limit active social engagement, as if they are trying to stay out of trouble by lying low.

Chimpanzees take this withdrawal tactic one step further: they are actually less aggressive when briefly crowded. Again, this reflects greater emotional restraint. Their reaction is reminiscent of people on an elevator, who reduce frictions by minimizing large body movements, eye contact and loud verbalizations. We speak of the elevator effect, therefore, as a way in which both people and other primates handle the risks of temporary closeness.

Our research leads us to conclude that we come from a long lineage of social animals capable of flexibly adjusting to all kinds of conditions, including unnatural ones such as crowded pens and city streets. The adjustment may not be without cost, but it is certainly preferable to the frightening alternative predicted on the basis of rodent studies.

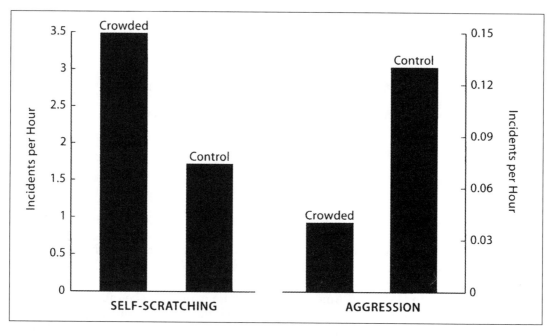

BRYAN CHRISTIE

During brief periods of crowding, people often limit social interaction—a way of avoiding any conflict. Chimpanzees do the same, reducing their aggressive interactions. This doesn't mean that crowded situations do not induce anxiety. Chimpanzees packed together tend to scratch themselves more often—a sign of stress.

We should add, though, that even the behavioral sink of Calhoun's rats may not have been entirely the product of crowding. Food competition seemed to play a role as well. This possibility contains a serious warning for our own species in an ever more populous world: the doomsayers who predict that crowding will inevitably rip the social fabric may have the wrong variable in mind. We have a natural, underappreciated talent to deal with crowding, but crowding combined with scarcity of resources is something else.

FURTHER INFORMATION

THE HIDDEN DIMENSION. E. T. Hall. Doubleday, 1966.

CROWDING. A. Baum in *Handbook of Environmental Psychology*, Vol. 1. Edited by D. Stokols and I. Altman. Wiley, 1987.

THE MYTH OF A SIMPLE RELATION BETWEEN SPACE AND AGGRESSION IN CAPTIVE PRIMATES. F. B. M. de Waal in *Zoo Biology* supplement, Vol. 1, pages 141–148; 1989.

INHIBITION OF SOCIAL BEHAVIOR IN CHIMPANZEES UNDER HIGH-DENSITY CONDITIONS. F. Aureli and F. B. M. de Waal in *American Journal of Primatology*, Vol. 41, No. 3, pages 213–228; March 1997.

RHESUS MONKEY BEHAVIOUR UNDER DIVERSE POPULATION DENSITIES: COPING WITH LONG-TERM CROWDING. P. G. Judge and F. B. M. de Waal in *Animal Behaviour*, Vol. 54, no. 3, pages 643–662; September 1997.

FRANS B. M. DE WAAL, FILIPPO AURELI and PETER G. JUDGE share a research interest in the social relationships and behavioral strategies of nonhuman primates. Their work on aspects of this topic will appear in Natural Conflict Resolution, *to be published by the University of California Press. De Waal, author of* Chimpanzee Politics *and* Good Natured, *worked for many years at the Arnhem zoo in the Netherlands before coming to the U.S., where he is now director of the Living Links Center at the Yerkes Regional Primate Research Center in Atlanta and professor of psychology at Emory University. Aureli is a senior lecturer in biological and earth sciences at Liverpool John Moores University in England. Judge is an assistant professor at Bloomsburg University in Pennsylvania and a research associate at Yerkes.*

From *Scientific American*, May 2000, pp. 76–81. © 2000 by Scientific American, Inc. Reproduced with permission. All rights reserved.

Nobody Left to Hate

by Elliot Aronson

In 1971 a highly explosive situation had developed in Austin, Texas—one that has played out in many cities across the United States. Austin's public schools had recently been desegregated and, because the city had always been residentially segregated, white youngsters, African American youngsters, and Mexican-American youngsters found themselves sharing the same classroom for the first time in their lives. Within a few weeks, long-standing suspicion, fear, distrust, and antipathy among the groups produced an atmosphere of turmoil and hostility, exploding into interethnic fistfights in corridors and schoolyards across the city.

The school superintendent called me in to see if I could do anything to help students learn to get along with one another. After observing what was going on in classrooms for a few days, my graduate students and I concluded that intergroup hostility was being exacerbated by the competitive environment of the classroom.

Let me explain. In every classroom we observed, the students worked individually and competed against one another for grades. Here is a description of a typical fifth-grade classroom we observed:

> The teacher stands in front of the class, asks a question, and waits for the children to indicate that they know the answer. Most frequently, six to ten youngsters raise their hands. But they do not simply raise their hands, they lift themselves a few inches off their chairs and stretch their arms as high as they can in an attempt to attract the teacher's attention. To say they are eager to be called on is an incredible understatement. Several other students sit quietly with their eyes averted, as if trying to make themselves invisible. These are the ones who don't know the answer. Understandably, they are trying to avoid eye contact with the teacher because they do not want to be called on.
>
> When the teacher calls on one of the eager students, there are looks of disappointment, dismay, and unhappiness on the faces of the other students who were avidly raising their hands but were not called on. If the selected student comes up with the right answer, the teacher smiles, nods approvingly, and goes on to the next question. This is a great reward for the child who happens to be called on. At the same time that the fortunate student is coming up with the right answer and being smiled upon by the teacher, an audible groan can be heard coming from the children who were striving to be called on but were ignored. It is obvious they are disappointed because they missed an opportunity to show the teacher how smart and quick they are. Perhaps they will get a chance next time. In the meantime, the students who didn't know the answer breathe a sigh of relief. They have escaped being humiliated this time.

The teacher may have started the school year with a determination to treat every student equally and encourage all of them to do their best, but the students quickly sorted themselves into different groups. The "winners" were the bright, eager, highly competitive students who fervently raised their hands, participated in discussions, and did well on tests. Understandably, the teacher felt gratified that these students responded to her teaching. She praised and encouraged them, continued to call on them, and depended on them to keep the class going at a high level and at a reasonable pace.

Then there were the "losers." At the beginning, the teacher called on them occasionally, but they almost invariably didn't know the answer, were too shy to speak, or couldn't speak English well. They seemed embarrassed to be in the spotlight; some of the other students made snide comments—sometimes under their breath, occasionally out loud. Because the schools in the poorer section of town were substandard, the African American and Mexican-American youngsters had received a poorer education prior to desegregation. Consequently, in Austin it was frequently these students who were among the "losers." This tended unfairly to confirm the unflattering stereotypes that the white kids had about minorities. The "losers" were considered stupid or lazy.

The minority students also had preconceived notions about the white kids: they considered them pushy show-offs and teachers' pets. These stereotypes were seemingly confirmed by the way most of the white students behaved in the competitive classroom.

After a while, the typical classroom teacher stopped trying to engage the students who weren't doing well. She or he felt it was kinder not to call on them and expose them to ridicule by the other students. In effect, a silent pact was made with the losers: to leave them alone as long as they weren't disruptive. Without really meaning to, the teacher gave up on these students—and so did the rest of the class. Without really meaning to, the teacher contributed to the difficulty the students were experiencing. After a while, these students tended to give up on themselves as well—perhaps believing that they *were* stupid—because they sure weren't getting it.

The jigsaw classroom facilitates interaction among all students in the class, leading them to value one another as contributors to their common task.

It required only a few days of intensive observation and interviews for us to have a pretty good idea of what was going on in these classrooms. We realized we needed to do something drastic to shift the emphasis from a relentlessly competitive atmosphere to a more cooperative one. It was in this context that we invented the *jigsaw strategy*.

THE JIGSAW CLASSROOM

Jigsaw is a specific type of group learning experience that requires everyone's cooperative effort to produce the final product. Just as in a jigsaw puzzle, each piece—each student's part—is essential for the production and full understanding of the final product. If each student's part is essential, then each student is essential. That is precisely what makes this strategy so effective.

Here's how it works. The students in a history class, for example, are divided into small groups of five or six students each. Suppose their task is to learn about World War II. In one jigsaw group, let us say that Sara is responsible for researching Hitler's rise to power in prewar Germany. Another member of the group, Steven, is assigned to cover concentration camps; Pedro is assigned Britain's role in the war; Lin is to research the contribution of the Soviet Union; Babu will handle Japan's entry into the war; and Monique will read about the development of the atom bomb. Eventually each student will come back to

her or his jigsaw group and will try to present a vivid, interesting, well-organized report to the group. The situation is specifically structured so that the only access any member has to the other five assignments is by listening intently to the report of the person reciting. Thus, if Babu doesn't like Pedro or he thinks Sara is a nerd, if he heckles them or tunes out while they are reporting, he cannot possibly do well on the test that follows.

To increase the probability that each report will be factual and accurate, the students doing the research do not immediately take it back to their jigsaw group. After completing their research, they must first meet with the students from each of the jigsaw groups who had the identical assignment. For example, those students assigned to the atom bomb topic meet together to work as a team of specialists, gathering information, discussing ideas, becoming experts on their topic, and rehearsing their presentations. This is called the "expert" group. It is particularly useful for those students who might have initial difficulty learning or organizing their part of the assignment for it allows them to benefit from listening to and rehearsing with other "experts," to pick up strategies of presentation, and generally to bring themselves up to speed.

After this meeting, when each presenter is up to speed, the jigsaw groups reconvene in their initial heterogeneous configuration. The atom bomb expert in each group teaches the other group members what she or he has learned about the development of the atom bomb. Each student in each group educates the whole group about her or his specialty. Students are then tested on what they have learned from their fellow group members about World War II.

What is the benefit of the jigsaw classroom? First and foremost it is a remarkably efficient way to learn the material. But even more important, the jigsaw process encourages listening, engagement, and empathy by giving each member of the group an essential part to play in the academic activity. Group members must work together as a team to accomplish a common goal—each person depends on all the others. No student can achieve her or his individual goal (learning the material, getting a good grade) unless everyone works together as a team. Group goals and individual goals complement and bolster each other. This "cooperation by design" facilitates interaction among all students in the class, leading them to value one another as contributors to their common task.

Our first intervention was with fifth graders. First we helped several fifth-grade teachers devise a cooperative jigsaw structure for the students to learn about the life of Eleanor Roosevelt. We divided the students into small groups—diversified in terms of race, ethnicity, and gender—and made each student responsible for a certain portion of Roosevelt's biography. Needless to say, at least one or two of the students in each group were already viewed as losers by their classmates.

Carlos was one such student. Carlos was very shy and felt insecure in his new surroundings. English was his second language. He spoke it quite well but with a slight accent. Try to imagine his experience: After attending an inadequately funded, substandard neighborhood school consisting entirely of Mexican-American students like himself, he was suddenly bussed across town to the middle-class area of the city and catapulted into a class with Anglo students who spoke English fluently and seemed to know much more than he did about all the subjects taught in the school—and were not reluctant to let him know it.

When we restructured the classroom so that students were now working together in small groups, this was terrifying to Carlos at first. He could no longer slink down in his chair and hide in the back of the room. The jigsaw structure made it necessary for him to speak up when it was his turn to recite. Carlos gained a little confidence by rehearsing with the others who were also studying Roosevelt's work with the United Nations, but he was understandably reticent when it was his turn to teach the students in his jigsaw group. He blushed, stammered, and had difficulty articulating the material he had learned. Skilled in the ways of the competitive classroom, the other students were quick to pounce on Carlos' weakness and began to ridicule him.

One of my research assistants was observing that group and heard some of its members make comments such as, "Aw, you don't know it, you're dumb, you're stupid. You don't know what you're doing. You can't even speak English." Instead of admonishing them to "be nice" or "try to cooperate," she made one simple but powerful statement. It went something like this: "Talking like that to Carlos might be fun for you to do, but it's not going to help you learn anything about what Eleanor Roosevelt accomplished at the United Nations—and the exam will be given in about fifteen minutes." What my assistant was doing was reminding the students that the situation had changed. The same behavior that might have seemed useful to them in the past, when they were competing against each other, was now going to cost them something very important: the chance to do well on the upcoming exam.

Old, dysfunctional habits do not die easily, but they do die. Within a few days of working with jigsaw, Carlos' groupmates gradually realized that they needed to change their tactics. It was no longer in their own best interest to rattle Carlos; he wasn't the enemy—he was on their team. They needed him to perform well in order to do well themselves. Instead of taunting him and putting him down, they started to gently ask him questions. The other students began to put themselves in Carlos' shoes so they could ask questions that didn't threaten him and would help him recite what he knew in a clear and understandable manner.

After a week or two, most of Carlos' groupmates had developed into skillful interviewers, asking him relevant questions to elicit the vital information from him. They became more patient, figured out the most effective way to work with him, helped him out, and encouraged him. The more they encouraged Carlos, the more he was able to relax; the more he was able to relax, the quicker and more articulate he became. Carlos' groupmates began to see him in a new light. He became transformed in their minds from a "know-nothing loser who can't even speak English" to someone they could work with, someone they could appreciate, maybe even someone they could like.

Moreover, Carlos began to see himself in a new light: as a competent, contributing member of the class who could work with others from different ethnic groups. His self-esteem grew, and as it grew his performance improved even more; and as his performance continued to improve, his groupmates continued to view him in a more and more favorable light.

Within a few weeks, the success of the jigsaw was obvious to the classroom teachers. They spontaneously told us of their great satisfaction over the way the atmosphere of their classrooms had been transformed. Adjunct visitors (such as music teachers and the like) were little short of amazed at the dramatically changed atmosphere in the classrooms. Needless to say, this was exciting to my graduate students and me. But, as scientists, we were not totally satisfied; we were seeking firmer, more objective evidence—and we got it.

Jigsaw students from poorer neighborhoods showed enormous academic improvement; they scored significantly higher on objective exams than the poorer students in traditional classes.

Because we had randomly introduced the jigsaw intervention into some classrooms and not others, we were able to compare the progress of the jigsaw students with that of the students in traditional classrooms in a precise, scientific manner. After only eight weeks there were clear differences, even though students spent only a small portion of their classtime in jigsaw groups. When tested objectively, jigsaw students expressed significantly less prejudice and negative stereotyping, showed more self-confidence, and reported that they liked school better than children in traditional classrooms.

Moreover, this self-report was bolstered by hard behavioral data. For example, the students in jigsaw classrooms were absent less often than those in traditional classrooms. In addition, the jigsaw students from poorer neighborhoods showed enormous academic improvement over the course of eight weeks; they scored significantly higher on objective exams than the poorer students in traditional classes, while those students who were already doing well continued to do well—as well as their counterparts in traditional classes.

JIGSAW AND BASKETBALL

You might have noticed a rough similarity between the kind of cooperation that goes on in a jigsaw group and the kind of cooperation that is necessary for the smooth functioning of an athletic team. Take a basketball team, for example. If the team is to be successful, each player must play her or his role in a cooperative manner. If each player is hellbent on being the highest scorer on the team, then each will shoot whenever the opportunity arises.

In contrast, on a cooperative team, the idea is to pass the ball crisply until one player manages to break clear for a relatively easy shot. If I pass the ball to Sam, and Sam whips a pass to Jameel, and Jameel passes to Tony, who breaks free for an easy lay-up, I'm elated even though I didn't receive credit for either a field goal or an assist. This is true cooperation.

As a result of this cooperation, athletic teams frequently build a cohesiveness that extends to their relationship off the court. They become friends because they have learned to count on one another. There is one difference between the outcome of a typical jigsaw group and that of a typical high-school basketball team, however, and it is a crucial difference. In high school, athletes tend to hang out with each other and frequently exclude nonathletes from their circle of close friends. In short, the internal cohesiveness of an athletic team often goes along with the exclusion of everyone else.

In the jigsaw classroom, we circumvented this problem by the simple device of shuffling groups every eight weeks. Once a group of students was functioning well together—once the barriers had been broken down and the students showed a great deal of liking and empathy for one another—we would re-form the groupings. At first the students would resist this re-forming of groups. Picture the scene: Debbie, Carlos, Tim, Patty, and Jacob have just gotten to know and appreciate one another and they are doing incredibly good work as a team. Why should they want to leave this warm, efficient, and cozy group to join a group of relative strangers?

Why, indeed? After spending a few weeks in the new group, the students invariably discover that the new people are just about as interesting, friendly, and wonderful as their former group. The new group is working well together and new friendships form. Then the students move on to their third group, and the same thing begins to happen. As they near the end of their time in the third group, it begins to dawn on most students that they didn't just luck out and land in groups with four or five terrific people. Rather, they realize that just about *everyone* they work with is a good human being. All they need to do is pay attention to each person, to try to understand her or him, and good things will emerge. That is a lesson well worth learning.

ENCOURAGING GENERAL EMPATHY

Students in the jigsaw classroom become adept at empathy. When we watch a movie, empathy is what brings tears or joy in us when sad or happy things happen to a character. But why should we care about a character in a movie? We care because we have learned to feel and experience what that character experiences—as if it were happening to us. Most of us don't experience empathy for our sworn enemies. So most moviegoers watching *Star Wars*, for example, will cheer wildly when the Evil Empire's spaceships are blown to smithereens. Who cares what happens to Darth Vader's followers.

Is empathy a trait we are born with or is it something we learn? I believe we are born with the capacity to feel for others. It is part of what makes us human. I also believe that empathy is a skill that can be enhanced with practice. It I am correct, then it should follow that working in jigsaw groups would lead to a sharpening of a youngster's general empathic ability, because to do well in the group the child needs to practice feeling what her or his groupmates feel.

To test this notion, one of my graduate students, Diane Bridgeman, conducted a clever experiment in which she showed a series of cartoons to ten-year-old children. Half of the children had spent two months participating in jigsaw classes; the others had spent that time in traditional classrooms. In one series of cartoons, a little boy is looking sad as he waves goodbye to his father at the airport. In the next frame, a letter carrier delivers a package to the boy. When the boy opens the package and finds a toy airplane inside, he bursts into tears. Diane asked the children why they thought the little boy burst into tears at the sight of the airplane. Nearly all of the children could answer correctly: because the toy airplane reminded him of how much he missed his father.

Then Diane asked the crucial question: "What did the letter carrier think when he saw the boy open the package and start to cry?" Most children of this age make a consistent error: they assume that everyone knows what they know. Thus, the youngsters in the control group thought the letter carrier would know the boy was sad because the gift reminded him of his father leaving.

But the children who had participated in the jigsaw classroom responded differently. They were better able to take the perspective of the letter carrier—to put themselves in his shoes. They realized that he would be confused at seeing the boy cry over receiving a nice present because the letter carrier hadn't witnessed the farewell scene at the airport. Offhand, this might not seem very important. After all, who cares whether kids have the ability to figure out what is in the letter carrier's mind? In point of fact, we should all care—a great deal.

Here's why: the extent to which children can develop the ability to see the world from the perspective of another human being has profound implications for empathy, prejudice, aggression, and interpersonal relations in general. When you can feel another person's pain, when you can develop the ability to understand what that person is going through, it increases the probability that your heart will open to that person. Once your heart opens to another person, it becomes virtually impossible to bully that other person, to taunt that other person, to humiliate that other person—and certainly to kill that other person. If you develop the general ability to empathize, then your desire to bully or taunt anyone will decrease. Such is the power of empathy.

This isn't a new idea. We see it, for example, in William Wharton's provocative novel *Birdy*. One of the protagonists, Alphonso, a sergeant in the army, takes an immediate dislike for an overweight enlisted man, a clerk typist named Ronsky. There are a great many things that Alphonso dislikes about Ronsky. At the top of his list is Ronsky's annoying habit of continually spitting—he spits all over his desk, his typewriter, and anyone who happens to be in the vicinity. Alphonso cannot stand the guy and has fantasies of punching him out. Several weeks after meeting him, Alphonso learns that Ronsky had earlier taken part in the Normandy invasion and had watched in horror as several of his buddies were cut down before they even had a chance to hit the beach. It seems that his constant spitting was a concrete manifestation of his attempt to get the bad taste out of his mouth. Upon learning this, Alphonso sees his former enemy in an entirely different light. He sighs with regret and says to himself, "Before you know it, if you're not careful, you can get to feeling for everybody and there's nobody left to hate."

Who CAN BENEFIT?

We now have almost thirty years of scientific research demonstrating that carefully structured cooperative learning strategies are effective. Students learn material as well as, or better than, students in traditional classrooms. The data also show that through cooperative learning the classroom becomes a positive social atmosphere where students learn to like and respect one another and where taunting and bullying are sharply reduced. Students involved in jigsaw tell us that they enjoy school more and show us that they do by attending class more regularly.

It goes without saying that the scientific results are important. But on a personal level, what is perhaps even more gratifying is to witness, firsthand, youngsters actually going through the transformation. Tormentors evolve into supportive helpers and anxious "losers" begin to enjoy learning and feel accepted for who they are.

The jigsaw classroom has shown us the way to encourage children to become more compassionate and empathic toward one another. Accordingly, it stands to reason that this technique could provide a simple, inexpensive, yet ideal solution to the recent epidemic of school shootings that is plaguing the United States.

However, it can be misleading to suggest that jigsaw sessions always go smoothly. There are always problems, but most can be prevented or minimized. And I don't mean to imply that competition, in and of itself, is evil; it isn't. But, at any age, a general atmosphere of exclusion that is ruthless and relentless is unpleasant at best and dangerous at worst.

The poet W. H. Auden wrote, "We must love one another or die." It is a powerful statement, but perhaps too powerful. Ideally, it's best to bring people together in cooperative situations before animosities develop. In my judgment, however, although loving one another is very nice, it isn't essential. What is essential is that we learn to *respect* one another and to feel empathy and compassion for one another—even those who seem very different from us in race, ethnicity, interests, appearance, and so on.

In Austin our goal was to reduce the bigotry, suspicion, and negative racial stereotyping that was rampant among the city's public school students. We didn't try to persuade students with rational or moral arguments, nor did we declare National Brotherhood Week. Such direct strategies have proven notoriously ineffective when it comes to changing deep-seated emotional attitudes of any kind.

Rather, we engaged the scientifically proven mechanism of self-persuasion: we placed students in a situation where the only way they could hope to survive was to work with and appreciate the qualities of others who were previously disliked. Self-interest may not be the prettiest of motives for changing behavior, but it is an opening—and an open door is better than one that is bolted shut.

Elliot Aronson is a distinguished social psychologist and fellow of the American Academy of Arts and Sciences. He has received a variety of national and international awards for his teaching, scientific research, and writing, including the American Psychological Association's highest award in 1999 for a lifetime of scientific contributions. This article is adapted from his new book, Nobody Left to Hate: Teaching Compassion After Columbine (W. H. Freeman and Company, April 2000).

From *The Humanist*, May/June 2000, pp. 17-21. © 2000 by The Humanist. Reprinted by permission.

Disaster and Trauma

Editor's Note: The initial shock of the September 11 tragedies has diminished for many people, but the mental health challenges will be with us for a much longer time. We hope readers will find this issue's... article helpful in addressing the trauma... and helping patients move beyond. [This] is a review of what is known about traumatic reactions in the aftermath of disaster.

The attacks of September 11 ended the lives of more than 5,000 people and transformed the lives of many more. Most directly affected were the tens of thousands of witnesses, rescue workers, and grieving family members and friends. Millions more read and heard the news and saw the images displayed repeatedly on television. This catastrophe has had a more devastating impact than a natural disaster or major accident, because we know that it was meant to sow terror and we have good reasons to fear that something like it may happen again. Even people not directly touched may feel temporarily shaken and helpless. This sad and anxious time is also a time for thinking about the psychological effects of trauma and how to cope with the emotional disorders that can follow.

Shock, anger, grief, and fear are normal reactions to such a devastating event. Almost all of us have lost something, if only some confidence in the future. Surveys conducted in the weeks after the attacks indicated a rise in the number of people—even among those not close to the scenes of the disaster—who felt depressed, had trouble sleeping, or couldn't concentrate. Fatigue, headaches, indigestion, nightmares, and intrusive images were common among the bereaved, witnesses, and relief workers. The number of new prescriptions for sleeping pills rose by a reported 28% and the number of new prescriptions for antidepressants by 17% in the New York area.

A person's immediate response to a disaster, no matter how extreme, is not an emotional disorder or a sign of mental illness. People who were far from the sites of the attack and even most who were nearby can expect to recover quickly. They should resume their normal lives as soon as possible, coming to terms with regret and concentrating on the future, keeping faith in their own capacities and getting help if necessary. Most symptoms of this kind go away in a week or two, and just being with others at community gatherings, religious services, and other meetings can be an important source of solace. Physical activity and other distractions often provide relief, and techniques such as meditation, breathing exercises, and muscle relaxation may help.

For most of the more immediate victims, thinking about the experience and discussing it may be better than suppressing the memories and images. Many will need listeners, even as they tell their stories repeatedly. The benefit of formal crisis counseling is disputed. One method—critical stress incident debriefing—was originally developed to help firefighters cope with their experiences but is now used more widely. A counselor in an informal setting encourages trauma survivors to recall the event and discuss their feelings in the immediate aftermath. Some studies have found these sessions to be helpful, but others suggest that they may actually do harm. What is clear is that no one should be forcefully persuaded to talk about the experience.

Post-traumatic stress disorder

While most people are recovering their balance and resuming their routines, a few will have lasting symptoms, including persistent severe depression and anxiety. And some will develop a chronic condition that is complex, pervasive, and difficult to treat—the lingering wound (the original meaning of "trauma") from an overwhelming assault on the emotions. According to the American Psychiatric Association's definition, post-traumatic stress disorder (PTSD) results from experiencing an event that involves a threat of death or serious injury or a threat to physical integrity. The experience causes intense fear, horror, and feelings of helplessness. A diagnosis of PTSD is made only after the symptoms have lasted at least a month. They may appear immediately but occasionally emerge after a long delay—sometimes even years later. These symptoms are:

1. Reexperiencing: Victims may relive the traumatic event in the form of intrusive memories, nightmares, and flashbacks (feeling or acting as though the experience is recurring). They may be upset when they are exposed to anything—an emotion, sensation, place, or person—that recalls or resembles some aspect of the experience. Even remote reminders can provoke intense physical stress reactions.

2. Avoidance: Victims often try to avoid the thoughts and feelings they had at the time of the trauma and all people, places, and activities that bring the experience to mind. In the process, their lives become restricted and their emotions numbed. They may be unable to recall all or part of the experience. They lose interest in everyday activities and feel estranged from others. They may suffer from a sense of futility and expect to die before

Normal and Abnormal Grief

When several thousand die, many thousands more are in mourning. Even normal grief can be surprisingly prolonged and take unexpectedly pervasive and debilitating forms. In one study of the widows and widowers of people who died in auto accidents, investigators found higher than average levels of anxiety and physical symptoms even 4–7 years later. More than half of the subjects still had painful memories or mental pictures that resembled intrusive reliving experiences.

For the bereaved, shock and numbness are often followed by feelings of emptiness and despair, inability to feel pleasure, headaches, and indigestion. Sadness may be mixed with anger that has no true object. Like people suffering from depression, the bereaved may be irritable and alienate their friends. And they may become angry with themselves, feeling guilty about what they did or failed to do at the time of death. Some sink into a clinical depression, which should be treated with medications and psychotherapy.

Although there are some losses from which we never fully recover, normal grief, however intense and devastating, is not a psychiatric disorder. Grieving persons should be reassured that their feelings are normal and acceptable. Most need only time and sympathetic company—especially people who are willing to listen when they talk about the deceased. When asked, they say they want to be with people who are close to them, and they are especially grateful for unexpected expressions of concern.

But long-lasting grief can also resemble a traumatic stress response, especially when death is unexpected, premature, and violent, as it was on Sept. 11. The terms "incomplete grief," "unresolved grief," "complicated grief," and "traumatic grief" are sometimes used. The symptoms may include intrusive thoughts and images of the deceased, obsessive longing, desperate loneliness, feelings of helplessness and futility, and loss of a sense of security and trust. Although closely linked to the trauma, this effect of sudden separation and loss does not necessarily include the characteristic PTSD symptoms of numbing, avoidance, tension, suspicion, and misdirected vigilance. For unresolved or traumatic grief, the treatments recommended for depression, PTSD, or both may be helpful.

Shear, K. M. et al. "Traumatic Grief Treatment: A Pilot Study," *American Journal of Psychiatry* (Sept. 2001): Vol. 158, No. 9, pp. 1506–1508.

constantly on guard (hypervigilant), as though they are still being threatened.

Few people will have all of these symptoms. A diagnosis of post-traumatic stress disorder formally requires at least one in the first group, three in the second, and two in the third. The symptoms may seem to be a strange mixture, even superficially incompatible in some ways, but there is a common theme—the traumatic event is controlling emotional life. The victim refers everything to it, constantly responding to that past experience as though it were present, unable to adapt to new circumstances and take advantage of new opportunities.

According to a nationwide survey, more than 50% of people in this country have undergone an experience that is potentially traumatic—chiefly a natural disaster, a life-threatening accident, or seeing another person badly injured or killed. Other surveys have found a lifetime PTSD rate of 8% in the United States and a current rate (previous year) of 1–3%, although it is difficult to separate pure PTSD from other mental disorders, such as mood or personality disorders. Mass destruction that affects a whole community, like the September attacks, is an especially potent source of PTSD. The disorder is common after airplane crashes and major fires, and the risk is especially high if the cause of the trauma is a deliberate assault rather than an accident or natural disaster.

Both circumstances and individual personality determine who is likely to develop PTSD. Most at risk, obviously, are those most directly exposed—people who are seriously injured or narrowly escape death, police officers, firefighters, healthcare and emergency rescue workers who are on the scene immediately afterward, and anyone who has lost a husband, wife, parent, child, co-worker, or close friend. Women are twice as vulnerable as men, and children are at even higher risk. According to one recent study, as many as 30% of children exposed to a trauma may develop symptoms of PTSD. Another powerful risk factor is previous traumatic experience—especially child abuse and chronic severe stress such as long periods of combat.

The danger is high for people who lack social support—someone to commiserate with, help they can count on from family, friends, and the community. Anyone who has a psychiatric disorder or a family history of psychiatric disorders is also vulnerable. In a situation like the present one, people with paranoid or other delusional tendencies are especially likely to suffer, but the trauma can worsen almost any existing symptoms, including anxiety, depression, personality problems, and addictions to alcohol and other drugs. It is often difficult to tell which of the symptoms are independent of the trauma and which are caused by it.

Chronic PTSD is especially common among people who suffer an acute stress reaction that lasts several days to a month. Although this response may include a number of PTSD symptoms, its distinguishing feature is dissociation. Victims feel detached and disconnected from others and from their own feelings. They are barely conscious of their surroundings. They suffer from a sense of unreality (depersonalization or derealization) and sometimes amnesia as well. Numbing or loss of awareness may provide some immediate shelter, but this re-

their time. It is as though their feelings are no longer fully real to them and the ordinary business of life no longer matters.

3. Heightened arousal: Victims may be irritable or subject to angry outbursts. Their sleep is troubled and their concentration is poor. They are jumpy (an exaggerated startle response) and

Talking to Children

Children suffering from grief or trauma have many of the adult symptoms and some that are peculiar to them. Very young children, up to the age of six, may be confused and have a tendency to cling—following their parents everywhere and insisting that the parents stay with them until they fall asleep at night. They may regress into bedwetting, thumbsucking, and other behavior they've outgrown. They often have stomachaches, headaches, appetite loss, and other physical symptoms.

At ages 6–11, children may feel guilty, as though they are somehow responsible for the disaster. They sometimes engage in repetitive play related to the traumatic experience. They can be irritable and unable to concentrate, and their school performance may deteriorate. Adolescents may express their feelings in a rebellious risk-taking, antisocial behavior, or through withdrawal and efforts to distance themselves—even pretending not to care in order to make themselves feel strong.

Without denying their own fears, adults have to make children feel safe, reassuring them that they will not be injured, killed, or orphaned. They should maintain routines and spend more time than usual with the children. It is important to find out what they know, let them say what they are thinking and feeling, and answer their questions. They can be told that it is normal and acceptable to admit fear, guilt, and even anger. Adults must also take care of themselves, because children often model their responses on what they see in their parents.

Very young children should not be exposed to reminders such as repeated television viewing, partly because they will often be confused and think that the attacks are continuing or that they and their families are in danger. If they have language, they can be helped to describe their feelings, and props such as toy ambulances may be useful. Older children can be told the truth about death. Their nightmares can be explained and schoolwork monitored. They should be reassured that "babyish" feelings and behavior are normal and will go away. It may be necessary to tolerate repetitive questions while calming specific fears: "Will this happen to me?" Adolescents can be encouraged to talk about their feelings to the family and one another.

Most children will eventually recover. Only a few will need professional help for serious long-term behavior problems, declining schoolwork, extreme withdrawal and depression, aggressive outbursts, or persistent nightmares.

A source of information and referrals on children's grief, reactions to trauma, and other emotional problems is: the American Academy of Child & Adolescent Psychiatry, 3615 Wisconsin Avenue N.W., Washington, D.C. 20016–3007. Telephone: 202–966–7300. Web: www.aacap.org.

sponse quickly loses any usefulness it may have, making it difficult to assimilate the memories and recover from the effects of the trauma. About 50% of people with acute stress reactions return to normal within three months, but an estimated 25% develop PTSD.

Physiology of stress

Reactions to stress involve the body as well as the mind. An automatic stress response is normal whenever an emergency disrupts or severely tests adaptive capacity. As the body mobilizes the confront the crisis, the adrenal hormones cortisol and adrenaline (epinephrine) begin to circulate, responding to signals passed through the pituitary gland from the hypothalamus, deep in the brain. The chemical messengers dopamine and norepinephrine are released in the sympathetic nervous system. Muscles tense and heart rate, blood pressure, and respiratory rate rise.

Both during a trauma like September 11 and when they recall it, people who develop PTSD show higher arousal levels than other survivors of the same catastrophe—more activity in the sympathetic nervous system, higher levels of adrenaline, and a greater rise in heart rate and blood pressure. But they have lower than average levels of cortisol, which supplies a feedback mechanism that turns off the alarm when the emergency is over. As soon as it reaches a certain level in the blood, the brain receives a signal and delivers a reply: turn down the sympathetic system and suppress the secretion of adrenaline. One theory about the origin of PTSD is that trauma makes some people hypersensitive to cortisol. In response, the adrenal glands stop releasing the hormone, and it never reaches a level high enough to curb the emergency response.

Meanwhile, the mind is undergoing changes. The sympathetic nervous system activates the amygdala, a brain region that coordinates responses to fear and anger, storing emotionally significant memories that are needed for survival. These memories in turn can influence later physical reactions. The form of the memories may also be affected. If the alarm is never completely turned off, the experience is not assimilated normally and may return as nightmares and other intrusive experiences.

The physiology of depression, another long-term effect of severe stress, is different; for example, depressed people tend to have a high rather than a low level of cortisol. Whether a person develops PTSD or other symptoms after a traumatic experience depends on individual differences we know too little about. Psychiatric researchers are trying to gain a better understanding of these vulnerabilities in order to develop more effective treatments.

Overcoming trauma

The aftereffects of trauma demand both intellectual and emotional resolution. While minds are calmed and bodies soothed, sufferers may want an explanation or a response from others that helps them make sense of the experience. For some, the first few days and weeks are a critical time in which an acute stress reaction may be prevented from turning into chronic PTSD. Physical comfort—massage, hugging—may mean a great deal to them. They can be educated about stress responses and helped to manage their anxiety. Psychotherapy or counseling may also be helpful.

People with PTSD need to regain the capacity to think and talk about the experience without unwanted intrusions, and exercise control over their feelings without avoidance and emotional numbing. If the treatment succeeds, they will be calm when they want to be and vigilant only when they have to be.

The most popular and well-studied treatments for PTSD are behavioral and cognitive. Exposure with systematic desensitization can reduce the fear of cues that evoke memories of the trauma. Patients review the experience under controlled conditions, gradually approaching its most disturbing aspects, until the memories no longer cause serious distress. In cognitive therapy, the techniques of reframing and reinterpretation are used to change unrealistic assumptions and probe automatic thoughts that provoke inappropriate fear, guilt, and other disturbing emotions. Training in problem solving and assertiveness may also be helpful.

Many people with PTSD make good use of group therapy or mutual support groups. They give meaning to their experience by telling their stories and listening to other victims whose similar experiences promote understanding and sympathy. By helping others, group participants come to feel more capable of helping themselves. They are reassured when they see others recover, and they tolerate their feelings better when many people are available to offer comfort.

Drugs are prescribed for trauma victims to relieve severe symptoms quickly, and in the longer term, to help them make use of psychotherapy. For the immediate treatment of restlessness and anxiety, beta-blockers like propranolol (Inderal) and benzodiazepines such as clonazepam (Klonopin) are often helpful. The most effective medications for the long haul (they take several weeks to begin working) are antidepressants, especially selective serotonin reuptake inhibitors (SSRIs) like sertraline (Zoloft) and fluoxetine (Prozac). (See *Harvard Mental Health Letter*, October and November 2000.) These drugs not only relieve depression but also improve sleep, suppress intrusive images, and calm explosive anger. Some of these symptoms can also be treated with mood stabilizers like lithium or anticonvulsants such as carbamazepine (Tegretol).

Systematic desensitization, cognitive therapy, and problem-solving training have all been found better than no treatment and in some studies more effective than simple counseling. In one study, cognitive-behavioral therapy was found to prevent the acute stress reaction from developing into PTSD. The rate of PTSD in patients given counseling alone was 83%, compared with 33% among those who had cognitive-behavioral therapy.

A 1998 review of 41 controlled studies of PTSD treatment found that psychotherapy was more effective than drugs alone, although SSRIs had some advantage in the treatment of depression related to trauma. Behavior therapy was particularly helpful, with results that persisted, according to follow-up studies, at least months after the end of treatment. There were few rigorous studies of group therapy.

The International Society for Traumatic Stress Studies has recently issued guidelines for the treatment of PTSD based on the tabulated opinions of more than 100 experts. Their collective conclusion is that psychotherapy should be continued at least once a week for three months after improvement, with booster sessions at longer intervals after that. The methods most often recommended are exposure with desensitization, cognitive therapy, and anxiety management (including muscle relaxation, meditation, and breathing exercises). Among drug treatments for PTSD, the experts prefer SSRIs and the newer antidepressants nefazodone (Serzone) and venlafaxine (Effexor).

Researchers at Dartmouth are conducting a nationwide study on the psychotherapy of PTSD among women in the military. More than 400 women at 12 sites will be assigned at random for ten weeks to either exposure with desensitization or a "present-centered" therapy (not further described). For six months afterward, they will be evaluated for depression, anxiety, and posttraumatic symptoms. The events of September 11, too, will stimulate research that provides new insight into ways of neutralizing the effects of traumatic stress.

RESOURCES

National Center for Post-Traumatic Stress Disorder, VA Medical and Regional Office Center (116D), 215 North Main Street, White River Junction, VT 05009. Telephone: 802–296–5132. Web: www.ncptsd.org.

Anxiety Disorders Association of America, 11900 Parklawn Drive, Suite 100, Rockville, Maryland 20852. Telephone: 301–231–9350. Web: www.adaa.org.

FOR FURTHER READING

Yehuda, R. "Psychoneuroendocrinology of Post-Traumatic Stress Disorder," *Psychoneuroendocrinology* (June 1998): Vol. 21, No. 2, pp. 359–79.

Ursano, R. J. et al. "Psychiatric Dimensions of Disaster: Patient Care, Community Consultation, and Preventive Medicine," *Harvard Review of Psychiatry* (November–December 1995): Vol. 3, No. 4, pp. 196–209.

Hembree, E. A. and Foa, E. B. "Posttraumatic Stress Disorder: Psychological Factors and Psychosocial Interventions," *Journal of Clinical Psychiatry* (2000): Vol. 61, Suppl. 7, pp. 33–39.

Foa, E. B. et al., eds. *Effective Treatments for PTSD: Practice Guidelines from the International Society for Traumatic Stress Studies*, New York: Guilford Press, 2000.

From the *Harvard Mental Health Letter*, January 2002, pp. 1-5. © 2002 by President and Fellows of Harvard College. Reprinted by permission.

PSYCHOLOGICAL HELP for the Terrorized

"No one knows all the answers as to how to help a nation heal."

BY RICHARD E. VATZ AND LEE S. WEINBERG

WHILE PSYCHOLOGISTS of various stripes have long offered counseling to help people cope with losses of loved ones, the sickening acts of terrorism that struck the U.S. on Sept. 11 seem different and worse. Tragic events often happen without warning in our lives, but the sheer scope of the death and destruction in New York, the fact that the jetliners' passengers were aware of their fate and that some struggled valiantly to overcome the hijackers, the symbols of America being attacked, and the number of people—survivors, relatives, and friends—suffering and struggling to regain their psychological balance put this tragedy in a category of its own.

It is different, too, in how Americans perceive it. The terror created by the image of jetliners smashing into the World Trade Center and the Pentagon, as well as the crashing of a hijacked plane near Pittsburgh, did not end with these events. In fact, there was and is deep fear that the "other shoe may drop." Anxiety concerning future terrorism as well as the ongoing dramatic economic ramifications of these attacks cannot easily be put to rest. Does anyone, therefore, really know what advice and/or counsel should be given to all those Americans upset by these horrible events (which would seem to include virtually everyone) and to those who are directly connected by blood or friendship to the victims?

Helping people cope with loss, brought about by terrorism or other causes, generally falls to professionals in the fields of psychology and psychiatry. In the wake of the tragedy of Sept. 11, there was—and continues to be—a spate of articles in the popular press on the psychological dimensions of the events of that

Photos courtesy of the New York City Fire Department Photo Unit
Grieving New York City firefighter mourns the loss of his comrades.

day, especially the effects on those close to the victims as well as those who were actual observers.

Singled out for much analysis are the cell phone calls made by passengers who knew or sensed that they were going to die. These passengers wished to call loved ones as a last goodbye. Several articles addressed whether it was better for survivors to have "closure" by receiving a call from a loved one to say a final goodbye from a doomed airplane. E. Fuller Torrey, among the U.S.'s most high-profile psychiatrists and brain researchers, concluded, "I'm not sure that the shrinks have any more insight to answer this question than the average folks on the street. I'm not sure that I have any more wisdom or knowledge than anyone else because nobody has done any studies on this." He added that it was his "gut reaction" that it is better to make the call if you can because it "would presumably provide some closure." Similarly unsure of the answer as to whether it is better or worse to receive such a call was Linda Kovalesky-McLaine, a clinical social worker, who said simply, "I can't answer that question. I think it would be a different answer for every person."

Mental health writer Sandra Boodman wrote in *The Washington Post* (Sept. 18, 2001) that the witnessing of the horrific events on television will lead to some people's not regaining their "psychological equanimity." In fact, she maintains that mental health professionals believe such witnessing can exacerbate or even "cause a diagnosable mental disorder." Psychologists and psychiatrists around the country seem to be divided on the issue of whether such severe psychological consequences are likely.

While most of them support making counseling readily available to survivors and observers at large, there are some psychiatrists who believe that there is too much of a rush to provide psychological "aid" to those who may not need it. In an interview with us, Sally Satel, a psychiatrist in Washington, D.C., and a fellow at the American Enterprise Institute, pointed out that, although those who feel the need to get "professional help" should seek it, there may be a self-fulfilling prophecy at work. When people are convinced that they surely are under unmanageable psychological stress, they tend to believe it and feel just that sort of stress. Moreover, many people will benefit—perhaps even more than from professional help—from support from traditional sources of comfort and love.

According to one article, the psychological effects of the terrorism are multifarious, with thousands of Americans seeking mental health assistance and, simultaneously, "therapists are reaching out to help the emotionally wounded" through "national and local hotlines, moderating Internet chats and in [mental health professionals'] offices." The American Red Cross reported in the week following the terroristic attacks over 15,000 "mental-health-related contacts," and also that calls to a hotline run by The National Mental Health Association increased by about one-third over normal periods. Moreover, referral calls for problem children are up substantially, and the increases in psychological distress could well continue to rise. New York radio psychologist Joy Browne notes that the number of calls have soared on her show, and Washington psychologist Faith Tanney indicates that her therapy clients are demanding more and longer psychological sessions.

It is widely believed by psychologists and psychiatrists that about one-fourth of those who experience or witness traumatic events that "involve actual or threatened death or serious injury" (according to The American Psychiatric Association's *Diagnostic and Statistical Manual of Mental Disorders*) suffer long-lasting post-traumatic stress disorder. Boodman maintains that "researchers have found that between 10 and 30% of people who directly experience trauma—in this case, that would in-

Exhausted firefighters take a much-needed break in their desperate search for survivors buried in the rubble of the World Trade Center. More than 300 firefighters who had rushed into the buildings following the terrorist attack were killed when both towers collapsed.

clude those who escaped from the infernos at the Pentagon or the World Trade Center—will develop PTSD."

A greater number, it is assumed, suffer the disorder's symptoms for a shorter length of time. However, Erica Goode of *The New York Times* warns that, for some, the terrorism that has struck the U.S. "will be memories that gradually turn malignant, as dangerous as any cancer." Many psychologists and psychiatrists are skeptical of such a pandemic. Goode, meanwhile, cites Robert Ursano, a professor of psychiatry at the Uniformed Services University of the Health Sciences specializing in assessing the effects of terrorism, who says that, "Over time, most people will do okay."

There is concern among various mental health practitioners that intervention sometimes actually may make the situation worse. In a letter posted on several Internet boards for mental health experts, sent to the American Psychological Association's *APA Monitor*, 20 mental health specialists and others wrote that there is evidence in studies of debriefing techniques, reported in the medical publication *The Cochran Library*, that proactive psychological "debriefing" can be ineffective and even debilitating. The writers state that, "in times like these it is imperative that we refrain from the urge to intervene in ways

New York Mayor Rudy Giuliani (right) and Fire Commisioner Thomas Von Essen (left) watch rescue and recovery efforts at the World Trade Center in the after math of the attack.

that—however well-intentioned—have the potential to make matters worse." They conclude with the commonsense advice that "psychologists can be of most help by supporting the community structures that people naturally call upon in times of grief and suffering... let us do whatever we can, while being careful not to get in the way." Almost immediately, there was a backlash from some leaders in crisis prevention who argued that the criticism was untimely and might discourage victims from receiving vital services that could forestall future psychological problems.

There are, however, some areas where psychologists can and do provide help in the wake of national tragedies. The American Psychological Association has published a guide called "Coping with Terrorism" (website: www.helping.apa.org and click on "The Trauma of Terrorism," located on the home page). Psychologists Rona M. Fields and Joe Margolin, who have researched the effects of terrorism and worked with its victims, created the guide. It focuses on people who directly experience terrorism and describes possible psychological impacts to watch for. The guide also warns against reactions such as xenophobia, as it can lead to discrimination and even persecution of innocent members of ethnic and racial groups whose members have committed acts of terrorism.

Fields and Margolin's guide specifically provides advice for "helping children cope," although they do not pinpoint the ages for which their advice is appropriate. Their counsel includes reassuring youngsters of the stability of our democracy and its institutions, as well as reminding them that they have a source of strength in their parents and that they can experience "a sense of empowerment" by talking about their experiences in previous scary circumstances with which they have now come to terms.

John Weaver, a grief counselor for the American Red Cross, emphasizes that reassuring children through parental presence is important. However, he cautions against "anxious reassurance," through which parents' own anxieties are transmitted to their offspring. He advises communicating to children that specific steps are being taken to enhance their safety and adds that it is important to teach them not to blame others who may simply share the ethnic background of the perpetrators of the terrorism.

One of the complexities of reassuring children concerning the events of Sept. 11 is that this terrorist attack occurred here in the U.S. In the terrorism of the last few years—the bombing of the *U.S.S. Cole* in Yemen and the bombing of the embassies in Africa were far away. Even the earlier bombing of the World Trade Center and the Murrah Federal Building in Oklahoma City seemed at the time to be isolated incidents, not likely to recur. Today, though, no one can be quite so smugly certain that the danger has passed.

In an article in *The Baltimore Sun* on the day following the mind-numbing crashes of the jetliners into the World Trade Center and the Pentagon, Richard M. Sarles, professor of child and adolescent psychiatry at the University of Maryland Medical Center, advocated offering "reassurance and protection [to children] and let[ting] them know we're here and that we're safe." However, Sarles points out the difficulty of reassuring children when events dictate otherwise: "The good news is that [massive terrorism] occurs rarely in this country... if you were living in Israel where terrorism is a daily event, it's very hard to reassure." Paramjit T. Joshi, chair of the psychiatry department at Children's National Medical Center in Washington, sees the other side and cautions against "falsely minimizing the danger." The trouble with inaccurately reassuring children—as well as older Americans—is that, if the reassurances are proved false by subsequent events, the source loses credibility.

The problems and depression caused by the terrorism that has struck the nation has not led Americans to seek help only in psychological sources. While some have taken advantage of counseling from mental health professionals, others look for solace elsewhere. It has been well-documented that there are tremendous variations geographically as to where Americans can seek comfort in times of stress—often due to simple realities of availability of mental health personnel as well as differing norms in the social acceptance of getting psychological help. *The Washington Post* reports that, even in areas where psychological counseling is readily available, such as Washington, D.C., many people look to religious institutions as well to deal with their insecurities at times of national crisis. The *Post* indicates that numerous individuals have "turned to houses of worship for treatment of their spiritual and psychological wounds." At such locations, many Americans pose religious and philosophical questions, such as the morality of military retaliation and others relating to the implications of the terrorism for the power of evil in the world.

No one can deny that there are critical psychological consequence to victims' experiencing or observing terrorist acts. Perhaps the most significant effect on the nation as a whole is the reduction in our sense of security, economic well-being, and self-identification as Americans. No one knows all the answers as to how to help a nation heal. Whether through counseling, family, or religious contacts, it is imperative that people regain their emotional footing in order to win intelligently and effectively what surely will be a long fight ahead against international terrorism.

Richard E. Vatz*, Associate Psychology Editor of* USA Today, *is professor of rhetoric and communication, Towson (Md.) University.* ***Lee S. Weinberg****, Associate Psychology Editor of* USA Today, *is an associate professor in the Graduate School of Public and International Affairs, University of Pittsburgh (Pa.).*

From *USA Today* magazine, November 2001. © 2001 by the Society for the Advancement of Education. Reprinted by permission.

LIFE IN AMERICA

AMERICAN FAMILIES
Are Drifting Apart

The sexual revolution, women's liberation, relaxation of divorce laws, and greater mobility are fracturing the traditional family structure.

BY BARBARA LEBEY

A VARIETY OF REASONS—from petty grievances to deep-seated prejudices, misunderstandings to all-out conflicts, jealousies, sibling rivalry, inheritance feuds, family business disputes, and homosexual outings—are cause for families to grow apart. Family estrangements are becoming more numerous, more intense, and more hurtful. When I speak to groups on the subject, I always ask: Who has or had an estrangement or knows someone who does? Almost every hand in the room goes up. Sisters aren't speaking to each other since one of them took the silver when Mom died. Two brothers rarely visit because their wives don't like each other.

A son alienates himself from his family when he marries a woman who wants to believe that he sprung from the earth. Because Mom is the travel agent for guilt trips, her daughter avoids contact with her. A family banishes a daughter for marrying outside her race or religion. A son eradicates a divorced father when he reveals his homosexuality. And so it goes.

The nation is facing a rapidly changing family relationship landscape. Every assumption made about the family structure has been challenged, from the outer boundaries of single mothers raising out-of-wedlock children to gay couples having or adopting children to grandparents raising their grandchildren. If the so-called traditional family is having trouble maintaining

harmony, imagine what problems can and do arise in less-conventional situations. Fault lines in Americans' family structure were widening throughout the last 40 years of the 20th century. The cracks became evident in the mid 1970s when the divorce rate doubled. According to a 1999 Rutgers University study, divorce has risen 30% since 1970; the marriage rate has fallen faster; and just 38% of Americans consider themselves happy in their married state, a drop from 53% 25 years ago. Today, 51% of all marriages end in divorce.

How Americans managed to alter their concept of marriage and family so profoundly during those four decades is the subject of much scholarly investigation and academic debate. In a May, 2000, *New York Times Magazine* article titled "The Pursuit of Autonomy," the writer maintains that "the family is no longer a haven; all too often a center of dysfunction, it has become one with the heartless world that surrounds it." Unlike the past, the job that fits you in your 20s is not the job or career you'll likely have in your 40s. This is now true of marriage as well—the spouse you had in your 20s may not be the one you will have after you've gone through your midlife crisis.

In the 1960s, four main societal changes occurred that have had an enormous impact on the traditional family structure. The sexual revolution, women's

liberation movement, states' relaxation of divorce laws, and mobility of American families have converged to foster family alienation, exacerbate old family rifts, and create new ones. It must be emphasized, however, that many of these changes had positive outcomes. The nation experienced a strengthened social conscience, women's rights, constraints on going to war, and a growing tolerance for diversity, but society also paid a price.

The 1960s perpetuated the notion that we are first and foremost *entitled* to happiness and fulfillment. It's positively un-American *not* to seek it! This idea goes back to that early period of our history when Thomas Jefferson dropped the final term from British philosopher John Locke's definition of human rights—"life, liberty, and... property"—and replaced it with what would become the slogan of our new nation: "the pursuit of happiness." In the words of author Gail Sheehy, the 1960s generation "expressed their collective personality as idealistic, narcissistic, anti-establishment, hairy, horny and preferably high."

Any relationship that was failing to deliver happiness was being tossed out like an empty beer can, including spousal ones. For at least 20 years, the pharmaceutical industry has learned how to cash in on the American obsession with feeling good by hyping mood drugs to rewire the brain circuitry for happiness through the elimination of sadness and depression.

Young people fled from the confines of family, whose members were frantic, worrying about exactly where their adult children were and what they were doing. There were probably more estrangements between parents and adult children during the 1960s and early 1970s than ever before.

In the wake of the civil rights movement and Pres. Lyndon Johnson's Great Society came the women's liberation movement, and what a flashy role it played in changing perceptions about the family structure. Women who graduated from college in the late 1960s and early 1970s were living in a time when they could establish and assert their independent identities. In Atlanta, Emory Law School's 1968 graduating class had six women in it, the largest number ever to that point, and all six were in the top 10%, including the number-one graduate. In that same period, many all-male colleges opened their doors to women for the first time. No one could doubt the message singer Helen Reddy proclaimed: "I am woman, hear me roar." For all the self-indulgence of the "hippie" generation, there was an intense awakening in young people of a recognition that civil rights must mean equal rights for everyone in our society, and that has to include women.

Full equality was the battle cry of every minority, a status that women claimed despite their majority position. As they had once marched for the right to vote, women began marching for sexual equality and the same broad range of career and job opportunities that were always available to men. Financial independence gave women the freedom to walk away from unhappy marriages. This was a dramatic departure from the puritanical sense of duty that had been woven into the American fabric since the birth of this nation.

For all the good that came out of this movement, though, it also changed forever traditional notions of marriage, motherhood, and family unity, as well as that overwhelming sense of children first. Even in the most-conservative young families, wives were letting their husbands know that they were going back to work or back to school. Many women had to return to work either because there was a need for two incomes to maintain a moderate standard of living or because they were divorced and forced to support their offspring on their own. "Don't ask, don't tell" day-care centers proliferated where overworked, undertrained staff, and two-income yuppie parents, ignored the children's emotional needs—all in the name of equality and to enable women to reclaim their identifies. Some might say these were the parents who ran away from home.

Many states began to approve legislation that allowed no-fault divorce, eliminating the need to lay blame on spouses or stage adulterous scenes in sleazy motels to provide evidence for states that demanded such evidence for divorces. The legal system established procedures for easily dissolving marriages, dividing property, and sharing responsibility for the children. There were even do-it-yourself divorce manuals on bookstore shelves. Marriage had become a choice rather than a necessity, a one-dimensional status sustained almost exclusively by emotional satisfaction and not worth maintaining in its absence. Attitudes about divorce were becoming more lenient, so much so that the nation finally elected its first divorced president in 1980—Ronald Reagan.

With divorced fathers always running the risk of estrangement from their children, this growing divorce statistic has had the predictable impact of increasing the number of those estrangements. Grandparents also experienced undeserved fallout from divorce, since, almost invariably, they are alienated from their grandchildren.

The fourth change, and certainly one of the most pivotal, was the increased mobility of families that occurred during those four decades. Family members were no longer living in close proximity to one another. The organization man moved to wherever he could advance more quickly up the corporate ladder. College graduates took the best job offer, even if it was 3,000 miles away from where they grew up and where their family still lived.

Some were getting out of small towns for new vistas, new adventures, and new job opportunities. Others were fleeing the overcrowded dirty cities in search of cleaner air, a more reasonable cost of living, and retirement communities in snow-free, warmer, more-scenic locations. Moving from company to company had begun, reaching what is now a crescendo of job-hopping. Many young people chose to marry someone who lived in a different location, so family ties were geographically severed for indeterminate periods of time, sometimes forever.

According to Lynn H. Dennis' *Corporate Relocation Takes Its Toll on Society*, during the 10 years from 1989 to 1999, more than 5,000,000 families were relocated one or more times by their employers. In addition to employer-directed moves, one out of five Americans relocated at least once, not for exciting adventure, but for economic advancement and/or a safer place to raise children. From March, 1996, to March, 1997, 42,000,000 Americans, or 16% of the population, packed up and moved from where they were living to another location. That is a striking statistic. Six million of these people moved from one region of the country to another, and young adults aged 20 to 29 were the most mobile, making up 32% of the moves during that year. This disbursement of nuclear families throughout the country disconnected them from parents, brothers, sisters, grandparents, aunts, uncles, and cousins—the extended family and all its adhesive qualities.

Today, with cell phones, computers, faxes, and the Internet, the office can be anywhere, including in the home. Therefore, we can *live* anywhere we want to. If that is the case, why aren't more people choosing to live in the cities or towns where they grew up? There's no definitive answer. Except for the praise heaped on "family values," staying close to family no longer plays a meaningful role in choosing where we reside.

These relocations require individuals to invest an enormous amount of time to reestablish their lives without help from family or old friends. Although nothing can compare to the experience of immigrants who left their countries knowing they probably would never see their families again, the phenomenon of Americans continually relocating makes family relationships difficult to sustain.

Our culture tends to focus on the individual, or, at most, on the nuclear family, downplaying the benefits of extended families, though their role is vital in shaping our lives. The notion of "moving on" whenever problems arise has been a time-honored American concept. Too many people would rather cast aside some family member than iron out the situation and keep the relationship alive. If we don't get along with our father or if our mother doesn't like our choice of mate or our way of life, we just move away and see the family once or twice a year. After we're married, with children in school, and with both parents working, visits become even more difficult. If the family visits are that infrequent, why bother at all? Some children grow up barely knowing any of their relatives. Contact ceases; rifts don't resolve; and divisiveness often germinates into a full-blown estrangement.

In an odd sort of way, the more financially independent people become, the more families scatter and grow apart. It's not a cause, but it is a facilitator. Tolerance levels decrease as financial means increase. Just think how much more we tolerate from our families when they are providing financial support. Look at the divorced wife who depends on her family for money to supplement alimony and child support, the student whose parents are paying all college expenses, or the brother who borrows family money to save his business.

Recently, a well-known actress being interviewed in a popular magazine was asked, if there was one thing she could change in her family, what would it be? Her answer was simple: "That we could all live in the same city." She understood the importance of being near loved ones and how, even in a harmonious family, geographical distance often leads to emotional disconnectedness. When relatives are regularly in each other's company, they will usually make a greater effort to get along. Even when there is dissension among family members, they are more likely to work it out, either on their own or because another relative has intervened to calm the troubled waters. When rifts occur, relatives often need a real jolt to perform an act of forgiveness. Forgiving a family member can be the hardest thing to do, probably because the emotional bonds are so much deeper and usually go all the way back to childhood. Could it be that blood is a thicker medium in which to hold a grudge?

With today's families scattered all over the country, the matriarch or patriarch of the extended family is far less able to keep his or her kin united, caring, and supportive of one another. In these disconnected nuclear families, certain trends—workaholism, alcoholism, depression, severe stress, isolation, escapism, and a push toward continuous supervised activity for children—are routinely observed. What happened to that family day of rest and togetherness? We should mourn its absence.

For the widely dispersed baby boomers with more financial means than any prior generation, commitment, intimacy, and family togetherness have never been high on their list of priorities. How many times have you heard of family members trying to maintain a relationship with a relative via e-mail and answering machines? One young man now sends his Mother's Day greeting by leaving a message for his mom on *his* answering machine. When she calls to scold him for forgetting to call her, she'll get a few sweet words wishing her a happy Mother's Day and his apology for being too busy to call or send a card! His sister can expect the same kind of greeting for her birthday, but only if she bothers to call to find out why her brother hadn't contacted her.

Right now, and probably for the foreseeable future, we will be searching for answers to the burgeoning problems we unwittingly created by these societal changes, but don't be unduly pessimistic. Those who have studied and understood the American psyche are far more optimistic. The 19th-century French historian and philosopher Alexis de Tocqueville once said of Americans, "No natural boundary seems to be set to the effort of Americans, and in their eyes what is not yet done, is only what they have not yet attempted to do." Some day, I hope this mindset will apply not to political rhetoric on family values, but to bringing families back together again.

Barbara LeBey, *an Atlanta, Ga.-based attorney and former judge, is the author of* Family Estrangements—How They Begin, How to Mend Them, How to Cope with Them.

From *USA Today* magazine, September 2001. © 2001 by the Society for the Advancement of Education. Reprinted by permission.

How to Multitask

By Catherine Bush

Who can remember life before multitasking? These days we all do it: mothers, air-traffic controllers, ambidextrous athletes, high-flying executives who manage to eat, take conference calls, write e-mail and conduct board meetings all at the same time. We lionize those who appear to multitask effortlessly and despair at our own haphazard attempts to juggle even two tasks, secretly wondering if there exists a race of superior beings whose brains are hard-wired for multitasking feats. Only recently have neurologists begun to understand what our brains are up to when we do it. What they've learned offers hope to all multitasking delinquents out there.

1. Don't think you can actually do two things at once. Even when you think you're doing more than one thing simultaneously—say, driving and talking on a cell phone—you aren't. Unlike a computer, the brain isn't structured as a parallel processor. It performs actions, even very simple actions, in a strict linear sequence. You must complete the first task, or part of that task, before moving on to the next. What we call multitasking is actually task switching.

Hal Pashler, a professor of psychology at the University of California at San Diego, conducted an experiment in which he tested the brain's ability to respond to two different sounds in quick succession. What he found is that the brain stalls fractionally before responding to the second stimulus. The second sound is heard (the brain can take in information simultaneously), but it requires time, if only milliseconds, to organize a response. "When you really study precisely what people's brains are doing at any moment, there's less concurrent processing than you might think," Pashler explains. "The brain is more of a time-share operation." He adds, "When fractions of a second matter, we're better off not doing another task."

2. Prioritize. To know when to switch tasks, you must distinguish between the tasks you must perform and those you can afford to blow off.

Consider the experiment that Jordan Grafman developed at the National Institute of Neurological Disorders and Stroke (N.I.N.D.S.) in Bethesda, Md. It's a driving simulation in which you must avoid errant cars and jaywalkers, all while reciting sequences of numbers called out to you. Typically, your driving skills will grow more erratic as you pay attention to the numbers (although, frighteningly, you may not be aware of this). But when a virtual pedestrian dashes into the road, you'll most likely abandon the recitation. That's because in a driving simulation, avoiding killing people is the one challenge that outranks all others.

Before approaching multiple tasks, recommends Grafman, clearly establish which tasks are more important than others. "Mentally rehearsing," he says, "definitely improves performance."

3. Immerse yourself in your immediate task, but don't forget what remains to be done next. To switch tasks successfully, the brain must marshal the resources required to perform the new task while shutting off, or inhibiting, the demands of the previous one. At the same time, you must maintain the intention to break off at a certain point and switch to another activity. During such moments of mental juggling, a section of the brain called Brodmann's Area 10 comes alive. (Area 10 is located in the fronto-polar prefrontal cortex—at the very front of the brain.)

The crucial role played by Area 10 in multitasking was documented in a 1999 study that Grafman helped conduct; the results were published in the journal Nature. Functional magnetic resonance imaging scans (functional M.R.I.'s) were given to subjects at the Institute of Neurological Disorders while they performed simple multitasking experiments. Blood flow to Area 10 increased when people kept a principal goal in mind while temporarily engaged in secondary tasks. "This is presumably the last part of the brain to evolve, the most mysterious and exciting part," Grafman says. "It's what makes us most human."

Paul Burgess, who researches multitasking at University College, London, has also been focusing on the role of Area 10. "If you're missing it due to injury or a birth defect," he explains, "you keep forgetting to do things." He points out that successful multitasking requires that you not continuously think about switching tasks. That is, the activation of Area 10 does not require constant, conscious rehearsing of the need to switch tasks. For instance, if you have to make an important phone call at the end of the day, you don't tend to make an explicit mental note of this fact every five minutes. Rather, you engage in a less explicit act of remembrance—a kind of low-level arousal, Burgess speculates, in which blood flow increases to Area 10.

4. Depend on routines—and compare new tasks with old ones. Multitasking becomes easier, scientists believe, when you make parts of the process routine. For example, driving, a familiar activity for many of us, becomes largely automatic—the parts of the prefrontal cortex involved in cognition surrender to the regions deeper in the brain that govern visual and motor control. Once a task has been learned, the brain will try to shift the load for performance to its deeper structures, freeing up the cortex for other tasks requiring active cognition. That way, if something unexpected happens (like a pedestrian bolting into the road), you'll have the resources to deal with it.

When you are thrown into a new task, it's helpful to search for a comparison to something you've done before. The brain thrives on analogies. If you're suddenly forced to fly a crashing plane, you might want to draw on your PlayStation skills. "We solve task-switching dilemmas by trying to retrieve similar circum-stances, similar situations being represented in similar regions of the prefrontal cortex," Grafman says. "If we don't, our experience will be totally chaotic, and we will clearly fail." He then laughs. "This cannot explain Art Tatum." The jazz pianist's wild two-handed improvising was pouring from his CD player when I entered his office. "With Tatum, nothing was routine. He must have had a great prefrontal cortex."

5. Make schedules, not to-do lists. And whatever you do, don't answer the phone. For those of us who find multitasking difficult, Burgess claims that the simplest aids—like timers and alarms—are the most effective. When the American astronaut Jerry Linenger was working aboard the space station Mir, he wore three or four watches with alarms set to notify him when to switch tasks.

"The alarm does not have to carry any information, just be a reminder that something has to be done," Burgess says. Studies have shown that neurologically impaired patients have been helped at multitasking by nothing more than someone clapping their hands at random intervals. An interruption breaks your train of thought and initiates a recall of what else needs to be done.

It's important, however, that the interruption itself not entail a task. For example, if the phone rings, don't answer it. Dealing with whatever the call is about will distract your brain from what you've already set out to do. Instead, use the in-terruption to see if you're on track with other activities. "Make calling others one of the things that needs to be scheduled," Burgess advises. "And if you have to answer the call, don't go straight back to what you were doing before the call arrived. Very deliberately check the time, and ask yourself if there was something else you should have been doing."

By following such an approach, you can actually change your brain. Visualizing the circumstances in which you need to switch tasks will establish a mental pathway that will be available when you really need it. As functional brain scans suggest, just by thinking about what we need to do and when we need to do it, we can increase blood flow to Area 10, our multitasking hot spot.

Age also improves us. Children are easily distracted from tasks by competing signals, and younger adults, with their maturing prefrontal cortexes, are best at learning and combining new tasks. As we age (and our brains atrophy), learning new tasks becomes harder, but we get better at extracting themes and prioritizing tasks.

"For tasks performed in a short period of time, the younger tend to do better," Burgess says. "Older people learn from their mistakes and begin to compensate over time. This is very encouraging science for those of us not 20 years old."

Catherine Bush is the author of the novel "The Rules of Engagement."

From *The New York Times Magazine,* April 8, 2001. © 2001 by The New York Times Company. Reprinted by permission.

Work **Work Work Work!**

It's taking over our lives—invading our homes, haunting our holidays, showing up for dinner. **Should we care?**

by Mark Hunter

YOU'VE HEARD THE JOKE BY NOW, BUT IT RINGS so true that it bears retelling: A guy reads a headline saying "Clinton creates 8 million jobs", and he cracks wearily, "Yeah, and I got three of 'em."

That gag may be the epitaph of the 1990s. In a very real sense, all of us—not just the 13 percent of us working two or three part-time jobs to survive—have three jobs. There's the work we do for a living, the work we do for ourselves (in many cases, to make sure we still can make a living tomorrow), plus the combination of housework and caregiving. Researchers differ on how much time we put into each of these categories, but most agree on one crucial point: The total keeps growing. As my brother Richard, a vice president of the Gartner Group, a high-tech advisory company, puts it: "It's like trying to fit a size 12 into a size eight shoe."

By far the biggest chunk of our time still goes to the work we do for a living. A survey of some 3,000 employees nationwide by the Families and Work Institute (FWI), a New York nonprofit organization that addresses work and family issues, discovered that over the past two decades, the average time spent at a full-time job has risen from 43.6 to 47.1 hours per week. Over a year, that comes to about four extra weeks—the same figure that Juliet B. Schor arrived at in her controversial 1991 study, *The Overworked American*, one of the first books to document what she called "the decline of leisure."

This fact hit home for me when I returned to the U.S. in 1996 after a decade abroad. I began to notice that not one of the other seven people in my office left their desks at lunchtime, the way folks used to. Throw in that traditional half-hour lunch break, and that's another two-and-a-half hours every week that many people give to work—or about three more weeks per year. Likewise, the Bureau of Labor Statistics reports that since 1985 paid vacation time has declined, and so has the average time that workers take off sick. Not surprisingly, more than one third of

the people in the FWI survey said that they "often or very often feel used up at the end of the workday." It's true that some researchers, like John Robinson, a sociology professor at the University of Maryland, argue that it's mainly the well-off among us who are working more, as a matter of choice, and that on average our leisure time has increased. But that's not what I see all around me.

Simultaneously, the old line between work life and private life is vanishing. In trying to understand why employees often refused to take advantage of maternity leave and flex-time, sociologist Arlie Hochschild, author of *The Time Bind*, discovered, to her amazement, that work has become a form of 'home' and home has become 'work.' "She reports that many people now see their jobs as a more appreciative, personal sort of social world" compared with their homes, where in the age of divorce and double careers, "the emotional demands have become more baffling and complex." When I interviewed 40 men about their work-life tradeoffs, every one of them said that it was easier to be a success on the job than in his personal relationships. Is it just a coincidence that hit TV shows like *Taxi* or *Murphy Brown* substituted the workplace "family" for the domestic setting of *The Brady Bunch*?

Work has penetrated the home in another potent way, notes market researcher Judith Langer, who has interviewed several hundred people on this subject over the past ten years: "People feel that what they're required to do at work has spilled over into the rest of their lives—reading, keeping up with trends in their fields, keeping up with e-mail and voice mail. We had a guy come into a focus group carrying all the publications that had hit his desk that day and complain, 'Monday weighs 20 pounds.'"

Personal technology has turned what once were hobbies into jobs: When my brother goes home from the office, he fires up his PC and checks the online orders for his self-produced harmonica records. And when the one third of Americans with managerial or professional jobs leave home, work follows them on a cell phone, pager, or modem. This past winter I received numerous business-related e-mail messages from an executive who was on a hiking trip deep in the mountains of Utah. (Emergency rescue crews have reported finding stranded hikers in the wilderness who had filled their backpacks with a portable computer, but forgotten to bring enough food and water.) The next time a cell phone rings in a restaurant at dinner-time, notice how many people automatically reach for theirs, because it might be a business call. In the 1960s and 1970s, stress experts called this kind of thing multiphasic behavior, otherwise known as doing several tasks at once. Nowadays we call it efficiency.

The distinction between work and leisure no longer exists

Ironically, the Baby Boomers, who came of age shout-ing their contempt for the man in the gray flannel suit, have done more than any other generation to erase the line between work and private life. Among the first to spot this paradox was Alvin Toffler in his 1980 futurist manifesto, *The Third Wave*. While most observers took those in the hippie movement for a bunch of unwashed, lazy bums, Toffler realized that they were really the pro-totype of a new kind of worker, the "prosumer"—people who, like frontier farmers, produce a share of what they consume, from home medicine to clothing (my fiancee creates a wardrobe every two years) to home-baked bread, instead of buying it all in the marketplace. "Once we recognize that much of our so-called leisure time is in fact spent producing goods and services for our own use," he noted, "then the old distinction between work and leisure falls apart."

Just as they turned the home into a workplace, Boomers redefined the ideal workplace as a playground. At the end of the 1970s, pollster Daniel Yankelovich found that this "New Breed" of Americans believed that work should be first and foremost a means to self-fulfill-ment—unlike their parents, who were taught by the Depression that any job that pays a secure wage was worth keeping. When Catalyst, a New York nonprofit or-ganization that seeks to advance women in business, sur-veyed more than 800 members of two-career couples about what mattered most to them on the job, at the top of the list were emotional benefits such as supportive management, being able to work on their own, and hav-ing control over their product.

Our careers now start earlier and end later, reversing a trend that reached its peak after World War II, when child labor virtually disappeared and retirement became a right. These days, so many teenagers have jobs—and as a result are cutting back on sleep, meals, and homework—that the National Research Council has called for strict new limits on the hours they're allowed to work. At the same time, the number of people 55 and older who still are in the labor force has increased by 6 million since 1950, and most of that increase is women. The Department of Labor projects that this number is going to grow by an-other 6 million by the year 2006.

None of this was supposed to happen. Only a genera-tion ago, the conventional wisdom among economists was that America was turning into an "affluent society", in which ever more efficient technology would produce an abundance of wealth that we could enjoy with less and less labor. Science-fiction novelists like Kurt Vonnegut imag-ined a society in which a tiny elite ran the show, while ev-eryone else sat around bored. In their vision, work would no longer be a burden, but a privilege for the happy few.

There are a lot of reasons why things didn't turn out quite that way. One is the Vietnam War, which heated the American economy to the boiling point just as the oil shocks of the 1970s arrived—a combination that led to double-digit inflation and sapped the value of wages. Then successive waves of recession, mergers, and down-sizing crashed through the American economy during the '80s. With few exceptions, one of the surest ways to raise a company's stock price—and along with it the value of its executives' stock options—was to fire a piece of its workforce. (Fortunately, downsizing appears to be losing steam, as Wall Street begins to suspect it as a des-perate attempt to make a company's bottom line look good in the short term.) Gradually, overtime pay replaced wage increases as the main way to stay ahead of the bills.

The Baby Boom played a role here, too. With so many Boomers competing for jobs, they became cheap for em-ployers: "For the first time in recent American history," marvels Landon Y. Jones in *Great Expectations: America and the Baby Boom Generation*, "the relative earnings of col-lege graduates *declined*." In order to maintain or, in many cases to surpass, the lifestyles of their parents—more Baby Boomers now own homes and, on average, bigger homes than Americans did in the 1950s—they have gone deeply into debt. About one fourth of the average fam-ily's income now goes to pay various creditors, more than in any previous generation.

Just as the feminist revolution was urging women to do something with their lives besides raise kids and clean house, it became difficult for the average family to make ends meet without two incomes. Today, in nearly four out of five couples—compared with one out of five in 1950—both partners are in the labor force, with women working nearly as many hours for pay as men. One posi-tive result is that since the late 1970s men have taken over a steadily growing (though still smaller) share of the childcare and household chores—nearly two hours' worth per day that used to be considered women's work.

Yet even visionary feminists like Dorothy Dinnerstein, who predicted this shift in her landmark 1976 book, *The Mermaid and the Minotaur*, did not foresee that it would also have a negative impact on our intimate lives. The Internet site BabyCenter recently polled roughly 2,000 of its new-mother visitors on whether they did or would return to work after their child was born. Two out of three survey participants said that they would go back to work within six months, but only one out of six said that she found the move "satisfying"; twice as many called it "wrenching." Men are also feeling the pinch." I have absolutely no time for myself or my friends," a married male executive and father complained to a Catalyst researcher. "Not enough time for us as a couple, and even the extended family say they don't see us enough."

Work is focusing us to constantly learn new ways of working

In previous decades, surveys showed that the biggest source of problems for married couples was money; now, when both partners are asked what is the biggest challenge they face, the majority of two-career couples answer "too little time." Not surprisingly, a growing number of leading-edge companies now offer working couples flexible schedules, expanded parental leave, and other benefits that allow their employees to reconcile their jobs with their personal lives.

Paradoxically, the same technology that was supposed to make us all wealthy loafers has contributed to the work-life squeeze. Computers and the changes they wrought have eliminated entire categories of jobs—when was the last time, for example, you talked to a human operator, instead of an automated phone tree, when you called a big company? In his book *The End of Work*, Jeremy Rifkin warned that this trend would end by puffing nearly all of us out of a job—a neat Doomsday inversion of the old "affluent society" prophecy. But many economists argue that new jobs will be created by new technology, just as they always have been. Perhaps, but the pressures to adapt to these rapid technological changes are greater than ever.

Computers have even changed the rhythm of our work, giving us more of a say in how the job is done because technology-savvy frontline personnel become responsible for decisions that managers used to make, as they constantly feed information up and down the line. The same applies to managers, whose desktop PCs, equipped with software that does everything from keeping appointments to formatting business letters and writing contracts, have largely replaced personal secretaries. We get more control—which happens to be one of the key measures of job satisfaction—but in return we end up giving more of ourselves to the job.

Beyond requiring us to put in longer hours for fear of losing our jobs, work is changing us in positive ways. In particular, it is literally forcing us to expand beyond the limits of what we previously thought we could accom-

plish, to constantly learn new ways of working. A lifelong career now means lifelong retraining. As the Radcliffe Public Policy Institute in Cambridge, Massachusetts, reports, "The qualities that once nearly guaranteed lifelong employment—hard work, reliability, loyalty, mastery of a discrete set of skills—are often no longer enough." That message has come through loud and clear. About one out of 12 Americans moonlights from his or her principal job in order to learn new skills or weave a "safety net" in case that job is lost. And American universities, starved for students only a few years ago as the Baby Boom grew up and out of the classrooms, have found a burgeoning new market in older workers. Census data show that by 1996 an incredible 468,000 college students were age 50 and older—an increase of 43 percent since 1990.

I don't have to look far to see that trend at work. My brother's wife earned her degree as a geriatric nurse in her late 40s, and it's now her part-time career. My mother, who runs her own public-relations agency, is working toward a degree as an English-language teacher, which will become her post-"retirement" career. And I'm riding that same train. This year I began teaching myself to write code for the Internet, just like my friend Randy, a former magazine editor who spent years of evenings learning to make Web pages in order to support his family. Why? Because by the year 2006 there will be fewer jobs for journalists, according to the Department of Labor. Like everyone else, I've got a choice between moving up—or out.

And there's real excitement in acquiring fresh skills—including the joy of proving wrong the adage that old dogs can't learn new tricks. But many older workers are not getting a chance to share in that excitement: They are being shunted aside from the retraining they will need to stay in the labor market at a moment when they are the fastest-growing share of the labor force. And the point at which a worker on the rise becomes a worker who's consigned to history is coming earlier in people's careers, usually around age 44, according to the Bureau of Labor Statistics. This situation persists at a time when a 77-year-old astronaut named John Glenn just went back into space—and while the minimum age for receiving Social Security benefits is rising.

Perhaps more managers should look at the hard science on this question. In a survey of the available research, Paula Rayman, director of the Radcliffe Public Policy Institute notes that there are "at least 20 studies showing that vocabulary, general information, and judgment either rise or never fall before age 60." Despite these results, they found that managers "consistently made different hiring, promotion, training, and discipline decisions based *solely* [my emphasis] on the age of the workers."

A recent survey of 405 human-resources professionals found that only 29 percent of them make an active effort to attract and/or retain older workers. Among those employers who have made such efforts, establishing opportunities for advancement, skills training, and part-time

six survival tips

THE RULES OF THE GAME MAY HAVE CHANGED, BUT midcareer and older workers still hold a number of aces—among them experience, wisdom, and adaptability. Here's some expert advice on how to play your cards and strengthen your hand for the future, gleaned from John Thompson, head of IMCOR, an interim executive placement firm in Stamford, Connecticut; Peter Cappelli, professor of management at The Wharton School in Philadelphia and author of *The New Deal at Work* (Harvard Business School Press 1999); and management gurus N. Fredric Crandall and Marc J. Wallace, authors of *Work and Rewards in the Virtual Workplace* (AMACOM, 1998)

LEARN WHILE YOU EARN If your company will pay for you to attend college-level courses to up-grade your skills, great. If not, take them anyway. Anything computer-related is a good bet. Microsoft offers training programs via organizations such as AARP.

FLEX YOUR MUSCLES By offering to work hours that younger workers may shun because of family and other commitments, you set yourself apart, especially in the eyes of employers in service industries who need 24-hour or seven-a-day week staffing. Employers such as the Home Shopping Network now rely on mature workers to fill a variety of positions.

CAST A WIDE NET The World Wide Web has radically changed the employment scene. A growing selection of jobs are being posted there, and so are résumés. Take a look at the Working Options section on AARP's Web site at www.aarp.org/working_options/home.html for career guidance and links to resources, including America's Job Bank.

BECOME AN MVP Do something to make yourself invaluable. For example, consider becoming a mentor to a young, up-and-coming manager who may need just the kind of guidance an experienced hand can offer. Another option: Seek out projects that matter to your boss and allow you to showcase your talents.

TEST THE WATERS Temporary workers are the fastest-growing segment of the labor force, for good reason. Companies faced with budget-cutting pressures are loathe to add full-time, permanent workers who drive up salary and benefit costs. It gives you an opportunity to try out an alternate career to see if it really fits. And temporary work often is the pathway to a permanent gig.

BE A COMEBACK KID Even if you're planning to retire or cut back from full-time work, don't forget job possibilities with your current employer. GE's information unit in Rockville, Maryland, offers a Golden Opportunity program that lets retirees work up to 1,000 hours a year, and many firms in Southern California use retirees to help with special engineering projects.

—*Tim Smart*

work arrangements are the most common. Overall, older employees are rated highly for loyalty and dedication, commitment to doing quality work, reliability in a crisis, solid work performance, and experience. This has given rise to a new phenomenon, in which downsized older workers are coming back to the workplace as consultants, temps. or contingent workers hired to work on specific projects.

Many who possess skills that are high in demand, like computer experts or financial advisers are finding fresh opportunities: Brokerage firms, for example, have discovered that their clients enjoy having investment counselors whose life experience is written on their faces.

Other countries are grappling with this issue as well. The Danish government, for example now offers salaried one-year training programs to unemployed workers over age 50. The German government has made it more costly for companies to downsize. And the French government is experimenting with ways to reduce the hours people spend on the job, to spread the work around. For Americans, however, the likely solution will depend on the ability of older workers to take control of their careers as never before, to think of themselves as independent contractors—units of one, so to speak—and, to do whatever they can to enhance their value. At a time when work has become, all-encompassing for many of us, it remains an eminently desirable endeavor. And although much is uncertain about the future, one thing is clear: Work will be part of it.

Mark Hunter is the author of five books, including The Passions of Men: Work and Love in the Age of Stress *(Putnam, 1988). He lives in Paris.*

From *AARP Modern Maturity*, May/June 1999, pp. 35–41. © 1999 by Mark Hunter. Reprinted by permission.

UNIT 6

Enhancing Human Adjustment: Learning to Cope Effectively

Unit Selections

Key Points to Consider

- According to the article on self-help books, what advice do such books provide? How should you evaluate a self-help book?

- Can most individuals successfully cope with everyday difficulties? When do you believe professional intervention is necessary?

- What can we do to overcome past psychological problems so that we can live happier, healthier lives?

- Why do some people make bad choices? Why do they continue to make bad choices; do they not learn from their behaviors?

- What is anxiety? What is an anxiety disorder?

- Describe symptoms of depression. Are mood disorders treatable? Explain.

- What are the important basic human needs that are related to happiness?

 **Links: www.dushkin.com/online/**
These sites are annotated in the World Wide Web pages.

John Suler's Teaching Clinical Psychology Site
  http://www.rider.edu/users/suler/tcp.html

Health Information Resources
  http://www.health.gov/nhic/Pubs/tollfree.htm

Knowledge Exchange Network (KEN)
  http://www.mentalhealth.org

Mental Health Net
  http://www.mentalhealth.net

Mind Tools
  http://www.mindtools.com/

NetPsychology
  http://netpsych.com/index.htm

On each college and university campus a handful of students experience overwhelming stress and life-shattering crises. One student learns that her mother, living in a distant city, has terminal cancer. Another receives the sad news that his parents are divorcing. A sorority blackballs a young woman who was determined to become a "sister"; she commits suicide. The sorority members now experience immense guilt.

Fortunately, almost every campus houses a counseling center for students. Some universities also offer assistance to employees. At the counseling service, trained professionals provide assistance and therapy to troubled members of the campus community.

Many individuals are able to adapt to life's vagaries, even to life's disasters. Other individuals flounder. They simply do not know how to adjust to change. These individuals sometimes seek temporary professional assistance from a therapist or counselor. For these professionals, the difficulty may be how and when to intervene. Very few individuals, fortunately, require long-term care.

There are as many definitions of maladjustment as there are mental health professionals. Some practitioners define mental illness as "whatever society cannot tolerate." Others define it in terms of statistics: "If a majority do not behave that way, then the behavior signals maladjustment." Some professionals suggest that an inadequate self-concept is the cause of maladjustment while others cite a lack of contact with reality. A few psychologists claim that to call one individual "ill" suggests that the rest are healthy by contrast, when, in fact, there may be few real distinctions among people.

Maladjustment is difficult to define and to treat. For each definition, a theorist develops a treatment strategy. Psychoanalysts press clients to recall their dreams, their childhoods, and their intrapsychic conflicts in order to analyze the contents of the unconscious. Humanists encourage clients to explore all of the facets of their lives in order to become less defensive. Behaviorists are usually concerned with observable and therefore treatable symptoms or behaviors. For behaviorists, no underlying causes are postulated to be the roots of adjustment problems. Other therapists, namely psychiatrists who are physicians by training, may utilize these therapies and add drugs and psychosurgery to the regimen.

This brief list of interventions raises further questions. For instance, is one form of therapy more effective, less expensive, or longer lasting than another? Is one diagnosis better treated by a particular form of therapy? Who should make the diagnosis? If two experts disagree on the diagnosis and treatment, how do we decide which one is correct? Should psychologists be allowed to prescribe psychoactive drugs? These questions continue to be debated.

Some psychologists question whether professional intervention is necessary at all. In one well-publicized but highly criticized study, researcher Hans Eysenck was able to show that spontaneous remission rates were as high as therapeutic "cure" rates. You, yourself, may be wondering whether professional help is always necessary. Can people be their own healers? Is support from friends as helpful as professional treatment?

The first two readings in this unit offer general information to individuals who are having difficulty adjusting and coping. Spe-

cifically, the articles pertain to the process of change as suggested by self-help books and by psychologists. In the first article in this unit, "Self-Help: Shattering the Myths," Annie Murphy Paul cross-examines advice provided in psychology books for lay persons. The author denounces the advice because it is contrary to scientific evidence. Several different myths perpetuated by self-help books are destroyed when held up to scientific scrutiny.

In a related article, Philip Goldberg suggests that we can heal ourselves. Goldberg claims that many of our adult dysfunctions are a consequence of childhood traumas or negative past experiences. He helps the reader identify this emotional pain and cope with it.

We next commence a review of situations in which people find themselves and which have the potential to cause coping problems. In the first article in this series, "Bad Choices: Why We Make Them, How to Stop," Mary Ann Chapman asserts that our own destructive behaviors are regulated by the immediate rewards we think we will receive rather than by the long-term destructive consequences. Once we learn how to manage the short-term effects, we can overcome self-destructiveness.

We next look at anxiety—a common consequence of modern life. In the article "The Science of Anxiety," anxiety disorders are described and differentiated from one another. Methods for treating anxiety disorders are also revealed.

Another very troubling but common disorder is depression. We all feel depressed at times, but for some individuals depression becomes overwhelming and chronic. The next article emphasizes the latter, known as clinical depression. In "Overcoming Depression," Sharon Doyle Driedger writes about her continuing struggle with depression and about the myriad of treatments that have been offered to her.

In order to end this anthology on an upbeat note, we look at something more positive in "Happiness Explained." Holly Morris tells us what happiness is and which situations generate happiness, such as family closeness. Happiness is created when basic and important human values are satisfied and thus create a pleasant upward spiral toward even greater happiness.

Self-Help:
Shattering the Myths

BOOKSTORES AND THE INTERNET ARE SPILLING OVER WITH ADVICE FROM THE LATEST SELF-HELP GURUS. PT *FINDS OUT WHETHER ANY OF IT MAKES SENSE.*

IT'S NO SURPRISE THAT AMERICA—LAND OF SECOND CHANCES, FABLED site of self-invention—also harbors an endless appetite for self-help. From Poor Richard to Dale Carnegie to Tony Robbins, we love the idea that we can fix what's broken by ourselves, without the expensive ministrations of doctor or shrink. The limits of HMOs, and the limitlessness of the Internet, have lately made self-help even more appealing: Americans spent $563 million on self-help books last year, and surfed more than 12,000 Web sites devoted to mental health. An estimated 40% of all health-related Internet inquiries are on mental health topics, and depression is the number-one most researched illness on the Web.

By Annie Murphy Paul

In the spirit of pioneers, we're concocting our own remedies and salving our own wounds. But is it good medicine? Once the preserve of charlatans and psychobabblers, self-help has undergone its own reinvention, emerging as a source of useful information presented by acknowledged authorities. That's not to say snake oil isn't still for sale. Often, the messages of self-help books tend to be vast oversimplifications, misrepresenting a part of the truth for the whole, as the following list of popular misconceptions and distortions demonstrates.

The antidote—the "good" kind of self-help, grounded in research—is also available to those who help themselves. Just keep in mind that even the best self-help may be too simplistic to manage complex problems, and that research, with its emphasis on straight science, may not always offer a clear course of action.

Does venting anger make you more angry?

DISTORTION 1
VENT YOUR ANGER, AND IT'LL GO AWAY.

SELF-HELP BOOKS SAY: "Punch a pillow or punching bag. And while you do it, yell and curse and moan and holler," advises *Facing the Fire: Expressing and Experiencing Anger Appropriately* (Bantam Doubleday Dell, 1995). "Punch with all the frenzy you can. If you are an-

gry at a particular person, imagine his or her face on the pillow or punching bag, and vent your rage physically and verbally."

RESEARCHERS SAY: Pillow punching, like other forms of vigorous exercise, might be helpful for stress management, but recent studies suggest that venting anger may be counterproductive. "Venting anger just keeps it alive," says Brad Bushman, Ph.D., a psychologist at Iowa State University. "People think it's going to work, and when it doesn't, they become even more angry and frustrated."

In addition, several studies show that the outward expression of anger leads to dangerously elevated cardiovascular activity, which may contribute to the development of cardiovascular disease.

THE BEST SELF-HELP BOOKS

GENERAL RESOURCES
The Authoritative Guide to Self-Help Resources in Mental Health By John C. Norcross, Linda Frye Campbell and Thomas P. Smith (Guilford, 2000)

THE BEST SELF-HELP AND SELF-AWARENESS BOOKS
A Topic-by-Topic Guide to Quality Information By Stephen B. Fried and G. Ann Schultis (American Library Association, 1995)

Caring for the Mind: The Comprehensive Guide to Mental Health By Dianne and Robert Hales (Bantam, 1995)

RESOURCES ON ANXIETY
An End to Panic: Breakthrough Techniques for Overcoming Panic Disorder By Elke Zuercher-White (New Harbinger Publications, 1998)

Anxiety & Depression: The Best Resources to Help You Cope Edited By Rich Wemhoff (Resource Pathways, 1998)

RESOURCES ON DEPRESSION
Feeling Good: The New Mood Therapy By David D. Burns (Avon, 1992)

Understanding Depression: A Complete Guide to Its Diagnosis and Treatment
By Donald F. Klein, M.D., and Paul H. Wender, M.D. (Oxford University Press, 1993)

SELF-HELP RESOURCES ON OBSESSIVE-COMPULSIVE DISORDER
Getting Control: Overcoming Your Obsessions and Compulsions By Lee Baier (Plume, 1992)

The OCD Workbook: Your Guide to Breaking Free from Obsessive-Compulsive Disorder By Bruce M. Hyman and Cherry Pedrick (New Harbinger Publications, 1999)

RESOURCES FOR TRAUMA AND PTSD
Coping with Post-Traumatic Stress Disorder By Carolyn Simpson and Dwain Simpson (Rosen Publishing Group, 1997)

Coping with Trauma: A Guide to Self-Understanding By Jon G. Allen (American Psychiatric Press, 1995)

THE BEST SELF-HELP WEB SITES

GOVERNMENT-SPONSORED WEB SITES:
Knowledge Exchange Network (operated by the U.S. Dept. of Health and Human Services, Substance Abuse and Mental Health Services Administration, and the Center for Mental Health Services) www.mentalhealth.org
•National Center for PTSD (operated by the U.S. Department of Veterans Affairs) www.dartmouth.edu/dms/ptsd
•National Institute of Mental Health www.nimh.nih.gov

NON-PROFIT SITES

•American Psychiatric Association www.psych.org
•Anxiety Disorders Association of America www.adaa.org
•The Help Center of the American Psychological Association www.helping.apa.org
•The International Society for Mental Health Online www.ismho.org
•National Alliance for the Mentally Ill www.nami.org
•National Depressive and Manic-Depressive Association www.ndmda.org

COMMERCIAL WEB SITES

•Online Psych www.onlinepsych.com
•Basic Information www.realpsychology.com
•Self-Help and Psychology Magazine www.shpm.com

Bushman recently put the so-called "catharsis hypothesis" to the test, deliberately inducing anger in a group of college students by marking nasty comments on essays they had written. Those who slammed a punching bag afterward were more, not less, aggressive to people they subsequently encountered.

"It may be better to do things incompatible with anger like watching a funny movie or listening to music"

WHAT TO DO INSTEAD: A better tack, says Bushman, is to do "anything that's incompatible with anger and aggression." That includes watching a funny movie, reading an absorbing novel, sharing a laugh with a friend, or listening to music. Given time, your anger will dissipate, and then you'll be able to deal with the situation in a more constructive way.

Though Bushman has found that exercise can actually heighten physical arousal and keep anger alive, other studies have concluded that sustained strenuous activity might indeed release anger and improve mood. And nontraditional exercise programs like tai chi, yoga and stretching may not only dissipate negative feelings such as anger but make people more conscious of their mood states, paving the way for them to do something constructive about them.

DISTORTION 2
WHEN YOU'RE DOWN IN THE DUMPS, THINK YOURSELF HAPPY BY FOCUSING ON THE POSITIVE.

SELF-HELP BOOKS SAY: "Close your mental doors behind you on unpleasant circumstances or failures you have experienced," commands Napoleon Hill's *Keys to Positive Thinking* (Plume, 1998). "Use your brain for controlled, optimistic thinking. Take possession of your mind and direct it to images of your choosing. Do not let circumstances or people dictate negative visual images."

RESEARCHERS SAY: Research shows that when we're anxious or stressed—in other words, exactly when we need a mood boost—our minds become unable to provide one.

That's because we're so preoccupied with our troubles that we don't have enough brainpower left over to suppress negative thoughts. And when we try to distract ourselves, pessimistic notions are the only ones that come to mind. "If you're really under stress, putting yourself in a good mood by thinking positive thoughts becomes not only difficult—in fact it backfires, and you get the opposite of what you want," says Daniel Wegner, Ph.D., a psychologist at the University of Virginia.

Feeling down? Go to the mall and lift your spirits

In an experiment, Wegner asked a group of people to put themselves in a good mood—which they did, fairly easily. But when they were also told to keep a nine-digit number in mind, they actually felt worse. The energy they had available to control their mood was reduced by the effort of remembering the number.

If you're upset or anxious, make a list of positive things

WHAT TO DO INSTEAD: "You have to enlist the help of other people," Wegner says. "Talk to friends or relatives or clergy or a therapist, or anyone else who might be able to help you think about other things." Or go to a place where people are enjoying themselves, like a party or the park or the mall, and you'll soon feel your spirits lift. Finally, if you know in advance that you're going to be upset or anxious about something, make a list of positive things that you can refer to when you need it most: your five favorite memories, say, or three occasions to look forward to.

DISTORTION 3
VISUALIZE YOUR GOAL, AND YOU'LL HELP MAKE IT COME TRUE.

SELF-HELP BOOKS SAY: "Hold the image of yourself succeeding, visualize it so vividly, that when the desired success comes, it seems to be merely echoing a reality that has already existed in your mind," suggests *Positive Imaging: The Powerful Way to Change Your Life* (Fawcett Book Group, 1996).

RESEARCHERS SAY: Sports psychologists have shown the power that visualization has on improving performance, but simply imagining that you've achieved your goal won't bring it any closer—and might even put it further out of reach.

Shelley Taylor, Ph.D., a psychologist at UCLA, has reservations about visualizing your goals. "First of all, it separates the goal from what you need to do to get it. And second, it enables you to enjoy the feeling of being successful without actually having achieved anything. That takes away the power of the goal"—and can even make you complacent, unwilling to work hard or take risks to get what you already have in your daydreams.

WHAT TO DO INSTEAD: In addition to picturing your goal as a fait accompli, "you should figure out what the steps to get there are, and then mentally rehearse them," says Taylor.

In an experiment, Taylor asked some students preparing for an exam to imagine their happiness at having received an 'A' on the test, and others to picture themselves sitting in the library, studying their textbooks and going over lecture notes. Those in the second group performed better on the test, and experienced less stress and worry.

For short-term goals, Taylor recommends running through the steps you've laid out once a day; for bigger dreams, you can revisit your plan every time you make some progress, and see if it needs adjusting.

DISTORTION 4
SELF-AFFIRMATIONS WILL HELP YOU RAISE LOW SELF-ESTEEM.

SELF-HELP BOOKS SAY: "Write affirmations on paper and put them in places you will see them—on the bathroom mirror, next to your bed, on the car dashboard," recommends *Life 101: Everything We Wish We Had Learned About Life In School—But Didn't* (Prelude Press, 1991). "You can also record them on endless-loop cassette tapes and play them in the background all day (and night)."

RESEARCHERS SAY: Psychologists say this technique may not be very helpful. Changing how we feel about ourselves is a lot more complicated, explains William Swann, Ph.D., of the University of Texas-Austin. "Self-esteem is based on two components: first, our sense of how likable and lovable we are, and second, our sense of how competent we are" at our jobs and at other activities that demand talent and skill. On those scores, we've been hearing from other people—parents, teachers, bosses, siblings, friends, romantic partners—all our lives, and their opinions of us continue to reinforce our notions of ourselves, good or bad. Self-affirmations, even when endlessly repeated, don't make much of a dent—and when they fail to work, they may leave us even more demoralized.

"The more specific the problem-solving strategies, the more useful. All the strategies presented should be based squarely on science or professional science."

What's more, people with low self-esteem may be especially unpersuaded by self-affirmations. Preliminary research by Swann's colleague at UT, Robert Josephs, Ph.D., indicates that those with poor self-images

SIFTING SCIENCE FROM SNAKE OIL:
How to Find Top Psychology in Pop Psychology

By Stephen B. Fried, Ph.D

AMERICANS TURN RELENTLESSLY TO BOOKS, MAGA-zines, radio, TV and the Internet in the hopes of finding their way to a better, less problem-filled life. But there's a catch. Some of this popular psychology is based on solid psychological science and practice, and some is not. How to distinguish which is which?

• Consider the source of the information. Does it come from a mental health professional? Beware of materials written by fellow sufferers who are laypersons. Experiencing a problem doesn't automatically confer the ability to help others. And what works for one may not work for all.

• The problem that's addressed has to be one that is amenable to change. Psychological states that are genetic, like manic-depressive disorder, are extraordinarily difficult to change. So are those that are at the core of what we think or do, such as sexual orientation. Depression is more responsive to deliberate efforts at change, and panic disorder and issues of sexual performance more susceptible still.

• The material must provide both facts about and specific strategies for dealing with the psychological concern. It's important that the information review the symptoms of any condition, and ideally a self-diagnosis questionnaire should be provided.

• Quality information also takes into account individual differences among readers. Most helpful is an array of techniques for tackling the problem. The more specific the problem-solving strategies, the more useful. And all of the strategies presented should be based squarely on science or professional practice.

• The material should refer the reader to authoritative sources, such as professional organizations. Does it contain a bibliography? A resource guide? These are important for possible follow-ups.

Along with G. Ann Schultis, I have analyzed self-help books and offer these additional guidelines in choosing good ones. The book's title should reflect its contents. The purpose of the book should be stated in the preface or the first chapter.

• Some radio and TV stations air entire programs devoted to psychological matters, often hosted by a "mental health professional." Highly dependent on the skills and knowledge of the host, these programs may play on the voyeuristic interests of listeners who may be titillated tuning into the intimate details of an anonymous caller's life. On the other hand, such programs may reach millions and motivate some to seek professional help because of what they heard.

• TV talk shows may feature "victims" of a particular problem—but they often encourage the very behaviors they are purporting to fix. For instance, a couple with poor interpersonal skills is goaded into fighting before the studio audience. Then a guest therapist (typically the author of a topical self-help book) suggests a quick fix to the problem. In this way, the program reinforces both the antisocial behavior and the idea of overly simple solutions to far more complex matters.

• Psychologically related sites have virtually exploded on the web. Look for those hosted by a reputable organization and that present in-depth coverage of issues. The best Web sites offer bibliographies of relevant articles and books; they also offer a listing of professional organizations.

No matter where you turn for information, you can't abandon your critical thinking skills.

Until he succumbed to a long-term illness last May, Dr. Fried was professor and chairman of psychology at Park University in Missouri.

---

simply don't believe the statements, because they don't value their own opinions very highly. In Josephs' experiment, high self-esteem people were able to pat themselves on the back for solving a set of problems, while "lows" had to hear praise from someone else before they would credit it.

WHAT TO DO INSTEAD: The only way to change the final product—your self-esteem—is to change what goes into making it—feedback from other people. "If you find yourself in bad relationships where your negative self-view is getting reinforced, then either change the way

those people treat you by being more assertive, or change who you interact with," says Swann. "If you're in a job where you're getting denigrated, insist that you be treated more appropriately, or change jobs. Try to do your job better than you've done it before."

IN OTHER WORDS: Stand up for yourself. Surround yourself with people who think you're great, and tell you so. Do your best to live up to their high opinions. And be patient. Self-esteem is the sum of your interactions with others over a lifetime, and it's not going to change overnight.

DISTORTION 5
"ACTIVE LISTENING" CAN HELP YOU COMMUNICATE BETTER WITH YOUR PARTNER.

SELF-HELP BOOKS SAY: "The technique of 'active listening' ensures that you not only hear, but really understand what your partner is trying to tell you," reads *Going the Distance: Finding and Keeping Life-long Love* (Plume, 1993). You do it by "paraphrasing your partner's words, then repeating in your own words what you believe your partner is trying to communicate to you."

RESEARCHERS SAY: There's only one problem with active listening: hardly anyone does it. Although the technique has been promoted by therapists for over three decades, research shows that actual couples—including the long-lasting, lovey-dovey ones—completely ignore it when they argue. "It just doesn't happen," says Sybil Carrere, Ph.D., a psychologist at the University of Washington who's been leading a six-year study of how newlyweds interact. "Intuitively it does make sense, but the fact is that when you look at happy couples, they're not doing it. They're being affectionate, they're using humor to break up tension, they're indicating interest in what their partner has to

say—they're doing a lot of positive things. But they're not doing active listening." In fact, one of the few studies that has been conducted on the effects of active listening shows that it does nothing to help couples in distress.

WHAT TO DO INSTEAD: According to Carrere, couples should focus their efforts on three other areas. First, women should try to present their complaints in a calm way: Research shows that men are more likely to listen if their partners tone down hostility and avoid contemptuousness. Second, men need to really listen to their partners, taking their feelings and opinions into account. And third, both sides should do what they can to keep the

male half cool and collected. "Men have a tendency when they get into conflict to get physiologically aroused, and then they tend to withdraw from the conflict in order to soothe themselves, which only makes the woman more angry," says Carrere. If the two of you can work together to head his anger off at the pass—by throwing in a joke, maybe, or offering a hug—you'll both be better off.

The five distortions presented here are only a few of the misconceptions you may encounter. To protect yourself against others, be sure to take self-help prescriptions with a measure of skepticism and a healthy dose of common sense.

Reprinted with permission from *Psychology Today*, March/April 2001, pp. 60-68. © 2001 by Sussex Publishers, Inc.

Make Peace with Your Past

A new study links an unhappy childhood to the most common causes of death in the U.S.

by Philip Goldberg

Are you doomed by long-ago traumas? No, says a prominent psychiatrist, who shows you how to rewrite your life story so that it has a happy ending

Diana(*) knew she was a walking time bomb. On any checklist of risk factors for heart disease and other killers, she ranked alarmingly high. Thirty pounds overweight, she had high blood pressure and soaring cholesterol. Her only exercise was walking to her car. She was also prone to depression, had chronic stress-related gastritis, and was a two-pack-a-day smoker. She knew she had to change her health habits.

"But I just couldn't do it," she says. "Every time I made some progress, I'd lose control and end up back where I started in no time."

What turned things around was an insightful physician who linked Diana's physical condition to her traumatic childhood. When Diana was 4 years old, her father died before her eyes. Two years later, her mother married a violent alcoholic. Diana was forced to watch him beat her mother and brother on a regular basis. She also witnessed her mother's suicide attempt.

"I couldn't really work on improving my health until I came to terms with all the pain and anger I'd suppressed as a child," Diana explains. "It was eating away at me."

How Your Past Can Hurt You

What do early traumas have to do with health decades later? "Adverse childhood experiences underlie the most common causes of death in the US," says Vincent J. Felitti, MD, an internist at the Southern California Permanente Medical Group in San Diego.

In a survey of more than 20,000 adults, Dr. Felitti and his colleagues from the Centers for Disease Control and Prevention found that those who suffered physical, psychological, or emotional abuse as children, or were raised in households marked by violence, substance abuse, mental illness, or criminal behavior, were far more likely to develop serious illnesses as adults—everything from diabetes and bronchitis to cancer and heart disease.

Is Your Past Hurting Your Health?

To assess how much the echoes of the past are disturbing your peace in the present, answer yes or no to the following questions:

- Are you holding a grudge against someone who hurt you?
- Do you think "Oh no, here I go again!" when personal problems arise?
- Are you plagued by thoughts such as "If I'd only..." or "I wish I hadn't..."?
- Do you feel ashamed of things you've done?
- Were you abandoned or abused (physically or verbally) as a child?
- Do you wish you could apologize to someone and be forgiven?
- Do you wish you could set the record straight about certain things?
- Do you often look back at your life and wonder what went wrong?
- In your mind, do you confront people from the past and finally tell them off?
- Do you replay old incidents and imagine better outcomes?
- Do you often feel like an innocent victim of fate?
- Does thinking about the "good old days" make you sad about the present?
- Are you still grieving the loss of a loved one?
- Does a voice in your head call you worthless, defective, despicable, or unlovable?
- Are you avoiding intimacy for fear of being hurt again?

The more yes answers you have, the more likely it is that old issues and traumatic incidents are jeopardizing your health—and the more urgent it is to make peace with your past.

"Adverse childhood experiences are likely to produce anger, anxiety, and depression," says Dr. Felitti. "To the degree that behavior such as overeating, smoking, and substance abuse are found to be effective coping devices, they would tend to be used chronically." Not exactly a recipe for wellness.

But that's only one way that traumatic experiences can destroy your health. "The chronic stress of unresolved emotional pain wreaks havoc on your immune and circulatory systems, cardiac function, hormone levels, and other physical functions," says psychiatrist Harold H. Bloomfield, MD, author of *Making Peace with Your Past* (HarperCollins, 2000). And it's not just childhood adversity that does the damage, he notes. The upheavals of adolescence and the losses and letdowns of adulthood also eat away at the body's resistance.

"We must make peace with our past," asserts Dr. Bloomfield, "because our life may literally depend on it."

10 Ways to Heal the Past

The good news is that our body and brain are remarkably resilient; we are fully capable of healing old wounds and reversing the damage of past adversity.

Here are 10 ways to rewrite your life story:

1. **Reframe the past.** "To the extent that you can find value in past adversity, you can neutralize its harmful effects and foster healing," says Dr. Bloomfield. You don't have the power to change the past, but you can control how you experience it now. Instead of responding in the same habitual way when disturbing incidents come to mind, pause, and take a deep breath. Then reinterpret them. Ask yourself "How did that experience make me stronger? What important life lessons did it teach me?"

2. **Break the shackles of shame.** Unlike remorse or guilt, shame isn't about feeling bad for what you've done but rather for what you are. "Shame is the cancer of the spirit," says Dr. Bloomfield. "It makes you feel worthless and unlovable, undeserving of happiness." A common result of an abusive childhood, shame leads us to make "psychic promises" to ourselves in an attempt to alleviate the agony. For example: "I'll be just like my parents, then they'll treat me better." Or: "If I shut down all my feelings, I won't have to feel this pain." Or: "I'll always be nice so no one will hurt me again." To stop these hidden contracts from destroying you, Dr. Bloomfield offers this advice. "Identify the promises you made, and give yourself permission to break them. And always remember that shame is a lie. You are worthy of love and respect."

3. **Release the pain.** Research shows that those who write about past traumas heal faster from illnesses, visit their doctor less often, and have stronger immune systems. "Set aside some time, and write letters to everyone who ever hurt you," suggests Dr. Bloomfield. No one needs to see these letters but you, so no holding back, censoring yourself, or worrying about spelling and grammar. Just let out all the rage that's been festering inside, contaminating your system.

4. **Stop the slow acid drip of regret.** The constant repetition of "If only …" and "I should have …" can destroy your health as well as your peace of mind. "An important aspect of healing is to stop punishing yourself for past mistakes," says Dr. Bloomfield. Instead, forgive yourself, learn the right lessons, and resolve to act differently in the future. Look back at the regrettable actions; recall who you were at the time. What did you know? What didn't you know? What were your actual choices? By reviewing the complete scenario, you might discover that you did okay under the circumstances.

5. **Move from grief to gain.** The emotional wounds of a devastating loss are as real as a contusion or a broken bone, says Dr. Bloomfield. Mending them requires moving through the three phases of grief: first, shock and denial; followed by anger, fear, and sadness; and finally, understanding and acceptance. You can get stuck in stage one, denying your pain or numbing your feelings. Or you can move through that stage, only to bog down in chronic depression or fear. In either case, the healing is incomplete.

    No matter how long ago the loss occurred, it's crucial to allow yourself to feel the emotions you may have suppressed. If you've lost a loved one, try writing that person a farewell letter, giving yourself permission to express everything that comes up—not just the sadness and love, but the rage, terror, and other emotions you may feel wrong for having.

6. **Practice acceptance.** Nothing perpetuates the impact of old hurts more than rehashing them in your mind. It's like watching the same movie over and over again in the hope that the ending will change. "Bemoaning your fate does not help you heal the past," says Dr. Bloomfield. "Peace comes from accepting what was for what it was and moving on."

7. **Cultivate gratitude.** Even better than acceptance is gratitude. No matter what happened in the past, remind yourself that you have gifts to be thankful for. You may even find that you're grateful for your troubles because of what you learned from them.

8. **Break the habit of blame.** Blaming your problems on people and events from your past means that you're not responsible for anything that happens to you, it protects you from self-doubt, and it brings you the cozy sympathy of others. But on the other

hand, it leads to chronic resentment, which is damaging to your mental and physical health.

"Blame is not something you heal," says Dr. Bloomfield. "It's something you choose to stop doing." Ending the bitterness of blame, he stresses, does not necessarily mean letting those who hurt you off the hook. You don't have to forgive them or reconcile with them. It simply means catching yourself in the act of blaming so you can break that self-destructive habit and take charge of your own well-being.

9. **Find inner peace.** No matter how traumatic your past has been, you can always find a peaceful place inside you, says Dr. Bloomfield. If you can tap that source, you can stop stress from building up, allowing your mind to clear for new solutions. There are countless ways to create calm: yoga, meditation, a walk in nature, a hot aromatic bath, a good massage, some soothing music, prayer, deep breathing, pleasant memories, and so on. In addition, suggests Dr. Bloomfield, when disturbing thoughts about the past rise up and snap at you, distract yourself: Focus on the physical sensation of breathing in and out, mentally recite a word such as "peace," or place your hand on a nearby object and focus on the textures that you feel.

10. **Create a satisfying future.** As the old saying goes, living well is the best revenge. A great way to make peace with your past is to become the person you always wanted to be. The grip of old patterns and perceptions may be so strong that you feel like a helpless victim. In fact, you are the author of your own life story, and you can start a new chapter anytime you choose.

Dr. Bloomfield recommends taking some time to visualize your life as you want it to be, then spell it out in writing. A day or two later, read your vision with a practical eye.

What do you have to do to make that dream come true? Which goals can you achieve this year? What steps can you take now?

You can create a life that is so fulfilling, so rich with meaning and purpose, says Dr. Bloomfield, "that the pain of the past loses its sting."

(*) not her real name

Philip Goldberg is a Los Angeles-based writer who is coauthor of *Making Peace with Your Past* (HarperCollins, 2000).

From *Prevention*, April 1, 2001, p. 147. © 2001 by Prevention.

BAD
Choices

WHY WE MAKE THEM
HOW TO STOP

If cigarettes, gambling, those last 10 pounds, that credit card habit and the one drink too many are standing in between you and your goals, this new formula may finally make the difference. And the good news is, it's all in your hands.

By Mary Ann Chapman, Ph.D.

As the police car pealed out behind Lynn with its lights blinking in her rear-view mirror, she remembered with dread that second glass of wine she drank just before leaving the party. Her heart raced as she considered the implications of getting a DWI ticket. She had been preparing to leave the party and knew she had to drive home, so why did she indulge?

Most of the bad choices we make in our lives involve an immediate reward—in Lynn's case, the taste and feel of the extra glass of wine. Like Lynn, we often choose to live now even though we're likely to end up paying the price later. This carpe-diem philosophy becomes even more powerful when the punishment is not a sure thing. In Lynn's case, the probability of her being pulled over by the police was not very high. If she had expected them to stop her, she might have reached for a ginger ale.

Our day-to-day bad choices have alarming results. For example, one-third of Americans are overweight, costing the U.S. government $100 billion each year in treatment of related illnesses.

We're also steeped in debt:

The Consumer Federation of America calculates that 60 million households carry an average credit card balance of $7,000, for a total national credit card debt topping $455 billion. Our failure to make sacrifices now for rewards later is particularly devastating when it comes to following prescribed medical regimens. Studies have found that only half of us take antidepressants, antihypertensives, asthma medications and tuberculosis drugs as prescribed. Such lack of compliance is the major cause of hospital admissions in people who have previously had heart failure, and it's entirely preventable.

Our desire to take the path of least resistance is so strong that we continue our sometimes destructive behavior even though we know, as in the cases of smoking and overeating, it literally may kill us. But we don't need to be slaves to instant gratification. Consider the ways we already suffer in the present for reward in the future: We get tetanus shots to protect against lockjaw and use condoms to reduce the risk of sexually transmitted diseases; we have money taken out of our paychecks for retirement, and parents routinely make sacrifices for

their children's future. The key to breaking a bad habit and adopting a good one is making changes in our daily life that will minimize the influence of the now and remind us of the later. It sounds difficult, but new tricks make it possible.

A look at the animal kingdom reveals clues as to how this is done. Working in a laboratory with pigeons, Howard Rachlin, Ph.D., of the State University of New York at Stony Brook, found that when birds were given a simple choice between immediate and delayed reward, they chose the immediate reward 95% of the time. This was true even though the delayed reward (food) was twice the size of the immediate one.

Then researchers made the task more complicated, giving birds the chance to choose between 1) the same immediate and delayed options as in the first part of the study, or 2) a no-option condition in which they were only allowed access to the delayed reward. This situation is analogous to the choice between going to a gym where you have the option of relaxing in the sauna or hopping on the stationary bicycle, and going to a gym that has only

PT's Good-Choice Guide

	BEHAVIOR	NOW	LATER	STRATEGIES FOR CHANGE
BAD CHOICES	Overeating	Food tastes good, is comforting	You get fat, unhealthy; suffer lowered self-esteem	Only snack when sitting at the table—never in front of the TV; keep inspiring picture or story on the fridge or cupboard; calculate how long it would take to burn off the calories of what you're about to eat
	Eating fast food	Quick; easy; tastes good	Too much fat; not nutritious; not healthful	Identify health-food places close to home; locate low fat/calorie menu items
	Anger	Temporary relief	Problems interacting with others	Apologize immediately for getting angry; reward yourself for situations in which you avoid anger
	Constant complaining	Sympathy from others	Viewed negatively; social repercussions	Tell friends to change topics when you start complaining
	Smoking	Pleasure from cigarette	Lung cancer; possible death	Confine smoking to one designated area (preferably one you don't like); keep a day calendar in your cigarette cupboard and rip off a day for every cigarette pack you open to symbolize days off your life
	Gambling	Occasionally win money	Lose money over the long term	Donate all winnings (preferably to a cause you dislike); keep track of losses, place them prominently; consider ways you could have spent the money you lost
GOOD CHOICES	Healthful eating	Extra effort; taste not as good	Good health; reduced chance of many diseases	Reduce effort by buying preprepared healthful foods or by preparing them over the weekend; dine with a friend who shares an interest in healthy eating
	Saving money	Less money to spend now	Avoid interest charges on loans or credit cards; can afford larger or more meaningful items	Have automatic deductions taken out of your paycheck
	Using condoms	Some say less pleasurable sex	Prevent AIDS, sexually transmitted diseases, pregnancy	Always keep condoms handy; use other techniques to enhance sex; donate money to AIDS causes
	Going to the dentist	Painful, scary	Avoid further pain of root canals, existing cavities	Find a friendly dentist; schedule appointments at the same time as a friend; give yourself a small reward each time you go
	Exercising	Extra effort; give up relaxation time	Improved circulation; reduced risk of disease; weight loss; increased energy; greater self-esteem	Move near a gym; buy weights or a bike; after a workout, write down how good you feel and read it next time you are in a slump
	Overcoming shyness	Disruption of "safe" pattern of behavior	More friends and social activities	Start by prolonging a conversation someone starts with you and make it a habit

exercise equipment—giving you no option but to exercise once you get there.

As the researchers increased the amount of time birds had to wait after selecting between the two alternatives, the birds increasingly chose the second option, to have only the delayed reward available. In this way, the researchers effectively altered the birds' environment to minimize the value of the immediate choice.

BREAKING A BAD HABIT

We can apply the same logic to help us break our bad habits: We need to 1) minimize or avoid the immediate reward, and

2) make the long-term negative consequence seem more immediate.

My friend John, for example, relies too much on his credit card. When the lunch bill comes, he charges the total tab and pockets his colleagues' cash. You may not know John, but I bet you know that he doesn't rush to the bank and deposit that money.

John needs to avoid the immediate positive effect of using his credit card. The most logical step would be to leave it at home—except that he might need it for travel or emergencies. John's best bet would be to do a little preplanning: He could stop by the bank after work to make sure he had enough money for the next day's lunch. Or he could locate an ATM near the restaurant to make it more convenient—and therefore more likely—for him to withdraw cash.

As a reminder of that big scary negative at the end of the month, John could paste his latest credit card bill near his computer, on the refrigerator or someplace he will see it every day. He might also tape the amount he owes to the face of the credit card. These nearly effortless gestures will make it hard for John to readily ignore his problem and help him bridge the gap between now and later.

STARTING A GOOD HABIT

You might be eager to start eating healthy meals, getting regular exercise or making new friends. Most likely, the going will be tough at first, but the potential long-term benefits are well worth it. Once again, the idea is to minimize the immediate—a negative this time—and bridge the distance to the future, the good stuff.

For the past couple of months, I have been trying to get myself to drink a small glass of soy milk every day. Each week I buy a carton of soy milk and after two weeks, I dump it down the drain. I have convinced myself that I need to drink soy milk for the protein and the long-term health benefits. But somehow, the immediate negative of drinking the milk (and even thinking about drinking the milk!) has been seemingly impossible to overcome.

What would help lessen the yuck of soy milk? I tried drinking it in my favorite special cup. That helped a little, but not enough. My new strategy is to mix half a cup of soy milk with regular milk. Every day I drink the soy milk I put an X on my calendar for that day, which makes me feel accomplished and helps me associate drinking the soy milk with a positive consequence. And to make the long-term benefits more immediately apparent, I tore out magazine articles that tout the health benefits of soy and taped them to my refrigerator.

WHEN OLD HABITS DIE HARD

It's never very easy to change, but for some people, it is exceptionally difficult. Twenty-two-year-old Jimmy is a good example. Jimmy's arms are bruised and scarred from his heroin habit. For him, the immense immediate pleasure of heroin far outweighs the long-term consequences of his habit: tuberculosis, lack of money and the inability to hold down a job.

You might not think you have anything in common with Jimmy—or a compulsive gambler or a kleptomaniac. But researchers are beginning to recognize that all of these behavioral patterns involve, to varying extents, maximizing immediate consequences despite huge negative long-term ones.

To find out if some people are more prone to favor the here and now than others, the University of Missouri's Alan Strathman, Ph.D., and his colleagues conducted surveys in Missouri and California. They asked survey participants how much they agreed with statements such as "I consider how things might be in the future and try to influence those things with my day-to-day behavior," and "Convenience is a big factor in the decisions I make or the actions I take." Strathman found that individuals did indeed have varying degrees of what he calls "future orientation"—preference for delayed consequences—and that this orientation remains stable over time. The individual differences were reflected in general health concerns and in environmentally friendly behaviors such as recycling.

The good news is that the behavioral change strategies can work just as well for people who tend to favor the here and now. They don't require special genes or exceptional chemistry. They are very simple and that's their beauty. Time and again, they have been used successfully to help people overcome problems from obesity to sulking to failing grades. These simple strategies are effective because behaviors are mostly learned and, therefore, can be unlearned. They can take us off autopilot and introduce ideas (namely, long-term consequences) that we normally wouldn't consider. Even if we have focused on the short-term all our lives, these strategies can help us maximize our chances of success.

FURTHER READING

Self-Help Without the Hype, R. Epstein (Performance Management Publications, 1997)

Self-Directed Behavior: Self-Modification for Personal Adjustment (seventh edition), D.L. Watson and R.G. Tharp (Books/Cole, 1996)

Managing Everyday Problems, T. A. Brigham (Guilford Press, 1988)

Mary Ann Chapman earned her Ph.D. in experimental psychology from Washington State University in 1994. She is a scientific communications writer in southern California.

Reprinted with permission from *Psychology Today*, September/October 1999, pp. 36–39, 71. © 1999 by Sussex Publishers, Inc.

THE SCIENCE OF ANXIETY

WHY DO WE WORRY OURSELVES SICK? BECAUSE THE BRAIN IS HARDWIRED FOR FEAR, AND SOMETIMES IT SHORT-CIRCUITS

By CHRISTINE GORMAN

IT'S 4 A.M., AND YOU'RE WIDE AWAKE—PALMS SWEATY, HEART racing. You're worried about your kids. Your aging parents. Your 401(k). Your health. Your sex life. Breathing evenly beside you, your spouse is oblivious. Doesn't he—or she—see the dangers that lurk in every shadow? He must not. Otherwise, how could he, with all that's going on in the world, have talked so calmly at dinner last night about flying to Florida for a vacation?

How is it that two people facing the same circumstances can react so differently? Why are some folks buffeted by the vicissitudes of life while others glide through them with grace and calm? Are some of us just born more nervous than others? And if you're one of them, is there anything you can do about it?

The key to these questions is the emotional response we call anxiety. Unlike hunger or thirst, which build and dissipate in the immediate present, anxiety is the sort of feeling that sneaks up on you from the day after tomorrow. It's supposed to keep you from feeling too safe. Without it, few of us would survive.

All animals, especially the small, scurrying kind, appear to feel anxiety. Humans have felt it since the days they shared the planet with saber-toothed tigers. (Notice which species is still around to tell the tale.) But we live in a particularly anxious age. The initial shock of Sept. 11 has worn off, and the fear has lifted, but millions of Americans continue to share a kind of generalized mass anxiety. A recent TIME/CNN poll found that eight months after the event, nearly two-thirds of Americans think about the terror attacks at least several times a week. And it doesn't take much for all the old fears to come rushing back. What was surprising about the recent drumbeat of terror warnings was how quickly it triggered the anxiety so many of us thought we had put behind us.

This is one of the mysteries of anxiety. While it is a normal response to physical danger—and can be a useful tool for focusing the mind when there's a deadline looming—anxiety becomes a problem when it persists too long beyond the immediate threat. Sometimes there's an obvious cause, as with the shell-shocked soldiers of World War I or the terror-scarred civilians of the World Trade Center collapse. Other times, we don't know why we can't stop worrying.

GLOSSARY

STRESS Any external stimulus, from threatening words to the sound of a gunshot, that the brain interprets as dangerous

FEAR The short-term physiological response produced by both the brain and the body in response to stress

ANXIETY A sense of apprehension that shares many of the same symptoms as fear but builds more slowly and lingers longer

DEPRESSION Prolonged sadness that results in a blunting of emotions and a sense of futility; often more serious when accompanied by anxiety disorder

There is certainly a lot of anxiety going around. Anxiety disorder—which is what health experts call any anxiety that persists to the point that it interferes with one's life—is the most common mental illness in the U.S. In its various forms, ranging from very specific phobias to generalized anxiety disorder, it afflicts 19 million Americans (*see* "Are You Too Anxious?").

And yet, according to a survey published last January by researchers from UCLA, less than 25% of Americans with anxiety disorders receive any kind of treatment for their condition. "If mental health is the stepchild of the health-care system," says Jerilyn Ross, president of the Anxiety Disorders Association of America, "then anxiety is the stepchild of the stepchild."

Sigmund Freud was fascinated with anxiety and recognized early on that there is more than one kind. He identified two major forms of anxiety: one more biological in nature and the other more dependent on psychological factors. Unfortunately, his followers were so obsessed with his ideas about sex drives and unresolved conflicts that studies of the physical basis of anxiety languished.

In recent years, however, researchers have made significant progress in nailing down the underlying science of anxiety. In just the past decade, they have come to appreciate that whatever the factors that trigger anxiety, it grows out of a response that is hardwired in our brains. They have learned, among other things:

ARE YOU TOO ANXIOUS?

Everybody feels a bit of anxiety from time to time, but a clinical anxiety disorder is a different matter. If you suspect you may be suffering from one, you should consult a professional for a diagnosis. The psychological diagnostic manual lists 12 anxiety conditions. Here are the signs of five of the most common ones:

PANIC DISORDER

WHAT IT IS: Recurrent, unexpected attacks of acute anxiety, peaking within 10 minutes. Such panic may occur in a familiar situation, such as a crowded elevator

WHAT IT ISN'T: Occasional episodes of extreme anxiety in response to a real threat

WHAT TO LOOK FOR: Palpitations; chest pains, sweating, chills or hot flushes; trembling; shortness of breath or choking; nausea; light-headedness or feeling of unreality; fear of losing control or dying

BOTTOM LINE: Four or more of these symptoms in at least two discrete episodes could spell trouble

SPECIFIC PHOBIA

WHAT IT IS: Consuming fear of a specific object or situation, often accompanied by extreme anxiety symptoms

WHAT IT ISN'T: Powerful aversion to certain places or things

WHAT TO LOOK FOR:

- Do you come up with elaborate ways to avoid the object or situation?
- Do you dread the next possible encounter?
- Are you aware that the fear is excessive but you are unable to control it?
- Does merely thinking about the thing you fear make you anxious?

BOTTOM LINE: Don't worry if you just plain hate, say, snakes or crowds or heights. The key is how powerful your feelings are—and how you handle them

OBSESSIVE-COMPULSIVE DISORDER

WHAT IT IS: A preoccupation with specific thoughts, images or impulses, accompanied by elaborate and sometimes bizarre rituals

WHAT IT ISN'T: Fastidious—even idiosyncratic—behavior that does not significantly interfere with your quality of life

WHAT TO LOOK FOR: Are the obsessive thoughts persistent and intrusive?

- Do you expend a lot of energy suppressing the thoughts, usually unsuccessfully?
- Are you generally aware that the thoughts are irrational?
- Is the anxiety temporarily eased by a repetitive ritual such as hand washing or a thought ritual such as praying?
- Are the rituals time consuming?

BOTTOM LINE: Some researchers question whether OCD is a genuine anxiety disorder. Whatever it is, it does respond to treatment—provided you seek help

POST-TRAUMATIC STRESS DISORDER

WHAT IT IS: Repeated, anxious reliving of a horrifying event over an extended period of time

WHAT IT ISN'T: Anxiety following a trauma that fades steadily over the course of a month or so

WHAT TO LOOK FOR: After witnessing, experiencing or hearing about an event that caused or threatened to cause serious injury, do you:

- Have recurrent recollections or dreams about the experience?
- Feel emotionally or physically as if the event were still occurring?
- Experience intense anxiety when something reminds you of the event?
- Try to avoid thoughts, feelings, activities or places associated with the event?
- Have difficulty recalling details of the event?
- Experience anxiety symptoms such as irritability, jumpiness, difficulty sleeping, feelings of detachment from others, diminished interest in things, feelings that your future is in some way limited?

BOTTOM LINE: Sometimes, PTSD will not appear until six months after the event. Seek help whenever symptoms occur

GENERALIZED ANXIETY DISORDER

WHAT IT IS: Excessive anxiety or worry, occurring more days than not for six months

WHAT IT ISN'T: Occasional serious worry that doesn't markedly diminish quality of life

WHAT TO LOOK FOR: Restlessness; difficulty concentrating or sleeping; irritability; fatigue; muscle tension

BOTTOM LINE: If you have three or more symptoms for the required six months, the diagnosis may fit

—*By Jeffrey Kluger*

- There is a genetic component to anxiety; some people seem to be born worriers.
- Brain scans can reveal differences in the way patients who suffer from anxiety disorders respond to danger signals.
- Due to a shortcut in our brain's information-processing system, we can respond to threats before we become aware of them.
- The root of an anxiety disorder may not be the threat that triggers it but a breakdown in the mechanism that keeps the anxiety response from careening out of control.

Before we delve into the latest research, let's define a few terms. Though we all have our own intuitive sense of what the words stress and fear mean, scientists use these words in very specific ways. For them, stress is an external stimulus that signals danger, often by causing pain. Fear is the short-term response such stresses produce in men, women or lab rats. Anxiety has a lot of the same symptoms as fear, but it's a feeling that lingers long after the stress has lifted and the threat has passed.

In general, science has a hard time pinning down emotions because they are by nature so slippery and subjective. You can't

THE ANATOMY OF ANXIETY

WHAT TRIGGERS IT...
When the senses pick up a threat—a loud noise, a scary sight, a creepy feeling—the information takes two different routes through the brain

... AND HOW THE BODY RESPONDS
By putting the brain on alert, the amygdala triggers a series of changes in brain chemicals and hormones that puts the entire body in anxiety mode

A THE SHORTCUT
When startled, the brain automatically engages an emergecy hot line to its fear center, the amygdala. Once activated, the amygdala sends the equivalent of an all-points bulletin that alerts other brain structures. The result is the classic fear response: sweaty palms, rapid heartbeat, increased blood pressure and a burst of adrenaline. All this happens before the mind is conscious of having smelled or touched anything. Before you know why you're afraid, you are

B THE HIGH ROAD
Only after the fear response is activated does the conscious mind kick into gear. Some sensory information, rather than traveling directly to the amygdala, takes a more circuitous route, stopping first at the thalamus—the processing hub for sensory cues—and then the cortex—the outer layer of brain cells. The cortex analyzes the raw data streaming in through the senses and decides whether they require a fear response. If they do, the cortex signals the amygdala, and the body stays on alert

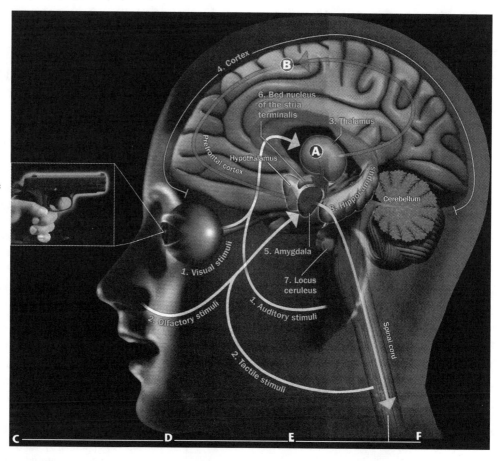

C Stress-Hormone Boost
Responding to signals from the hypothalamus and pituitary gland, the adrenal glands pump out high levels of the stress hormone cortisol. Too much cortisol shortcircuits the cells in the hippocampus, making it difficult to organize the memory of a trauma or stressful experience. Memories lose their context and become fragmented

D Racing Heartbeat
The body's sympathetic nervous system, responsible for heart rate and breathing, shifts into overdrive. The heart beats faster, blood pressure rises and the lungs hyperventilate. sweat increases, and even the nerve endings on the skin tingle into action, creating goose bumps

E Fight, Flight or Fright
The senses become hyperalert, drinking in every detail of the surroundings and looking for potential new threats. Adrenaline shoots to the muscles, preparing the body to fight or flee.

F Digestion shutdown
The brain stops thinking about things that bring pleasure, shifting its focus instead to identifying potential dangers. To ensure that no energy is wasted on digestion, the body will sometimes respond by emptying the digestive tract through involuntary vomiting, urination or defecation

Source: Dennis S. Charney, M.D., National Institute of Mental Health.   TIME Diagram by Joe Lertola.   Text by Alice Park

(Continued on following page)

THE ANATOMY OF ANXIETY

continued

1. Auditory and visual stimuli

Sights and sounds are processed first by the thalamus, which filters the incoming cues and shunts them either directly to the amygdala or to the appropriate parts of the cortex

2. Olfactory and tactile stimuli

Smells and touch sensations bypass the thalamus altogether, taking a shortcut directly to the amygdala. Smells, therefore, often evoke stronger memories or feelings than do sights or sounds

3. Thalamus

The hub for sights and sounds, the thalamus breaks down incoming visual cues by size, shape and color, and auditory cues by volume and dissonance, and then signals the appropriate parts of the cortex

4. Cortex

It gives raw sights and sounds meaning, enabling the brain to become conscious of what it is seeing or hearing. One region, the prefrontal cortex, may be vital to turning off the anxiety response once a threat has passed

5. Amygdala

The emotional core of the brain, the amygdala has the primary role of triggering the fear response. Information that passes through the amygdala is tagged with emotional significance

6. Bed nucleus of the stria terminalis

Unlike the amygdala, which sets off an immediate burst of fear, the BNST perpetuates the fear response, causing the longer-term unease typical of anxiety

7. Locus ceruleus

It receives signals from the amygdala and is responsible for initiating many of the classic anxiety responses: rapid heartbeat, increased blood pressure, sweating and pupil dilation

8. Hippocampus

This is the memory center, vital to storing the raw information coming in from the senses, along with the emotional baggage attached to the data during their trip through the amygdala

Source: Dennis S. Charney, M.D., National Institute of Mental Health.   Text by Alice Park

ask a rat if it's anxious or depressed. Even most people are as clueless about why they have certain feelings as they are about how their lungs work. But fear is the one aspect of anxiety that's easy to recognize. Rats freeze in place. Humans break out in a cold sweat. Heartbeats race, and blood pressure rises. That gives scientists something they can control and measure. "You can bring on a sensory stimulus that makes an animal—or human—fearful and study its effects," says Dr. Wayne Drevets of the National Institute of Mental Health (NIMH). "Then you can take the stimulus away and see how the animal calms down."

Indeed, a lot of what researchers have learned about the biology of anxiety comes from scaring rats and then cutting them open. Just as the Russian physiologist Ivan Pavlov showed 100 years ago that you could condition a dog to salivate at the sound of a bell, scientists today have taught rats to fear all kinds of things—from buzzers to lights—by giving them electrical shocks when they hear the buzzer or see the light. The animals quickly learn to fear the stimulus even in the absence of a shock. Then researchers destroy small portions of the rats' brains to see what effect that has on their reactions (an experiment that would be impossible to conduct in humans). By painstakingly matching the damaged areas with changes in behavior, scientists have, bit by bit, created a road map of fear as it travels through the rat's brain.

The journey begins when a rat (we'll get to humans later) feels the stress, in this case an electric shock. The rat's senses immediately send a message to the central portion of its brain, where the stimulus activates two neural pathways. One of these pathways is a relatively long, circuitous route through the cortex, where the brain does its most elaborate and accurate processing of information. The other route is a kind of emergency shortcut that quickly reaches an almond-shaped cluster of cells called the amygdala.

What's special about the amygdala is that it can quickly activate just about every system in the body to fight like the devil or run like crazy. It's not designed to be accurate, just fast. If you have ever gone hiking and been startled by a snake that turned out to be a stick, you can thank your amygdala. Joseph LeDoux, a neuroscientist at New York University, calls it "the hub in a wheel of fear."

But while the amygdala is busy telling the body what to do, it also fires up a nearby curved cluster of neurons called the hippocampus. (A 16th century anatomist named it after the Greek word for seahorse.) The job of the hippocampus is to help the brain learn and form new memories. And not just any memories. The hippocampus allows a rat to remember where it was when it got shocked and what was going on around it at the time. Such contextual learning helps the poor rodent avoid dangerous places in the future. It probably also helps it recognize what situations are likely to be relatively safe.

By this point, the other half of the stress signal has reached the cortex, which confirms that there's a danger present and figures out that it's causing pain. Once the shock has worn off, a part of the brain called the prefrontal cortex sends out an all-clear message and lets the amygdala know that it's O.K. to stand down. At least it's supposed to. It seems that it's harder to turn off a stress response than to turn it on. This makes sense, in terms of survival. After all, it's better to panic unnecessarily than to be too relaxed in the face of life-threatening danger.

Discovering this basic neural circuitry turned out to be a key breakthrough in understanding anxiety. It showed that the anx-

WHAT CAN YOU DO

There are as many ways to relieve anxiety as there are things that make us anxious. The key is to find the way that works for you—and use it

BEHAVIORAL THERAPY

When the brain sets anxiety alarms ringing, our first inclination is to find the off switch. Behavioral scientists take the opposite approach. They want you to get so accustomed to the noise that you don't hear it anymore. The standard behavioral treatment for such anxiety conditions as phobias, obsessive-compulsive disorder (OCD) and panic disorder is to expose patients to a tiny bit of the very thing that causes them anxiety, ratcheting up the exposure over a number of sessions until the brain habituates to the fear. A patient suffering from a blood phobia, for example, might first be shown a picture of a scalpel or syringe, then a real syringe, then a vial of blood and so on up the anxiety ladder until there are no more rungs to climb. There is a risk that if treatment is cut short (before the patient has become inured to the anxiety triggers), the anxious feelings could be exacerbated. But done right, behavioral therapy can bring relief from specific phobias in as little as two or three sessions. Social anxiety takes somewhat longer, and OCD may take a good deal longer still.

COGNITIVE THERAPY

Rather than expect patients to embrace anxiety, cognitive therapists encourage them to use the power of the mind to reason through it. First popularized in the 1980s, cognitive therapy teaches people who are anxious or depressed to reconfigure their view of the world and develop a more realistic perspective on the risks or obstacles they face. Patients suffering from social-anxiety disorder, for example, might see a group of people whispering at a party and assume the gossip is about them. A cognitive therapist would teach them to rethink that assumption. Some behavioral therapists question cognitive techniques, arguing—not without some justification—that a brain that was so receptive to reason wouldn't be all that anxious in the first place. Cognitive therapists dispute that idea, though some have begun incorporating behavior-modification techniques into their treatment.

ANTIDEPRESSANTS

When talk therapy doesn't work—or needs a boost—drugs can help, especially the class of antidepressants called selective serotonin reuptake inhibitors. Prozac is the best known of these drugs, which work by preventing the brain from reabsorbing too much of the neurotransmitter serotonin, leaving more in nerve synapses and thus helping to improve mood. Another SSRI, Paxil, was recently approved by the Food and Drug Administration specifically for the treatment of social-anxiety disorder, though the others seem to work as well. A third, Zoloft, has been approved for OCD and panic disorder. Each formulation of SSRI is subtly different—targeting specific subclasses of serotonin. And side effects—which can include dry mouth, fatigue and sexual dysfunction—will vary from person to person. A new group of antidepressants, known as serotonin-norepinephrine reuptake inhibitors, may be even more effective in treating anxiety disorders than the SSRIs are. As the name implies, SNRIs target a second neurotransmitter called norepinephrine, which is secreted by the adrenal fight-or-flight response—thus actually increasing anxiety symptoms in many situations. However, norepinephrine also helps control emotion and stabilize mood, and, properly manipulated along with serotonin, may be able to do just that for the anxious person.

MINOR TRANQUILIZERS

If the antidepressants have a flaw, it's that they sometimes don't start working for weeks—a lifetime for the acutely anxious. For this reason, many doctors recommend judicious doses of fast-acting relaxants such as the benzodiazepines Xanax, Valium or Klonopin to serve as a temporary bridge until the SSRIs have a chance to kick in. The downside of such drugs is that they can be highly addictive and may merely mask symptoms. For this reason, doctors will prescribe them very carefully and strictly limit refills.

EXERCISE

Before turning to drugs or talk therapy, many people prefer to try to bring their anxiety under control on their own. Unlike most emotional or physical conditions, anxiety disorders respond well to such self-medication—provided you know how to administer the treatment. One of the most effective techniques is simple exercise. It's no secret that a good workout or a brisk walk can take the edge off even the most acute anxiety. Scientists once believed the effect to be due to the release of natural opiates known as endorphins, but new research has called this into question. Regardless, working out regularly—most days of the week, if possible for at least 30 minutes or so—may well help recalibrate the anxious brain.

ALTERNATIVE TREATMENTS

One of the most popular self-treatments is yoga, which is both a form of exercise and a way to quiet the mind by focusing attention on breathing. Indeed, even without yoga, breathing exercises can help quell an anxiety episode, if only by slowing a racing heart and lengthening the short, shallow breaths of a panic attack. Many anxiety sufferers have relief through meditation or massage—even just a 10-min. foot treatment. For those willing to travel a little farther from the mainstream there's aromatherapy (enthusiasts recommend rose and lavender scents), guided imager (a form of directed meditation used with some success by people recovering from cancer and open-heart surgery) and acupuncture.

LIFESTYLE CHANGES

If all else fails, go back to basics and try cleaning up your lifestyle. For starters, you can cut back or eliminate the use of sugar, caffeine, nicotine, alcohol and any recreational drugs you may be taking. Are you eating right and getting enough sleep and leisure time? Finally, if your job or the place you live is making you anxious, you might consider moving to a less stressful environment or finding a different line of work.

—By Jeffrey Kluger. With reporting by Sora Song/New York

iety response isn't necessarily caused by an external threat; rather, it may be traced to a breakdown in the mechanism that signals the brain to stop responding. Just as a car can go out of control due to either a stuck accelerator or failed brakes, it's not always clear which part of the brain is at fault. It may turn out that some anxiety disorders are caused by an overactive amygdala (the accelerator) while others are caused by an underactive prefrontal cortex (call it the brake).

It may also be that an entirely different part of the brain holds the key to understanding anxiety. Michael Davis, a behavioral neuroscientist at Emory University in Atlanta, has spent six years studying a pea-size knot of neurons located near the amygdala with an impossible name: the bed nucleus of the stria terminalis, or BNST. Rats whose BNST has been injected with stress hormones are much jumpier than those that have got a shot in their amygdala. Could the BNST be at the root of all anxiety disorders? The clues are intriguing, but as scientists are so fond of saying, more research is needed.

Of course, what you would really like to know is whether any of the work done in rats applies to humans. Clearly researchers can't go around performing brain surgery on the amygdalas of living patients to see if it affects their anxiety levels. But the fascinating case of a woman known only by her research number, SM046, suggests that when it comes to fear, rodents and hominids really aren't so different.

Owing to an unusual brain disorder, SM046 has a defective amygdala. As a result, her behavior is abnormal in a very particular way. When scientists at the University of Iowa show SM046 pictures of a series of faces, she has no trouble picking out those that are happy, sad or angry. But if the face is displaying fear, she cannot recognize the feeling. She identifies it as a face expressing some intense emotion, but that is all. Her unusual condition strongly suggests that even in *Homo sapiens*, fear takes hold in the amygdala.

But studying brain-damaged patients can teach scientists only so much. They would also like to know how anxiety works in normal, intact brains. For this, brain scans have proved invaluable.

For years, doctors have used CAT scans and MRIs to help them diagnose strokes, brain tumors and other neurological conditions. But as the technology has become more sophisticated, researchers have started to employ it to tease out some of the subtle changes associated with mental illness. "We're not yet able to use these scans in a diagnostic way," says Dr. David Silbersweig of the Weill Cornell Medical College in New York City. "But we're getting pretty specific about the areas of the brain that are implicated in a number of psychiatric disorders."

One type of brain scan helps identify structures that are the wrong size or shape. Two years ago, researchers at the University of Pittsburgh showed that the amygdalas of a group of overanxious young children were, on average, much larger than those of their unaffected peers. Perhaps they just had more fear circuits to contend with? Neuroscientists are tempted to say yes, but they admit the conclusion is pretty speculative. Another group of researchers found that patients with post-traumatic stress disorder had a smaller hippocampus than normal. Perhaps their stressful experiences had somehow interfered with the hip-

pocampus' ability to make new memories and, just as important, forget the old ones? Again, no one knows for sure.

Another type of brain scan tells scientists which brain cells are using the most oxygen or soaking up the most nutrients. The idea, explains Dr. Scott Rauch of Massachusetts General Hospital, is that any area that seems more active than usual while someone is anxious may play an important role in making the person that way. Rauch's team has spent the past eight years scanning groups of combat veterans, some with post-traumatic stress disorder and some without, to see which areas of the brain light up when they hear tapes recounting their most troubling memories. So far, the signals in the amygdala appear to be more active in those with PTSD than in those without. In addition, signals to the prefrontal cortex of PTSD subjects seem to be weaker than in those without the disorder. Perhaps this explains why the patients still feel threatened even when they are perfectly safe.

The next step, Rauch says, is to scan groups of people who are likely to be thrust into dangerous situations—fire fighters, say, or police officers. Then it may be possible to determine if any changes in their brains are the result of traumatic situations or if the changes predate them. Either is plausible. The stress of surviving a building collapse, for example, could turn a normal amygdala into an overactive one. Or an already overactive amygdala may overwhelm the brain in the wake of a disaster.

Eventually, researchers would like to learn what role our genes, as opposed to our environment, play in the development of anxiety. "It has been known for some time that these disorders run in families," says Kenneth Kendler, a psychiatric geneticist at Virginia Commonwealth University in Richmond, Va. "So the next logical question is the nature-nurture issue." In other words, are anxious people born that way, or do they become anxious as a result of their life experiences?

Kendler and his colleagues approached the question by studying groups of identical twins, who share virtually all their genes, and fraternal twins, who, like any other siblings, share only some of them. What Kendler's group found was that both identical twins were somewhat more likely than both fraternal twins to suffer from generalized anxiety disorder, phobias or panic attacks. (The researchers have not yet studied twins with post-traumatic stress disorder or obsessive-compulsive disorder.)

The correlation isn't 100%, however. "Most of the heritability is in the range of 30% to 40%," Kendler says. That's a fairly moderate genetic impact, he notes, akin to the chances that you will have the same cholesterol count as your parents. "Your genes set your general vulnerability," he concludes. "You can be a low-vulnerable, intermediate-vulnerable or a high-vulnerable person." But your upbringing and your experiences still have a major role to play. Someone with a low genetic vulnerability, for example, could easily develop a fear of flying after surviving a horrific plane crash.

There is plenty to learn about how anxiety and fear shape the brain. One of the biggest mysteries is the relationship between anxiety and depression. Researchers know that adults who suffer from depression were often very anxious as children. (It's also true that many kids outgrow their anxiety disorders to become perfectly well-adjusted adults.) Is that just a coincidence, as many believe, or does anxiety somehow prime the brain to become depressed later in life? Brain scans show that the amygdala is very active in depressed patients, even when they are sleeping. Studies of twins suggest that many of the same genes could be involved. "There's a lot of overlap," says Dr. Dennis Charney, chief of the research program for mood and anxiety disorders at the NIMH. "Anxiety and depression have a similar underlying biology, and the genetics may be such that anxiety surfaces early in life and depression later on." Still, no one can say for sure.

Certainly antidepressants, like the serotonin reuptake inhibitors (Prozac and others) have proved very helpful in treating anxiety; some doctors think they are even more effective against anxiety than they are against depression. Although no one knows exactly why these antidepressants work, one important clue is that their effects don't show up until after a few weeks of treatment. The pathways for toning down anxiety are apparently much more resistant than those for ratcheting it up.

It's a mistake, however, to think that pills alone can soothe your neurochemistry. Remember the cortex? That's where you would expect psychotherapy to work, increasing the repertoire of calming messages that can be passed along to the amygdala. Certain desensitization techniques can also help the brain learn, through the hippocampus, to be less reactive. Of course, you have to do it right. Reliving a trauma too soon after it happened could also make the memory harder to erase.

There are no guidebooks to tell you when it's safe to venture out again. In many ways, the whole country last September was made part of an unwitting experiment in mass anxiety. Our brains are even now in the process of rewiring themselves. How successfully we navigate this delicate transition will depend a lot on our genes, our environment and any future attacks.

—*Reported by Alice Park/Bethesda, Leslie Whitaker/Chicago and Dan Cray/Los Angeles*

From *Time*, June 10, 2002, pp. 47-54. © 2002 by Time, Inc. Magazine Company. Reprinted by permission.

OVERCOMING DEPRESSION

One woman's terrifying odyssey through a nightmare of despair

BY SHARON DOYLE DRIEDGER

Depression hit me at a time when dreams were coming true. In April, 1998, I climbed the Eiffel Tower and strolled along the Thames with my husband and our teenage son and daughter. It was a special family holiday and my first European vacation, slightly less wacky but with a lot more laughs than the Chevy Chase version. In May, I won a National Magazine Award, unexpected recognition for work I love. I liked my life. How could I be a woman on the verge of a nervous breakdown? Well, OK. Looking back, I remember feeling tired all the time. But that's normal for a working mother, isn't it? I remember feeling vaguely unwell and I remember a gnawing fear that the breast cancer I fought several years earlier had returned. But the test results were all clear. There was no catastrophe, no trauma that would explain what happened to me next.

On an ordinary, rainy November morning, for no particular reason, my life fell apart. The surreal scene plays over and over in a far corner of my mind, like a third-rate horror movie. I am at the office, working at my computer, when a dark, foggy presence closes in on me. My vision falters and the words on the screen blur into meaninglessness. In a panic, I scroll through the lines I had just written, but they are indecipherable, foreign. I can't read. I can't think. I can't move. A black, animate nothingness has clamped my brain, shut down my body. I feel numb and empty. I cry for an hour before I realize I can't stop.

Somehow I manage to find my way home. When I turn the key in my front door just after noon, everything is familiar, except me. I watch myself walk from room to room, like a stranger. The emptiness I feel is raw, alarming. I sit in my favourite chair, I stand in the kitchen doorway, I pick up a photo, trying to feel something, anything. Nothing touches me. I am strangely detached, as if I had crossed some invisible line. Is this, I wonder, what it's like to lose your mind? I see no way back. I feel hopeless and helpless. And the worst is yet to come. I had no idea then that I suffered from a clinical depression so severe I would be unable to return to work for more than a year. I didn't know that the conventional treatments would ultimately fail me. All I wanted to do was sleep. I went upstairs to lie down and when I woke up after an hour or so, I couldn't move.

Depression is a lonely place. That is a sad and strange fact, given that nearly one in five Canadians will suffer from clinical depression at some point in their lives. Like most, I tried to hide it, even from myself. In the months preceding my breakdown, I experienced a few symptoms—insomnia, difficulty concentrating and inexplicable tears—that made me wonder if I maybe, possibly, sort of, might have depression. But I am woman, I have hormones. Probably just perimenopausal blues, I thought. My family doctor prescribed Prozac to help me ride out the slump. It made me feel weird, spacey. Besides, I don't like being lumped in with the pill-popping crowd who can't cope without a designer drug.

A CASE HISTORY AMID THE COLLECTIVE PAIN

It was with a sense of mission that I began earlier this year to write about my experience with clinical depression. Then, on Sept. 11, everything changed. What, I wondered, was the relevance of one person's mental pain in the aftermath of horrific death and destruction? My depression remains a tiny puddle next to a sea of anguish. Yet the symptoms of depression are easily confused with grief. Like depression, grief reveals itself in individuals as appetite loss, sleep problems, a sense of foreboding, an inability to focus. But the gloom that many continue to feel is, in most cases, a normal and mainly passing response to catastrophe, and not clinical depression—a persistent and debilitating illness that may be unconnected to external events. And while the terrorist attacks could push a small number of people into the hell of depression, there is help, and hope.

S.D.D.

So I stopped. Really, I should be able to get over it myself. I tell my kids: "You can do anything you put your mind to."

I am an optimistic depressive, but after four or five drugs
I lose patience. When eight drugs fail, I am convinced I am a hopeless case, doomed to spend the rest of my life in a foggy gloom.

Why couldn't I think my way out of depression?

The diagnosis—a major depressive episode—feels like an accusation. Slumped in a leather chair in a psychiatrist's office, I am ready to take the blame. "What did I do wrong?" I ask, weeping and pulling clumps of Kleenex out of the box on the small oak coffee table. "Depression is an illness, like diabetes," the kindly, upbeat doctor assures me. "Nobody knows precisely what causes depression." Depression, he explains, is a disorder of the brain that produces physical and mental symptoms. No matter what the initial trigger—genes, ill health, severe stress—people suffering from depression have an imbalance in serotonin and other brain chemicals linked to mood. "Depression is treatable," he tells me. With the help of SSRIs—selective serotonin reuptake inhibitors—and other antidepressants, roughly 50 per cent of patients recover and another 30 per cent show substantial improvement, sometimes within weeks. I feel incredible, if passing, relief. My neurochemistry is out of whack. I won't have to spend hours on a shrink's couch, digging into my psyche for something that may have gone wrong in my childhood. I leave his office with a prescription for Serzone and a sliver of hope.

I stare at the little white capsule of Serzone rolling around in the palm of my hand. I flashback to my earlier encounter with Prozac. The pharmacist hadn't meant to scare me. "Prozac is a good drug," he told me when I went to pick up my prescription. "There were reports that it could lead to suicide, but they were later discounted." Just the notion scared me so much it once took me 10 days to work up the nerve to take Prozac. Now, I don't care. In the perversity of

depression, that grim downside starts to look attractive.

I ignore the list of "possible side-effects" on the pharmacist's handout—headache, dry mouth, nausea, drowsiness, dizziness, weakness, constipation, lightheadedness. My misery is so unrelenting, I can't imagine how I could feel any worse. Besides, it says side-effects may go away during treatment. And, hey, maybe it will magically lift me out of the abyss of depression, or even make me feel "better than well," like the patients in Peter Kramer's *Listening to Prozac*. For a fleeting moment, I consider the pill-popping stigma. But in the grip of a disabling depression, pride is a luxury. So I swallow the Serzone and wait for my serotonin levels to shift back to normal.

In my first desolate weeks on sick leave, my depression deepens. It reaches into every cell of my body and weighs me down with a crushing fatigue. I can't move out of bed. I don't have the energy to lift a fork, to chew my food. I lose 20 lb. in less than two months. I can't sleep. I can't talk. Mouthing words takes too much effort. I find out the hard way that depression is not just in my head. It's a real, physical ailment.

The Serzone starts to kick in after a few weeks. It gives me short bursts of nervous energy, enough to propel me to the shower, maybe to get dressed. But after an hour or two, the effect wears off and I slide back into tears and inertia. My doctor increases the dose. The drug holds me up, partway out of the well of misery, for as long as half a day. But the side-effects become more intense—dry mouth, so extreme the thirst wakes me at night, blurred vision, ringing in my ears, eye pain, bladder problems, nervous agitation, stiff neck—the list goes on. By the end of January, it is clear the drug is not helping.

Before I can switch to Manerix, an antidepressant that could be dangerous if combined with an SSRI, I have to let the Serzone wash out of my system. Withdrawal is a hell of fever, nausea, night sweats and achy bones that lasts for more than a week. Then, sweet relief and surprise. I feel—almost—like myself again. The confusion, grogginess, memory problems, anxiety—symptoms I thought were caused by the depression—seem to disappear along with the Serzone. I curse the drug and revel, briefly, in my newfound clarity.

Three days later, I fall into a deeper, sharper depression. I realize I need the drugs. They blur my mind and afflict my body, but they dull the unbearable pain. I'm willing to pay the price.

Scientists are trying to figure out why some antidepressants work for some patients and not others. In the meantime, treatment is a matter of trial and error. "There are lots of other drugs," my doctor tells me. "We will find one that will help you." Although most antidepressants work on the same principle—of modifying levels of neurotransmitters linked to mood—their chemical configurations vary, producing somewhat different effects. Some antidepressants increase serotonin levels, others enhance norepinephrine. Some drugs energize, others are calming. The most up-to-date treatment for depression relies on the science, and art, of administering and combining any of the dozens of available antidepressants, along with a chaser of tranquillizers, anti-seizure drugs or other medications that might balance or augment their effects. In my two-year pharmaceutical odyssey, my doctor prescribes nine different drugs: Prozac, Paxil, Serzone, Zoloft, Wellbutrin, Manerix, Effexor, nortriptyline and Celexa.

A pattern emerges: my hopes soar with each new drug. I wait and I watch

Sometimes, from the smug perspective of restored health, I wonder why I endured so many side-effects. But the truth is, if I had not found SAMe, I may have stuck with the dreaded antidepressants.

for the smallest sign of improvement. My doctor monitors my reactions, adjusts the dosages. It's tricky. Antidepressants may cause so-called paradoxical effects—memory loss, confusion, anxiety, insomnia—the very symptoms they are intended to cure. Some provide no relief, others help a little. In every case, the side-effects become intolerable. Wellbutrin revs me up so much I can't sleep. Manerix merits a note in my journal for sending "a wonderful, caressing flow through my body." I end up in emergency five days later with swollen lips and a rash around my neck. Unfortunately, I am allergic to Manerix. Effexor makes my hands tremble, my mind spacey. Nortriptyline, a tricyclic, one of a class of drugs that fell out of favour when Prozac went on the market in 1989, lifts my mood, concentration and energy levels. But the side-effects—dry mouth, weight gain, constipation, urine retention, dizziness, fainting, hot flashes, agitation, anxiety, panic attacks—are numerous, intense and, ultimately, unbearable.

I am an optimistic depressive, but after four or five drugs I lose patience. Family and friends can only watch and listen. I am alone in the ring with an invisible illness. My disability leave is stretching on and on. Will I have to waste another two months coping with debilitating side-effects only to find another drug won't work? I pester my doctor about Saint-John's-wort. Why shouldn't I try the popular herbal remedy? He points to studies that show it only works for mild to moderate depression and challenges my assumption that natural means safe and side-effect free. When eight drugs fail, I am convinced I am a hopeless case, doomed to spend the rest of my life in a foggy gloom.

There's nothing funny about depression, although I almost laugh when

Bobby McFerrin's light and breezy *Don't Worry, Be Happy* plays on the office speakers as I sit, forlorn and teary-eyed, in the psychiatrist's waiting room. But as Andrew Solomon, American author of the brilliant memoir *The Noonday Demon*, writes, all too accurately: "Depression is ridiculous." I mean, I know *Analyze This* should not hold such deep meaning for me. I understand, on some level, that spotting a spider on the bathroom wall really is no reason to conclude my house should be demolished. And I question my ability to identify so completely with Tony Soprano that I, too, resent his Uncle Junior.

In the darkest moments, I wish for a recurrence of my breast cancer. At least that would be a real illness. I look for any escape. In one black fantasy, I picture myself as an extra in a crowd scene in a movie. The crowd disperses and I am gone. Conveniently, painlessly, I fade into the background.

Mostly, I feel flat. I sleepwalk through bleak, vacant days. Months pass. Life in slow motion. I cry everywhere, in funny movies, on the phone with friends, on the subway. The tears flow randomly, absurdly unconnected to my feelings. My thoughts are muddled. Simple tasks, like organizing the cutlery tray, are intellectually daunting. I make it to the grocery store one day, but in the middle of the canned goods aisle I am overcome with confusion trying to find the four items on my list.

I'd be crazy not to want a quick fix. That's why I focus on the search for the right drug. Exercise, too, my doctor tells me. I'm a jogger and I know about endorphin highs. Good idea, if I had the energy to move. Eventually, I drag myself out of bed, go to the gym and walk, crying, once around the track. I run for half a lap, produce more tears than sweat, and then collapse. It's a start.

My doctor is not a believer but he encourages me to pray. There is evidence that meditation can have a positive influence on brain chemistry. I force myself to move, to do something, anything, even for a few minutes. I start with small victories. I get up, get dressed. Gradually, I try talk therapy, art therapy, bibliotherapy, light therapy, yoga, meditation—anything that might help pull me out of depression. I collect names of people with depression. Winston Churchill, J. K. Rowling, Mother Teresa. I try not to think about Sylvia Plath. I add omega-3 oils to my diet.

In May, 1999, my doctor writes me a prescription for Celexa, a brand-new drug. Although its side-effects are milder than other SSRIs, there are several—dry mouth, a dragging fatigue and a feeling of weakness in my muscles and bones. A breakthrough comes in July. I snap out of the fog, and for a few hours, I am alert, optimistic, even happy. The moment passes but it is enough to convince me I have finally found the right drug. I start the long, achingly slow climb to recovery. There are no sudden bursts of energy, just slight, gradual easings of debilitating fatigue and despair. Slowly, subtly, slipping back, moving forward, Celexa lifts me out of depression. Is this as good as it gets?

In January, 2000, hoping that my lingering depression would soon fade, I ease back to work. Two weeks later, a suspicious shadow appears on my annual mammogram. A biopsy shows I have breast cancer again. The diagnosis is discouraging but cancer is, at least, a tangible enemy. It's a disease with a slogan: "Cancer can be beaten." It's possible to gather the courage to fight it. Depression not only kills the will to live, it disconnects the inner resources and strengths

A PILL THAT WORKS FOR MANY IS IN A LEGAL LIMBO

The latest alternative to Prozac is not a herb, a vitamin or a high-tech pharmaceutical. SAMe—the common name for S-adenosylmethionine—is a component of every living cell. Italian researchers discovered the compound, produced naturally in the body from an essential fatty acid found in meat and other protein, in the 1950s. It took two decades to figure out how to manufacture a usable form of the unstable molecule. But by the early 1970s, scientists began to notice that SAMe could help alleviate symptoms of osteoarthritis and improve mood and liver function, with few and mild side-effects.

Widely used in Europe as a prescription treatment for depression since 1976, SAMe only appeared in North America in 1999. Sold as a nutritional supplement, it became an instant hit in health-food stores. But after six months of booming sales, Health Canada reclassified SAMe as a new drug and ordered it off the shelves. Government regulations require manufacturers and retailers of new products to substantiate health claims—an expensive undertaking.

"That could cost $1 million and we would never recover our costs," says Don Beattie, Vancouver-based director of regulatory affairs for Quest Vitamins, a division of multinational Boehringer Ingelheim Canada Ltd. Like other manufacturers, Quest is waiting for a cheaper approval process to be established soon by Health Canada. So SAMe is caught in an administrative limbo at least until sometime next year. In the meantime, Health Canada allows consumers to import a three-month supply for personal use. In the United States,

it's available over the counter in pharmacies and health-food stores.

"A lot of patients know about SAMe," says Toronto psychiatrist Anthony Levitt, who has prescribed it for drug-resistant depression since 1988, under a special access program. "The data are very promising." Trials have found it effective for 60 per cent of people who try it, making it roughly comparable to other antidepressants.

SAMe typically starts to relieve depression in seven days, compared with two to four weeks for standard antidepressants. Some patients report mild, transient headaches, gastrointestinal complaints or a caffeine-like agitation. Levitt believes the chance of serious, long-term side-effects is low. "It is such a ubiquitous substance in the body," he says. "When you are taking SAMe, you are merely supplementing something that is already present in every cell."

Still, he and most other doctors hesitate to recommend SAMe until it attains the scientific clout of rigorous large-scale studies. "I have reservations," says Levitt. "We don't know the long-term effects. Just because a product is 'natural' doesn't necessarily mean it is safe or effective."

Besides, as with any unregulated product, it's hard to be sure what you're actually getting in a bottle, says Teodoro Bottiglieri, a Texas-based neuropharmacologist and co-author of Stop Depression Now, a 1999 book about SAMe. Measuring the level of SAMe in several brands sold in the United States, Bottiglieri found three that contained "zero per cent." So far, it's a case of buyer beware.

---

that would make it possible to fight it. In June, I finish four weeks of radiation therapy and carry on what feels like a never-ending struggle with depression.

I resign myself to the possibility of taking Celexa for years, if not the rest of my life. But March, 2001, brings a new complication—a twitchiness around my eyes. I blink uncontrollably, for minutes at a time, even at night in a darkened room. Annoying but insignificant, I think. When I mention it to my doctor, he has me gradually, carefully, wean off Celexa. Tics—caused by malfunctions in the part of the brain that controls body movement—are a little-known but serious and, possibly irreversible, side-effect that may emerge after prolonged use of SSRIs.

Am I a rare case? Maybe. There is simply not enough data to know for sure. There was no evidence in initial clinical trials that SSRIs could cause tics, but they—and other so-called extrapyramidal side-effects like muscle spasms and a drug-induced form of Parkinsonism—are common with psychiatric drugs that block dopamine levels. Now, scientists understand that an increase in serotonin levels in the brain leads to a corresponding drop in dopamine. At the same time, after widespread use of the SSRIs in large populations, reports are surfacing of tics and other troublesome side-effects including, rarely, irregular heartbeat.

So now what?

My doctor recommends SAMe—short for S-adenosylmethionine—a natural supplement that is wildly popular in the United States. SAMe (pronounced sammy) has been used for more than 25 years in Europe, where it is available as a treatment for depression and osteoar-

thritis. Several studies show it to work as well as standard antidepressants, with only a few mild side-effects. Still, my doctor warns: "The long-term safety is unknown."

At first, I can't find SAMe. The health-food stores and pharmacies I visit no longer carry it, since the federal government prohibited its sale in 1999. One helpful clerk suggests that I order it over the Internet, since Health Canada allows consumers to bring in a three-month supply from the United States, where it is classified as a dietary supplement. But after several inquiries, one downtown proprietor looks me over, pulls a bottle of pills out from under the counter and says, with a wink: "I have my sources." At $500 for a one-month supply, SAMe is expensive. But I'm worth it.

My first week on SAMe is nerve-racking. The therapeutic dose is eight tablets a day. I start with two. SAMe has few known side-effects—mild, transient headaches, gastrointestinal complaints and a caffeine-like jitteriness—and I experience them all. I persevere, gradually increasing my intake. After five or six days on SAMe, I notice a small improvement. After just two weeks, I feel balanced, steady. SAMe is by no means a cure, but it set the stage for a recovery. Now, after six months, I continue to notice a growing sense of well-being.

Sometimes, from the smug perspective of restored health, I wonder why I endured so many side-effects. I want to go back in time and shake myself and yell: "Junk those drugs." And the truth is, depression is so unspeakably painful that if I had not found SAMe, and had not responded to it, I may have decided to stick with the dreaded antidepressants. Besides, it's the government regulators, pharmaceutical companies and the medical establishment that need the shaking up. Why can't I buy SAMe here? Why do I have to order it from the United States? Why are we protected from the potential dangers of SAMe, which has a clean record as a prescription drug in Europe? Where are the warnings about the emerging side-effects of SSRIs? Why are they prescribed for children?

Although it has worked wonders for me, I know SAMe is not a magic bullet. There are risks with it, too. And it could simply stop working. Depression is a complex illness with myriad causes and, for many of us, healing takes more than a pill. In the two years it took to find my "quick fix," I slowly, painstakingly reclaimed my health through exercise, better sleep and diet, counselling, meditation, yoga and prayer. In my case, it helps to have SAMe in the mix. Why shouldn't I try it? I have more dreams to pursue.

From *Maclean's*, November 12, 2001, pp. 34-38. © 2001 by Maclean Hunter Ltd. Reprinted by permission.

NEWS YOU CAN USE

Happiness Explained

New science shows how to inject real joy into your life

BY HOLLY J. MORRIS

There's an ancient tale of happiness that appears in many cultures, and it goes something like this: Once there was a prince who was terribly unhappy. The king dispatched messengers to find the shirt of a happy man, as his advisers told him that was the only cure. They finally encountered a poor farmer who was supremely content. Alas, the happy man owned no shirt.

Ahhh, happiness. Ineffable, elusive, and seemingly just out of reach. For most of the 20th century, happiness was largely viewed as denial or delusion. Psychologists were busy healing sick minds, not bettering healthy ones. Today, however, a growing body of psychologists is taking the mystery out of happiness and the search for the good life. Three years ago, psychologist Martin Seligman, then president of the American Psychological Association, rallied colleagues to what he dubbed "positive psychology." The movement focuses on humanity's strengths, rather than its weaknesses, and seeks to help people move up in the continuum of happiness and fulfillment. Now, with millions of dollars in funding and over 60 scientists involved, the movement is showing real results. Far from being the sole product of genes, luck, delusions, or ignorance, happiness can be learned and cultivated, researchers are finding.

CONTENTMENT

WHAT IT IS: Feeling safe and calm.

WAYS TO GET IT: A friendly, nonthreatening environment is key. If you're not so lucky, relaxation exercises may mimic the body's response to contentment. **Rebecca Shaw** finds it in marriage to Ray Shaw, and in her two children, Christian, 3, and Sierra, 2—and by not putting up with mean people.

Decades of studying depression have helped millions become less sad, but not necessarily more happy—a crucial distinction. When you alleviate depression (no mean task), "the best you can ever get to is zero," says Seligman, a professor at the University of Pennsylvania. But "when you've got a nation in surplus and at peace and not in social turmoil," he explains, "I think the body politic lies awake at night thinking about 'How do I go from plus 2 to plus 8 in my life?'"

Indeed, people in peaceful, prosperous nations aren't necessarily getting any happier. Though census data show that many measures of quality of life have risen since World War II, the number of people who consider themselves happy remains flat. And people are 10 times as likely to suffer depression as those born two generations ago. Researchers have scads of information on what isn't making people happy. For example, once income provides basic needs, it doesn't correlate to happiness. Nor does intelligence, prestige, or sunny weather. People grow used to new climates, higher salaries, and better cars. Not only does the novelty fade but such changes do nothing to alleviate real problems—like that niggling fear that nobody likes you.

Happiness helpers. Scientists also know what works. Strong marriages, family ties, and friendships predict happiness, as do spirituality and self-esteem. Hope is crucial, as is the feeling that life has meaning. Yes, happy people may be more likely to have all these things at the start. But causality, researchers find, goes both ways. Helping people be a little happier can jump-start a process that will lead to stronger relationships, renewed hope, and a general upward spiraling of happiness.

The average person has a head start. Decades of international survey research suggest that most people in developed nations are basically happy. This tendency toward mild cheerfulness may have evolved to keep peo-

CHANGE

WHAT IT IS: What you need when your goals aren't satisfying you.

WAYS TO GET IT: Figure out why what you're doing isn't working. **Allison Waxberg**, a scientist in the cosmetics industry, wanted more creativity in her life. She took art classes, realized she had talent, and now attends Brooklyn's Pratt Institute.

ple moving—glum ancestors would have moped, not mobilized.

Some have more of a head start than others. University studies of twins suggest that about half of one's potential for happiness is inherited. Researchers think happiness is influenced not by a single "happy gene," but by inborn predispositions toward qualities that help or hinder happiness, such as optimism or shyness. And personality doesn't fluctuate that much over an average life span. People seem to have "happiness set points"—base lines that mood drifts back to after good and bad events.

There's a lot of wiggle room on either side of that base line, though. Most positive psychologists refer to a set range. "If you're a more gloomy, pessimistic person, you're probably never going to be really deliriously happy, but you can get into the high end of your possible range and stay there," says psychologist Ken Sheldon of the University of Missouri.

Michael Lee, too, believes happiness can be learned. "You practice it day in and day out," says the 28-year-old marketing director from San Jose, Calif. He has always been pretty happy but has seen his joy grow. A Catholic, he started a faith-sharing group with childhood friends. Under guidance from Jesuit priests, they learned to take time each night to reflect on the positive in their everyday lives—"subtle things like meeting a new person… or kids sitting out in the yard playing." In cultivating his appreciation of the routine, and surrounding himself with other happy people, Lee grew happier. Boosting your happiness isn't always easy, though: Moving up within your range can mean working against your inborn personality traits, learned thinking habits, environment, or all three. But the latter two can change. "If you want to keep your happiness at the higher end of the set range," says Sonja Lyubomirsky, a psychologist at the University of California-Riverside, "you have to commit yourself every day to doing things to make you happy."

One way is to find the right goals and pursue them. Sheldon's research suggests that goals reflecting your interests and values can help you attain and maintain new levels of happiness, rather than returning to base line. By setting and achieving a progression of goals, you can boost your well-being. Even when you fail, you can better

---

MOOD MEASUREMENT
How happy are you? Find out

One way scientists measure happiness is by simply asking people to evaluate their overall satisfaction with their lives. This scale of life satisfaction was developed by psychologist Ed Diener of the University of Illinois-Urbana-Champaign and is used worldwide to gather data on happiness. The scoring at the bottom shows how you compare with other Americans.

Taking the test

For each of the five items below (A-E), select an answer from the O-to-6 response scale. Place a number on the line next to each statement, indicating your agreement or disagreement with that statement.

6: Strongly agree
5: Agree
4: Slightly agree
3: Neither agree or disagree
2: Slightly disagree
1: Disagree
0: Strongly disagree

A _____Your life is very close to your ideal.
B _____The conditions of your life are excellent.
C _____You are completely satisfied with your life.
D _____So far you have obtained the important things you want in your life.
E _____If you could live your life over, you would change nothing.
_____**TOTAL**

26 to 30: Extremely satisfied, much above average
21 to 25: Very satisfied, above average
15 to 20: Somewhat satisfied, average for Americans
11 to 14: Slightly dissatisfied, a bit below average
6 to 10: Dissatisfied, clearly below average
0 to 5: Very dissatisfied, much below average

maintain that higher level next time you reach it, though you'll probably top out at the high end of your range.

Allison Waxberg, 30, wasn't miserable and wasn't depressed—but she wasn't especially happy, either. After six years as a skin scientist in the cosmetics industry, she longed for more-creative work. "I grew up drawing, but I always felt like I had to do something like be a doctor or a lawyer or something professional," she says. When people feel they have no choice in the goals they pursue, they're not going to be satisfied. Goals that derive from

GAGGLE OF GIGGLES

Laughter as its own punch line

Peals of laughter cut through the persistent early-morning drizzle at Seattle's Green Lake Park. As passers-by gape—and then grin—four men and women titter, giggle, chortle, and guffaw, in what looks like a yoga class gone goofy. Led by energetic Stephanie Roche, they alternate rhythmic chanting and clapping with penguinlike waddling and pretend sneezing—all while howling with laughter. There's no punch line; there's not even a joke. This is a laughing club, one of at least 20 begun in the United States this year. They are held in parks, churches, and often in nursing homes, where the gentle cheer is especially welcome.

Laughing clubs are an export from India, where they're familiar sights in hundreds of neighborhoods. Invented by physician Madan Kataria in 1995, the clubs don't rely on humor or jokes. Rather, they focus on the act of laughing, which releases stress and promotes deep, healthy breathing. At first, the ha-has and hee-hees can be forced. Eye contact is required, which helps break the ice. But few can resist breaking into spontaneous laughter during the "lion laugh"—

stick out your tongue, google your eyes, and use your hands as paws. "Sometimes people have to fake it," says psychologist Steve Wilson, 60, of Columbus, Ohio, whose World Laughter Tour trains laughter-club leaders. "And then it flips and it just becomes hysterical."

Roche's laughing club started a mere two weeks ago. After she saw a documentary, *The Laughing Club of India*, at a Seattle film festival (it airs August 28 on Cinemax), she became a "certified laughter leader" at one of Wilson's workshops. She patterned her club after the Indian versions, holding it in a neighborhood park three days a week at 7 a.m. Clubs are encouraged to create their own laughs: Wilson can reel off a long list of obscure ones, such as the "airline safety instruction laugh," in which you gesture at exits and don an imaginary oxygen mask. The Seattle group is already customizing. Karen Schneider-Chen, a 49-year-old jail outreach worker, mimics raindrops with fluttering fingers. "We're working on a Seattle rain laugh," she says.

—H.J.M., with Bellamy Pailthorp in Seattle

FLOW

WHAT IT IS: The state of intense concentration that occurs during challenging, goal-directed activities.

WAYS TO GET IT: Flow can arise from pastimes, like playing sports or music, but also from reading and good conversation. College sophomore **Jason Vincens** finds flow in competitive wrestling.

fear, guilt, or social pressure probably won't make you happier, even if you attain them. "Ask yourself, 'Is this intrinsically interesting and enjoyable?' If it isn't, do I at least believe in it strongly?" says Sheldon. "If I don't, why the hell am I doing it?"

Waxberg tried a series of jobs, including making prosthetic limbs, but had yet to combine her technical and creative sides. Finally, she took some art classes and proved to herself that she had talent. She's now earning an industrial design master's from Brooklyn's Pratt Institute, where she has won acclaim for her ceramics, and is doing her thesis on skin. She hopes to start a new career as a design consultant this year.

For Waxberg, finding the right goal was key—but first she had to figure out why the old ones weren't working. The trick is to know what kind of goals you have. Diffuse

goals, such as "be someone," are next to impossible to achieve. More-concrete goals ("get a job") that relate back to the abstract goal ("be a success") are more satisfying. That also goes for the goal of "being happy." "You'll be happier if you can get involved in things and do well at them, but don't be thinking too much about trying to get happier by doing them," says Sheldon. "It's really kind of Zen in a way."

Out with the bad. Another path to greater happiness is cultivating positive emotions. They're good for more than warm fuzzies: Good feelings broaden thinking and banish negative emotions, says Barbara Fredrickson, a psychologist at the University of Michigan. Negative emotions narrow thought, by necessity. Ancestors didn't have time to sift through creative escape options when fears loomed. But positive emotions open new routes for thinking. When researchers induce positive emotions, thinking becomes more expansive and resourceful.

Most people can't feel positive emotions at will. But you can approach events in a way that gets them going, then let momentum take over. Jay Van Houten made a decision to see the positive when faced with a potentially fatal brain tumor. The 54-year-old business manager from Boise, Idaho, listed the benefits, such as "a built-in excuse for not hearing things like 'Please take out the trash,' " as the surgery left him deaf in one ear.

Though laughing at yourself is fleeting, Fredrickson believes such moments have lasting consequences. "Pos-

HIGHS AND LOWS

Taking one's happy temp

Scientists also measure happiness with "experience sampling," in which mood is assessed on multiple occasions over time. With Palm devices that beeped at random intervals, two *U.S. News* writers answered questions such as "How pleasant are you feeling?" several times a day for a week. Researcher Christie Scollon of the University of Illinois analyzed the data. The red and orange lines combine positive and negative emotions to show overall mood. Person A is happier than the average American—she feels more positive than negative emotions. Person B is unhappier than most—and she's moody. She feels a log of bad along with the good. This illustrates an important notion: Feeling good is more than just not feeling bad.—*H.J.M.*

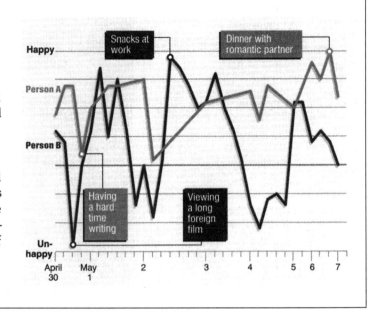

PERSPECTIVE

WHY GET IT: It helps peolple see the good in their lives when things are going badly.

WAYS TO GET IT: Comparing one's situation with a worst-case scenario really can make people feel better. After a potentially fatal brain tumor, not much fazes **Jay Van Houten** these days. ...he volunteers with the mentally and physically disabled.

itive emotions and broadened thinking are mutually building on one another, making people even more creative problem-solvers over time, and even better off emotionally," she says. Coping with one problem well—as Van Houten did with humor—may make people more resilient next time trouble comes along. Van Houten says he's much happier now, especially as nothing seems as bad as a potentially fatal brain tumor. After his surgery, he had to relearn balance. "I still drill into the ground if I turn too fast," he says. "You've got to approach it with a certain amount of humor to get you through the day."

Using humor to feel better works because thinking can't be both narrow and broad. To test this idea, Fredrickson had subjects prepare a speech, then let them off the hook. As they calmed, she showed them video clips that sparked various emotions: a puppy playing with a flower (joy), ocean waves (contentment), a scene from the 1979 tear-jerker *The Champ* (sadness), and a computer screen-saver (neutral). Those who felt joy and contentment calmed down faster. This doesn't mean you should think about puppies when you're down (though if it helps, go for it), but that when you've done all you can

about a problem, a positive distraction can banish lingering bad feelings.

One of the worst enemies of positive emotions is feeling threatened, says Fredrickson. A safe environment is key. Rebecca Shaw found that happiness just needed a chance to flourish. "The day I met my husband was the day my boyfriend broke up with me, and I was pregnant," says the 32-year-old of Ridge, Md. Miserable, lonely, and despairing, she had just moved back in with her parents to get her bearings. Then she ran into an old friend, Ray Shaw. As they spent time together in the following weeks, happiness "stole up" on her. "Suddenly I was just smiling and didn't even realize it—it was just such a subtle turn," she says. Now, four years after their marriage, the defense contractor, inventor, and stay-at-home mom doubts she could be happier. "My husband didn't replace any of the things that were missing," she says. "He just kind of gave me the sanctuary to go and find them myself."

Part of seeking positive emotions is being open to them in everyday life. Mindfully approaching sources of good feelings can be more lasting than seeking instant gratification. Distinctions can disappear. "Overeating ice cream and shopping get lumped in with spending time with your family or pursuing an interesting activity," says Fredrickson. People may choose shortcuts with little meaning over activities with positive consequences. A more nuanced appreciation of good feelings—"experiential wisdom," Fredrickson calls it—may help people benefit more from positive emotions. So think: Is ice cream really going to make me feel better for longer than the time it takes to eat it?

Some emotions simply aren't that hard to feel, if you take the time. Take gratitude. Robert Emmons of the University of California-Davis found that people who wrote down five things for which they were grateful in weekly or daily journals were not only more joyful; they were healthier, less stressed, more optimistic, and more likely to help others. You don't have to write things down to be grateful for them, of course, though it helps to make them concrete. During difficult times, "I just tend to focus on the things I'm grateful for and the parts of life that are good," says Sean David Griffiths, 38, a project officer at the Centers for Disease Control and Prevention in Atlanta. And gratitude could help ward off mindless materialism, says Emmons. "When you don't appreciate stuff is when you get rid of it and get something else."

Researchers are also finding more positive emotions than once were thought to exist. Anyone who has witnessed a touching good deed will recognize the heart-warming tingling in the chest that follows. Psychologist Jonathan Haidt of the University of Virginia dubbed this uplifting emotion "elevation," and finds that it makes people want to be kind. Such emotions break down mental barriers and help people see the world in new ways. Even mild feelings of elevation can change minds. Haidt found that students who watched a documentary about Mother Teresa were more interested in activities like volunteer work. (In contrast, the subjects who watched clips of *America's Funniest Home Videos* were interested in self-focused activities like watching TV and eating.)

The feeling of hope is one reason spirituality may correlate with well-being. Hope fosters optimism, and faith is, by definition, hope for the future. And the churchgoing form of faith can be a built-in social support network. This is not to say that atheists can't be happy, but it helps explain why so many do find happiness in faith, and why researchers continue to find connections between faith, optimism, and physical health.

Teaching positive. Nurturing optimism is a key way to help hope and happiness flourish. Optimism predisposes people toward positive emotions, whereas pessimism is a petri dish for depression. Over 20 years ago, Seligman and his colleagues developed a method to teach optimism by helping people recognize and dispute inaccurate thoughts. Called "learned optimism" (and outlined in the book of the same name), they found it could inoculate against depression as well. Teaching optimistic thinking styles to middle schoolers lowered the occurrence of depression as the children aged. Even optimistic children grew happier. "These are sticky skills," says Karen Reivich, codirector of the Penn Resiliency Project. "Once you start using them, you feel better, and you keep using them."

The skills of learned optimism are based on findings that pessimists blame themselves for problems, figure they will last forever, and let them invade every corner of their lives. Good events are freak occurrences. Optimists look for outside causes of bad events and assume they will be fleeting—but take credit for good events and bet they'll keep happening. (Because optimism tends to act as a self-fulfilling prophecy, they often do.) By learning new ways to explain events, pessimists can become more optimistic and more resilient, leaving them better equipped to appreciate the good and cope with the bad. Today, these skills are taught in Pennsylvania schools by teachers trained through Adaptiv Learning Systems, which also offers a more grown-up version to the corporate world.

One of the most positive states of all is easy enough to come by—if you're willing to concentrate. Dubbed "flow" by psychologist Mihaly Csikszentmihalyi, director of the Quality of Life Research Center in Claremont, Calif., it's the single-minded focus of athletes and artists, scientists and writers, or anyone doing anything that poses a challenge and demands full attention. People in flow are too busy to think about happiness, but afterward they think of the experience as incredibly positive. And it's followed by well-earned contentment.

People find flow in myriad ways—any hobbyist or athlete can tell you that. "The secret to my happiness isn't a secret at all," says 19-year-old Jason Vincens, a sophomore at the University of Illinois. "I found something I love and I'm doing it." He has been wrestling competitively since sixth grade. When he wrestles, he doesn't worry about anything else. Afterward, he doesn't have the energy. But you don't have to take up tennis or the violin to find flow: A discussion with good friends can do the trick.

The paradox of flow is that many people have it, but don't appreciate it. Csikszentmihalyi is endlessly puzzled that adults and teenagers feel more creative and excited while working but would rather be doing something else. "I think it's basically a set of assumptions for many people, that work is something that we do simply for our paycheck," he says. So rather than enjoy it, people tend to rush home and watch TV, which rarely provides much pleasure. It's the same principle that causes people to put off activities they enjoy, but which require effort, such as swimming laps.

With age, serenity. Wait around if you must, as some research suggests that people grow happier with age. You don't have the high highs of youth, but neither do you have the low lows. Older people often pursue goals less out of guilt or social pressure and more for their own satisfaction. Also, age often brings wisdom, which adds depth to happiness. You could think of happiness growing out, rather than up.

And yet the stereotype that happy people are shallow persists. "Me being a chronically happy person doesn't mean that I haven't had some real down spells," says Lars Thorn, 24, who works in marketing in Manchester, Vt. During a difficult breakup, he told a friend he was feeling terrible. "And she said, 'Oh, no you're not—you're Lars!'" he recalls. "I was perceived as being a cardboard cutout of a person with no real emotion." But new research suggests happy people may be more realistic than unhappy folks. Psychologist Lisa Aspinwall of the University of Utah finds that optimists are more open to negative information about themselves than pessimists.

Positive mood gives them the resources to process bad news. Optimists are also more likely to accept what they cannot change and move on, says Aspinwall. Indeed, she says, they have an intuitive grasp of the Serenity Prayer, which asks for the wisdom to know the difference between what one can and cannot change.

There's no disputing that positive psychology's findings echo the exhortations of ancient wisdom, and let's face it—Oprah. Be grateful and kind and true to yourself. Find meaning in life. Seek silver linings. But then, what did you expect—be mean to children and animals?

So are people just not listening to their grandmothers and gurus? Psychologist Laura King of the University of Missouri has found that people at least say they know these things and consistently rate meaning and happiness above money. But in a study with colleague Christie Scollon, she found that people were all for meaning, yet most said they didn't want to work for it. Other evidence echoes her findings: People *say* one thing but do another. "One of the problems," says King, "might be that people don't understand that lives of happiness and meaning probably involve some hard work."

Will people work to learn happiness? Positive psychologists think that if they can tease out the best in people, happiness will follow. To Seligman, happiness is "the emotion that arises when we do something that stems from our strengths and virtues." And those, anyone can cultivate. "There's no set point for honesty," he says. The idea that happiness is the sum of what's best in people may sound suspiciously simple, but it's a whole lot easier than finding that happy man's shirt.

SPIRITUALITY

WHAT IT DOES: People with some form of spirtual belief (not just religion) are often happier and more optimistic.
WHY IT WORKS: Possibly because it can promote hope and social support. **Michael Lee** started Lighthouse, a faith-sharing group. ...he prays with his wife, **Agatha Chung**, at a meeting.

From *U.S. News & World Report,* September 3, 2001, pp. 46-55. © 2001 by U.S. News & World Report, L.P. Reprinted by permission.

Glossary

This glossary of psychology terms is included to provide you with a convenient and ready reference as you encounter general terms in your study of psychology and personal growth and behavior that are unfamiliar or require a review. It is not intended to be comprehensive, but taken together with the many definitions included in the articles themselves, it should prove to be quite useful.

abnormal behavior Behavior that contributes to maladaptiveness, is considered deviant by the culture, or that leads to personal psychological distress.

absolute threshold The minimum amount of physical energy required to produce a sensation.

accommodation Process in cognitive development; involves altering or reorganizing the mental picture to make room for a new experience or idea.

acculturation The process of becoming part of a new cultural environment.

acetylcholine A neurotransmitter involved in memory.

achievement drive The need to attain self-esteem, success, or status. Society's expectations strongly influence the achievement motive.

achievement style The way people behave in achievement situations; achievement styles include the direct, instrumental, and relational styles.

acquired immune deficiency syndrome (AIDS) A fatal disease of the immune system.

acquisition In conditioning, forming associations in first learning a task.

actor-observer bias Tendency to attribute the behavior of other people to internal causes and our own behavior to external causes.

acupuncture Oriental practice involving the insertion of needles into the body to control pain.

adaptation The process of responding to changes in the environment by altering responses to keep a person's behavior appropriate to environmental demands.

adjustment How we react to stress; some change that we make in response to the demands placed upon us.

adrenal glands Endocrine glands involved in stress and energy regulation.

adrenaline A hormone produced by the adrenal glands that is involved in physiological arousal; adrenaline is also called epinephrine.

aggression Behavior intended to harm a member of the same or another species.

agoraphobia Anxiety disorder in which an individual is excessively afraid of places or situations from which it would be difficult or embarrassing to escape.

alarm reaction The first stage of Hans Selye's general adaptation syndrome. The alarm reaction is the immediate response to stress; adrenaline is released and digestion slows. The alarm reaction prepares the body for an emergency.

all-or-none law The principle that states that a neuron only fires when a stimulus is above a certain minimum strength (threshold), and when it fires, it does so at full strength.

alogia Individuals with schizophrenia that show a reduction in speech.

alpha Brain-wave activity that indicates that a person is relaxed and resting quietly; 8–12 Hz.

altered state of consciousness (ASC) A state of consciousness in which there is a redirection of attention, a change in the aspects of the world that occupy a person's thoughts, and a change in the stimuli to which a person responds.

ambivalent attachment Type of infant-parent attachment in which the infant seeks contact but resists once the contact is made.

amphetamine A strong stimulant; increases arousal of the central nervous system.

amygdala A part of the limbic system involved in fear, aggression, and other social behaviors.

anal stage Psychosexual stage during which, according to Sigmund Freud, the child experiences the first restrictions on his or her impulses.

anorexia nervosa Eating disorder in which an individual becomes severely underweight because of self-imposed restrictions on eating.

antidepressants Drugs used to elevate the mood of depressed individuals, presumably by increasing the availability of the neurotransmitters norepinephrine and/or serotonin.

antisocial personality disorder Personality disorder in which individuals who engage in antisocial behavior experience no guilt or anxiety about their actions; sometimes called sociopathy or psychopathy.

anxiety disorder Fairly long-lasting disruption of a person's ability to deal with stress; often accompanied by feelings of fear and apprehension.

applied psychology The area of psychology that is most immediately concerned with helping to solve practical problems; includes clinical and counseling psychology as well as industrial, environmental, and legal psychology.

aptitude test Any test designed to predict what a person with the proper training can accomplish in the future.

archetypes In Carl Jung's personality theory, unconscious universal ideas shared by all humans.

arousal theory Theory that focuses on the energy (arousal) aspect of motivation; it states that we are motivated to initiate behaviors that help to regulate overall arousal level.

asocial phase Phase in attachment development in which the neonate does not distinguish people from objects.

assertiveness training Training that helps individuals stand up for their rights while not denying rights of other people.

assimilation Process in cognitive development; occurs when something new is taken into the child's mental picture.

attachment Process in which the individual shows behaviors that promote proximity with a specific object or person.

attention Process of focusing on particular stimuli in the environment.

attention deficit disorder Hyperactivity; inability to concentrate.

attitude Learned disposition that actively guides us toward specific behaviors; attitudes consist of feelings, beliefs, and behavioral tendencies.

attribution The cognitive process of determining the motives of someone's behavior, and whether they are internal or external.

autism A personality disorder in which a child does not respond socially to people.

autonomic nervous system The part of the peripheral nervous system that carries messages from the central nervous system to the endocrine glands, the smooth muscles controlling the heart, and the primarily involuntary muscles controlling internal processes; includes the sympathetic and parasympathetic nervous systems.

aversion therapy A counterconditioning therapy in which unwanted responses are paired with unpleasant consequences.

avoidance conditioning Learning situation in which a subject avoids a stimulus by learning to respond appropriately before the stimulus begins.

avolition Individuals with schizophrenia who lack motivation to follow through on an activity.

Glossary

backward conditioning A procedure in classical conditioning in which the US is presented and terminated before the termination of the CS; very ineffective procedure.

basal ganglia An area of the forebrain that is important to smooth muscle movement and actions. This area works in conjunction with the midbrain to help us avoid moving in choppy, fragmented ways.

behavior Anything you do or think, including various bodily reactions. Behavior includes physical and mental responses.

behavior genetics How genes influence behavior.

behavior modification Another term for behavior therapy; the modification of behavior through psychological techniques; often the application of conditioning principles to alter behavior.

behaviorism The school of thought founded by John Watson; it studied only observable behavior.

belongingness and love needs Third level of motives in Maslow's hierarchy; includes love and affection, friends, and social contact.

biological motives Motives that have a definite physiological basis and are biologically necessary for individual or species survival.

biological response system Systems of the body that are important in behavioral responding; includes the senses, muscles, endocrine system, and the nervous system.

biological therapy Treatment of behavior problems through biological techniques; major biological therapies include drug therapy, psychosurgery, and electroconvulsive therapy.

bipolar disorder Mood disorder characterized by extreme mood swings from sad depression to joyful mania; sometimes called manic depression.

blinding technique In an experiment, a control for bias in which the assignment of a subject to the experimental or control group is unknown to the subject or experimenter or both (a double-blind experiment).

body dysmorphic disorder Somatoform disorder characterized by a preoccupation with an imaginary defect in the physical appearance of a physically healthy person.

body language Communication through position and movement of the body.

bottom-up processing The psychoanalytic process of understanding communication by listening to words, then interpreting phrases, and finally understanding ideas.

brief psychodynamic therapy A therapy developed for individuals with strong egos to resolve a core conflict.

bulimia nervosa Eating disorder in which an individual eats large amounts of calorie-rich food in a short time and then purges the food by vomiting or using laxatives.

California Psychological Inventory (CPI) An objective personality test used to study normal populations.

Cannon-Bard theory of emotion Theory of emotion that states that the emotional feeling and the physiological arousal occur at the same time.

cardinal traits In Gordon Allport's personality theory, the traits of an individual that are so dominant that they are expressed in everything the person does; few people possess cardinal traits.

catatonic schizophrenia A type of schizophrenia that is characterized by periods of complete immobility and the apparent absence of will to move or speak.

causal attribution Process of determining whether a person's behavior is due to internal or external motives.

central nervous system The part of the human nervous system that interprets and stores messages from the sense organs, decides what behavior to exhibit, and sends appropriate messages to the muscles and glands; includes the brain and spinal cord.

central tendency In statistics, measures of central tendency give a number that represents the entire group or sample.

central traits In Gordon Allport's personality theory, the traits of an individual that form the core of the personality; they are developed through experience.

cerebellum The part of the hindbrain that is involved in balance and muscle coordination.

cerebral cortex The outermost layer of the cerebrum of the brain where higher mental functions occur. The cerebral cortex is divided into sections, or lobes, which control various activities.

cerebrum (cerebral hemisphere) Largest part of the forebrain involved in cognitive functions; the cerebrum consists of two hemispheres connected by the corpus callosum.

chromosome Bodies in the cell nucleus that contain the genes.

chunking Process of combining stimuli in order to increase memory capacity.

classical conditioning The form of learning in which a stimulus is associated with another stimulus that causes a particular response. Sometimes called Pavlovian conditioning or respondent conditioning.

clinical psychology Subfield in which psychologists assess psychological problems and treat people with behavior problems using psychological techniques (called psychotherapy).

cognition Mental processes, such as perception, attention, memory, language, thinking, and problem solving; cognition involves the acquisition, storage, retrieval, and utilization of knowledge.

cognitive behavior therapy A form of behavior therapy that identifies self-defeating attitudes and thoughts in a subject, and then helps the subject to replace these with positive, supportive thoughts.

cognitive development Changes over time in mental processes such as thinking, memory, language, and problem solving.

cognitive dissonance Leon Festinger's theory of attitude change that states that, when people hold two psychologically inconsistent ideas, they experience tension that forces them to reconcile the conflicting ideas.

cognitive expectancy The condition in which an individual learns that certain behaviors lead to particular goals; cognitive expectancy motivates the individual to exhibit goal-directed behaviors.

cognitive learning Type of learning that theorizes that the learner utilizes cognitive structures in memory to make decisions about behaviors.

cognitive psychology The area of psychology that includes the study of mental activities involved in perception, memory, language, thought, and problem solving.

cognitive restructuring The modification of the client's thoughts and perceptions that are contributing to his or her maladjustments.

cognitive therapy Therapy developed by Aaron Beck in which an individual's negative, self-defeating thoughts are restructured in a positive way.

cognitive-motivational-relational theory of emotion A theory of emotion proposed by Richard Lazarus that includes cognitive appraisal, motivational goals, and relationships between an individual and the environment.

collective unconscious Carl Jung's representation of the thoughts shared by all humans.

collectivistic cultures Cultures in which the greatest emphasis is on the loyalty of each individual to the group.

comparative psychology Subfield in which experimental psychologists study and compare the behavior of different species of animals.

compulsions Rituals performed excessively such as checking doors or washing hands to reduce anxiety.

concept formation (concept learning) The development of the ability to respond to common features of categories of objects or events.

concrete operations period Stage in cognitive development, from 7 to 11 years, in which the child's ability to solve problems with reasoning greatly increases.

conditioned response (CR) The response or behavior that occurs when the conditioned stimulus is presented (after the CS has been associated with the US).

conditioned stimulus (CS) An originally neutral stimulus that is associated with an unconditioned stimulus and takes on the latter's capability of eliciting a particular reaction.

conditioned taste aversion (CTA) An aversion to particular tastes associated with stomach distress; usually considered a unique form of classical conditioning because of the extremely long interstimulus intervals involved.

conditioning A term applied to two types of learning (classical and operant). Conditioning refers to the scientific aspect of the type of learning.

conflict Situation that occurs when we experience incompatible demands or desires; the outcome when one individual or group perceives that another individual or group has caused or will cause harm.

conformity Type of social influence in which an individual changes his or her behavior to fit social norms or expectations.

connectionism Recent approach to problem solving; the development of neural connections allows us to think and solve problems.

conscientiousness The dimension in the five-factor personality theory that includes traits such as practical, cautious, serious, reliable, careful, and ambitious; also called dependability.

conscious Being aware of experiencing sensations, thoughts, and feelings at any given point in time.

conscious mind In Sigmund Freud's psychoanalytic theory of personality, the part of personality that we are aware of in everyday life.

consciousness The processing of information at various levels of awareness; state in which a person is aware of sensations, thoughts, and feelings.

consensus In causal attribution, the extent to which other people react as the subject does in a particular situation.

conservation The ability to recognize that something stays the same even if it takes on a different form; Piaget tested conservation of mass, number, length, and volume.

consistency In causal attribution, the extent to which the subject always behaves in the same way in a situation.

consolidation The biological neural process of making memories permanent; possibly short-term memory is electrically coded and long-term memory is chemically coded.

contingency model A theory that specific types of situations need particular types of leaders.

continuum of preparedness Martin Seligman's proposal that animals are biologically prepared to learn certain responses more readily than they are prepared to learn others.

control group Subjects in an experiment who do not receive the independent variable; the control group determines the effectiveness of the independent variable.

conventional morality Level II in Lawrence Kohlberg's theory, in which moral reasoning is based on conformity and social standards.

conversion disorder Somatoform disorder in which a person displays obvious disturbance in the nervous system without a physical basis for the problem.

correlation Statistical technique to determine the degree of relationship that exists between two variables.

counterconditioning A behavior therapy in which an unwanted response is replaced by conditioning a new response that is incompatible with it.

creativity A process of coming up with new or unusual responses to familiar circumstances.

critical period hypothesis Period of time during development in which particular learning or experiences normally occur; if learning does not occur, the individual has a difficult time learning it later.

culture-bound The idea that a test's usefulness is limited to the culture in which it was written and utilized.

cumulative response curve Graphed curve that results when responses for a subject are added to one another over time; if subjects respond once every 5 minutes, they will have a cumulative response curve value of 12 after an hour.

curiosity motive Motive that causes the individual to seek out a certain amount of novelty.

cyclothymia disorder A moderately severe problem with numerous periods of hypomanic episodes and depressive symptoms.

death instinct (also called Thanatos) Freud's term for an instinct that is destructive to the individual or species; aggression is a major expression of death instinct.

decay Theory of forgetting in which sensory impressions leave memory traces that fade away with time.

defense mechanisms Psychological techniques to help protect ourselves from stress and anxiety, to resolve conflicts, and to preserve our self-esteem.

delayed conditioning A procedure in classical conditioning in which the presentation of the CS precedes the onset of the US and the termination of the CS is delayed until the US is presented; most effective procedure.

delusion The holding of obviously false beliefs; for example, imagining someone is trying to kill you.

dendrites The branch-like structures of neurons that extend from the cell body (soma). The dendrites are the receivers of neural impulses (electrical and chemical signals) from the axons of other neurons. Although there are some areas of the body that contain dendrites that can act like axon terminals, releasing neurotransmitters in response to impulses and local voltage changes, most dendrites are the receiving branches of the neuron.

dependent variable In psychology, the behavior or response that is measured; it is dependent on the independent variable.

depersonalization disorder Dissociative disorder in which the individual escapes from his or her own personality by believing that he or she does not exist or that his or her environment is not real.

depolarization Any change in which the internal electrical charge becomes more positive.

depression A temporary emotional state that normal individuals experience or a persistent state that may be considered a psychological disorder. Characterized by sadness and low self-esteem.

descriptive statistics Techniques that help summarize large amounts of data information.

developmental psychology Study of physical and mental growth and behavioral changes in individuals from conception to death.

Diagnostic and Statistical Manual of Mental Disorders (DSM) Published by the American Psychiatric Association in 1952, and revised in 1968, 1980, 1987, and 1994, this manual was provided to develop a set of diagnoses of abnormal behavior patterns.

diffusion of responsibility Finding that groups tend to inhibit helping behavior; responsibility is shared equally by members of the group so that no one individual feels a strong commitment.

disorganized schizophrenia A type of schizophrenia that is characterized by a severe personality disintegration; the individual often displays bizarre behavior.

displacement Defense mechanism by which the individual directs his or her aggression or hostility toward a person or object other than the one it should be directed toward; in Freud's dream theory, the process of reassigning emotional feelings from one object to another one.

dissociative disorder Psychological disorder that involves a disturbance in the memory, consciousness, or identity of an individual; types include multiple personality disorder, depersonalization disorder, psychogenic amnesia, and psychogenic fugue.

dissociative fugue Individuals who have lost their memory, relocated to a new geographical area, and started a new life as someone else.

dissociative identity disorder (multiple personality disorder) Dissociative disorder in which several personalities are present in the same individual.

distinctiveness In causal attribution, the extent to which the subject reacts the same way in other situations.

Down syndrome Form of mental retardation caused by having three number 21 chromosomes (trisomy 21).

Glossary

dream analysis Psychoanalytic technique in which a patient's dreams are reviewed and analyzed to discover true feelings.

drive Motivational concept used to describe the internal forces that push an organism toward a goal; sometimes identified as psychological arousal arising from a physiological need.

dyssomnia Sleep disorder in which the chief symptom is a disturbance in the amount and quality of sleep; they include insomnia and hypersomnia.

dysthymic disorder Mood disorder in which the person suffers moderate depression much of the time for at least two years.

ego Sigmund Freud's term for an individual's sense of reality.

egocentric Seeing the world only from your perspective.

eidetic imagery Photographic memory; ability to recall great detail accurately after briefly viewing something.

Electra complex The Freudian idea that the young girl feels inferior to boys because she lacks a penis.

electroconvulsive therapy (ECT) A type of biological therapy in which electricity is applied to the brain in order to relieve severe depression.

emotion A response to a stimulus that involves physiological arousal, subjective feeling, cognitive interpretation, and overt behavior.

empiricism The view that behavior is learned through experience.

encoding The process of putting information into the memory system.

encounter group As in a sensitivity training group, a therapy where people become aware of themselves in meeting others.

endorphins Several neuropeptides that function as neurotransmitters. The opiate-like endorphins are involved in pain, reinforcement, and memory.

engram The physical memory trace or neural circuit that holds memory; also called memory trace.

episodic memory Highest memory system; includes information about personal experiences.

Eros Sigmund Freud's term for an instinct that helps the individual or species survive; also called life instinct.

esteem needs Fourth level of motives in Abraham Maslow's hierarchy; includes high evaluation of oneself, self-respect, self-esteem, and respect of others.

eustress Stress that results from pleasant and satisfying experiences; earning a high grade or achieving success produces eustress.

excitement phase First phase in the human sexual response cycle; the beginning of sexual arousal.

experimental group Subjects in an experiment who receive the independent variable.

experimental psychology Subfield in which psychologists research the fundamental causes of behavior. Many experimental psychologists conduct experiments in basic research.

experimenter bias Source of potential error in an experiment from the action or expectancy of the experimenter; might influence the experimental results in ways that mask the true outcome.

external locus of control In Julian Rotter's personality theory, the perception that reinforcement is independent of a person's behavior.

extraversion The dimension in the five-factor personality theory that includes traits such as sociability, talkativeness, boldness, fun-lovingness, adventurousness, and assertiveness; also called surgency. The personality concept of Carl Jung in which the personal energy of the individual is directed externally.

factor analysis A statistical procedure used to determine the relationship among variables.

false memories Memories believed to be real, but the events never occurred.

fast mapping A process by which children can utilize a word after a single exposure.

fetal alcohol syndrome (FAS) Condition in which defects in the newborn child are caused by the mother's excessive alcohol intake.

five-factor model of personality tracts A trait theory of personality that includes the factors of extraversion, agreeableness, conscientiousness, emotional stability, and openness.

fixed action pattern (FAP) Unlearned, inherited, stereotyped behaviors that are shown by all members of a species; term used in ethology.

fixed interval (FI) schedule Schedule of reinforcement where the subject receives reinforcement for a correct response given after a specified time interval.

fixed ratio (FR) schedule Schedule of reinforcement in which the subject is reinforced after a certain number of responses.

flashbulb memory Memory of an event that is so important that significant details are vividly remembered for life.

forgetting In memory, not being able to retrieve the original learning. The part of the original learning that cannot be retrieved is said to be forgotten.

formal operations period Period in cognitive development; at 11 years, the adolescent begins abstract thinking and reasoning. This period continues throughout the rest of life.

free association Psychoanalytic technique in which the patient says everything that comes to mind.

free recall A verbal learning procedure in which the order of presentation of the stimuli is varied and the subject can learn the items in any order.

frequency theory of hearing Theory of hearing that states that the frequency of vibrations at the basilar membrane determines the frequency of firing of neurons carrying impulses to the brain.

frustration A cause of stress that results from the blocking of a person's goal-oriented behavior.

frustration-drive theory of aggression Theory of aggression that states that it is caused by frustration.

functionalism School of thought that studied the functional value of consciousness and behavior.

fundamental attribution error Attribution bias in which people overestimate the role of internal disposition and underestimate the role of external situation.

gate-control theory of pain Theory of pain that proposes that there is a gate that allows pain impulses to travel from the spinal cord to the brain.

gender-identity disorder (GID) Incongruence between assigned sex and gender identity.

gender-identity/role Term that incorporates gender identity (the private perception of one's sex) and gender role (the public expression of one's gender identity).

gene The basic unit of heredity; the gene is composed of deoxyribonucleic acid (DNA).

general adaptation syndrome (GAS) Hans Selye's theory of how the body responds to stress over time. GAS includes alarm reaction, resistance, and exhaustion.

generalized anxiety disorder Anxiety disorder in which the individual lives in a state of constant severe tension, continuous fear, and apprehension.

genetics The study of heredity; genetics is the science of discovering how traits are passed along generations.

genotype The complete set of genes inherited by an individual from his or her parents.

Gestalt therapy Insight therapy designed to help people become more aware of themselves in the here and now and to take responsibility for their own actions.

grandiose delusion Distortion of reality; one's belief that he or she is extremely important or powerful.

group therapy Treatment of several patients at the same time.

groupthink When group members are so committed to, and optimistic about, the group that they feel it is invulnerable; they become so concerned with maintaining consensus that criticism is muted.

GSR (galvanic skin response) A measure of autonomic nervous system activity; a slight electric current is passed over the skin, and the more nervous a subject is, the easier the current will flow.

hallucinations A sensory impression reported when no external stimulus exists to justify the report; often hallucinations are a symptom of mental illness.

hallucinogens Psychedelic drugs that result in hallucinations at high doses, and other effects on behavior and perception in mild doses.

halo effect The finding that once we form a general impression of someone, we tend to interpret additional information about the person in a consistent manner.

Hawthorne effect The finding that behavior can be influenced just by participation in a research study.

health psychology Field of psychology that studies psychological influences on people's health, including how they stay healthy, why they become ill, and how their behavior relates to their state of health.

heuristic Problem-solving strategy; a person tests solutions most likely to be correct.

hierarchy of needs Abraham Maslow's list of motives in humans, arranged from the biological to the uniquely human.

hippocampus Brain structure in the limbic system that is important in learning and memory.

homeostasis The state of equilibrium that maintains a balance in the internal body environment.

hormones Chemicals produced by the endocrine glands that regulate activity of certain bodily processes.

humanistic psychology Psychological school of thought that believes that people are unique beings who cannot be broken down into parts.

hyperphagia Disorder in which the individual continues to eat until he or she is obese; can be caused by damage to ventromedial hypothalamus.

hypersomnia Sleep disorder in which an individual falls asleep at inappropriate times; narcolepsy is a form of hypersomnia.

hypnosis Altered state of consciousness characterized by heightened suggestibility.

hypochondriasis Somatoform disorder in which the individual is obsessed with fears of having a serious medical disease.

hypothalamus Part of the brain's limbic system; involved in motivational behaviors, including eating, drinking, and sex.

hypothesis In the scientific method, an educated guess or prediction about future observable events.

iconic memory Visual information that is encoded into the sensory memory store.

id Sigmund Freud's representation of the basic instinctual drives; the id always seeks pleasure.

identification The process in which children adopt the attitudes, values, and behaviors of their parents.

identity diffusion In Marcia's adolescent identity theory, the status of individuals who have failed to make a commitment to values and roles.

illusion An incorrect perception that occurs when sensation is distorted.

imitation The copying of another's behavior; learned through the process of observation.

impression formation Developing an evaluation of another person from your perceptions; first, or initial, impressions are often very important.

imprinting A form of early learning in which birds follow a moving stimulus (often the mother); may be similar to attachment in mammals.

independent variable The condition in an experiment that is controlled and manipulated by the experimenter; it is a stimulus that will cause a response.

indiscriminate attachment phase Stage of attachment in which babies prefer humans to nonhumans, but do not discriminate among individual people.

individuation Carl Jung's concept of the process leading to the unification of all parts of the personality.

inferential statistics Techniques that help researchers make generalizations about a finding based on a limited number of subjects.

inferiority complex Adler's personality concept that states that because children are dependent on adults and cannot meet the standards set for themselves they feel inferior.

inhibition Restraint of an impulse, desire, activity, or drive.

insight A sudden grasping of the means necessary to achieve a goal; important in the Gestalt approach to problem solving.

insight therapy Therapy based on the assumption that behavior is abnormal because people do not adequately understand the motivation causing their behavior.

instinct Highly stereotyped behavior common to all members of a species that often appears in virtually complete form in the absence of any obvious opportunities to learn it.

instrumental conditioning Operant conditioning.

intelligence Capacity to learn and behave adaptively.

intelligence quotient (IQ) An index of a person's performance on an intelligence test relative to others in the culture; ratio of a person's mental age to chronological age.

interference Theory of forgetting in which information that was learned before (proactive interference) or after (retroactive interference) causes the learner to be unable to remember the material of interest.

internal locus of control In Rotter's personality theory, the perception that reinforcement is contingent upon behavior.

interstimulus interval Time interval between two stimuli; in classical conditioning, it is the elapsed time between the CS and the US.

intrinsic motivation Motivation inside the individual; we do something because we receive satisfaction from it.

introspection Method in which a subject gives a self report of his or her immediate experience.

introversion The personality concept of Carl Jung in which the personal energy of the individual is directed inward; characterized by introspection, seriousness, inhibition, and restraint.

James-Lange theory of emotion Theory of emotion that states that the physiological arousal and behavior come before the subjective experience of an emotion.

kinesthesis The sense of bodily movement.

labeling of arousal Experiments suggest that an individual experiencing physical arousal that cannot be explained will interpret those feelings in terms of the situation she or he is in and will use environmental and contextual cues.

language acquisition device (LAD) Hypothesized biological structure that accounts for the relative ease of acquiring language, according to Noam Chomsky.

latent dream content In Sigmund Freud's dream theory, the true thoughts in the unconsciousness; the true meaning of the dream.

latent learning Learning that occurs when an individual acquires knowledge of something but does not show it until motivated to do so.

law of effect Edward Thorndike's law that if a response produces satisfaction it will be repeated; reinforcement.

learned helplessness Condition in which a person learns that his or her behavior has no effect on his or her environment; when an individual gives up and stops trying.

learned social motives Social motives that are learned; include achievement and affiliation.

learning The relatively permanent change in behavior or behavioral ability of an individual that occurs as a result of experience.

Glossary

learning styles The preferences students have for learning; theories of learning styles include personality differences, styles of information processing, and instructional preferences.

life instinct (also called Eros) Sigmund Freud's term for an instinct that helps the individual or species survive; sex is the major expression of life instinct.

life structure In Daniel Levinson's theory of adult personality development, the underlying pattern of an individual's life at any particular time; seasonal cycles include preadulthood, early adulthood, middle adulthood, and late adulthood.

linguistic relativity hypothesis Proposal that the perception of reality differs according to the language of the observer.

locus of control Julian Rotter's theory in which a person's beliefs about reinforcement are classified as internal or external.

long-term memory The permanent memory where rehearsed information is stored.

love An emotion characterized by knowing, liking, and becoming intimate with someone.

low-ball procedure The compliance technique of presenting an attractive proposal to someone and then switching it to a more unattractive proposal.

magic number 7 The finding that most people can remember about seven items of information for a short time (in short-term memory).

magnetic resonance imaging (MRI) A method of studying brain activity using magnetic field imaging.

major depressive disorder Severe mood disorder in which a person experiences one or more major depressive episodes; sometimes referred to simply as depression.

maladjustment Condition that occurs when a person utilizes inappropriate abilities to respond to demands placed upon him or her.

manic depressive reaction A form of mental illness marked by alternations of extreme phases of elation (manic phase) and depression.

manifest dream content In Sigmund Freud's dream theory, what is remembered about a dream upon waking; a disguised representation of the unconscious wishes.

maturation The genetically controlled process of growth that results in orderly changes in behavior.

mean The arithmetic average, in which the sum of scores is divided by the number of scores.

median The middle score in a group of scores that are arranged from lowest to highest.

meditation The practice of some form of relaxed concentration while ignoring other sensory stimuli.

memory The process of storing information so that it can be retrieved and used later.

memory attributes The critical features of an event that are used when the experience is encoded or retrieved.

mental age The age level on which a person is capable of performing; used in determining intelligence.

mental set Condition in which a person's thinking becomes so standardized that he or she approaches new problems in fixed ways.

microexpressions Facial expressions that last a fraction of a second. Since microexpressions do not last long, they go undetected in our everyday lives. Microexpressions are a type of nonverbal communication.

Minnesota Multiphasic Personality Inventory (MMPI-2) An objective personality test that was originally devised to identify personality disorders.

mnemonic technique Method of improving memory by combining and relating chunks of information.

modeling A process of learning by imitation in a therapeutic situation.

mood disorder Psychological disorder in which a person experiences a severe disruption in mood or emotional balance.

moral development Development of individuals as they adopt their society's standards of right and wrong; development of awareness of ethical behavior.

motivated forgetting (repression) Theory that suggests that people want to forget unpleasant events.

motivation The forces that initiate and direct behavior, and the variables that determine the intensity and persistence of the behavior.

motivator needs In Federick Herzberg's theory, the factors that lead to job satisfaction; they include responsibility, the nature of the work, advancement, and recognition.

motive Anything that arouses the individual and directs his or her behavior toward some goal. Three categories of motives include biological, stimulus, and learned social.

Müller-Lyer illusion A well-known illusion, in which two horizontal lines have end lines either going in or out; the line with the end lines going in appears longer.

multiple approach-avoidance conflict Conflict that occurs when an individual has two or more goals, both of which have positive and negative aspects.

multiple attachment phase Later attachment stage in which the baby begins to form attachments to people other than the primary caretaker.

multiple intelligences Howard Gardner's theory that there exists several different kinds of intelligence.

Myers-Briggs Type Indicator (MBTI) Objective personality test based on Carl Jung's type theory.

narcotic analgesics Drugs that have an effect on the body similar to morphine; these relieve pain and suppress coughing.

naturalistic observation Research method in which behavior of people or animals in their normal environment is accurately recorded.

Necker cube A visual illusion. The Necker cube is a drawing of a cube designed so that it is difficult to determine which side is toward you.

negative reinforcement Removing something unpleasant to increase the probability that the preceding behavior will be repeated.

NEO Personality Inventory (NEO-PI) An objective personality test developed by Paul Costa Jr. and Robert McCrae to measure the five major factors in personality; consists of 181 questions.

neodissociation theory Idea that consciousness can be split into several streams of thought that are partially independent of each other.

neuron A specialized cell that functions to conduct messages throughout the body.

neurosis A Freudian term that was used to describe abnormal behavior caused by anxiety; it has been eliminated from *DSM-IV*.

neutral stimulus A stimulus that does not cause the response of interest; the individual may show some response to the stimulus but not the associated behavior.

norm A sample of scores representative of a population.

normal curve When scores of a large number of random cases are plotted on a graph, they often fall into a bell-shaped curve; as many cases on the curve are above the mean as below it.

observational learning In social learning theory, learning by observing someone else behave; people observe and imitate in learning socialization.

obsessions Fears that involve the inability to control impulses.

obsessive compulsive disorder Anxiety disorder in which the individual has repetitive thoughts (obsessions) that lead to constant urges (compulsions) to engage in meaningless rituals.

object permanence The ability to realize that objects continue to exist even if we can no longer see them.

Oedipus complex The Freudian idea that the young boy has sexual feelings for his mother and is jealous of his father and must identify with his father to resolve the conflict.

olfaction The smell sense.

openness The dimension in the five-factor personality theory that includes traits such as imagination, creativity, perception, knowledge, artistic ability, curiosity, and analytical ability; also called intellect.

operant conditioning Form of learning in which behavior followed by reinforcement (satisfaction) increases in frequency.

opponent-process theory Theory that when one emotion is experienced, the other is suppressed.

optimum level of arousal Motivation theory that states that the individual will seek a level of arousal that is comfortable.

organic mental disorders Psychological disorders that involve physical damage to the nervous system; can be caused by disease or by an accident.

organizational psychology Area of industrial psychology that focuses on worker attitudes and motivation; derived primarily from personality and social psychology.

orgasm The climax of intense sexual excitement; release from building sexual tension, usually accompanied by ejaculation in men.

paired-associate learning A verbal learning procedure in which the subject is presented with a series of pairs of items to be remembered.

panic disorder Anxiety disorder characterized by the occurrence of specific periods of intense fear.

paranoid schizophrenia A type of schizophrenia in which the individual often has delusions of grandeur and persecution, thinking that someone is out to get him or her.

partial reinforcement Any schedule of reinforcement in which reinforcement follows only some of the correct responses.

partial reinforcement effect The finding that partial reinforcement produces a response that takes longer to extinguish than continuous reinforcement.

pattern recognition Memory process in which information attended to is compared with information already permanently stored in memory.

Pavlovian conditioning A bond or association between a neutral stimulus and a response; this type of learning is called classical conditioning.

perception The active process in which the sensory information that is carried through the nervous system to the brain is organized and interpreted; the interpretation of sensation.

persecutory delusion A delusion in which the individual has a distortion of reality; the belief that other people are out to get him or her.

person perception The process of using the information we gather in forming impressions of people to make evaluations of others.

personal unconscious Carl Jung's representation of the individual's repressed thoughts and memories.

personality disorder Psychological disorder in which there are problems in the basic personality structure of the individual.

phantom-limb pain Phenomenon in which people who have lost an arm or leg feel pain in the missing limb.

phobias Acute excessive fears of specific situations or objects that have no convincing basis in reality.

physiological needs First level of motives in Abraham Maslow's hierarchy; includes the biological needs of hunger, thirst, sex, exercise, and rest.

placebo An inert or inactive substance given to control subjects to test for bias effects.

plateau phase Second phase in the human sexual response cycle, during which the physiological arousal becomes more intense.

pleasure principle In Freudian theory, the idea that the instinctual drives of the id unconsciously and impulsively seek immediate pleasure.

positive reinforcement Presenting a subject something pleasant to increase the probability that the preceding behavior will be repeated.

Positron Emission Tomography (PET) Similar to the MRI, this method enables psychologists and doctors to study the brain (or any other living tissue) without surgery. PET uses radioactive glucose (instead of a strong magnetic field) to help study activity and locate structures in the body.

postconventional morality Level III in Lawrence Kohlberg's theory, in which moral reasoning is based on personal standards and beliefs; highest level of moral thinking.

posttraumatic stress disorder (PTSD) Condition that can occur when a person experiences a severely distressing event; characterized by constant memories of the event, avoidance of anything associated with it, and general arousal.

Prägnanz (law of) Gestalt psychology law that states that people have a tendency to group stimuli according to rules, and that people do this whenever possible.

preconscious mind In Sigmund Freud's psychoanalytic theory of personality, the part of personality that contains information that we have learned but that we are not thinking about at the present time.

preconventional morality Level I of Lawrence Kohlberg's theory, in which moral reasoning is largely due to the expectation of rewards and punishments.

prejudice An unjustified fixed, usually negative, way of thinking about a person or object.

Premack principle Principle that states that, of any two responses, the one that is more likely to occur can be used to reinforce the response that is less likely to occur.

preoperational thought period Period in cognitive development; from two to seven years, the period during which the child learns to represent the environment with objects and symbols.

primary appraisal Activity of determining whether a new stimulus event is positive, neutral, or negative; first step in appraisal of stress.

primary narcissism A Freudian term that refers to the oral phase before the ego has developed; the individual constantly seeks pleasure.

primary reinforcement Reinforcement that is effective without having been associated with other reinforcers; sometimes called unconditioned reinforcement.

probability (p) In inferential statistics, the likelihood that the difference between the experimental and control groups is due to the independent variable.

procedural memory The most basic type of long-term memory; involves the formation of associations between stimuli and responses.

projection Defense mechanism in which a person attributes his or her unacceptable characteristics or motives to others rather than himself or herself.

projective personality test A personality test that presents ambiguous stimuli to which subjects are expected to respond with projections of their own personality.

proximity Closeness in time and space. In perception, it is the Gestalt perceptual principle in which stimuli next to one another are included together.

psyche According to Carl Jung, the thoughts and feelings (conscious and unconscious) of an individual.

psychoactive drug A drug that produces changes in behavior and cognition through modification of conscious awareness.

psychoanalysis The school of thought founded by Sigmund Freud that stressed unconscious motivation. In therapy, a patient's unconscious motivation is intensively explored in order to bring repressed conflicts up to consciousness; psychoanalysis usually takes a long time to accomplish.

psychobiology (also called biological psychology or physiological psychology) The subfield of experimental psychology concerned with the influence of heredity and the biological response systems on behavior.

psychogenic amnesia A dissociative disorder in which an individual loses his or her sense of identity.

psychogenic fugue A dissociative disorder in which an individual loses his or her sense of identity and goes to a new geographic location, forgetting all of the unpleasant emotions connected with the old life.

Glossary

psychographics A technique used in consumer psychology to identify the attitudes of buyers and their preferences for particular products.

psycholinguistics The psychological study of how people convert the sounds of a language into meaningful symbols that can be used to communicate with others.

psychological dependence Situation in which a person craves a drug even though it is not biologically needed by the body.

psychological disorder A diagnosis of abnormal behavior; syndrome of abnormal adjustment, classified in *DSM*.

psychological types Carl Jung's term for different personality profiles; Jung combined two attitudes and four functions to produce eight psychological types.

psychopharmacology Study of effects of psychoactive drugs on behavior.

psychophysics An area of psychology in which researchers compare the physical energy of a stimulus with the sensation reported.

psychosexual stages Sigmund Freud's theoretical stages in personality development.

psychosomatic disorders A variety of body reactions that are closely related to psychological events.

psychotherapy Treatment of behavioral disorders through psychological techniques; major psychotherapies include insight therapy, behavior therapy, and group therapy.

psychotic disorders The more severe categories of abnormal behavior.

puberty Sexual maturation; the time at which the individual is able to perform sexually and to reproduce.

quantitative trait loci (QTLs) Genes that collectively contribute to a trait for high intelligence.

rational-emotive therapy A cognitive behavior modification technique in which a person is taught to identify irrational, self-defeating beliefs and then to overcome them.

reaction formation Defense mechanism in which a person masks an unconsciously distressing or unacceptable trait by assuming an opposite attitude or behavior pattern.

reality principle In Freudian theory, the idea that the drives of the ego try to find socially acceptable ways to gratify the id.

reciprocal determinism The concept proposed by Albert Bandura that the behavior, the individual, and the situation interact and influence each other.

reciprocal inhibition Concept of Joseph Wolpe that states that it is possible to break the bond between anxiety provoking stimuli and responses manifesting anxiety by facing those stimuli in a state antagonistic to anxiety.

reflex An automatic movement that occurs in direct response to a stimulus.

regression Defense mechanism in which a person retreats to an earlier, more immature form of behavior.

reinforcement Any event that increases the probability that the behavior that precedes it will be repeated; also called a reinforcer; similar to a reward.

reinforcement therapy A behavior therapy in which reinforcement is used to modify behavior. Techniques in reinforcement therapy include shaping, extinction, and token economy.

REM Sleep There are two main categories of sleep, Non-Rapid Eye Movement Sleep (NREM; which contains stages 1–4; basically everything except REM), and Rapid Eye Movement Sleep (REM). REM sleep is a sleep period during which your brain is very active, and your eyes move in a sharp, back-and-forth motion as opposed to a slower, more rolling fashion that occurs in other stages of sleep. People often believe mistakenly that humans only dream during REM sleep, although humans also dream during slow wave sleep (stages 3 and 4). However it is true that the majority of our dreaming occurs during REM sleep.

repression Defense mechanism in which painful memories and unacceptable thoughts and motives are conveniently forgotten so that they will not have to be dealt with.

residual schizophrenia Type of schizophrenia in which the individual currently does not have symptoms but has had a schizophrenic episode in the past.

resistance Psychoanalytic term used when a patient avoids a painful area of conflict.

resolution phase The last phase in the human sexual response cycle; the time after orgasm when the body gradually returns to the unaroused state.

Restricted Environmental Stimulation Technique (REST) Research technique in which environmental stimuli available to an individual are reduced drastically; formerly called sensory deprivation.

retrograde amnesia Forgetting information recently learned because of a disruptive stimulus such as an electric shock.

reversible figure In perception, a situation in which the figure and ground seem to reverse themselves; an illusion in which objects alternate as the main figure.

Rorschach Inkblot Test A projective personality test in which subjects are asked to discuss what they see in cards containing blots of ink.

safety needs Second level of motives in Abraham Maslow's hierarchy; includes security, stability, dependency, protection, freedom from fear and anxiety, and the need for structure and order.

Schachter-Singer theory of emotion Theory of emotion that states that we interpret our arousal according to our environment and label our emotions accordingly.

scheme A unit of knowledge that the person possesses; used in Jean Piaget's cognitive development theory.

schizophrenia Severe psychotic disorder that is characterized by disruptions in thinking, perception, and emotion.

scientific method An attitude and procedure that scientists use to conduct research. The steps include stating the problem, forming the hypothesis, collecting the information, evaluating the information, and drawing conclusions.

secondary appraisal In appraisal of stress, this is the evaluation that an individual's abilities and resources are sufficient to meet the demands of a stressful event.

secondary reinforcement Reinforcement that is effective only after it has been associated with a primary reinforcer; also called conditioned reinforcement.

secondary traits In Gordon Allport's personality theory, the less important situation-specific traits that help round out personality; they include attitudes, skills, and behavior patterns.

secure attachment Type of infant-parent attachment in which the infant actively seeks contact with the parent.

self-actualization A humanistic term describing the state in which all of an individual's capacities are developed fully. Fifth and highest level of motives in Abraham Maslow's hierarchy, this level, the realization of one's potential, is rarely reached.

self-efficacy An individual's sense of self-worth and success in adjusting to the world.

self-esteem A measurement of how people view themselves. People who view themselves favorably have good self-esteem whereas people who view themselves negatively have poor self-esteem. Self-esteem affects a person's behavior dramatically.

self-evaluation maintenance model (SEM) Tesser's theory of how we maintain a positive self-image despite the success of others close to us.

self-handicapping strategy A strategy that people use to prepare for failure; people behave in ways that produce obstacles to success so that when they do fail they can place the blame on the obstacle.

self-serving bias An attribution bias in which an individual attributes success to his or her own behavior and failure to external environmental causes.

semantic memory Type of long-term memory that can use cognitive activities, such as everyday knowledge.

sensation The passive process in which stimuli are received by sense receptors and transformed into neural impulses that can be carried through the nervous system; first stage in becoming aware of environment.

sensitivity training group (T-group) Therapy group that has the goal of making participants more aware of themselves and their ideas.

sensorimotor period Period in cognitive development; the first two years, during which the infant learns to coordinate sensory experiences with motor activities.

sensory adaptation Tendency of the sense organs to adjust to continuous stimulation by reducing their functioning; a stimulus that once caused sensation and no longer does.

sensory deprivation Situation in which normal environmental sensory stimuli available to an individual are reduced drastically; also called REST (Restricted Environmental Stimulation Technique).

serial learning A verbal learning procedure in which the stimuli are always presented in the same order, and the subject has to learn them in the order in which they are presented.

sex roles The set of behaviors and attitudes that are determined to be appropriate for one sex or the other in a society.

shaping In operant conditioning, the gradual process of reinforcing behaviors that get closer to some final desired behavior. Shaping is also called successive approximation.

short-term memory Part of the memory system in which information is only stored for roughly 30 seconds. Information can be maintained longer with the use of such techniques as rehearsal. To retain the information for extended periods of time, it must be consolidated into long-term memory where it can then be retrieved. The capacity of short-term memory is also limited. Most people can only store roughly 7 chunks of information plus or minus 2. This is why phone numbers only have seven digits.

signal detection theory Research approach in which the subject's behavior in detecting a threshold is treated as a form of decision making.

similarity Gestalt principle in which similar stimuli are perceived as a unit.

simple phobia Excessive irrational fear that does not fall into other specific categories, such as fear of dogs, insects, snakes, or closed-in places.

simultaneous conditioning A procedure in classical conditioning in which the CS and US are presented at exactly the same time.

Sixteen Personality Factor Questionnaire (16PF) Raymond Cattell's personality test to measure source traits.

Skinner box B. F. Skinner's animal cage with a lever that triggers reinforcement for a subject.

sleep terror disorder (pavor nocturnus) Nonrapid eye-movement (NREM) sleep disorder in which the person (usually a child) wakes up screaming and terrified, but cannot recall why.

sleepwalking (somnambulism) NREM sleep disorder in which the person walks in his or her sleep.

social cognition The process of understanding other people and ourselves by forming and utilizing information about the social world.

social cognitive theory Albert Bandura's approach to personality that proposes that individuals use observation, imitation, and cognition to develop personality.

social comparison Theory proposed by Leon Festinger that we tend to compare our behavior to others to ensure that we are conforming.

social exchange theory Theory of interpersonal relationships that states that people evaluate the costs and rewards of their relationships and act accordingly.

social facilitation Phenomenon in which the presence of others increases dominant behavior patterns in an individual; Richard Zajonc's theory states that the presence of others enhances the emission of the dominant response of the individual.

social influence Influence designed to change the attitudes or behavior of other people; includes conformity, compliance, and obedience.

social learning theory An approach to social psychology that emphasizes observation and modeling; it states that reinforcement is involved in motivation rather than in learning, and proposes that aggression is a form of learned behavior.

social phobia Excessive irrational fear and embarrassment when interacting with other people. Social phobias may include fear of assertive behavior, fear of making mistakes, or fear of public speaking.

social psychology The study of how an individual's behavior, thoughts, and feelings are influenced by other people.

sociobiology Study of the genetic basis of social behavior.

sociocultural Emphasizes the importance of culture, gender, and ethnicity in how we think, feel, and act.

somatic nervous system The part of the peripheral nervous system that carries messages from the sense organs and relays information that directs the voluntary movements of the skeletal muscles.

somatization disorder Somatoform disorder in which a person has medical complaints without physical cause.

somatoform disorders Psychological disorders characterized by physical symptoms for which there are no obvious physical causes.

specific attachment phase Stage at about six months of age, in which the baby becomes attached to a specific person.

split-brain research Popular name for Roger Sperry's research on the syndrome of hemisphere deconnection; research on individuals with the corpus callosum severed. Normal functioning breaks down in split-brain subjects when different information is presented to each hemisphere.

SQ5R A technique to improve learning and memory. Components include survey, question, read, record, recite, review, and reflect.

stage of exhaustion Third stage in Hans Selye's general adaptation syndrome. As the body continues to resist stress, it depletes its energy resources and the person becomes exhausted.

stage of resistance Second stage in Hans Selye's general adaptation syndrome. When stress is prolonged, the body builds some resistance to the effects of stress.

standardization The process of obtaining a representative sample of scores in the population so that a particular score can be interpreted correctly.

Stanford-Binet Intelligence Scale An intelligence test first revised by Lewis Terman at Stanford University in 1916; still a popular test used today.

state-dependent learning Situation in which what is learned in one state can only be remembered when the person is in that state of mind.

statistically significant In inferential statistics, a finding that the independent variable did influence greatly the outcome of the experimental and control group.

stereotype An exaggerated and rigid mental image of a particular class of persons or objects.

stimulus A unit of the environment that causes a response in an individual; a physical or chemical agent acting on an appropriate sense receptor.

stimulus discrimination Responding to relevant stimuli.

stimulus generalization Responding to stimuli similar to the stimulus that had caused the response.

stimulus motives Motivating factors that are internal and unlearned, but do not appear to have a physiological basis; stimulus motives cause an individual to seek out sensory stimulation through interaction with the environment.

stimulus trace The perceptual persistence of a stimulus after it is no longer present.

strange-situation procedure A measure of attachment developed by Mary Ainsworth that consists of eight phases during which the infant is increasingly stressed.

Glossary

stress Anything that produces demands on us to adjust and threatens our well-being.

Strong Interest Inventory An objective personality test that compares people's personalities to groups that achieve success in certain occupations.

structuralism First school of thought in psychology; it studied conscious experience to discover the structure of the mind.

subject bias Source of potential error in an experiment from the action or expectancy of a subject; a subject might influence the experimental results in ways that mask the true outcome.

subjective organization Long-term memory procedures in which the individual provides a personal method of organizing information to be memorized.

sublimation Defense mechanism; a person redirects his or her socially undesirable urges into socially acceptable behavior.

successive approximation Shaping; in operant conditioning, the gradual process of reinforcing behaviors that get closer to some final desired behavior.

superego Sigmund Freud's representation of conscience.

surface traits In Raymond Cattell's personality theory, the observable characteristics of a person's behavior and personality.

symbolization In Sigmund Freud's dream theory, the process of converting the latent content of a dream into manifest symbols.

systematic desensitization Application of counterconditioning, in which the individual overcomes anxiety by learning to relax in the presence of stimuli that had once made him or her unbearably nervous.

task-oriented coping Adjustment responses in which the person evaluates a stressful situation objectively and then formulates a plan with which to solve the problem.

test of significance An inferential statistical technique used to determine whether the difference in scores between the experimental and control groups is really due to the effects of the independent variable or to random chance. If the probability of an outcome is extremely low, we say that outcome is significant.

Thanatos Sigmund Freud's term for a destructive instinct such as aggression; also called death instinct.

Thematic Apperception Test (TAT) Projective personality test in which subjects are shown pictures of people in everyday settings; subjects must make up a story about the people portrayed.

theory of social impact Latané's theory of social behavior; it states that each member of a group shares the responsibility equally.

Theory X Douglas McGregor's theory that states that the worker dislikes work and must be forced to do it.

Theory Y Douglas McGregor's theory that states that work is natural and can be a source of satisfaction, and, when it is, the worker can be highly committed and motivated.

therapy In psychology, the treatment of behavior problems; two major types of therapy include psychotherapy and biological therapy.

time and motion studies In engineering psychology, studies that analyze the time it takes to perform an action and the movements that go into the action.

tip-of-the-tongue phenomenon A phenomenon in which the closer a person comes to recalling something, the more accurately he or she can remember details, such as the number of syllables or letters.

token economy A behavior therapy in which desired behaviors are reinforced immediately with tokens that can be exchanged at a later time for desired rewards, such as food or recreational privileges.

trace conditioning A procedure in classical conditioning in which the CS is a discrete event that is presented and terminated before the US is presented.

trait A distinctive and stable attribute in people.

trait anxiety Anxiety that is long-lasting; a relatively stable personality characteristic.

transference Psychoanalytic term used when a patient projects his feelings onto the therapist.

transsexualism A condition in which a person feels trapped in the body of the wrong sex.

trial and error learning Trying various behaviors in a situation until the solution is found.

triangular theory of love Robert Sternberg's theory that states that love consists of intimacy, passion, and decision/commitment.

triarchic theory of intelligence Robert Sternberg's theory of intelligence that states that it consists of three parts: componential, experiential, and contextual subtheories.

Type-A behavior A personality pattern of behavior that can lead to stress and heart disease.

unconditional positive regard Part of Carl Rogers's personality theory; occurs when we accept someone regardless of what he or she does or says.

unconditioned response (UR) An automatic reaction elicited by a stimulus.

unconditioned stimulus (US) Any stimulus that elicits an automatic or reflexive reaction in an individual; it does not have to be learned in the present situation.

unconscious mind In Sigmund Freud's psychoanalytic theory of personality, the part of personality that is unavailable to us; Freud suggests that instincts and unpleasant memories are stored in the unconscious mind.

undifferentiated schizophrenia Type of schizophrenia that does not fit into any particular category, or fits into more than one category.

variable interval (VI) schedule Schedule of reinforcement in which the subject is reinforced for the first response given after a certain time interval, with the interval being different for each trial.

variable ratio (VR) schedule Schedule of reinforcement in which the subject is given reinforcement after a varying number of responses; the number of responses required for reinforcement is different for every trial.

vestibular sense Sense that helps us keep our balance.

vulnerability-stress model Theory of schizophrenia that states that some people have a biological tendency to develop schizophrenia if they are stressed enough by their environment.

Weber's Law Ernst Weber's law that states that the difference threshold depends on the ratio of the intensity of one stimulus to another rather than on an absolute difference.

Wechsler Adult Intelligence Scale (WAIS) An intelligence test for adults, first published by David Wechsler in 1955; it contains verbal and performance subscales.

Wechsler Intelligence Scale for Children (WISC-III) Similar to the Wechsler Adult Intelligence Scale, except that it is designed for children ages 6 through 16, and helps diagnose certain childhood disorders such as dyslexia and other learning disabilities.

Wechsler Preschool and Primary Scale of Intelligence (WPPSI-R) Designed for children between the ages of 4 and 7; helps diagnose childhood disorders, such as dyslexia and other learning disabilities.

withdrawal Unpleasant physical reactions that a drug dependent user experiences when he or she stops taking the drug.

within-subject experiment An experimental design in which each subject is given all treatments, including the control condition; subjects serve in both experimental and control groups.

working memory The memory store, with a capacity of about 7 items and enduring for up to 30 seconds, that handles current information.

Yerkes-Dodson Law Popular idea that performance is best when arousal is at a medium level.

Sources for the Glossary: *The majority of terms in this glossary are from* Psychology: A ConnecText, *4th Edition, Terry F. Pettijohn. ©1999 Dushkin/ McGraw-Hill, Guilford, CT 06437. The remaining terms were developed by the* Annual Editions *staff, 2001.*

Index

Index

Test Your Knowledge Form

We encourage you to photocopy and use this page as a tool to assess how the articles in *Annual Editions* expand on the information in your textbook. By reflecting on the articles you will gain enhanced text information. You can also access this useful form on a product's book support Web site at *http://www.dushkin.com/online/*.

NAME: _____ DATE: _____

TITLE AND NUMBER OF ARTICLE: _____

BRIEFLY STATE THE MAIN IDEA OF THIS ARTICLE:

LIST THREE IMPORTANT FACTS THAT THE AUTHOR USES TO SUPPORT THE MAIN IDEA:

WHAT INFORMATION OR IDEAS DISCUSSED IN THIS ARTICLE ARE ALSO DISCUSSED IN YOUR TEXTBOOK OR OTHER READINGS THAT YOU HAVE DONE? LIST THE TEXTBOOK CHAPTERS AND PAGE NUMBERS:

LIST ANY EXAMPLES OF BIAS OR FAULTY REASONING THAT YOU FOUND IN THE ARTICLE:

LIST ANY NEW TERMS/CONCEPTS THAT WERE DISCUSSED IN THE ARTICLE, AND WRITE A SHORT DEFINITION:

We Want Your Advice

ANNUAL EDITIONS revisions depend on two major opinion sources: one is our Advisory Board, listed in the front of this volume, which works with us in scanning the thousands of articles published in the public press each year; the other is you—the person actually using the book. Please help us and the users of the next edition by completing the prepaid article rating form on this page and returning it to us. Thank you for your help!

ANNUAL EDITIONS: Personal Growth and Behavior 03/04

ARTICLE RATING FORM

Here is an opportunity for you to have direct input into the next revision of this volume.
We would like you to rate each of the articles listed below, using the following scale:

1. **Excellent: should definitely be retained**
2. **Above average: should probably be retained**
3. **Below average: should probably be deleted**
4. **Poor: should definitely be deleted**

Your ratings will play a vital part in the next revision.
Please mail this prepaid form to us as soon as possible.
Thanks for your help!

RATING	ARTICLE	RATING	ARTICLE
	1. The Benefits of Positive Psychology		37. Disaster and Trauma
	2. The Trouble With Self-Esteem		38. Psychological Help for the Terrorized
	3. Repression Tries for Experimental Comeback		39. American Families Are Drifting Apart
	4. Why Our Kids Are Out of Control		40. How to Multitask
	5. In Search of a Leader		41. Work, Work, Work, Work!
	6. The Tangled Skeins of Nature and Nurture in Human Evolution		42. Self-Help: Shattering the Myths
	7. Nature vs. Nurture: Two Brothers With Schizophrenia		43. Make Peace With Your Past
	8. The Personality Genes		44. Bad Choices: Why We Make Them, How to Stop
	9. Where We Come From		45. The Science of Anxiety
	10. The Secrets of Autism		46. Overcoming Depression
	11. Altered States of Consciousness		47. Happiness Explained
	12. Brain-Based Learning		
	13. Resolved: No More Dumb Resolutions		
	14. The Biology of Aging		
	15. Fetal Psychology		
	16. Four Things You Need to Know About Raising Baby		
	17. Childhood Is for Children		
	18. Parenting: The Lost Art		
	19. Disarming the Rage		
	20. You Can Help Your Adolescent in the Search for Identity		
	21. The Funmasters		
	22. Living to 100: What's the Secret?		
	23. Start the Conversation		
	24. Got Time for Friends?		
	25. What's Your Emotional IQ?		
	26. Nurturing Empathy		
	27. Faces of Perception		
	28. How to Spot a Liar		
	29. Shy Squared		
	30. Revealing Personal Secrets		
	31. Welcome to the Love Lab		
	32. Prescription for Passion		
	33. Forgiveness: Who Does It and How Do They Do It?		
	34. The Betrayal of the American Man		
	35. Coping With Crowding		
	36. Nobody Left to Hate		

(Continued on next page)

NO POSTAGE
NECESSARY
IF MAILED
IN THE
UNITED STATES

BUSINESS REPLY MAIL
FIRST-CLASS MAIL PERMIT NO. 84 GUILFORD CT

POSTAGE WILL BE PAID BY ADDRESSEE

McGraw-Hill/Dushkin
530 Old Whitfield Street
Guilford, Ct 06437-9989

Ill....ll...l..l..ll.l...ll.l.l.l.l...l.l.l..l.l

- -

ABOUT YOU

Name   Date
_____

Are you a teacher? ❐   A student? ❐
Your school's name
_____

Department
_____

Address   City   State   Zip
_____

School telephone #
_____

YOUR COMMENTS ARE IMPORTANT TO US!

Please fill in the following information:
For which course did you use this book?
_____

Did you use a text with this ANNUAL EDITION?   ❐ yes ❐ no
What was the title of the text?
_____

What are your general reactions to the *Annual Editions* concept?
_____

Have you read any pertinent articles recently that you think should be included in the next edition? Explain.
_____

Are there any articles that you feel should be replaced in the next edition? Why?
_____

Are there any World Wide Web sites that you feel should be included in the next edition? Please annotate.
_____

May we contact you for editorial input?   ❐ yes ❐ no
May we quote your comments? ❐ yes ❐ no